I0135097

The Morning Chronicle's

LABOUR AND THE POOR

Volume VI

THE RURAL DISTRICTS

The Morning Chronicle's

LABOUR AND THE POOR

Volume VI

THE RURAL DISTRICTS

ALEXANDER MACKAY & SHIRLEY BROOKS

Edited By
Rebecca Watts & Kevin Booth

Ditto Books
www.dittobooks.co.uk

First Published by Ditto Books 2020

© Ditto Books 2020

All rights reserved

A catalogue record for this book is available
from the British Library

ISBN 978-1-913515-06-5 (hardback)
ISBN 978-1-913515-16-4 (paperback)

Cover Image:
Mullion Cove, Cornwall
From "Our Own Country. Descriptive, Historical, Pictorial"
Published 1891
Image courtesy of The British Library

"The eldest boy, twelve years old, appeared, as he walked, more like a moving heap of rags and tatters than anything bearing the semblance of a human being. How his rags were kept on was a mystery which I believe none could solve, and if they had been taken off, it would have been impossible for the owner to have put them on again. They were never taken off; in fact he slept in the rags, as did his other brothers and sisters, for in the upper room there were no beds, no sheets, no blankets, no counterpanes."

Contents

List of Illustrations

Preface

This work attempts to be a faithful reproduction of the "Labour and the Poor" letters as printed in *The Morning Chronicle*. Only obvious typographical errors and omissions have been corrected. Variations in the spelling and hyphenation of words have largely been retained. We hope any such inconsistencies prove to be of some historical interest to the reader.

As much as possible we have tried to recreate the original layout and styling of the text and all factual tables have been reproduced as closely to the originals as possible with only minimal alterations made where necessary to improve readability.

Not all letters were titled. Where missing we have added titles to the Table of Contents to assist navigation and explanation of content. The letters themselves are as per the originals.

A handful of illustrations have been added to each volume. These did not appear in the original text but hopefully provide added interest.

R. W.
K. B.

Introduction

In 1849 a leading London-based newspaper, *The Morning Chronicle*, undertook an investigation into the working and living conditions of the poor throughout England and Wales in the hope that their findings might lead to much needed change.

The reputed catalyst for their "Labour and the Poor" series was an article written by Henry Mayhew recording a journey into Bermondsey, one of the most deprived districts of London, which was printed in September 1849. Following this it was proposed that an in-depth investigation be carried out and "Special Correspondents", the investigators, were selected and distributed around the country. The first article or "Letter" appeared on the 18th of October 1849 and the series would run for almost 2 years and 222 letters.

The well-known and respected writers and journalists recruited for the task included Henry Mayhew who was assigned to the Metropolitan districts, Angus Bethune Reach to the Manufacturing districts, Alexander Mackay and Shirley Brooks to the Rural districts and Charles Mackay to investigate the cities of Birmingham and Liverpool. The author of the letters from Wales is as yet unknown.

It is clear from references made in the letters that Alexander Mackay commenced his investigation in the counties of Buckinghamshire, Berkshire, Oxfordshire and Wiltshire, before examining the south western counties of Devon, Cornwall, Somerset and Dorset. He then proceeded eastward through Hampshire, Surrey, Sussex and Kent. He began an inquiry into the counties of Gloucestershire, Monmouthshire, Herefordshire, Worcestershire and Shropshire, but only one letter of this was published. In 1850 he accepted the task of travelling to India to investigate the viability of expanding the cotton producing areas and trade in the East Indies.

It is most likely that Shirley Brooks commenced his portion of the investigation in the eastern counties of Norfolk, Suffolk and Essex, continuing on to cover Hertfordshire, Bedfordshire,

Huntingdonshire and Cambridgeshire, before proceeding to the midland counties of Northamptonshire, Leicestershire, Rutland, Nottinghamshire and Derbyshire.

The "Labour and the Poor" letters were extremely popular at the time, being widely read throughout the nation and even abroad. The revelations in them caused quite a stir amongst the middle and upper classes of Victorian society. *Letters to the Editor* poured in with donations for specific cases of distress that appeared in the letters and also for the general alleviation of the suffering of the poor. A special fund was set up by *The Morning Chronicle* to collect and distribute these donations.

These *Letters to the Editor* have been included in this series, predominantly in the Metropolitan district volumes whose letters elicited the majority of responses. They provide a unique window into the thoughts and sentiments of the Victorian readership as they react to the incredible accounts of misery and desperation being unveiled.

The Morning Chronicle's extraordinary and unsurpassed "Labour and the Poor" investigation provides an unparalleled insight into the people of the period, their living and working conditions, their feelings, their language, their sufferings and their struggles for survival amidst the poverty and destitution of 19th century Britain. An investigation of such magnitude had never before been attempted and the undertaking was truly of epic proportions. Its impact at the time was profound. Its historical importance today is without question.

LABOUR AND THE POOR.

——◆——

THE RURAL DISTRICTS.

[FROM OUR SPECIAL CORRESPONDENT.]

Letter I.

At no previous time, perhaps, has the attention of thinking men been so generally or so anxiously directed to questions of a social character as at present. The events of the last two years have led to this, indicating, as they have done beyond all dispute, that the political systems of Europe were, and still are, tainted with a more deeply-seated malady than that which assumes the type of mere political defects. The extent to which the social systems of the Continent were rotten to their core, became evident from the suddenness with which Government after Government crumbled beneath the shock of the French Revolution. Two States alone stood firm amid the storm, and these two (England and Russia) represented respectively the two extremes of political existence in Europe. In the one, order was maintained by the absolute supremacy of force; in the other, it was preserved by the ascendancy of sound opinion.

Proud of it as we may be, and thankful, as we no doubt are, for our escape from the ravages of the revolutionary tempest, we must carefully guard against the error of supposing that the social edifice which gave us shelter is absolutely perfect, because in the day of trial it did not prove itself utterly defective. Strong and compact as it showed itself, as a whole, there were, nevertheless, points at which it gave indications of weakness, which it would be folly to disregard. That which withstands one rude assault is not necessarily proof against a succession of shocks. Whilst to systems which had fewer strong points than weak ones the storm carried destruction and overthrow, it but indicated in ours such as were weak, that we might strengthen them for the future. Shall we profit by the warning, or are we, too, to wait until we see the hand-writing on the wall? There can be no greater enemy to the fortunes of England than the unqualified panegyrist of her institutions. Even had we enjoyed a complete immunity from the

1

dangers of the recent upheavings of the moral elements throughout the world, it would be presumption as well as folly in us to suppose that we had not much to do to render our exemption from such dangers perpetual. But we had no such immunity. If order maintained its ascendancy, it cannot be forgotten that disaffection was in our streets. The revolutionary wave spread to our very doors, and, for the moment, threatened to involve us, too, in the inundation. If the movement here led to discomfiture instead of to a catastrophe, it was simply because the elements of order amongst us were stronger than those of confusion. But the elements of confusion were with us, and are with us still. It is true that they may not be formidable enough to overthrow the Government, or bring down society about our ears; but it is the tendency of weeds, if unplucked, to monopolize the soil, and of cancerous growths, if not carefully removed, speedily to involve the more vital parts of the system. So it is with society. Its weak points, if left to extend, will soon spread to the danger of the strong. What are the weak points of our system? Is it the political machine that is out of gear? The bulk, even of its most ardent admirers, admit that it has its defects, but these are less organic in their nature than defects of detail. Where, then, is the real difficulty? Is it in our social system? If here, it is all the more serious, for it is, in general, much easier to adjust a political difficulty than to cure a deep-rooted and wide-spread social derangement.

To some the very suggestion may seem strange, that there may be something radically wrong with the structure of English society. We are so much in the habit of regarding ourselves in the van of civilization, and as taking strides in the direction of improvement which no other people can equal, that we can with difficulty be brought to suspect the existence of serious blemishes in our social system. But it would be well for us to content ourselves less with superficial observation, and betake ourselves more to searching scrutiny. Such a course may possibly reveal to us a state of things which prejudice would at once stamp as unreal, and to which even candour itself would be inclined to turn the ear of disbelief. Is our social fabric that sound compact and harmonious whole which it appears to be, or is it, after all, but a deceptive image, with (as was said of the Russian empire) its body of brass and its feet of clay? In times like these, when political fabrics elsewhere are being engulphed in the quicksands at their foundations, this is a question into which it is not only desirable but necessary to inquire. And in pursuing the inquiry, let us not be misled by appearances. Society with us may look not only ornate, but also firm and stable; but is it in reality so from its base upwards? If it has improved, and is still improving, has it done and is it still doing so, as a whole, or only in some of its parts? If the latter, which is the laggard part? It is to be feared that the lower orders have not kept pace in the race of improvement with the upper classes; and the question is, why are they not better off?

Public attention in this country is daily concentrating itself more and more on this important subject. The relation subsisting, and which ought to subsist, between the different classes of society, is fast becoming the question of questions. Are our social duties towards each other adequately performed, or the obligations attaching to our respective positions properly fulfilled? Does wealth properly acquit itself of its obligations to poverty? Does ignorance find as active a foe in intelligence as it should? Is the punishment of crime on its right footing; and are the temptations to crime not unnecessarily multiplied? Are the relations between labour and capital satisfactorily adjusted; and are the physical, moral, and religious wants of the masses sedulously cared for? These, and others like these, are the great practical questions which are now rapidly supplanting in men's minds discussions on mere speculative topics. There are none more interested in their proper solution than the upper classes themselves. The chain of mutual dependence is complete, extending upwards as well as downwards; albeit the extremes of society are so far apart, that they scarcely seem to belong to the same general system. But let circumstances separate them as much as they may, they cannot escape the common tie which binds them together in the chain of mutual dependence. As well might the gilded weathercock, which overlooks half a county from the top of Salisbury Cathedral, fancy itself independent of the foundations of the spire, as the upper classes imagine that their interests are separate from those of the lower orders of the State. Their interests, when properly understood, are found to be common interests; their wrongs common wrongs. But there is this difference between them, that the upper classes have at their disposal means for pushing their interests and redressing their wrongs, which the lower have not at command. The question, therefore, as regards the safety and stability of society, resolves itself into a consideration of the condition of the lower orders. There could be no more fitting time than the present for embarking on such an inquiry. The times are tranquil. But let us not be deceived by the smoothness of the surface. If we have surmounted some dangers, we have others still to meet.

Sub-soil ploughing is frequently resorted to as a remedy for exhausted soils. It is useful thus to bring that which is below occasionally to the surface. It is equally beneficial to bring now and then to light the truths which may be extracted from the depths of society. On others has devolved the task of doing this in the metropolis and the manufacturing districts, whilst to me has been assigned that of driving a deep furrow through the moral soil of the counties. In doing so I shall take them in groups, confining my observations in the first place to the counties of Bucks, Berks, Wilts, and Oxford.

To this group there are many features which are common, whilst in other respects they are distinguished from each other by marked peculiarities. They are all inland counties, and all chiefly dependent upon the same species of industry, being mainly, if not wholly, agricultural. They have every variety of soil, from the heavy clay of the Vale of Aylesbury, to the drier and lighter slopes of Salisbury Plain. They are also characterized by considerable diversity of climate, not varying so much as regards heat and cold, as in respect to dryness and humidity. The consequence is, that agriculture, in almost every form which it can assume, is extensively prosecuted in the district. The combined area of the four counties is 2,812,300 acres, being about one-eleventh part that of all England. There are few spots throughout the whole of this wide expanse in which agriculture could not be pushed to its highest development. The largest tracts incapable of high cultivation are to be found in the southern division of Wiltshire, the surface of which is broken by the low chalk hills, which, stretching through Hampshire, run through Wilts, to the borders of Dorset and Somerset. But in parts, even of this bleak and rugged district, such as Salisbury Plain, corn is produced in abundance. In some tracts, however, the chalk comes so close to the surface as to preclude the possibility of converting them into arable land, and there is no alternative but to leave them as downs for the pasture of sheep. With scarcely any other exception, the whole area of the counties in question is divided between arable and pasture lands; dairy farming, to which the latter are chiefly turned, forming a larger feature in the agriculture of Bucks and Wiltshire than in that of Berks or Oxfordshire, but being more or less common to all. There is a great deal of pasture land in the northern division of Wilts, which is low and flat, and dairy farms are not unfrequent in its central and south-western districts. Throughout the greater portion of the centre of Buckinghamshire, stretching from Thame to near Leighton, particularly from Aylesbury to Leighton, dairy farming is the rule, the raising of crops being the exception. The same may be said of the tract lying between Aylesbury and Bicester. Most of this district is comprised in what is generally known as the Vale of Aylesbury. In the southern portion of the county, the plough is very generally used, whilst in the northern, that abutting upon Northamptonshire, the higher style of farming common to that county, comprising green crops, is in vogue. In Berks and Oxfordshire, on the other hand, the dairy farms are more isolated, there being in neither of them such continuous stretches of pasture land as in the other counties of the group. In addition to a fertile soil, thus yielding every variety of production common to this country, they have scattered over them, as stimulants to their agricultural industry, such market towns as Reading, Windsor, Salisbury, Marlborough, Devizes, Warminster, Trowbridge, Westbury, Calne, Chippenham, Oxford, Thame, Aylesbury, Buckingham, Wycombe, &c. They are intersected by numerous and excellent roads, and some of them are well irrigated by canals, whilst they are now all directly connected by railway with the great mart of the nation, and the chief focus of its industrial energies—the metropolis.

Having thus briefly glanced at their great physical features, let us now view them in their moral aspect.

The population of England was, by the last census, about 15,000,000 of souls. This, distributed over the whole area of the country, which is about 32,247,600 acres, would give about one person to every 2 1-7 acres. The population of the four counties under consideration was 737,496, which, distributed over their combined area, already noticed as being 2,812,390 acres, gave one person to about every 3 1-6 acres. The population of Wilts was 258,733 souls, its area 874,880 acres, giving one person to about every 3½ acres. In Bucks, the proportion was one to a little over 3 acres, its population being 155,983 souls, and its area 472,320 acres. In Berks, having 161,447 inhabitants, it was one to scarcely 3 acres, the whole area of the county being 431,280 acres; whist in Oxford, with an area of 483,840 acres and 161,643 inhabitants, it was about one to every 3 acres. In Wilts the pressure of population upon the soil is the least, in Berks it is the greatest in the group; but even in the latter it is considerably less than the average pressure throughout England. Taking the average of the group there is in it above an acre more to each individual than there is throughout the whole of England; in other words, the population of these four counties, before it could press in the same degree upon their surface as the whole population of England does upon the whole area of England, would have to increase about 45 per cent.

In 1841 there were:—

	Farmers and Graziers.		Agricultural Labourers.
In Wilts	4,456	—	31,099
— Berks	1,876	—	18,649
— Bucks	2,465	—	18,860
And in Oxford	2,365	—	17,909

That is to say, there were in Wiltshire scarcely seven labourers to each farmer, in Berks somewhat more than nine, and in Bucks and Oxfordshire about seven and a half. Of the whole number of agricultural labourers in Wiltshire, there are about 5,700 under 20 years of age, of which number about 700 are females. In Berks the number under 20 years of age is 3,330, of whom only 318 are females; in Bucks 2,838, of whom only 136 are females; and in Oxford 2,937, of whom only 14 were returned as females. In none of them does the number of females of all ages employed come near the number of males employed under 20 years of age. The number of males under 20 years of age returned as employed in agricultural labour in Wilts was less than one-fifth of the whole number of males in the county returned as under 20 and over 10 years of age, including the town as well as the country population. In Oxford the proportion was also less than one-fifth; in Berks it was about a sixth, and in Bucks about one-seventh.

In 1841, there were engaged in trade, commerce, and manufactures in Wilts, 28,027 persons, against 36,390 engaged in agriculture. In Berks the numbers were 16,479, against 21,249; in Bucks, 19,664, against 21,897; and in Oxford, 17,369, against 30,789. It will be seen that it is in Wilts and Bucks that the proportion of those engaged in commerce, trade, and manufactures approaches the nearest to an equality with that of those engaged in agriculture. The extent to which lace-making and straw platting are carried on in the latter accounts for this. In the former the proportion of the first-mentioned class of persons was at one time much greater than now, the manufacturing industry of Wilts having, in common with that of the whole south-west of England, fallen greatly back of late years, owing to causes which will be explained hereafter. The total number of persons returned as engaged in all occupations in Wilts, was 88,756; in Berks, 55,678; in Bucks, 54,340; and in Oxford, 53,238. In the first three counties more than one-third of the whole population were returned as employed, and in the last, somewhat less than one-third. Of the residue of the population of each, the great bulk consists of women and children of tender age, the rest being such as were returned as independent, and those represented as pensioners, paupers, almspeople, and beggars. The number returned as independent in Wilts was 5,996, or about 2.32 per cent. of the whole population. In Berks the number was 4,779, being nearly 3 per cent. of the whole population. In Bucks it was 3,084, or less than 2 per cent.; and in Oxford, 3,857, or 2.38 per cent. of the whole. Taking the four counties together, the average number returned as independent was about 2.40 per cent. of their aggregate population. The numbers returned, at the same time, as paupers, almspeople, and beggars, were—in Wilts, 3,790; in Berks, 2,229; in Bucks, 1,695; and in Oxford, 1,622; making in all 9,336 returned as absolutely dependent—being about 1.23 per cent. of their aggregate population. The annual value of real property, as rated to the income tax, is in Wilts, £1,424,545; in Berks, £1,016,474; in Bucks, £832,889; and in Oxford, £1,025,620—making the total aggregate annual value of the property of the four counties, as thus rated, £4,299,528, or about 5.22 per cent. of the whole real property rateable to the income tax in England. The amount expended in each county in 1847, for the relief of the poor, was, in Wilts, £141,133—being an increase of 6 per cent. over the expenditure in 1846; in Berks, £85,252—being an increase of 8 per cent. over that of the previous year; in Bucks, £82,838—showing an increase of 7 per cent. in one year; and in Oxford, £87,033—also showing an increase of 7 per cent. Thus, the aggregate increase of expenditure for the poor in 1847, as compared with that for 1846, was almost 7 per cent. The greatest increase was in Berkshire, but that was far below the increase in some other counties, such as Nottingham, in which, for the year, it was no less than 19 per cent.

Having thus taken a rapid survey of the four counties in question, in their physical and moral aspects, it is now time to proceed to the consideration of what is proposed as the more particular subject of inquiry—the condition of the labouring classes engaged in agriculture. The general summary which has been made of the capabilities, resources, wealth, burdens, and population of the district, will be useful, inasmuch as it will enable the reader, before the real state of the case is laid before him, to form his own estimate of what should be the condition of the different classes of people inhabiting such a district, with which estimate he can afterwards contrast the real circumstances of the peasantry as they will be divulged to him. In laying bare what these circumstances are, it will be my first endeavour to give as accurate a description as possible of the labouring classes in their physical condition, in doing which I shall first deal with them in connection with their dwellings and persons, leaving the subjects of wages and diet for a future communication.

It is a generally received opinion that the condition of the female in a community indicates the stage attained by it in civilization. This, however, would only appear to be a correct standard of judgment after several steps in advance have already been taken: for it is generally found that society has made considerable progress from its rude starting point, ere the condition of the female undergoes any visible amelioration. The first symptom of man's progress is furnished in the character of his habitation. Whatever progress he may make in other directions, every future step he takes is marked by improvement in this. First the hovel, then the hut, and lastly the house, progressing in perfection until, having become comfortable, it is rendered elegant and ornate. Such is the result when man is left free to develop his condition. Every step he takes in the higher walks of civilization, is accompanied, if not preceded, by a superior degree of comfort and refinement in his external life. Hence it is that his physical condition becomes the test of his intellectual and moral development. To judge of the progress of a nation, we must consider its people in their relations to external nature; and in doing so it will not do to confine our observations to any one class of society. To estimate aright the civilization of England, we must not confine ourselves to such tests as Buckingham Palace, Stafford House, or Chatsworth. It frequently happens that the centre can only be raised at the expense of the circumference, and the greatest monuments to the glory of a nation have frequently been the most striking proofs of its wretchedness. There is a high and there is a low grade of civilization in every country, and its average advancement can only be known by considering them along with the grades which intervene. The distance between the two extremes of English civilization is as great as that between St. Paul's and a mud hovel. To keep the fabric together, it is as well that we should keep its extremes constantly in view.

There is nothing attended with unmixed good—not even railways. They have called into existence a larger travelling class than before; and it is the tendency of travelling to bring more or less to light every phase of national life. But although men travel now by hundreds where they formerly travelled by tens, less is known now than formerly of the rural life of England. In the old coaching days a traveller was dragged along the highways of the country, on which its towns and villages were standing—giving him an opportunity of observing every form of English life, from that of the peasant to that of the peer. At the end of his journey some definite impressions remained on his mind of the scenes through which he had passed. He had observed the nature and capabilities of the different rural districts, and the extent to which they were neglected or turned to account. He had seen the dwellings of the labourer clustered in hamlets and villages along the road, and the mansions of the proprietors peering, one after another, through the foliage which embowered them; and as he drove up the main street of each town, he discerned its peculiarities and the direction of its industry. He had thus an opportunity of studying the life of his country in its lowest and its highest stages of development, and in the phase which it assumes when, under the stimulus of numbers and competition, it puts forth its most concentrated energies. But to the great bulk of travellers this opportunity is no longer extended. We have made a small England of it by means of our railways and electric telegraphs. Thoughts now travel with the swiftness of lightning, and men travel almost with the speed of thought. We are wafted from London to Liverpool in one-fifth the time formally occupied in the journey. But what do we see and learn by the way? The lines of the old highways are forsaken, the least populous parts of the country are traversed, towns are shunned instead of passed through, and the impressions left upon the traveller are of the most unsatisfactory and confused description. At his journey's end, he has but a dim recollection of fields, hedges, and trees; tunnels, embankments, and cuttings; towns, now on this hand and now on that: but all flying past him, like the phantasmagoria of a dream—his senses alternately excited by the dread of an accident and the shrieking of the locomotive. He has a less definite impression even of the physical features of the country, than he can get of the Mississippi from a visit to the monster picture at the Egyptian Hall. He has little or no chance of learning the different modes of life and the varied circumstances of the people. Men now travel over, where they formerly travelled through, the country.

In undertaking a journey they now think only of its extremes—the chief consideration attached to the intermediate space being that it comprises so many miles to be rapidly overcome. The consequence is, that, although the gain to trade and commerce may be incalculable, the stock of general knowledge derived from a varied and extensive personal observation is diminished. It therefore results that the generation of Englishmen now springing up, will know less of the rural life of England than their forefathers, unless the information which they cannot now so readily gather for themselves is supplied them from other sources. It is of the last importance to the well-being of society that this information should be constantly and extensively furnished; for it is to be feared that, whilst the material improvements of the day are such as are in their direct benefits confined almost exclusively to the upper and middle classes, their effect is to elevate those classes to a point where they, more or less, lose sight altogether of the lower orders. The danger of this is obvious, especially at a time when material and social considerations are exciting such an influence on political conditions. At this moment, in all quarters of the land, a cry is coming up to us from the lower orders. Is it the plaint of want, or the wail of despair? If either, it is as well that we should both understand and meet it, lest it come upon us with yet more startling echoes. To know the ground on which we stand, we must ascertain what the depths of society can reveal.

LABOUR AND THE POOR.

—◆—

THE RURAL DISTRICTS.

[FROM OUR SPECIAL CORRESPONDENT.]

BUCKS, BERKS, WILTS, AND OXFORD.

THE LABOURER'S HOME.

Letter II.

Having, in a former communication, taken a general survey, both in a moral and material point of view, of the district to which my inquiry is for the present confined, I now proceed, according to the arrangement proposed, to furnish as succinct a description as possible of the physical condition of the agricultural labourer in the counties composing it.

The importance of the investigation can only be estimated by considering, not simply the number of agricultural labourers in these counties, but also the number of those who are directly dependent for their subsistence upon agricultural labour. The number of labourers in 1841 was 85,910. Of these there were—

Adult males	66,790
Adult females	4,540
Males and females under 20 years of age	14,580
Total	85,910

But although these were all the labourers employed in the counties in question at the time of the last census, it does not follow that they comprised all dependent upon the labour in which they were engaged. The census, after enumerating those engaged in all occupations, together with those of independent means, and such as were absolutely dependent on charity, sets down the remainder in one gross total as the "residue of the population." This residue comprises two classes of persons—females not engaged in any specific occupation, and children either attending school or too young to work. These are all, or

11

mostly all, dependent upon the two other classes returned as occupied and independent, the great bulk of them being of course dependent upon the former class. Of these it is fair to infer that the greatest portion are dependent on those following agricultural occupations, for by far the greatest proportion of those returned as actually occupied in the four counties follow such occupations. An approximation to the gross number dependent for subsistence on agricultural labour, which is all that can be looked for, may be had as follows.

Of the 66,790 adult males employed as labourers, the greater proportion may be taken as married men. The system which obtains in so many parts of the country, of paying married men more for their labour than single men, is one of the many premiums upon marriage held out to the lower orders by our agricultural system. It will certainly not be over the mark to take three-fifths, or about 40,000 of them, as married. This would leave 26,790 as the number of unmarried adult male labourers. To the 40,000 married must be added 40,000 adult females, as their wives. The adult females, returned as occupied in agricultural labour may be included in the category of married females. The number of children in each family will, on a low average, be three, exclusive of the unmarried male adults and of the number of males and females returned as occupied under 20 years of age. The whole number, therefore, dependent in the four counties on agricultural labour may be taken to be—

Unmarried males	26,790
Married ditto	40,000
Married women, including 4,540 adult females returned as occupied in agricultural labour	40,000
Children, 3 to a family	120,000
Males and females under 20 years of age returned as occupied	14,580
Total	241,370

It thus appears that one-third of the aggregate population of the four counties, which is 737,496 souls, are directly dependent for their subsistence upon agricultural labour. The inquiry, therefore, into their physical condition is an inquiry into that of one-third of the entire population of the district.

Amongst those not practically conversant with rural affairs, the impression prevails that the bulk of the labourers live in detached residences on the different farms, with a certain tie existing between them and the soil, and, by consequence, between them and its occupiers. In Scotland, and in some portions of the north of England, this is the case to a great extent, although not now to the same extent in Scotland as formerly. The times are past when, in the Lowlands, the farmer and his workman were mutually on such a footing that, after toiling together in the same fields, they sat down together at the same table, and in many cases slept under the same roof. But still the bulk of the labourers there live yet upon the farms, accommodation being generally, in such cases, afforded them in the "square," the term frequently applied to the farm buildings. The consequence is, that farm labourers are in Scotland a less distinct and detached class than they are in England, and they are far less frequently to be found, bearing in mind the relative proportions of the two countries as to numbers, clustered together in towns and villages, of which they chiefly constitute the population. In England the case is different. Many labourers are hired, with their board included, when accommodation is of course provided them on the farm. But the great bulk of them form a distinct class of society, inhabiting the outskirts of the rural towns and the villages, which they monopolise to themselves, having no capital or resource but their labour, no certainty that that will be called into exercise, and no guarantee for its employment, even when it is called into use, beyond a week at a time. It were better for them, as a class, to be kept more apart from each other than they are—for it is not under all circumstances that men improve from the constant intercourse which is the result of their congregating in masses together. In some cases, the sites of their villages belong to one proprietor—in others, to several; but it by no means follows that they are employed either on the farm of which a village site may form a part, or even on the property of which the farm may be but a portion. Indeed, it frequently happens that the only connection between them and the proprietor or occupier of the soil on which their habitations are erected, is that of landlord and tenant. Their labour is at the command of any one who bids for it; and as their employment is precarious, and their wages fluctuating, their lives are spent, in the majority of cases, in constant oscillation between their homes and the workhouse, with no alternative beyond but starvation or the gaol.

Much has of late years been said in this country in reference to the dwellings of the poor, and public sympathy has been largely excited on the subject. Both in the towns and in the country districts the matter has been widely investigated, and facts brought to light which were

a disgrace to the nation, because revolting to humanity. The consequence has been that much has been done for the amelioration of the
domiciliary condition of the lower orders, but, though much, it has
fallen far short of what is required. The very fact that, notwithstanding the extent to which the subject has been agitated, such frightful
revelations in reference to the dwellings of the poor have lately been
made in the metropolis, where one would have supposed their horrible condition was least likely to have escaped observation, will of
itself suffice to indicate the trifling extent to which improvement in
this respect has been pushed in the country districts, where its absence is less likely to obtrude itself upon the public attention. What
has been done has not been effected on any large preconcerted plan,
calculated to embrace the whole of a neglected class in the benefits of
its operation. The effect has been local and partial, not national. Here
and there a proprietor, from motives either of shame, benevolence,
or interest, has, by improving their dwellings, enhanced the comforts
of some of, or perhaps of all, the peasantry on his estates. But there
has been no general action in this direction, and ordinary comfort is a
thing yet estranged from the great bulk of the habitations of the poor.
For one good cottage, with adequate accommodation for a family,
numbers are still met with utterly unfit for human occupancy. There
is no large district in the group of counties now under consideration
in which the improvements have been universal, and there are few
estates on which the bad are not yet largely intermingled with the
cottages of a better description.

What is wanted for a poor man and his family is a cottage with
sufficient room, in a healthy situation, and with adequate provision
made for light, drainage, and ventilation. There is nothing extravagant in this demand, for it comprises nothing but what is absolutely
required for health, comfort, and decency. To these the poorest, when
industrious, as well as the richest, are entitled, as far as the resources
of the nation can supply them; whilst every class is interested in their
possession of them. In selecting the situation, the nature of the soil,
as affecting the climate, should be one of the circumstances attended
to, for on this greatly depends the extent to which provision should be
made for the purposes of drainage and ventilation. The cottage should
be constructed of stone or bricks, and covered with tiles or slate. It
should contain at least five rooms—two below, viz., one for a kitchen
and general purposes, and another for a pantry and washing-room;
and three bed-rooms above, one for the parents, and the other two for

the children, the boys and girls occupying separate rooms. It should not be built back to back with another cottage, which would prevent its having those openings in front and behind so necessary to proper ventilation. The flooring of the lower rooms should be of wood, bricks, or flags—never of mud. It should have a moderately sized garden attached to it, and should be provided, at a convenient distance, with a necessary, care being taken, by drainage and otherwise, to prevent the *excreta* from exercising a pestiferous influence upon the health of the family. This is not asking too much for a class who, by their industry and energies, add so much to the general stock of comfort and wealth. There is nothing in it beyond what is necessary for their physical health and moral purity; nothing, be it remembered, beyond what is sedulously provided for the pauper and the culprit.

But where are such domiciles to be found in the possession of the agricultural labourer? In few places, indeed, and these situated at great distances from each other. Here and there a benevolent landlord has built them, and let them at moderate rents to the labourers on his estate. Nor does it occur to any one, on seeing them, that their occupiers are too comfortably housed. To a large family, accommodation short of this is privation, which is more or less the lot of nine-tenths of the labouring class. But it would be unfair to lead the reader to suppose that the few cottages which have thus been built on an adequate scale comprise all that has been done in the shape of improvement in this direction. Between the home thus depicted as his right, and the wretched hovel which he frequently inhabits, there is vast room for improvement and the amelioration of his condition. Much has been done within the intermediate space, small as may have been the amount of improvement which has been pushed to the desirable point. In many cases cottages have been built coming more or less short of the standard referred to, but still being, as regards both position, accommodation, and other circumstances, a very great advance, indeed, upon the miserable tenements which they have superseded. In some instances these comprise three rooms—one below, and two (sleeping apartments) above; in others, four rooms, two below and two above. Although, when a family is large, and some of the children are approaching maturity, a cottage with even four rooms, unless one of the lower rooms be converted into a bedroom, is wanting in the accommodation necessary to decency and moral purity—such a tenement, or even one with three apartments, is a vast improvement upon such as had but one, or two rooms, at the most. This intermediate class of cottages I found existing in many sections of the four counties, having, in some instances, entirely superseded the tenements of the worst description, but in others only partly so. On Lord Pembroke's estates, in the neighbourhood of Wilton, an example has thus been set which it were prudent as well as just in other proprietors more extensively to imitate. Neat brick cottages have been erected of different sizes, enabling the tenants, when leasing them, to consult their family necessities—the rent of the cottages, with some ground attached to each of them, being of the most moderate amount. Even admitting that in this his lordship submits to a slight pecuniary loss, he is more than compensated by the gratitude, respect, and attachment entertained towards him by the humble occupants. In addition to this, his tenantry are greatly benefited, for as every improvement in their condition begets improved habits in the labourers, labour is cheapened to the farmers, inasmuch as they get more work for their money, whilst they are saved from those systematic depredations too often practised in many parts of the country, to make up for deficiencies of food and fuel. At Amesbury, too, about eight miles north of Salisbury, I found many cottages of a comfortable description. New cottages have not been erected here to any great extent, but much has been done by Sir E. Antrobus, one of the proprietors in the neighbourhood, to improve the general character of those already existing. The rents are not, on the whole, so moderate here as on Lord Pembroke's property; but I heard none of the cottagers speak in any but the most favourable terms of their landlord. Several of the cottages in this neighbourhood are owned by a Mr. Camm, who would do well both in extending the accommodation which they afford, and in lowering the rents paid for them. In some parts of the neighbourhood of Westbury, Warminster, Devizes, and Calne, the labourers are also comparatively well housed; but, taking Wilts as a whole, their condition, as regards their domiciles, is anything but favourable. Of Berks and Bucks the same may be said, with the exception of a few districts in each; whilst in Oxford, Mr. Henley, M.P., is one of the very few who has taken an active interest in the physical well-being of the poorer classes. "They know that they have a landlord," was the expression made use of to indicate to me the position assumed by Mr. Henley towards the labourer on his property. The expression is certainly capable of a double interpretation, but it was understood as it was meant, for Mr. Henley deals kindly, justly, and firmly by his people.

As with those of the better order, so there are different grades of cottages amongst those of the inferior description. Some of them, by undergoing considerable alteration, might be rendered habitable with some degree of comfort to the inmates, provided their number was not great; whilst others are in such plight, that no alteration of which they are capable would suffice to make them fitting receptacles for human beings. If the reader will accompany me, I shall lead him into a cabin constituting the abode of some of his contemporaries and fellow-subjects.

The approach to it is by a narrow road, flanked on either side by mouldering banks, crowned with decaying hedge-rows. The road leads down into a vale of rather limited surface, along the bottom of which, having cut a serpentine channel for itself through the deep alluvial deposit, extends a small and sluggish stream—so sluggish, indeed, that it seems at a loss to know which way to direct its course. It glides, though almost imperceptibly, through rich and well-wooded meadows, with clumps of willows here and there trailing in its muddy waters. At the foot of the descent you have a high stone wall on your left, the bank and hedge-row continuing on the right. It has rained hard for a day or two previously, and the lower part of the wall is immersed in water, which lies, to the depth of several inches, and of varying width, along the side of the road flanked by the wall. Having no visible outlet, it has now been exposed for many hours to the bright sun; and the scum with which it is already, in parts, covered, gleams in the sunshine like so much mother-o'-pearl. The air is close and stifling, the spot seeming to have been designed for engendering malaria of the most pestilential description. At the end of the short vista formed by the wall and the bank, stands the hovel to which we are directing our steps. It is one of a cluster, two or three being attached to it—the others standing at a little distance apart. They are overhung with foliage, which, in a healthier and more exposed position, would be their ornament and their shelter, but which here has the effect, by keeping them constantly in the shade, of rendering them cold, comfortless, and damp.

The cabin is so rude and uncouth that it has less the appearance of having been built than of having been suddenly thrown up out of the ground. The length is not above 15 feet, its width between 10 and 12. The wall, which has sunk at different points, and seems bedewed with a cold sweat, is composed of a species of imperfect sandstone, which is fast crumbling to decay. It is so low that your very face is

A Rural Cottage

almost on a level with the heavy thatched roof which covers it, and which seems to be pressing it into the earth. The thatch is thickly encrusted with a bright green vegetation, which, together with the appearance of the trees and the mason-work around, well attests the prevailing humidity of the atmosphere. In front it presents to the eye a door with one window below, and another window—a smaller one— in the thatch above. The door is awry from the sinking of the wall; the glass in the window above is unbroken, but the lower one is here and there stuffed with rags, which keep out both the air and the sunshine. As you look at the crazy fabric, you marvel how it stands. It is so twisted and distorted, that it seems as if it never had been strong and compact, and as if, from the very first, it had been erected, not as a human abode, but as a humble monument to dilapidation. But let us enter.

You approach the door-way through the mud, over some loose stones, which rock under your feet in using them. You have to stoop for admission, and cautiously look around ere you fairly trust yourself within. There are but two rooms in the house—one below, and the other above. On leaving the bright light without, the room which you enter is so dark that for a time you can with difficulty discern the objects which it contains. Before you is a large but cheerless fireplace—it is not every poor man that may be said to have a hearth—with a few smouldering embers of a small wood fire, over which still hangs a pot, recently used for some culinary purpose. At one corner stands a small ricketty table, whilst scattered about are three old chairs—one without a back—and a stool or two, which, with a very limited and imperfect washing apparatus, and a shelf or two for plates, tea-cups, &c., constitute the whole furniture of the apartment. What could be more cheerless or comfortless? and yet you fancy you could put up with everything but the close earthy smell, which you endeavour in vain to escape by breathing short and quickly.

As you enter, a woman rises and salutes you timidly. She is not so old as she looks, for she is careworn and sickly. She has an infant in her arms, and three other children, two girls and a boy, are rolling along the damp uneven brick floor at her feet. They have nothing on their feet, being clad only down to the knees in similar garments of rag and patchwork. They are filthy; and on remarking it, we are told whiningly by the mother that she cannot keep them clean. By-and-by another child enters, a girl, with a few pieces of dry wood, which she has picked up in the neighbourhood for fuel. Nor is this the whole family yet. There are two boys, who are out with their father at work, the three being expected in every moment to dinner. They enter shortly afterwards. The father is surprised, and, for a little, evidently somewhat disconcerted at the intrusion, doubtful as to whether it may bode him good or evil. We soon put him at his ease, and the family proceed to dine. The eldest girl holds the child, whilst the mother takes the pot from the fire, and pours out of it into a large dish a quantity of potatoes. This, together with a little bread and some salt butter for the father and the two eldest boys, forms the entire repast. There is neither beef, bacon, nor beer. Bread, potatoes, and water form the dinner as well of the growing child as of the working man. They had a little bacon on Sunday last—it is now Thursday—and they will not taste bacon till Sunday again, and perhaps not even then. But whilst they are over their scanty repast, let us take a glance at their sleeping accommodations.

These are above, and are gained by means of a few greasy and ricketty steps, which lead through a species of hatchway in the ceiling. Yes, there is but one room, and yet we counted nine in the family! And such a room! The small window in the roof admits just light enough to enable you to discern its character and dimensions. The rafters, which are all exposed, spring from the very floor, so that it is only in the very centre of the apartment that you have any chance of standing erect. The thatch oozes through the wood work which supports it, the whole being begrimed with smoke and dust, and replete with vermin. There are no cobwebs, for the spider only spreads his net where flies are likely to be caught. You look in vain for a bedstead; there is none in the room. But there are their beds, lying side by side on the floor almost in contact with each other, and occupying nearly the whole length of the apartment. The beds are large sacks, filled with the chaff of oats, which the labourer sometimes gets, and at others purchases from his employer. The chaff of wheat and barley is used on the farm for other purposes. The bed next the hatchway is that of the father and mother, with whom sleeps the infant, born but a few months ago in this very room. In the other beds sleep the children, the boys and girls together. The eldest girl is in her twelfth year, the eldest boy having nearly completed his eleventh, and they are likely to remain for years yet in the circumstances in which we now find them. With the exception of the youngest children, the family retire to rest about the same hour, generally undressing below, and then ascending and crawling over each other to their respective resting places for the night. There are two blankets on the bed occupied by the parents, the others being covered with a very heterogeneous assemblage of materials. It not unfrequently happens that the clothes worn by the parents in the day time form the chief part of the covering of the children by night. Such is the dormitory in which, lying side by side, the nine whom we have just left below at their wretched meal will pass the night. The sole ventilation is through the small aperture occupied by what is termed, by courtesy, a window. In other words there is scarcely any ventilation at all. What a den in the hour of sickness or death! What a den, indeed, at any time! And yet when the sable goddess stretches forth her leaden sceptre over the soft downy couch in Mayfair, such are the circumstances in which, in our rural parishes, she leaves a portion of her slumbering domain.

Let it not be said that this picture is overdrawn, or that it is a concentration for effect into one point of defects, spread in reality over a large surface. As a type of the extreme of domiciliary wretchedness in the rural districts, it is underdrawn. The cottage in question has two rooms. Some have only one, with as great a number of inmates to occupy it. Some of them, again, have three or four rooms, with a family occupying each room; the families so circumstanced amounting each, in some cases, to nine or ten individuals. In some cottages, too, a lodger is accommodated, who occupies the same apartment as the family. Such, fortunately, is not the condition of all the labourers in the agricultural districts; but it is the condition of a very great number of Englishmen—not in the back woods of a remote settlement, but in the heart of Anglo-Saxon civilization, in the year of grace 1849. It behoves the

> "——gentlemen of England,
> Who live at home at ease,"

to ponder seriously upon the condition of such of their fellow-subjects as are so wretchedly circumstanced. Such anomalies but ill accord with the civilization to which we lay claim. In its main outline our national fabric may be brilliant and imposing; but is it sound in all its component parts? Whilst improvement has brushed over the prominent points, burnishing them brightly, it has passed over many of the deep crevices which intervene, and in which the gangrene is being engendered which is silently eating into the very vitals of society.

Illustrations are both by way of resemblance and of contrast. It is by contrast that the condition even of a backwoodsman illustrates that of many an English peasant. The first rude hut which the settler builds for himself in the woods is, in every way, more comfortable than the home of many an agricultural labourer. Even the wigwam of the Indian far surpasses it in this respect. I have seen one pitched in the forest in the course of a night, when the snow lay four feet deep around, which was dry, light, warm, and commodious, as compared with the hut which has just been described. The inmates, too, were well clad in their warm mocassins, dressed skins, and ample blankets, profusely decorated with beads, the stained porcupine quill, and the hair of the moose deer. Yet these are they whom we term savages. The difference between a savage and a civilized man is a mere difference of condition. So far as his physical condition is concerned, the American Indian is in advance of a large proportion of the English peasants. He has better shelter, better clothing, and more substantial food. If the Indian's mind is untutored, the intellectual training of the peasant is unfortunately not such as to make the contrast, on this side, very favourable to him. Yet the one is, in our estimate, a civilized and Christian man—the other a savage who paints himself. But a dash of paint is better any day than dirt.

But we are told that society is necessarily and immutably a system of inequalities. Granted; but it may remain so without its extremes being so far apart. It is not differences of condition, but the greatness of the contrasts—the brilliancy of some points, and the depths of shadow in which others are plunged—that is to be reprehended and dreaded. How great, how dangerous, the distance between the palace and the hovel. It is not with the palace that we have to find fault, but with the hovel. If there is no reason why some Englishmen should not enjoy their palaces, neither is there any why comfort, self-respect, and decency should not be the concomitants of the lot of all. Let society have its inequalities, but let its foundations at least be high and dry.

But it may be urged that the misery here depicted is exceptional, and that it cannot be accepted as the type of the condition of any numerous body of the peasantry. I speak now of only four of the forty counties of England, and assert that it is the type of the condition of the great bulk of the peasantry in these counties. They may not be all equally wretched as regards some of the comforts of life, because they are not all equally burdened with large families. But the house accommodation of the great majority of them is of the lowest and most miserable description. The universal testimony, indeed, of those in better circumstances on the spot, is, that the accommodation of the peasantry in this respect is far from what it should be. There is ground for this opinion in the condition of the labourer on the great bulk of what was once the Duke of Buckingham's property, as also in that of some of the peasantry on the Marlborough estates. The state of their domiciles in the vicinity of Aylesbury, Wycombe, and Crendon, will also attest its truth. Leaving Bucks and passing into Oxfordshire, we have not to go far for evidences of its soundness. Taking the town of Thame as a centre, and describing around it a circle with a radius of about seven miles, we have abundant proof in the portions of the circle which fall within that county—again excepting the property of Mr. Henley—that the house accommodation afforded to the labourer is not what it should be. Close to the town of Thame is the hamlet of Moreton, where any change made must almost necessarily be one in the direction of improvement. The same may be said of the village of Tetsworth, about three miles from Thame, and of Lord Churchill's property in the vicinity of Crendon. But, perhaps, the climax of misery in this respect, in the district, is to be found in the village of Towersey, about a mile distant from Thame. One house was pointed out to me there with four rooms, each room occupied by a separate family, some of the families being very numerous. It was a two-story house, covered with tiles. There was no communication between the upper and lower stories, the former being approached from the outside by a flight of stone steps, which rose over the door leading into the latter. One of the families counted eight or ten, of both sexes, some of whom had attained maturity. The immorality to which their domestic condition gives rise I shall have occasion hereafter to refer to. There was a common necessary for all, situated at a little distance from the house. It had no door, and its occupant, of either sex, was exposed to the gaze of the passer-by. This relation may shock delicate nerves, but it is as well that the truth should be told without mincing it. All around was filthy in the extreme. As the soil about was heavy and wet, the drainage was most imperfect. Something has recently been done in the way of improvement under the Sanitary Act, but the state of the village is still such that the work seems yet to be begun. Such is a specimen of the condition of British subjects within twelve miles of the greatest seat of learning in the world, and one of the *foci* of British Christianity.

Passing into Berkshire, we find insufficiency and even wretchedness of accommodation to be the rule in almost every direction. In the neighbourhood of Lambourn and Hungerford, not far from Reading, and almost under the shadows of old Windsor itself, this is found to be the case. In Wiltshire, it is notoriously and extensively so. Not far from Calne are cottages of a very inferior description. Near Chippenham, in excellent situations, like that of Colerne, not far from Bowood, in the vicinity of Marlborough, in the north-east, and of Mere in the south-west of the county; in the Winterbourns, and along the whole line leading from Salisbury towards Hungerford, they are, in the majority of cases, worse than bad. Almost midway between Old and New Sarum, too, specimens of a very questionable description may be seen. The Old and the New are here brought within the compass of a single vision, showing the advance which society has made in the lapse of centuries. But the peasantry seem not to have participated in that advance. The old seems to have gradually merged into the new without including them in the change. How far they have been left behind is well illustrated by their condition, in the near neighbourhood of these two monuments to time past and time present. Commencing our study of English society at its foundation, and confining for the time being our attention to that, we could scarcely escape the inference, judging from the physical condition of the people, that our whole system had been stationary for the last three centuries. I shall hereafter consider how far the extension of the inquiry into the intellectual state of the people would tend to dispel the illusion.

A considerable proportion of the agricultural labourers live in the outskirts of the larger rural towns. Here, as in the villages more exclusively appropriated to themselves, their domiciles are of the most wretched kind. Salisbury, Aylesbury, and Windsor are pre-eminent in this respect. Salisbury lies low, the Cathedral itself being sometimes inundated after long-continued and heavy rains. Nevertheless, it is most imperfectly drained, although a stream of water runs in an open channel through almost every street. During the prevalence of the cholera here, many of the inhabitants were encamped in tents in the fields whilst their filthy habitations were being cleansed and ventilated. Salisbury, notwithstanding, lost about one out of every forty of its population. The "Duck-end" part of Aylesbury almost baffles description, whilst Windsor remains as it was when reported upon in 1842, as being about the filthiest and worst drained town in the kingdom. It would almost seem as if, in these and other places which might be named, filth was regarded as a distinct department of industry, in which men were emulous to excel.

Even were the diet of the peasantry good and ample, personal and domestic cleanliness would be indispensable to their health. But, existing as they do on insufficient food, to which they are condemned by the scantiness of their wages, their only chance of preserving health is by keeping clean their persons and dwellings. Soap and soda, the chief ingredients in the process of washing, are now cheap, and many keep their cottages, persons, and wearing apparel as clean as possible under the circumstances. But whilst their miserable condition gives many an excuse for the filthiness to which they are prone, it drives others, originally better disposed, into careless and untidy habits. There is a point at which man ceases to struggle with his fate, and resigns himself to the seeming necessities of his condition. Many an English peasant is, in his circumstances, sunk so far below the line of comfort, decency, and self-respect, that the effort to reach it seems beyond his power. He convinces himself that he cannot better himself, and ceases the endeavour. At length he does not even cherish the wish, and becomes indifferent. "How can we be clean with eight in a room?" replied one of them, on my alluding to the state of his lodging. Hence the complicated forms of disease with which the small communities in the rural districts are so often inflicted. Diseases of a catarrhal character, dysentery, and fevers, particularly of the typhoid type, are constantly lurking about their wretched habitations. Hence, too, the vice which so alarmingly prevails, for impurity of mind becomes the invariable concomitant of habitual impurity of body.

Soil has, in respect of health, a great influence on a peasant's dwelling. The cottage which might be healthy in one locality might be the very reverse in another. A hut which would not harbour disease on Salisbury Plain or amongst the Chilterns, might not be a safe dwelling-place if erected on the heavy clay soils of Bucks, Berks, or Oxford. Proper drainage should always be had; but in some localities where it is not had, it is absolutely indispensable.

It is not always easy to discern the laws by which epidemic diseases are directed in their course. The pestilence, which is now disappearing, whilst it has spared some, has made terrible havoc amongst others of the rural communities. Hearing at Aylesbury of a village, named Gibraltar, about five miles distant, on which it fell with terrible severity, I proceeded to the spot to ascertain, if possible, the cause of a visitation so peculiar in its malignity. The situation of the village is suggestive of health, being about half way between Aylesbury and Thame, on an elevated ridge, looking upon the Chilterns to the south-east. The first thing I inquired into was the state of the drainage, but was told by one of the villagers that there was but little water to draw off. "There is not a pond in the neighbourhood," said he, "and sometimes for weeks we are very ill off for water." The village consists of a very few houses of an inferior description, and its whole population did not exceed fifty-six previous to the visitation of the cholera. "How many died here?" I inquired. "Nineteen," replied an old woman, to whom the question was put. "Twenty," said a man in a smock frock, standing by. "Well, to be sure," said the crone; "one of the women that died was near her confinement, and that makes twenty, if you like." Nineteen deaths out of a population of fifty-six! Dumfries has been held up as a model of affliction, because its deaths by cholera ascended to one in thirty-seven. But here was one out of every three carried off! "I helped to lay out five in one day," said a woman about thirty, who herself lost her husband by the scourge. The population was thus decimated in a day. Sixteen died the first week, and three the second. It then disappeared. One family, consisting of a man and his wife and six children, entirely disappeared, with the exception of one child. The worst feature in the case is that the mortality was chiefly amongst the heads of families. Thirty-seven of the population have been spared, but eleven of them are orphan children. They were almost all sent to the union, but "after having been there a week, and being well cleaned," they were taken out again by their relatives, who are now eking out their subsistence by the proceeds of the children's labour in the fields. During the height of the disease the surviving children were kept in a tent some distance from the village. "All that we can say is that it was the work of Providence," said a woman to me who had been a resident on the spot for forty-seven years; "but they were a wicked set," she added, "and perhaps deserved it." "But were they not an underfed, and, from the want of water, a filthy set?" I asked. "Well," said she, "perhaps they were; but they were not that way much worse off than their neighbours." Since the plague has left, the huts have been whitewashed, and additional holes have been made in the walls to serve as windows for the admission of more light, and the promotion of a better ventilation.

For the accommodation which they possess, insufficient and scanty as it is, the cottagers almost invariably pay rent, and in some cases a high rent. The rent varies from 6d. to 2s. per week, the amount of rent not being so much determined by the character of the house as by that of the landlord. Mr. Camm's tenants pay much higher rents than Lord Pembroke's, for which they are in general far less comfortably lodged. In most cases a small piece of ground is attached to the cottage by way of a garden. In Bucks, Oxford, and part of Berks, this, which seldom exceeds the eighth of an acre, is included in the rent; but in other parts of Berks, and throughout Wilts, generally, it is not. Here again the Pembroke estates are an exception. When extra rent is charged, the lowest is three-halfpence a pole. In some cases it is three-pence, and in others as high as a shilling. Now the average rental of land in Wilts is about £1 per acre, or about three-halfpence a pole. The poor wretch, therefore, who rents, say twenty poles, and pays 2s. 6d. a year for it, pays the farmer's rent *pro tanto*. In cases in which he pays beyond that, the farmer makes a profit out of him. In addition to this, allotments are sometimes made to them in the fields. This is particularly the case in Bucks and Oxford, where they take each, on the average, from a quarter to half an acre, for which they pay at the rate of about 30s. per acre. On the estate of Dodershall, the property of Mr. Pigott, I witnessed a large field thus appropriated. In general, the little plots of ground seemed well and carefully cultivated, and the poor creatures seemed happy to be in possession of them. Their homes are in the adjacent village of Quainton, where they were made as happy as possible by the constant and benevolent attentions of the worthy rector of the parish and his lady. There are many cottages without any ground attached to them at all. But these are often times such as have been built as investments. The demolition of cottages, particularly in close parishes, has been one of the results of the Law of Settlement. This has, in some places, led parties with money to buy small lots of land, and build houses upon them for the poor, where cottages were scanty. For these houses the highest rents are generally charged, it being seldom, as already stated, that they have any garden annexed to them.

If this paper has swelled to a great length, it must be borne in mind that it was no easy matter to generalize the varied results of one's observations over a surface embracing so many diversities of circumstance, and extending to nearly three millions of acres.

Considering the extent to which, in all ranks of life, their domestic circumstances influence the views and conduct of families, the condition, in this respect, of the great mass of the peasantry affords matter for serious reflection. If the description here given be applicable—and I challenge an assertion to the contrary—to the domiciliary condition of a great proportion, if not the great majority of them, it is evident that our social system is based upon a quicksand—for where privation is left to usurp so largely the place of comfort, men's notions of right and wrong are apt to become confused, modesty will succumb to impurity, recklessness supersede self-respect, and vice of every kind gain the mastery over religion and morality.

LABOUR AND THE POOR.

———◆———

THE RURAL DISTRICTS.

[FROM OUR SPECIAL CORRESPONDENT.]

BUCKS, BERKS, WILTS, AND OXFORD.

WAGES AND DIET OF THE AGRICULTURAL LABOURER.

Letter III.

In each of the counties forming the group now under consideration, I found two distinct sets of opinions current respecting the condition of the labourer, traceable to the different points of view from which the parties entertaining them made their observations. In one respect there was a concurrence of opinion amongst all parties, every one admitting, that not only was the condition of the lower order considerably below the standard of ordinary comfort, but that it was also such as was calculated, by its continuance, to give rise to the most serious apprehensions. But, in making this admission, those in better circumstances almost invariably couple it with an assertion to the effect that, bad as their state was, the labourers were better off in that particular county than in the surrounding districts. The opinion prevalent amongst the labourers themselves was quite the reverse of this, their notion being that they could not be worse off anywhere than where they were. This betrays everywhere a conviction on their minds, that their circumstances are so low and abject, that it would be impossible to push them further in the descending scale.

I was told, for instance, that in Bucks, Oxford, and part of Berks, I would find the wages of the labourer intermediate in amount between the higher rate paid in the neighbourhood of the metropolis and the lower scale prevalent in the west and south-west. In this I was not deceived, so far as Bucks, the greater part of Oxford, and a small portion of Berks are concerned. But when I was also told that the same might be said of the other elements which enter into the sum total of the labourer's condition, I was prepared to find his circumstances, with regard to his household accommodation, his food, clothing, education, and moral culture in these counties far in advance of what, in the main, I actually found them. As compared with his class in other parts of the country, there is little in the circumstances of his physical condition to indicate the superiority of his wages. More, in proportion to their whole number, may be better housed, clothed, and fed than in the west; but in all these respects the great bulk of them in the counties named are about as low in their circumstances as it is possible for them to be, compatible with mere existence. But when I was informed that in Wilts, proverbial for the low scale of its wages, the labourers were better off as a class than some of their neighbours, I could not avoid ejaculating—God help them elsewhere!

These statements, on either side, do not, so far as they were not borne out by the fact, originate in all cases in any wilful perversion of the truth. They are the result more of ignorance than of design. Not only are the circumstances of one county little known or inquired into in another, but ignorance of their respective conditions pervades the different districts of one and the same county to a degree which must be witnessed to be fully comprehended. The higher orders, who are more in the habit than others of holding intercourse and interchanging opinions with each other, may be well acquainted with the circumstances of their county; but the middle classes, the traders, merchants, and artisans, know little of what is transpiring beyond the bounds of their own districts. Ask any of them what are the circumstances of the labourer in the parish adjoining his own, and separated from it, not by a barrier of impassable hills, but by a low fertile ridge, well intersected by good roads, and in nine cases out of ten the answer will be, "Well, sir, I have lived here these twenty years, but never thought of askin' particularly." It is seldom that from these persons you can get any definite information as to the ownership of the soil in their own localities—their ignorance in this respect being partly to be attributed to the non-residence of many of the proprietors. Buckingham, for instance, is notorious for absenteeism. Of course the labourers themselves are profoundly ignorant of what is happening around them. The consequence is, that to obtain an adequate knowledge of the state of a county, one is compelled to make a personal inspection of almost every district within it.

In inquiring into the condition of the agricultural labourer there is nothing more important to be considered than his wages, as upon them mainly hinge his physical circumstances. They are characterized by great variety, not only as regards amount, but also in respect of their kind and the time of their payment. The wages in one county do not differ more from those in another than do the wages in one district from those in another district of the same county. To some extent they depend, as to amount, upon the quality and the quantity of the work in return for which they are given; but, generally speaking, their amount is determined without any direct relation to the nature of the labour to be performed. There are higher grades of work connected with farming for which superior wages are paid, such as carters' work—that is to say, the work of those who are entrusted with horses in the fields, and the work to be performed by shepherds, who are generally as well paid, because it is indispensable that they should be a trustworthy class. There are also species of work which do not necessarily involve the consideration of trustworthiness, but which, from their acknowledged severity, secure the higher scale of wages to those employed in them. Of this class "breast-ploughing" is an instance, the first, as well as the most laborious, process in the cleaning of foul land. It need surprise no one to find a distinction drawn as regards wages between these occupations and the inferior kinds of work connected with tillage. But that which does very naturally excite surprise, is the different rates paid, not only in different counties, but even in different parishes, for the same species of work. The ploughman who gets £12 a year, with his board, in one parish, might not be able to procure more than £10 in that adjoining it; whilst the ordinary farm labourer may have 10s. a week for doing in one county that which would only bring him 8s. in the county adjacent to it. It is this discrepancy that strikes one as singular, especially when the circumstances of adjoining districts, between which it may exist, are similar as to the soil to be operated upon, and the skill required, or the labour to be undergone in working it. The existence of such a discrepancy at once suggests that the circulation of labour is less free than it should be. This leaves the standard of wages a matter almost entirely regulated by the *arbitrium* of the employers. How otherwise is a man compelled to take 7s. a week in the neighbourhood of Salisbury for doing that which would bring him 9s. in the vicinity of Aylesbury? This could not be so if the labourer were less ignorant of the circumstances of surrounding districts, and more free than he is to transfer his labour to the best market. With this discrepancy there is, of course, a high and a low standard of wages in each county; the low standard in one being, perhaps, the high standard in another. But, although it is low in all as compared with the point at which it has stood, I found, go where I would, that the apprehension was general amongst the labourers that it was to be still further reduced. Nor is this a vague presentiment with them, but a conviction arising from the fact that the contemplated reduction has already, in numerous instances, been partially effected. But before inquiry into the extent to which this has been done, and is still further threatened, it will be as well to glance cursorily at the average standard of wages in the four counties during the portion of the current year which is now past.

In Buckinghamshire and the greater part of Oxfordshire the wages have been comparatively high; throughout most of Berkshire and the whole of Wiltshire they have been very low. In the first-named counties 10s. a-week have been earned by the labourer; whilst 8s. was the maximum rate, except during harvest time, in the greater part of those last mentioned. In all the agricultural districts the wages of course vary with the season of the year and the work required to be done. It is from April to November that the highest wages are had, including the harvest time, when they everywhere reach their maximum. From November to April again the scale of remuneration is comparatively low and employment precarious, particularly during the winter months, when, sometimes for weeks at a time, great numbers are out of work. In Buckinghamshire and Oxfordshire 10s. 6d. and even 11s. a-week, the latter rarely, have been paid to those at work in the neighbourhood of the larger rural towns. These have since been reduced to 10s. and 9s. 6d. Taking the wages paid since January over the greater portion of the surface of these counties, 9s. 6d. is an ample figure at which to place their average weekly amount. If the reductions already made, and those still contemplated for the remainder of the year be taken into account, the average for the whole year will certainly not exceed 9s. a-week. In Berks and Wiltshire, even including the higher rates paid during harvest time, the average for the last nine months will scarcely exceed 8s. a week; whilst, taking the reductions made and contemplated, as in the other case, the average for the whole year will be but little above 7s. 6d. per week. As much as 12s. a week have been earned during the present harvest in Wiltshire; but it must be remembered that against the high rates there paid, must, in order to get the average, be put the very low rates of winter, and the time when, longer or shorter as it may be, they may receive no wages at all, because there is no work to be had. We must also bear in mind that when a poor wretch is prevented for a day, or even half a day, by heavy rain from working, his wages are stopped for the time. It is not every employer that deals in this way by his workmen; but the majority of the labourers themselves will tell you that this is the manner in which they are generally treated. This is a parsimony by which nothing in the long run is gained; for from men so treated it is impossible to expect, or even to get, full and efficient work when they are actually employed. A farmer carefully attends to the wants of any agricultural machine which he may possess, and in the purchase of which capital may have been invested. If it goes to wreck before it has replaced this capital, it is so much lost, and fresh capital must be applied to the purchase of another. But if, from neglect and privation, a human machine becomes useless, no capital is required to procure another. The human machine reproduces itself, and he can have it to work for him at his bidding. But for this he would be more careful of its well-being than he too generally is. Both the slave and the horse are fed even when circumstances compel them to be idle. But a heavy rain on a summer afternoon frequently consigns an English labourer and his family to want for the day.

If the earnings of a working man are to be taken as indicating the extent to which both he and his family can command the necessaries and comforts of life, what are we to infer as the condition of families whose dependence is here upon 9s., and there on from 7s. 6d. to 8s. a week? But it may be urged that this is not to be looked upon as their sole reliance, inasmuch as the wife and some of the children not unfrequently, by their labour in the fields, add considerably to the common stock. Let us consider, for a moment, how far they do so. In some counties, classed amongst those that are purely agricultural, petty manufactures are carried on, which furnish employment to the children (particularly girls) of the labourer. There is little of that species of work to be had in the counties in question, except in the western part of Wilts, where manufacturing is carried on to some extent, in the neighbourhood of Abingdon, in Berks, and in Bucks, where many females are still employed in lace making and the plaiting of straw. But it is with the purely agricultural districts that we have now to deal. It is generally said that a woman, by working in the fields, earns half as much as a man. This, however, is not the rule, but the exception. It is seldom that a woman, except during harvest, earns more than 7d. a-day, and this even when a man's wages may be from 9s. to 10s. a week. The extent of their earnings is frequently not more than 6d. a-day, and in some parts of Wilts women have worked this year, during the harvest, for no more than 3s. 6d. a week. I was informed by one woman, near Mere, in the south-west part of that county, that she had worked ten hours a day for 5d.—that is, at the rate of one halfpenny per hour! Taking the year round, a woman's earnings will not average 3s. a week. In Bucks and Oxford, the earnings of a man and wife would thus together make 12s. a week; in Berks and Wilts, scarcely 11s. If this additional sum were procured without any countervailing disadvantages—if it were a clear money gain, without drawback of any kind, it should not and could not be omitted in our estimate of a family's circumstances. But it is not a gain without drawback, and the first drawback is one of a pecuniary nature. When a married woman goes to the fields to work, she must leave her children at home. In many cases they are too young to be left by themselves, when they are generally left in charge of a young girl hired for the purpose. The sum paid to this vicarious mother, who is generally herself a mere child, is from 8d. to 1s. per week, in addition to which she is fed and lodged in the house. This is nearly equivalent to an addition of two more members to the family. If, therefore, the mother works in the fields for weekly wages equal to the maintenance of three children for the week, it is, in the first place, in many cases, at the cost of having two additional mouths to feed. But this is far from being all the disadvantages attending out-door labour by the mother. One of the worst features attending the system is the cheerlessness with which it invests the poor man's house. On returning from work, instead of finding his house in order and a meal comfortably prepared for him, his wife accompanies him home, or perhaps arrives after him, when all has to be done in his presence which should have been done for his reception. The result is, that home is made distasteful to him, and he hies to the nearest ale-house, where he soon spends the balance of his wife's earnings for the week, and also those of his children, if any of them have been at work. A great deal is lost also through the unthrifty habits of his wife. Her expertness at out-door labour has been acquired at the expense of an adequate knowledge of her in-door duties. She is an indifferent cook—a bad housewife in every respect. She is also in numerous instances lamentably deficient in knowledge of the most ordinary needlework. All that she wants in these respects she might acquire, if she stayed more at home and was less in the fields. In addition to this, her children would have the benefit of being brought up under her own eye, instead of being, as they are, utterly neglected and left to themselves; for the party left in charge of them—and it is not always that any one is so—is generally herself a child, having no control whatever over them. It is under these circumstances that the seeds of future vice are plentifully sown. On the whole, as regards the system of married women working in the fields, I cannot, when the children are young, but look on the balance as being on the side of disadvantage. In that case I think it would be decidedly better for the poor man, having reference only to his physical comforts, that his wife stayed at home. And this is the position of many a labouring man. In many cases, when the family is large, some of the children are at work, adding their scanty wages of from 1s. 6d. to 2s. a week to the common fund. But I have known numerous cases of families of seven children, of which the eldest was not eight years old. Besides, when they are fit to work and earn wages of their own, his children soon become independent of him, and set up for themselves. This is in one way a relief to him, unless his family, while diminishing at one end, is increasing at the other. There can be no doubt but that a family is frequently aided by the earnings of the children, but in by far the greater number of cases the means of support are procured by the parents themselves. From what has been already said of the disadvantage to the whole family at which the wife bears her share in procuring them, it will be evident that the husband's earnings are, after all, the true test and standard of his own condition and that of those dependent upon him.

Moreover, in a very large proportion of cases, the wife remains at home, attending to duties more appropriate to her sex and position, in which case there is no other test to be had, unless it be the trifling and fitful earnings of one or two of the children. We have seen that, in the counties in question, there are about 40,000 married couples, who, with their children, numbering about 120,000, depend exclusively upon agricultural labour for support. Of the 40,000 mothers, fully one-half stay at home, some being compelled to do so on account of the extreme youth of their children, and others, save when their families are somewhat advanced, preferring from calculation to do so, as being the best mode of turning their scanty means to good account. This may be taken as the case with half the married couples, who, with their families, will number about 100,000 individuals. So far, therefore, as these are concerned, the children, in about the same proportion of families, being too young to add anything to the common stock, there is nothing else to adopt as the test of their condition and the standard of their comforts but the earnings of the husband. Let us inquire, therefore, into the condition of a family thus solely

dependent upon such wages as the husband has, on the average, received during the past portion of the current year. I can best illustrate
that condition by one of the numerous cases which came under my
consideration in Wiltshire. The labourer in that case had had 8s. a
week, but he was then only in receipt of 7s. He had seven children,
the eldest of whom, a girl, was in her eighth year. Two of his children
had been at a "dunce's school," but they were not then attending it,
simply because he could not afford the 4d. a week which had to be
paid for their education. To ascertain how far he was really incapable,
in this respect, I requested him to detail to me the economy of his
household for a week, taking his earnings at 8s. The following is the
substance of the conversation, discarding, for the reader's sake, the
portions in which the names are given.

When are your wages paid?—On Saturday night, but often only
once a fortnight.

What do you do with the money on receiving it?—I first lay by
my rent, which is a shilling a week. I then go to the grocer's and lay
in something for Sunday and the rest of the week. I buy a little tea,
of which I get two ounces for 6d. Sugar is cheap, but I cannot afford
it. We sometimes sweeten the tea with a little treacle, but generally
drink it unsweetened.

Do you purchase any butcher meat?—Generally for a Sunday we
buy a bit of bacon.

How much?—It is seldom that I can afford more than half a
pound.

Half a pound amongst nine of you?—Yes; it is but a mere taste,
but we have not even that the rest of the week. It costs me about 5d.

Do you buy your bread, or make it at home?—We buy it. We have
not fire enough to make it at home, or it would be a great saving to
us.

Do you buy a quantity at once, or a loaf when you need it?—We
buy it as we need it.

Have you a garden attached to your cottage?—I have about 15
poles, for which I pay three ha'pence a pole. It is less than the 8th of
an acre.

What do you raise from it?—We raise some potatoes and cabbages.

Do you raise a sufficient quantity of potatoes to serve you for the
year?—No, not even if they were all sound.

In addition to the potatoes and the cabbages which you raise, how much bread do you require for your own support, and that of your wife and seven children for the week?—We require seven gallons of bread at least.

What is a gallon of bread?—It is a loaf which used to weigh 8 lb. 11 oz., but which now seldom weighs above 8 lbs. Those who supply bread to the union seldom make it over 8 lb.

What is the price of the gallon loaf?—Tenpence. It is cheaper than it was, but then there is not always so much of it. It is often of short weight.

Seven gallons of bread at 10d. a gallon would make 5s. 10d., would it not?—I believe it would make about that—you ought to know.

Do you always get seven gallons a week?—No, seldom more than six.

Then you spend 5s. in bread, and make up for the want of more by potatoes and cabbages?—Yes.

You have still some money left; what do you do with it?—It costs us something for washing. For soap and soda, and for needles and thread for mending, we pay about 5d. a week.

Do you buy fuel?—We get a cwt. of coal sometimes, which would cost us about 1s. or 1s. 1½d. if we took in any quantity and paid ready money. When we do neither it costs us about 1s. 4d. a cwt. If there is one poor man who can afford to buy it in any quantity for ready money, there are forty who cannot.

How long would a cwt. of coals serve you?—We make it last one way or another for two weeks.

Your fuel, therefore, will cost you about 8d. a week?—It will.

Is there anything else you have?—We buy a little salt butter sometimes, which we can get from 6½d. to 10d. a pound. We are obliged, of course, to take the cheapest; "and really, sir, it is sometimes not hardly fit to grease a waggon with."

But your money is already all gone, how do you pay for your butter?—It is not always that we have it, and we can only have it by stinting ourselves in other things.

You have said nothing about your clothing—how do you procure that?—But for the high wages we get during the harvest time we could not get it at all.

How long does the time last when you get high wages?—About ten weeks, and but for what we then get I do not know how we could get on at all.

From this recapitulation it must certainly appear a mystery to the reader how they get on as it is. The weekly expenditure, in our view, is as follows, the family being nine, and the weekly receipts 8s.:—

	s.	d.
Rent	1	0
Tea	0	6
Bacon	0	5
Bread	5	0
Soda, soap, &c.	0	5
Fuel	0	8
Total	8	0

The provision for clothing is in the extra wages paid at harvest time, whilst the family cannot be treated to the luxury of bad butter without sacrificing the tea, two ounces of which must serve for a week, the half pound of bacon, which affords but a "mere taste" on Sunday to each; some of the bread, which is already but too scantily supplied; or a portion of their fuel, the absence of which renders their home still more cheerless and desolate. Sugar, too, is out of the question, without trenching upon items more absolutely necessary. Nor is there any reserved fund for medicines, too often required by a family of nine thus miserably circumstanced. What, in short, have we here? We have nine people subsisting for seven days upon 60 lbs. of bread—scarcely a pound a day for each, half a pound of bacon, and two ounces of tea, the rest being made up by a provision too scanty, in nine cases out of ten, of potatoes and cabbages raised in the garden. Could they descend much lower in the scale of wretchedness, especially when we couple with their stinted supply of the less nutritious kinds of food the miserable hovels in which it is taken by them, either shivering in the winter's frosts, or inhaling the pestilential odours engendered around them by the summer heats?

I could no longer express any surprise at 4d. a-week being grudged for the education of two children.

This being the mode in which his weekly wages were expended, I asked the same individual to give me an account of his daily life, including his labour and fare. In reply to my questions on this point he answered, in substance, as follows:—

At what hour do you go to work?—At six in the morning generally in summer, but I have gone much earlier. In winter time work begins at a later hour.

Do you breakfast at home?—When I do not go out very early, I generally do.

Of what does your breakfast consist?—Principally of bread, and sometimes a little tea. Sometimes, too, we have a few potatoes boiled.

When do you dine?—About twelve.

Of what does your dinner consist?—On the Monday my wife gets a little flour and makes a pudding, which, with a few potatoes, forms my dinner. Sometimes we have a pudding on other days, but generally our dinner is bread and potatoes, with now and then a little cabbage. When the family is not large, there may be a bit of bacon left that has not been used on Sunday, but that is never the case with us.

You return to work again?—I do, and when I come home at night may have a little tea again, with the bread which forms my supper. The tea is never strong with us, but at night it is very weak.

Do your children get tea?—We have not enough for that.

What is their drink?—Water; sometimes we get them a little milk.

What is your own drink?—Water.

Do you never drink beer?—Never, but when it is given me; I can't afford to buy it.

When your dinner consists of bread, potatoes, and water, have you nothing to season it or make it palatable?—Nothing but a little salt butter, and we can only afford that when the bread or potatoes happen not to be very good, or when we are ailing, and our stomachs are a little dainty.

When your bread or potatoes are bad, or your stomachs are dainty, you take as a relish the butter which you said was scarcely fit to grease a waggon with?—We have nothing better to take.

Suppose you had nothing but bread to eat, how much would you require to sustain you at work in the course of a day?—Two pounds at least.

And how much would one of your children require?—About the same. A child, although not at work, will eat as much as a man; children are always growing, and always ready to eat; and one does not like to refuse food to them when they want it. I would sooner go without myself, than stint my children, if I could help it.

Then, at the rate of two pounds a-day for each, you would require for all about 126 pounds for the week?—I suppose about that.

And, as you only get about sixty pounds of bread a week, you have to rely on your potatoes and cabbages, your half pound of bacon, and two ounces of tea, to make up for the sixty-six pounds which you cannot get?—We have nothing else to rely on.

Have you enough of these to afford you as much nourishment as there would be in 66 lbs. of bread?—Not nearly enough.

Is what you have stated your manner of living from week to week?—It is, when I have work.

And when you have not work, how is it with you?—"In the winter months we have sometimes scarcely a bit to put in our mouths."

Such is the substance of the statement, as regards his own and his family's circumstances, made to me by a labouring man in receipt of the average rate of wages for the last nine months in Wiltshire. Comment is scarcely needed, the facts speaking but too plainly for themselves. Had the family been smaller, or the wages a little higher, instead of a "taste," they might have had a meal of bacon once a week. But even then it would be but once a week, potatoes and bread still constituting the staple of their diet, and even these not being had by them in sufficient quantity. Besides, even if they had it more frequently, bacon is not the most nourishing food in the shape of butcher meat. It is fat, and goes to fat. The little lean that is in it is almost destroyed by the process of curing. But it is greasy, and soon satisfies. "It fills us sooner than any other kind of meat," was the reply given to me, when I asked why they preferred it to beef? But the fault is that it does not fill them. It satiates, without filling them. Bulk is required as well as nutriment in food. The stomach has a mechanical as well as a chemical action to perform. A man could not live on cheese, nor could he exist on pills having in them the concentrated essence of beef. They buy bacon because it goes a longer way than other meat. In truth, they buy it because it soon cloys them. Nor is it always that they have even a "taste" of it once a week. I have seen several families who had not tasted butcher meat of any kind for weeks at a time. When French and English workmen came together during the construction of some of the French railways, it was found that the Englishman could perform far more work than his French competitor. This was universally attributed to the superiority of his diet, it being supposed but reasonable on all hands to expect more work from the man who fed on beef and porter than from him whose fare was bread and grapes. But the fare of the man who is expected by his labour to develop, year after year, the agricultural wealth of England, is, in a large proportion of cases, little better than bread and water— the fare of the condemned cell! Contrast the condition of the English farm labourer with that of the farm labourer in Canada. In England, he eats butcher meat once a week, and not always that; in Canada, he has as much of it as he wants, once, at least, and frequently twice, a day. Contrast his condition even with that of the slave in the southern states of America. In Virginia, the great slave state, it is seldom that a day passes without the slave eating butcher meat of some kind or other. In addition to this, when he is old and infirm, he has a claim on his master for support. But the English labourer, if he has a family to sustain, has not, even during the days of his strength, when he can do and does work, the same nutritious diet as the slave; whilst, when he is disabled, or loses his work, he must starve, or, as the alternative, become a vagrant, or the recipient of a formal and organized charity. In the words of one of themselves, "it is not a living, sir, it is a mere being we get;" by which he intended to convey that their reward for their toil was their being barely enabled to exist.

It may be said that the case put is an extreme one. It is the case, however, of nearly one-half of those who are dependent upon labour in the fields. But it may be said that I have omitted to take into account some little privileges which the labourer has, and which, when he avails himself of them, tend to enhance his comforts. He may keep a pig, for instance, and his employer will sometimes find him straw for it, which, in process of time, will serve as manure for his little garden. This looks very well on paper, but that is chiefly all. In the four counties under consideration the number of labourers keeping pigs is about one in twelve. It is also a striking illustration of the condition of the labourers, that even such of them as do feed a pig, seldom participate in the eating of it. Then we hear a great deal about the coal and clothing clubs, to which I shall hereafter more particularly advert, and the chief merit of which is, that they tend to render life not pleasant, but barely tolerable to the poor.

The class of labourers best circumstanced is, of course, that composed of unmarried men. When not boarded and lodged on the farm, they generally stay with their relatives, or with some other family. But by the pernicious system which obtains throughout the country, of giving them lower wages than married men, a direct premium is set upon marriage. The result of this ill-advised distinction is, that it drives many away from the culture of the soil, and hurries others into premature marriages. During my peregrinations through the county of Oxford, I was driven from Thame to the city of Oxford by a young man possessed of acuteness and intelligence superior to those of most of his class. "How long have you been connected with the inn?" I inquired. "For some years now, sir," he answered. "Did you leave any other employment to take to the stables?" I then asked him. "I was born in the hamlet (Moreton) to the left there, and brought up to farming; but I left it, and took to stabling, because the farmers would not give me fair wages for my work." "Was there any difference between your work and that of others?" "No," said he, "but I was single and others were married. I didn't want to marry, and I wouldn't work for less wages than others worked for, and so I left." To have got the higher rate of wages, he must have married had he remained. "Then," continued he, "they make no distinction between one who knows how to do his work and one who doesn't. I learnt to work properly on the farm, but I was never paid more than other single men who knew nothing about their work." This practice of discriminating between married and single men is fraught with no little mischief.

Such being the condition of so large a proportion of the labourers and their families in Wiltshire and Berkshire, where 8s. a week has been the average maximum rate of wages—a condition but little improved in Bucks and Oxford, where the maximum has been little if anything above 1s. higher—it becomes important to inquire into the prospect more immediately before them, with a view to ascertaining whether that condition is likely to be bettered or deteriorated. If I mistake not, rumours of an intended reduction of wages were recently very prevalent. Incredible as it may appear, these rumours have proved in general but too true. Throughout the four counties which I have already traversed the reduction either is or will be general. There is scarcely a district in either of them where the work of reducing wages has not already commenced, and there is scarcely a district in which the poor are not apprehensive that that work is to be carried still further. I had an excellent opportunity at Thame of discovering how things were tending, in this respect, in Bucks and Oxford. It so happened that I was there on the day of the annual fair, when a great many cattle change hands, and servants are hired for the year. The town was very full of booths, travelling shows, whirligigs, jugglers, tumblers, and barrel organs; pigs, horses, and oxen; labourers in clean smock-frocks, and farmers in top-boots. The gaiety and uproariousness of the day were succeeded by the multiform debaucheries of the night. The servants hired at this fair are generally such as are boarded and lodged on the farm, but the wages offered them were a good indication of what was likely to be the rate in vogue, so far as the ordinary farm labourer was concerned. Lower rates were almost invariably offered and accepted. In some parts of Bucks, where 11s. a week were paid, 10s. are now given, and where 10s. were paid, 9s. are now taken. Almost throughout the whole of Wilts a reduction has taken place, to a greater or less extent. Even as early as last June, wages in some districts were reduced from 8s. to 7s. It is true there was a temporary rise during harvest, but they have again sunk to 7s., and apprehensions are everywhere entertained that they will be reduced to 6s. Indeed, in numerous instances it is known that this has been determined upon by the farmers at their meetings, both in Wilts and Berks. "My master," said one man to me, "is not going to reduce, but what he pays away in one way he saves in another." "How much does he pay?" I asked. "He pays 8s.," replied he. "And how will he save the difference between 8s. and 6s.?" I demanded. "Why, sir," said he, "he is going to discharge some that he was in the habit of keeping during the winter. He's going to save in that way, but he has already saved in other ways. I have myself hoed turnips for a third more than I got this year, hoeing them by the job as usual." "You speak," said I, "of your master discharging some of you. Are you likely to be included in the number?"—"I can't say, sir," he answered; "when they discharge, they generally first send off such as have no families, lest by discharging those that have, a greater burden should fall on the parish. They then send off those with the smallest families for the same reason. You see, sir, it's made a matter of pounds shillings and pence throughout, and not of rewarding them that faithfully serve them." "Are you engaged for any length of time?" I asked. "No," said he, "none but the carters and shepherds are so. They are engaged from Michaelmas to Michaelmas. The rest of us may be sent away on a moment's notice. To be sure, if we are sent away on a Monday we may demand a whole week's wages. But then to entitle us to that, we must do nothing else during the week for hire." "Is there any combination amongst yourselves to keep up wages?" I inquired. "None, sir. We are too much in their power for that. If any man complains they call him saucy, and discharge him at once. The employers all understand each other, and won't employ him again until he has learnt better manners, or is punished enough for his impudence." "On what ground," I then asked, "are they lowering the wages around you?" "On the ground that living is cheaper," he replied. "And is it so?" was my next inquiry. "It is," said he; "bread is a good deal cheaper, and so are tea and sugar for such as can buy them. Meat, too, is a little cheaper, but not much."

"Are provisions now so cheap, that you could live comfortably with your family on 8s. 3d.?" "Lord bless you, no," he answered; "we can live better now on 8s. than before, but not comfortably yet." "What will they do who are reduced to 6s.?" asked I. "I don't know what will become of them," he replied. "As it is, it's wonderful how they get along. The hand of God is in it, sir, or they couldn't do it. But how they can live on 6s. a week, sir, I don't know. They can't do it, sir, they can't do it," he added, with a scowl upon his face, and an asperity in his tone, which contrasted strangely with his bearing and utterance throughout. He was from Amesbury, and my conversation with him took place in front of the "Old Castle," a small inn on the high-road to Salisbury, and just outside the outer mound of Old Sarum.

The same day, whilst strolling in a neighbouring parish, I espied an old man proceeding along the highway in front of me. He was very infirm, tottering along with the aid of a large staff which he carried, and I soon overtook him. After saluting him I got into conversation with him, and found that he had been long resident in the parish, and was now an out-door pauper receiving relief. "I have been off work these two years," he said, "and now get two shillings and half a gallon of bread a week from the union." "Do you pay any rent?" I asked. "Yes," said he, "sixpence a week. Aye, aye," he continued, "I have been in the King's service, and have worked here for more than thirty years, and it has all come to that at last," pointing to the repulsive looking walls of the workhouse, which rose over some tree-tops in the distance. "When were you discharged from the King's service?" I inquired. "I can't remember," said he, "it's so long ago, but it was the year after the battle of Waterloo." I then ascertained that he had returned to his parish and worked as a labourer, married, and had two sons, who were since dead, but not, he said, before they had known what it was to toil for a scanty reward. Their death was a great blow to him at the time, but he said that he had been since glad, for their sakes, that they were gone, for he could have left them nothing as an inheritance but his own misery and toil. "Do you hear anything about wages coming down?" I asked him. "Hear anything about it!" he exclaimed, "it's what all the poor people are talking about. They expect to be told next pay day, that they must come down to 6s." "Why are they to be brought down?" I inquired. "The farmers say," he replied, "that the poor people can now live cheaper, and that they themselves can get hardly anything for their corn." "Can they live more cheaply?" asked I. "A little," was his answer. "Since you have been in the parish have you known wages as low as they are now?" "Never," said he. "Have you known them much higher?" "A little higher," he replied. "Have you known corn much higher than now?" "Much," was his answer. "And were wages high in proportion?" "No," said he. "When corn was twice as high as now, wages were but very little higher. They beat the poor people down when things are cheap, but they won't raise their wages much when things are dear. They do the same with the landlords. They want to beat down rents when things are cheap, but they won't raise them when corn is high. They won't pay their poor people because they say they can't; but they ride their nags and keep their greyhounds for all that."

But, as regards the threatened reduction of wages, the worst has not yet been told. In the neighbourhood of Mere, some of the farmers have come to an understanding with each other to force upon the labourer 6s. in money, and a bushel of wheat at 6s., for a fortnight's work. Now, what is generally thus given to the labourer is what is called "tailings." At this moment the best grain is not selling in the markets of Wilts at more than 5s. a bushel, and to force upon the labourer an inferior grain at a superior price is an injustice of the grossest kind. Taking the grain which they would receive as equal in value with the best wheat, it would be but 5s. worth. But it is not worth 5s., and it would cost them nearly a shilling more to convert it into a shape fit for food. The value of the fortnight's wages would thus be about 10s., that is to say, *about 5s. a week!* Such is the prospect before the labourer, for the ensuing winter, in a part of Wilts.

Is it any wonder that, with such a prospect before them, the agricultural labourers should brood over their circumstances with the ominous sullenness of despair? What is that prospect? The winter is approaching—the season when most is required by us all to administer to our comforts. They are entering upon that season with here 8s., there 6s., and there again but 5s. a week for the support of their families. How far will these pitiful portions go in households of 5, 6, 7, 8, 9, or 10 individuals? We cannot, in estimating a labourer's comforts at any given time, apply to them the test of his average wages. It is his wages for the time being that decide the measure of his condition. Had he at any time more than was necessary to carry him and his family up to the line of comfort, he might lay by the surplus for adverse times. But he never has what secures him perfect comfort, and is always more than tempted to spend all he gets. He therefore commences this winter, as he does every winter, without any reserve fund to fall back upon; and the fact is appalling that, in this month of October, thousands of families in the very heart of England have no better prospect before them than that of living on 8s., 6s., and even 5s. a-week, in their cold, damp, cheerless, and unhealthy homes.

LABOUR AND THE POOR.

—◆—

THE RURAL DISTRICTS.

[FROM OUR SPECIAL CORRESPONDENT.]

BUCKS, BERKS, OXFORD, AND WILTS.

LETTER IV.

The low physical condition which I have depicted as the unfortunate lot of nine-tenths of the labouring poor in Wiltshire, of five-sixths of them in Berks, and of the great bulk of them in Bucks and Oxford, is utterly incompatible with the existence amongst them of a high standard of intellectual and moral attainment. Startling as may have been the disclosures made in reference to the household accommodation, the wages and diet of the agricultural labourers, they will not be found to be more so than the revelations of their intellectual and moral condition, which it is now my painful duty to make. I have no desire but one, in reference to the matter, and that is to tell a plain unvarnished tale. My object is to conduct, as impartially as possible, the branch of this extensive inquiry which has been committed to my hands, leaning neither towards nor against the poor, but dealing fairly by all classes concerned, and relating only what I have myself witnessed, or that of the existence of which I have had the most ample proof. The reader may be both shocked and astonished at what I shall relate, but not more so than I myself have been on finding that I had no alternative but to relate it.

In what I have heretofore said in regard to the physical circumstances of the agricultural labourers, I have carefully guarded against its being supposed that there were no exceptions in the four counties in question to the picture drawn of their miserable condition. These exceptions do exist, scattered over these counties in greater or less proportion, being most numerous, perhaps, in Buckingham, and least so in Wilts. But they are but mere exceptions after all, the description which I have given of their physical lot being applicable to the great bulk of the labourers in all the four counties. To the sketch which I am about to draw of their condition, intellectually and morally, the

47

exceptions, I regret to say, are still rarer in them all. I shall first consider them in reference to their intellectual state, treating this branch of the subject in connection with the condition of the present and the prospects of the rising generation.

Of the intellectual training of the present generation of labourers little need be said, indeed little can be said of that which has scarcely an existence. We hear much of the want now of a proper educational system for the poor, but there is this difference between the present time and that which is just past, that whilst now something is being done, however imperfect that may be, there was then little or nothing effected for the education of the lower orders. There are, at this moment, in the counties under consideration about 120,000 adults, both male and female, who are either themselves engaged in out-door agricultural work, or are dependent upon those so employed. Of these how many can read or write? The question is more aptly put by framing it, how few can read or write? A clergyman in Berkshire, who had been for eleven years in his parish, informed me that in seven cases out of ten the parties whom he married could not sign their own names. It may not be so bad as this everywhere, for the education of the people, like their physical comforts, has been more left to the benevolence and caprice of individuals, than it has been largely and comprehensively cared for by the state. Here and there you meet with endowed schools and other appliances of education, the existence of which, for many years past, is traceable either to private munificence or to local bounty, and the result of which has been to illumine, with a few feeble rays, in their different localities, the intellectual gloom which surrounded them. But for these, the prevailing ignorance, amongst this class of our countrymen, would be universal and supreme. This may be denounced as a strong assertion, but its strength is that of truth. He who doubts has but to examine for himself, and I care not into which of the four counties he goes for this purpose, for either of them will furnish him with abundant proof of the correctness of my statement. The mental degradation, so characteristic of the labouring class in the counties, does not arise from their want of intellectual parts, but from the absence of tuition and instruction. These same parties, when they remove into a large town, or a manufacturing district, display an acuteness and aptitude, which, if not equal to those of others more favourably situated from their youth, is in striking contrast with their previous intellectual torpidity. Nor are those who live in the larger rural towns so stolid, or so intellectually inert, as those

who inhabit the villages, or live detached in the more thoroughly ru-
ralized districts. It is amongst them that ignorance has so completely
established her dominion, and has so long swayed her sceptre undis-
turbed, that in many cases it is difficult to trace even the vestiges of
intelligence in the countenances of the people. Their intellectual range
is as limited as is the horizon of the mariner when in the deep trough
between two heavy seas. Their perceptive powers are feeble, for their
opportunities of observation are few. Their stock of acquired or communicated knowledge is in all cases small—in some it has scarcely an
existence. Unfortunate though it be, it is, nevertheless, true, that the
greatest mental activity that they display is in general in the exercise
of cunning and the pursuit of vice.

So far even as the routine of their daily labour is concerned, their
knowledge is not always sufficient. There are some who work intel-
ligently, others who work mechanically, and the number of the mechanical is far greater than that of the intelligent workmen. The little
knowledge which they possess as a class is almost entirely confined to
the round of their occupations. They can weed well, and hoe well, and
do the ordinary work of harvest well, but there are but few of them
who can plough well. There are operations in the practical conduct
of husbandry which, to the superficial observer, appear to be merely
mechanical, for which multitudes of them are incompetent. But, however limited their knowledge may be in many cases, even of the different branches of their own occupation, the range of their intellectual
acquirement is, in seven cases out of ten, bounded by that occupation. They may or may not, as the case may be, display acuteness and
intelligence when you question them in connection with their daily
avocations, but when you transcend the line of their own pursuits, and
endeavour to make them follow you beyond it, they become confused
and bewildered; and the degree of intelligence which may have previously irradiated their countenances, is superseded by a vacancy of
aspect which it is distressing to contemplate. I speak now not of all,
but of the great bulk of the men and women employed in the fields
in the four counties. They have grown up at their daily tasks without
anything like proper intellectual culture, and are, both in their mental darkness and moral obliquities, a standing disgrace to the nation,
and living monuments to its educational shortcomings. We vent our
indignation upon the Carolinian planter, who takes positive steps to
prevent the light of education from dawning upon the darkened soul
of his slave. But, if we have not exactly followed his example, with re-

gard to the rural labourers, we have, at all events, refrained, as a people, from extending to them those means of enlightenment which,
as a people alone, we could afford them. It is not this, that, or the
other class that is to blame, but the nation at large, which has too
long consigned to the chance efforts of individuals and localities the
all-important subject of popular education. The consequence is, that,
to this day, a large proportion of the lower orders are utterly ignorant
of the veriest elements of instruction—an intellectual destitution of
which hundreds and thousands of examples may be found within the
counties in question. I have spoken to hundreds of them, and tested
their knowledge of subjects bearing upon their social, moral, and religious duties, and found them generally with notions of morality lax
and undefined—with their knowledge of the obligations of society
towards them as limited as that of their duties towards society; and
with ideas upon religion, in many cases, too crude and too fantastic
to be very efficacious in the practical regulation of their lives. But for
them there is no better prospect held out, so far at least as regards
their intellectual improvement. They must toil away listlessly and mechanically as they have ever toiled, and die as ignorant as they have
lived. But there is hope for the generation that is to succeed them
at their avocations. For them more is being done than was done for
their fathers, and I propose now to inquire into the means actually in
operation for the instruction of the young in the agricultural districts,
and to ascertain how far we are in this respect atoning by our present
exertions for our past neglect.

Nothing is more difficult than to obtain an adequate idea of the
educational machinery of an English county. This may sound odd,
but there is a very obvious reason for it. Were education with us a ma-
tured and general system, extending on a uniform plan to every corner
of the land, its appliances in one municipal sub-division would be but
the *fac simile* of those in another, and indeed of those in all. Thus in
the state of New York, one has only to acquaint himself with the educational apparatus of any one school district to become master of
the whole plan of education throughout the state. Each district is,
in this respect, but the repetition of its neighbour. But in England
our whole system of public instruction is ragged and incomplete. In
no particular district has the system pursued any necessary relation
to that followed in adjoining districts. Schools which are common to
one locality may or may not be found in another, but the machinery at work in each is not, as in the United States and in Prussia,

part and parcel of one grand, comprehensive, and national scheme. The efforts made in this, that, or the other district in behalf of popular instruction, are more or less isolated and independent, having no direct or necessary identity with any great educational operation homogeneous to this country. So essentially local, incomplete, and disjointed, is our whole system, that not only can one not predicate upon his knowledge of what is going on in one county an assertion as to the proceedings in another adjoining it, but the same may also be said as regards contiguous parishes. Next to the inspectors of schools, whose duty it is to acquaint themselves thoroughly with the educational appliances of their respective districts, one would expect that the parties most likely to be well informed on such a subject would be the resident rural clergy. But, even from them, the information to be derived is scanty and imperfect. They know what is being done in their own parishes; but they are not necessarily informed of what is being effected in the same direction elsewhere. I am, therefore, compelled to present to the reader not a detailed, but a very general picture of what is being done for the promotion of popular instruction in the counties now under consideration.

Baffled in my endeavours to obtain very explicit information from those resident on the spot, I betook myself to official records, in the hope that they would furnish me with the intelligence which from other sources I had been unable to obtain. But here again I was disappointed, for on referring to the reports presented to the Education Committee of the Privy Council for the year 1847-8, by the different inspectors of schools throughout the kingdom, I found that, whilst they communicated some information, they, too, left much, very much, to speculation and conjecture. And this may be as fitting an occasion as may present itself for alluding to the manner in which the public are actually misled by some of the "Blue Books" published by authority of Parliament. In conducting this investigation your correspondents have necessarily very frequently to refer to numerous and bulky tomes of parliamentary literature. But it so happens that some of them, although ostensibly published for general information, are so prepared as to be convertible with accuracy only to official purposes. In this category are the important returns in connection with the poor. Looking into these returns, the public would be led to infer that from 1,800,000 to 2,000,000 of people were paupers in the regular receipt of relief, in other words, that every seven Englishmen, in addition to supporting themselves, had to find the means amongst them of supporting an eighth. Thousands have recoiled with horror from this appalling statement, and have been led to despair of the fortunes of the country, when, believing that already one-eighth of the population were regular paupers, they saw that pauperism was still rapidly on the increase amongst us. But the truth is, that these returns were prepared more for the Poor-law Board than for the public. And in preparing them, the practice is, if a man, from the sickness of his wife, or any of his children, is induced to apply for aid and receives it from the workhouse, to put him and his whole family down as paupers receiving relief. If the family consisted of nine, this transaction would add nine to the list of those returned as paupers. Nay more, if, some time afterwards, a second application were made, under similar circumstances, and complied with, the nine would count up again, thus making eighteen to be added to the number to be returned as poor. And this, when the reality may be that neither the man nor any of his family can justly be reckoned amongst the class called paupers. So far as they go, the returns of the school inspectors are curious, interesting, and valuable; but they do not go far enough, affording but an incomplete picture of an imperfect system. One, for instance, states that the schools *under inspection* in his district are 282 in number. This may, or it may not, imply that that is the whole number *liable to inspection*. Again, he states what proportion of them receive grants from the Committee, and what from the Lords of the Treasury. So far as these grants are concerned the return is sufficiently perfect, provided the number of schools given comprises all liable to inspection. But a portion of the number given consists of schools which, not having received any grants, have nevertheless "invited inspection." But we are not informed whether or not there are other schools which, not having received grants, have *not* invited inspection, or, if any, how many. There is no record whatever of the private schools in the district, and yet it is essential that we should know what is being done by private efforts to enable us to appreciate all that is being done in any locality for education. There is no reason why the number of these private schools, and of the number attending them, at least should not be given. They form an item in the returns presented to other Governments, and are necessary to enable us to compare our educational system with that of other countries. In the returns, for instance, made to the Government of Connecticut, the private schools are as carefully enumerated as are those of a public description. Again, when in this same report information is given as to the number of children in attendance, and their ages, it is confined to seventy-five schools of the 282. The only way in which one can come at the whole number of children attending these schools, is by laboriously adding together whole pages of tabulated statistics, each page containing at least two dozen columns of figures! Again, the inspector within whose district Oxford falls, tells, that in that county there are thirty-three schools liable to inspection; but not a word is there about private schools in the whole report. The inspectors in this are not to blame, as in all probability they were instructed to confine themselves to schools of a particular class. It is the whole system which is to blame, which seems to be as imperfect in its separate parts as it is as a whole. And with re-gard to the thirty-three schools in Oxford, we have no general results given us. For these we must wade through a fresh succession of sta-tistical tables similar to those alluded to—a task from which a mind ordinarily constituted recoils with horror. Nor is there any uniformity in the plan on which the several reports are drawn up. In fact, we are so much in the infancy of our educational career as a nation, that the department superintending it seems yet at a loss to know how to deal properly with the subject. I repeat it, therefore, that these reports con-vey no adequate idea of the machinery actually employed in the work of popular instruction in England. The reports on the parochial union schools are more complete and satisfactory; but, with this exception, we are left to grope comparatively in the dark in reference to a subject so all-important as that of public instruction.

Imperfect as they are in many respects, they nevertheless serve to show how utterly defective our whole system of education is. Many are led away by what has recently been done for the education of the masses, both of a public and private nature, into the belief that the business of popular instruction has now attained at least a respectable footing in this country. But this is a mistake which a very little obser-vation will suffice to dissipate. What has been done to give rise to such a belief? The public grants have, in the course of a few years, swelled from £30,000 to somewhat upwards of £100,000 per annum. This is consolatory, but it is still trifling as compared with what is being done elsewhere in the same sacred cause. The private efforts which have been made, particularly amongst some of the dissenting bodies, have been on a most munificent scale; but they have been, more or less, confined to particular districts of the country, the rural districts, as a whole, have participated but very little in their advantage. In nu-merous parishes in the country districts the dissenters have scarcely a footing; in others they are too feeble and too poor to take any effective measures for the instruction of the people. That which has been done, both of a public and of a private nature, in this country, falls far short of the mere public provision made for education in some of the states of the Continent, and in almost all the states of the American Union.

The number of schools for which public provision has, to some extent, been made in Wiltshire, is only 68, being one school for every 3,800 of the population. In Oxford the number is only 33, being but one school for every 4,900 of the population. In Berks it is still lower, being only 25, which gives but one school for every 6,200 of the population. The precise number in Bucks is not given; but giving that county as its proportion the average number of the other three counties, that proportion would be about 36 schools, or one for every 4,500 of the population. This will give us for the four counties but 162 schools, or one for every 4,420 of their aggregate population. Let us compare this with what is being done elsewhere. The latest returns which we have in reference to education in Holland are those of 1846. In that year there were in Holland 3,214 schools for a population of about 3,857,000 souls, being one school for about every 950 of the population. But of this number 639 are returned as "private schools," and 165 as schools on "special foundation," leaving 2,410 as the number of the "public parish schools." Now, taking these alone as the schools for which public provision is made, we have one school for every 1,600 of the population. In Prussia, during the same year, the number of elementary and other public schools amounted to upwards of 25,000, which for a population of 16,000,000 gave one school for about every 650 people. The contrast to our own presented by the educational system established on the other side of the Atlantic is still more striking. In New York, the population of which is about 3,000,000, the number of common public schools is about 10,000, being one for every 300 of the population. In Connecticut, again, there is one school for about every 250 of the population. Of Canada I cannot speak with the same degree of exactness, having no returns from the province before me; but this much I can say from personal knowledge, that in Canada West an ample and a munificent provision has been made for popular instruction as in most of the states of the Union. As compared, therefore, with the public provision made for education in the four counties in question, we find that that made in Holland is at least three times, that in Prussia nearly seven times, that in New York fourteen times, and that in Connecticut seventeen times as ample as it is in these counties. The educational machinery of the state of Connecticut furnishes the most striking example of what may be done, when a people is in earnest, for the promotion of public instruction. Although its population is but about one forty-fifth part that of England alone, its revenue arising from the school-fund, and available for the purposes of education for the year, is nearly one-fourth as great as the sum last voted for education by the British Parliament. There are in the state about 1,660 common schools, attended by about 90,000 children, being one school for about every sixty children. In New York, again, the lowest municipal sub-division is the school district, of which there are somewhat upwards of 10,000 in the state. Each district has its common school, the area of the district being in the great majority of cases not more than four square miles, generally forming a square the length of whose side is two miles. The school is planted as near the centre as possible, so that few of the children in the state are two miles removed from a place of public instruction. There is at present one school for about every 70 children. Instead of a school, for which public provision appears to have been made, in the four counties in question, for every four square miles, we have but one for every 22½ square miles; and instead of there being one school for every 60 or 70 children, we have in these counties but one for 1,090, between the ages of 5 and 15. In making these comparisons, I have in all cases excluded from my calculations such schools as are more strictly of a private nature.

Were the schools thus established in the four counties as perfect and efficient as they might be, a great deal of good might be effected by 162 schools, in addition to private institutions, amongst a population of about three-quarters of a million, and extending over an area of from three to four thousand square miles. But, in a great many instances, they are wofully deficient as regards those appliances with which they should be liberally supplied. Taking a bird's-eye view of a county in its educational aspect, we find that the combined machinery at work consists of the national schools, British schools, diocesan schools, sometimes connected with the National Society, and at other times not; endowed schools, private schools, and the schools of parochial unions. Of these the British and private schools are, generally speaking, the most active and efficient. The national and diocesan schools are, in many cases, perfect in their organization, adequate in their machinery, and efficient in their operation. But both the national and the British schools, which are the chief recipients of the public money, and particularly the former, are in too many instances deplorably wanting in what is essential to constitute a good elementary school. Some of the national schools are but caricatures of a proper educational establishment. To say nothing of inadequate accommodation, or of their deficient supply of books, apparatus, &c., they are in the character and attainments of their teachers lamentably behind what they should be. Many of them are able men, not only well educated, but also thoroughly instructed in the art of communicating their knowledge to others. But there is a large proportion of them who are rigid disciplinarians and honest in their efforts to do their duty, but who are each, nevertheless, a species of intellectual fossil, far behind as regards the knowledge of the day, and utterly unprepared, either by education or antecedent habits, for the important and by no means easy task of imparting instruction to the young. For these and for other reasons, to which I shall hereafter advert, the education acquired in these schools is, for the most part, of the most imperfect kind. The Bishop of Oxford, who has certainly done much to put the educational institutions of his diocese on a better footing than they formerly occupied, has issued a circular to the teachers of his diocese, stating what, in his judgement, should be the subjects on which the pupils in the national and diocesan schools should be instructed. It is a large and liberal catalogue, but one which will not be properly embraced in the round of instruction in one school out of ten, until the whole system is remodelled and rendered more efficient. One of the inspectors, again, gives the following list of subjects on which he thinks the children should be taught more or less:— Biography (of good men), natural history, the preservation of health, domestic economy, horticulture, mechanism, agriculture, geography, history, grammar, natural and experimental philosophy, money matters, political economy, and popular astronomy. A stranger would think, from scanning this list, that we were, throughout, the most erudite and philosophical people in the world. But we must not be misled by sounds or names. A lad who is taught the nature of wages and the names of the heavenly bodies may be described as receiving instruction in political economy and popular astronomy. It is true that most of the subjects mentioned are taught in the elementary schools of America; but how many of them are taught with us the following fact may attest. In the county of Oxford, under the four heads of geography, grammar, etymology, and history of England, there is not one child returned as receiving instruction. Whether this is a defect in the return, or arises from the fact that no children in the county are receiving instruction at the inspected schools on these subjects, I cannot exactly say. The simple fact is, that none are returned as receiving such instruction. The columns are there to receive the numbers, if there were any, but they are all blank—whilst the columns beside them are more or less filled up. But however this may be, geography is not as thoroughly and universally taught as it should be. This is a great mistake; for there is no greater drawback to the extensive emigration of the lower orders than that arising from their almost total ignorance of the capabilities, position, and even names of the places to which they should go. I have questioned them, old and young, on this subject, and have found their ignorance as universal as profound. Yet it is a subject on which they are most eager to acquire information. Many of them—men far advanced in life—were as much taken aback on my asking them what a colony was, as they could have been had I questioned them to unfold to me the mysteries of the Principia. They could give me no distinct notion of Canada, as to what or where it was. Their only idea seemed to be that it was somewhere across the sea, and very far off; whilst some of them entertained the most exaggerated notions of its climate. One man told me that he believed it was a country where it was winter all through the summer; whilst very few of them could give me any reason why it was more competent for them to go and settle in Canada than in France. On my telling them that there were portions of Canada where melons, peaches, apricots, and grapes grew luxuriantly in the open air, and that the same toil, which here brought them but a bare subsistence, might, in a very few years, make them landed proprietors there, they pricked up their ears, and looked at me in mute astonishment. Some of them had heard of New Zealand, others had not; but none of them had any practical knowledge of it. With the name of Australia they almost exclusively associated the idea of transportation. It is this ignorance that keeps them at home wedded to their misery here, instead of transferring themselves and their only capital, their labour, to spheres in which the willing hand need never want work, and labour is sure of its reward. But wretched though they be here, they will not leave to encounter the undefined evils with which ignorance associates emigration in their minds. Not only should geography be sedulously taught to the young, but something might be done to atone for the ignorance in which the existing generation of labourers was allowed to grow up, by teaching even them that which might in its results be of such service, both to themselves and others. It is not in connection with this department alone that our system is deficient. A large proportion of those who attend these schools never learn to read or write well, and have but a slight knowledge of arithmetic beyond its most elementary rules. Grammar is a branch of which few acquire more than the merest smattering—many not even that.

I have alluded to the parochial union schools, as constituting a feature of our educational system; but as no room is left me in this paper to enter into a detailed account of them, and as I shall have occasion hereafter to refer more particularly to their working, and that of the other schools in simultaneous operation with them, I shall content myself for the present with a general remark upon them, that, I regret to say, has reference to their utter inefficiency in the vast majority of cases for the accomplishment of their professed object. They are invariably connected with the workhouses of the different unions, their object being the instruction of pauper children, and are in most cases found within the walls of the workhouse. That at Aylesbury is the best arranged and the most efficient of any that I have seen, but even its efficiency cannot date much further back than a year. But in general the whole scheme is as ill devised as it is badly executed. It presents such a wreck, such an aspect of dilapidation throughout, that it looks more like the ruins of an educational system which had gone irretrievably into decay than like one which purports to be in active operation.

The list of schools which I have mentioned as constituting the main features in our scheme are all to be found, but in varying proportions, in the different counties of the kingdom. But it would be a mistake to suppose that they are to be found in the different parishes constituting the counties. If each parish had its National and British school, or either of them, it would be well off, provided they were efficient, without the others. But it is seldom that you find two parishes similarly provided with the means of education. They differ from each other both as regards the amount and the nature of the machinery at command. In one parish may be a National school, in that adjoining it a British school, or one may have both and its neighbour none. Again, there are some in which there are private schools, whilst there are none in others, and the same may of course be said with regard to endowed schools. But so irregularly and arbitrarily are the means of instruction distributed amongst them, that some parishes may be utterly destitute, whilst others have, more or less converged, all the means of education at command. The educational destitution of some of them may be illustrated by the condition in this respect of one in Berkshire.

The parish alluded to is that of Sutton Courtney, near the town of Abingdon. It has an area of 4,040 acres, and, with the exception of one or two farmers who own the land which they farm, cannot boast of a single resident proprietor. There is, consequently, no rent spent within it, and although tithe to the amount of about £3,000 is collected, that too is abstracted and spent elsewhere. The tithe belongs to the Dean and Chapter of Windsor, who, however, do not draw the tithe, having leased it to different parties on lives, the leases being renewable, and the dean and chapter receiving a fine on every renewal. The lessees are one or two parties in the neighbourhood, and another in Exeter. The case of Sutton Courtney is, in this respect, the parallel of that of Wokingham, which was presented by petition to the House of Commons in 1848. There the tithe, to the amount of about £2,000, had been alienated; and the consequence was that a large and important parish, which requires for its proper spiritual superintendence the undivided energies of two clergymen, did not enjoy the undivided attention of even one. And so in Sutton Courtney. Although nearly £3,000 are raised there in the shape of tithe, the stipend allowed to the vicar of the parish is but £150, although he has two churches to serve. The parish has a population of upwards of 1,500, who chiefly inhabit the village of Sutton Courtney, which has a thousand inhabitants, and the hamlets of Appleford and Sutton Wyck, with 200 and 300 respectively. Although situated in the midst of a healthy district, it would be difficult to conceive a more filthy and unwholesome locality than Sutton Courtney was, until within the last three or four months. Even yet, after much has been done to purify it, the nose of the wayfarer is assailed, on his descending the wide street, of which the village chiefly consists, by the most loathsome and sickening odours, proceeding from foul pools of reeking filth close to the doors of some of the cottages, and the short but slimy and pestilential tributaries, which, proceeding from most of the houses, discharge their contents into a putrid but covered drain at the side of the road. Bad as it is even yet, what must it have been when this drain, the sluggish receptacle of the accumulated filth of an uncleanly population, was uncovered, and glistened and simmered in the hot sun? And yet this was so as late as a few months back. The suns of May and June last quickened into fatal activity this hot-bed of disease and death, and fevers and other kindred diseases were the necessary consequence. The improvement which has taken place is owing to the vigilance and energy of the present vicar, who took steps which resulted in the covering of the drain. It was well that they did so, for by and bye the shadow of the cholera, in its fearful flight over the land, fell upon Sutton Courtney, as upon other places around it. First came several severe cases of diarrhœa, which spread alarm throughout the community. The clergyman endeavoured to calm their apprehensions from the pulpit, told them how to treat the disease in its premonitory stages, and above all insisted upon the necessity of sobriety and cleanliness both of person and domicile. At length a case of decided cholera was announced, and all was consternation. The vicar was absent on duty, but he returned at night. In the meantime, some of the inhabitants waited on a farmer in the neighbourhood to know what could be done. He was *nonplussed*, and advised them to "chance it." Not so the vicar. On returning and hearing what occurred, he immediately procured lime, and by torchlight, with the aid of his own stall boys, scattered it in the filthiest localities in the neighbourhood of the house which had been stricken by the plague. Next morning he procured more lime, and had the same operation performed over nearly the whole village. He had also about twenty necessaries emptied of their contents, which had been in a state of pestilential overflow for years, and the filthy contents of which were in some cases constantly oozing through thick stone walls into the highway. He had dung-heaps innumerable removed from the backs and from the fronts of houses—and in one heap, which was behind a cottage, in a small garden, not much larger than an ordinary room, and between a pig-stye and a necessary, he found, a few inches below the surface, the carcases of a sow and nine young pigs, which had all died, and which had been thrown there, scarcely covered, to decompose into manure. He had also an extensive reform effected in the internal economy of many of the houses, some of which were of the lowest class, comprising but two rooms, in one of which, in more cases than one, ten of a family slept together. In company with the vicar, I ascended to several of the dormitories. It was quite common to find three beds in one room. One of them, not more than twelve feet square, was thus furnished. The rafters were covered, and the room appeared to have been recently whitewashed. So far well—but the air seemed nevertheless sour and stifling. The light struggled through a small window, which was shut. The vicar opened it, exclaiming as he did so, "They never will ventilate their rooms." On descending, he asked the mother if nine of them did not sleep in the room up-stairs. "There's ten of us sleeps there, since she's come home," she replied, pointing to a girl, between thirteen and fourteen, who was then combing her hair at a broken piece of looking-glass, which was hanging against the window. She, her husband, and the two youngest children, one an infant at the breast, slept in one, the largest bed of the three, the rest being huddled together night after night in the other beds. Fortunately, the cholera did not spread, another instance of the baffling caprice of this singular disease—for if any place seemed to promise it a harvest it was Sutton Courtney. But I have here made a digression, which I am sure the reader will pardon for what it contains. Besides, as I shall illustrate another branch of my subject by the condition of Sutton Courtney, I thought it as well at once to pave the way for what I shall then relate of its morals by apprising the reader of the physical habits of its people. But to return to the subject of education.

Incredible as it may seem, it is nevertheless true, that, four years and a half ago, when the present vicar came to the living, with the exception of two "dame schools" in Sutton Courtney and an endowed school at Appleford, the parish was entirely destitute of the means of instruction. Now, those who know anything of a "dame school" are aware that it is just no school at all; and as to the endowed school, I shall show that it also was a nullity. Having got the people into the habit of attending church, which he deemed to be his first duty, his next object was to provide them with the means of instruction. He soon established a school, which he divided into four departments— the first an infant school for boys and girls, the second a day-school for boys and girls above the degree of infants; the third a night school for men and boys above the degree of children, and the fourth a night school for women and girls above the degree of children. He thus assailed ignorance in every stronghold which it possessed. For attendance at the night school a penny a week is paid by each individual, which, of course, entails a loss, as the fees will not cover the expense of coals and candles, pens, ink, and paper, &c. For attendance at the day-school twopence a week is paid by each. The school has not, as yet, been sufficiently long in operation to have produced any striking results. Its influence, however, will soon manifest itself, and an intellectual glimmering at least will be cast over this long-benighted portion of the land. The vicar has also established a small school at

Appleford, where the endowed-school already alluded to is situated. The principle of the foundation of this school is, that twenty children belonging to the parish should be educated at it. But that principle has long since been departed from. To sustain the school, a few hundreds a year, with a free house and garden, were left to the master. The present incumbent is a lieutenant in the navy. What his qualifications were for the office of teacher, the trustees can best explain. The average attendance at the school at present is a dozen instead of twenty. Instead of grounding them in the ordinary branches of instruction, he has given an almost exclusively industrial turn to their education, the boys being more employed in digging and cultivating his garden than they are occupied in the school-room. Their proficiency may be appreciated from the fact that one of them, after having been for three years at the school, had actually to be put to the very first lessons in writing on entering the school at Sutton Courtney. It was not, therefore, too much to say that, previously to the establishment of the latter school, this parish, which is within eight miles of Oxford, was utterly destitute of the means of instruction. The public little know to what extent this malappropriation of educational funds is carried on in England. The vicar had no little difficulty in establishing his school, the majority of the ratepayers being insensible to the necessity which existed for it. He at length, however, got it established, and now pays £40 a year towards its support, the ratepayers amongst them paying only £3! It must be admitted, however, that they contributed to the purchase of the schoolhouse and piece of ground attached to it, which cost about £300. But, having built the mill, they take no interest in keeping the machinery at work. Fortunately for the vicar, the Rev. Mr. Gregson, who has had a terrible struggle of it, he is a man of independent means. The working machinery of his parish, including his school, costs him more than his stipend. But suppose he had entirely to depend upon his stipend, where would the parish, as regards education, be at this moment? Just where it was when he entered it—at zero in destitution. And this it is which so closely connects the question of the tithes with that of education. Were the £3,000 raised spent in the parish, there would be more than sufficient to provide amply for its spiritual wants. The proper destination of the surplus would then be obvious. As it is, the parish is insufficiently provided with spiritual, whilst it has been left utterly destitute as regards secular instruction. This, it may be said, is an extreme case. It is to be hoped that it is so. It may be an extreme, but it is not a singular case. There are many not far from it which approximate it, in point of destitution, if there are not many which equal it. It would be scarcely possible to surpass it in this respect. But, even admitting it to be an extreme case, it is by such cases that our educational system can be best illustrated, as regards its deficiency. But one person may die of starvation out of a community of 100,000, but the death of one, under such circumstances, would indicate very great privation amongst a large proportion of the survivors. The educational system which admits of such a case, even as an extreme one, must be radically defective. I have dwelt more particularly on this parish as affording evidence of its defects, not because it was the only illustration at hand, but because I was desirous of citing a striking one, limited as I am, in these communications, as regards space.

Of how many of the 16,000 parishes in England is Sutton Courtney the type? I do not adduce it here as an exception, but as an illustration. There are, as already said, too many similar cases around it—similar even as to the extent of their destitution. But between that destitution, and the state of those parishes which are even the best supplied, how many grades of educational insufficiency intervene? It requires but little investigation into the subject to perceive that the great work of national education has yet to be begun in England.

There are many other topics connected with this subject which I shall have ample opportunity hereafter of adverting to.

LABOUR AND THE POOR.

—◆—

THE RURAL DISTRICTS.

[FROM OUR SPECIAL CORRESPONDENT.]

DEVON, SOMERSET, CORNWALL, AND DORSET.
PHYSICAL CONDITION OF THE LABOURER IN DEVON
AND SOMERSET.

LETTER V.

Before entering into a consideration of the moral and religious
condition of the labouring classes in the agricultural districts, it is advisable that I should extend over a large surface my observations as to
their physical and intellectual state. The group of counties of which I
now propose to treat, in reference to these branches of the general inquiry, comprises Devon, Somerset, Cornwall, and Dorset. As regards
the house accommodation, and the wages and diet of the labourer, I
shall deal with them separately; after which I shall take a general survey of the state of education in all; and then it will be time to deal with
the moral aspect of the subject—in doing which, I shall comprehend
with this the other group of counties already partly disposed of. In
prosecution of this plan, the present communication will be devoted
to an inquiry into the physical condition of the labouring classes in
the counties of Devon and Somerset.

These counties have an aggregate area of 2,707,200 acres. It would
be difficult to select another district in England presenting a greater
variety of surface, both as regards its general aspect and its capabilities
in an agricultural point of view. Portions of it are as wild and impracticable as is the Black Mount—once a royal forest—which extends in
such waste and monotonous succession from Glenorchy to Glencoe.
The sterility of these parts is most conspicuous in the districts comprehended under the names Dartmoor and Exmoor. The chief value of
these districts is in the pasture which they afford to sheep, and in the
treasures contained in some of the spurs and ridges which shoot off
from them in the direction of the estuary of the Severn. For the most

part, too, they are intersected by valleys, which are cultivated generally by small farmers, some to a greater, and some to a less extent, according to their circumstances and capabilities. In other directions, we find marshy tracts, composed of the debris washed down into the sea, during the lapse of ages, from the higher grounds of the interior. These marshes are more commonly met with along the northern than along the southern coast of the counties, and are more prevalent on some portions of the coast of Somerset than anywhere else. They constitute, however, but a small portion of the whole area, by far the greater part of which exposes to the sun a charming succession of gentle but rich alluvial undulations. In Somerset, the richer tracts are chiefly appropriated to the purposes of grazing, that county having been famous for its dairy farming ever since the time when tillage was so largely superseded in England by pasturage. Somerset has, indeed, long ceased to raise sufficient grain for its own consumption. Dairy farming is also very prevalent in Devon, particularly in that part of it which abuts upon the southern boundary of Somerset, and in the neighbourhood of Totnes. But a large proportion of the land of Devon is arable, tillage being the rule, and pasture the exception, especially along the line extending from Torquay to Honiton and Axminster.

The combined population of the two counties was, in 1841, 968,000 souls. This gave one person to every 2 4-5th acres—the average throughout all England being, as frequently observed, one to every 2 1-7th acres. The great pressure of population upon surface in this district, as compared with that in the district formerly considered, is accounted for by the presence of numerous and large towns in the counties now under consideration. The number of people employed in them in commerce, trade, and manufactures, in 1841, was 120,000; the number employed in agriculture, 99,009. Of those employed in agriculture 75,392 were agricultural labourers. Of this number no less than 58,596 were adult males, upwards of 20 years of age. This, making the same calculation as in the former case, would give 226,336 as the whole number in the two counties dependent upon agricultural labour for support; in other words, about one-fourth of the whole population is thus dependent. In the four counties already treated of, the proportion was much greater, the disparity being accounted for by the employment of various kinds afforded to immense numbers of people by the seaport and manufacturing towns (the latter on rather a small scale) with which the two counties abound. In addition to this, the greater proportion of their surface which is under pasture leads to the employment of a smaller number of people upon the land than would be thus employed were more of their acres devoted to the plough.

Devon and Somerset have long been classed in the unenviable category of counties presenting the agricultural labourer in his most deplorable circumstances. With Dorset and Wilts they are generally regarded as exhibiting the unfavourable—whilst Lincolnshire exhibits the favourable—extreme in the labourer's condition. Well aware of this, and of the difficulty of conquering a prepossession which may have been received on insufficient grounds, I divested myself, as much as possible, of preconceived notions, determined to judge, so far as I could, not from hearsay, but from personal observation. With this view I have been over the greater part of the two counties, and I have found the state of the labouring class to be such, in every respect, as to justify the prevailing impression.

In traversing both counties, more especially Devonshire, I was particularly struck with the utter absence of new cottages. Along the highways and byways, their absence is observable; and not only this—but in many places there are abundant evidences that cottages, which a few years ago were tenanted, are now, if not altogether untenantable, going rapidly into decay. Many are so rickety and ruined, that, to inhabit them any longer is impossible; whilst, as regards others, the process of demolition or decomposition has only commenced—confining the wretched tenants, who had formerly two rooms, to the only apartment which remains, and which they can with difficulty keep together. In search of these, one has not to go into remote and sequestered parts, where things are done which would not be exposed in the neighbourhood of the highways. I have seen specimens of cottages in this state along the line from Exeter to Honiton, and in the district traversed by the high road to London. One in particular struck my attention, from its dilapidated appearance, and the discomforts to which it obviously subjected its inmates. The upper part of one of the end walls was entirely away, exposing the crazy anatomy of the roof, and laying the whole of what used to form the sleeping apartment of the family bare to every tempest that swept around their miserable house. I entered this fragment of a cottage and found the family to consist of seven. The dilapidated wall had, for some years, shown signs of weakness, but no effort was made to repair it. At length it became so shaken that the only resource left appeared to be to pull down its upper part, and leave the lower and sounder portion standing. This was done, but nothing—not even a boarding—was put to supply its place, so that the family were driven to occupy the lower apartment only, unless they could contrive to sleep in a room exposed on one whole side to the elements. The lower room, which was about sixteen feet square, with a mouldering brick floor, served as kitchen, sitting-room and bed-room for seven people. The ceiling, which was rickety, bulged downwards, as if oppressed with its own weight—whilst through the gaping beams, with which it was replete, trickled the rain, whenever it was driven by the wind into the dismantled room above. The approaching winter will be the second spent by them in this wretched ruin. Back from the highways, and in the more secluded parishes, much of this state of things may be observed. Not only are no new cottages being erected to meet the exigencies of an increasing population, but old ones, instead of being kept in repair, are suffered to crumble to pieces—if, indeed, decay is not aided by more active means. In a parish between Honiton and the coast, a great part of which is owned by Sir Edward Elton, this process of cottage clearing seems to be a marked feature in proprietary policy. On Sir Edward Elton's property I am told that the average rate of decay or demolition is about six cottages per annum. As each cottage would contain a family of seven on the average, the proprietor thus clears his estate of about 42 poor persons each year, unless they can find room in their neighbours' hovels, which can, in most cases, be but ill spared. By this means this estate, and others similarly dealt with, will, by-and-by, become eased of one incumbrance at least which presses upon them—a large and unemployed population. But it may be said that this process of clearing has a tendency to raise wages, if its result should be to lessen the permanent charges upon the property. Into this subject I shall have occasion to inquire more at large in a subsequent communication.

Whilst, in many parts of Devon and Somerset, the process of the demolition of cottages has been going on far more rapidly than that of building new ones, the population of the two counties has been fast increasing. "We don't find room for them," said a farmer, with whom I conversed on this subject, "and they are drafted off to other places." But they are not thus drafted off in all cases, and the real effect of the demolition of cottages is to reduce, if possible, to a still lower point of wretchedness, the physical condition of the labourer.

The clergyman of one of the parishes of Devon pointed out to me an addition which had recently been made to the parish church. As it stood, the church was but a small one, but the addition made to it was larger than the original edifice. "Why was the addition made?" I asked. "Because the population of the parish has increased," was the reply. This answer was obvious, and I had anticipated it, but I wished to obtain it in order to base upon it another question. "How comes it," I inquired, "that, if the population has increased so as to require so large an addition to be made to the church, there is not a single new cottage to be found in your parish?" "That is difficult to say," he answered. "It does not appear to me," I added, "that there is a cottage in your whole parish which has been built within the last fifty years." "They all seem to be of that age at least," he replied, "and many much older." "And when was the addition made to the church?" I inquired. "Within the last twenty years," said he. This simple story speaks for itself. The population of the parish in question has largely increased, but the house accommodation has not increased in the slightest degree to meet the exigencies of a growing population. It is evident that the new comers were not drafted off elsewhere as fast as they came, otherwise the church might have remained of its original dimensions. The truth of course is, that most of them stayed in the parish—every cottage in it becoming more and more crowded with inmates every year. The consequences of this, both in a moral and a physical point of view, are shocking to contemplate. And this is the process which is going on in more parishes than one in the counties of Devon and Somerset. Whilst population is increasing within them, not only is house accommodation not increasing, but it is actually diminishing.

The points in Devon at which I more particularly inspected the dwellings of the poor, were—in the south, in the neighbourhood of Exeter, along the line between that city and Exmouth, in the direction of Totnes, and throughout a great part of the union of Kingsbridge; in the vicinity of Axminster, between that town and Honiton, and between Honiton and Sidmouth; and in the north, around Barnstaple, and along the more northerly part of the vale of the Torridge. In Somerset I examined them with some care in the neighbourhood of Minehead and Dunster in the north-west, near Bridgewater in the centre, and about Wells, Chewton, Mendip, &c., in the north-eastern part of the county. In the great majority of instances I found the condition of the cottages to be deplorably bad. It is not to be denied that I encountered some, and even many, exceptions. At many points there were cottages to be found well situated and commodious, but they were exceptions to the general character of the peasant's dwellings. My present object being to state the points at which accommodation is deficient, it would be unnecessary for me to dwell upon those instances in which I found it good, even were they more numerous than they are; and if, in what follows, I pass them without notice, it is because of their being merely exceptional.

It is impossible fully to estimate the wretchedness to which the inmates of the hovels which meet the eye at all points are exposed, without a close personal inspection of them. We are accustomed to associate with the idea of a country village, or with a cottage situated in a winding vale, or hanging upon the side of a rich and fertile slope, nothing but health, contentment, and happiness. A rural dwelling of this class, with its heavy thatch and embowering trees, makes such a nice pencil sketch, that we are naturally inclined to think it as neat and comfortable as it appears. But to know it aright it must be turned inside out, and its realities exposed to the gaze of the observer. Could the internal be always given with the external view, it would moderate our enthusiasm for the little sketches which work so early and so powerfully upon our fancies, and which are suggestive of nothing but contentment and happiness. How often does the cot, which looks so attractive and romantic upon paper, conceal an amount of wretchedness, filth, squalor, disease, privation—and frequently of immorality—which, when exposed in their reality, are perfectly appalling. And as to health—nowhere, perhaps, is the pure air of heaven more tainted than in the neighbourhood of these rustic dwellings. You will encounter odours in a country village which it would be difficult to match in Westminster or St. Giles. Indeed, the most sickening and offensive that I ever came in contact with had nestled themselves on the summit of Beacon-hill, in the neighbourhood of Bath. It is high time that people divested themselves of the false impressions too generally entertained of the character of our rural cottages. They are chiefly drawn from descriptions which at one time may have suited the reality, when the condition of the agricultural labourer was much better than it is now. For, that it was much better than at present is evident from the information derived from a variety of valuable sources. To go a considerable way back—we find Fortescue alluding to their condition in his day as one of great comfort and happiness, inasmuch as they lived chiefly upon butcher meat, of which they had plenty, and had abundance of good ale with which to accompany it at their meals. In regard to their diet at least, their condition now seems the very reverse of what it was then; and as it is impossible that they could have fallen back so much in this important element of their physical condition without having all the others deteriorated in proportion, it is fair to infer that their house accommodation was better formerly than now. It was better in this, if in no other respect, that fewer people were to be found under one and the same roof—a state of things much more favourable to health, cleanliness, and good morals, than that which now prevails. We must, therefore, judge of the labourer's condition, not from past descriptions of it, but from the sad realities of the present hour.

Between Exeter and Exmouth I found several cottages of a very low order, although not exactly of the worst description. East of Exmouth, and in the direction of Sidmouth, they were, in many instances, of an inferior description to those in the locality just named—being, in many cases, so overcrowded as to render almost impossible the preservation of health. In many instances I was deceived by the exterior of their hovels; for here, as elsewhere, they have recently been cleansed and whitewashed, in anticipation of a visit of the cholera. They therefore look at present, when only examined from the outside, much more attractive than they did two or three months ago—requiring an inspection of their interior to dispel the illusion which many of them, with their sparkling white walls, no matter how low and rickety they may seem, are calculated to produce. The cleaning which they so extensively underwent was not confined to the outside, but in the great majority of cases it would already be difficult to tell that the inside had been touched at all. I was scarcely prepared for the extent to which dung heaps were to be found close to the dwellings. When the drainage is bad, which is too often the case, and when there are a pig-stye and a dung heap attached to a cottage, the character of the atmosphere inhaled by the inmates may be easily conceived. The practice of keeping a pig is, in some counties, much more prevalent than in others. It is a boon, in one sense, to the labourer where he can keep one—but, in another, it is a nuisance of the first order. When he has a patch of ground attached to his house, it is almost invariably so small that the pig-stye, if not directly under his window, is not removed to the distance of thirty feet from it. The system of giving field allotments, too, has to some extent affected injuriously the sanitary state of some of the villages. These allotments are not universally granted—but where they are so, the land is generally well manured, the garbage used for this purpose having been collected for months at the very doors of the allottees. I have been told of several instances in which a decided change for the worse has thus been wrought in the sanitary state of village communities. Previously to their procuring allotments they had but little or no inducement to collect manure—but since they have been granted to them, it is one of the conditions on which they hold them that they shall be well manured. Besides being compelled to manure them well, they are themselves anxious to do so, inasmuch as they pay tolerably high rents for them, and are therefore anxious to get as good a return as possible. It thus happens that, either from the want of accommodation or from the absence of inclination to keep the neighbourhood of their dwellings clean and healthy, they collect the filthy heaps at the ends of their houses, and sometimes close to their very doors—so close indeed that you occasionally step upon them in entering the cottages. This is certainly no argument against the system of allotments, which is an admirable one in many points of view; but it shows how much has to be done to improve the condition of the class in question. It is not enough that a movement is made in their behalf, in this or that particular direction. Their condition is so wretched and low that, unless several movements are made in different directions for its improvement, the very measures which are designed to ameliorate it are accompanied with evils almost as great as those which they mitigate.

In some of the small valleys in the undulating district around Totnes I found several specimens of the worst description of cottages. Indeed it was a matter of surprise to me that some of them were inhabited at all, notwithstanding the miserable accommodation with which a labouring family will put up. The same may be said of the district, both in Dorset and Devon, lying around Axminster. Here the population is very dense—both on account of the clearing system having been carried to only a trifling extent, since few of the parishes around are close parishes, and of the demand for labour which at one time existed in Axminster, when it had some pretensions to being a place of manufacturing importance. But it is no longer so. Who hears of Axminster carpets now? The population which formerly collapsed upon the town has recently been thrown back again upon the adjoining parishes, in such numbers as to have a sensible effect both upon wages and rates, and to raise the value of cottages, whilst they have trenched upon their accommodation. I have been told of more than one instance in which this has taken place. As new cottages were not

at first built to meet the increasing demand for them by those returning to their parishes in search of employment, many persons were
obliged to lodge with those occupying such dwellings as existed. For
this accommodation they of course paid so much per week; the result
of which was, that the price of cottages was raised in some cases to
the tenants. If a small family could accommodate two or three lodgers,
which they frequently did, a considerable addition was made to their
weekly receipts; and as this addition came from the cottage, the landlord compelled them to share its enhanced value with him. In some
cases in which this was mentioned to me, the tenants looked upon this
increase of rent as the work of stewards or agents alone; in others they
were of opinion that the proprietors not only sanctioned but enjoined
it, with a view, if possible, of driving the poor people away, so as to
get rid of the cottages. I inquired of several of them if they felt very
generally the inconvenience of over-crowding, and if it had recently
increased. They replied, that it was the greatest inconvenience suffered
by them, and that, of late, its increase had been very great, both from
the natural growth of population, and from the large addition which
had been made to their numbers within the last few years, from the
decay of manufactures in Axminster. In one hovel with two rooms, I
found no fewer than eleven people. The sleeping apartment was upstairs as usual, directly under the thatch. There were three beds, two
of which were on the floor. In that having a bedstead slept the father
and mother and two children—a not uncommon arrangement—the
remaining seven occupying the beds on the floor. The eldest of the
family was a girl 16 years of age, the next a girl about 15, and the third
a boy of 14. They sometimes had a large tattered shawl hanging between the bed occupied by the parents and those on the floor, but in
winter they generally had it down, to serve as an additional covering
for the children. The family was scarcely ever free from disease, the
younger children being pale and emaciated, and diarrhœa being a very
common ailment with them all. Their diet was scanty, and the situation of the cottage bad. There was no drainage, and in wet weather
a strong infusion of manure from a neighbouring dung-heap would
trickle in at the cottage door. They were dirty in their habits, but to
have kept their house anything like clean would have required so constant and energetic a warfare with filth that they shrunk from engaging in it. In addition to this, the greater portion of the time of the
elder members of the family, including the parents, was occupied in
the fields, and when they came home at night from their toil, they

were too fatigued to address themselves to the task of keeping their house in decent order. It will very often be found that the filthy state in which cottages are kept arises more from the habits of the inmates, than from the character or situation of their domicile; but habits, if not exactly formed, are greatly influenced by circumstances. The circumstances of the agricultural labourer are such as frequently to call away from his home to work in the fields those whose proper duty it is to stay at home and keep the house neat and cleanly. But this necessity of his lot should only stimulate landlords to do all in their power to surround him with facilities for, and incentives to, cleanliness. This some landlords are doing on an extensive scale, and in a judicious manner. I have been given to understand that the Duke of Bedford has ordered no less than £16,000 to be expended in the erection of new cottages on his property in the vicinity of Tavistock, and in the mining district within the Cornish border. The plan on which these cottages will be built will be very commodious, and, in this respect, many believe that his grace is going somewhat too far. Unless the labourers inhabiting them be placed in a position to live comfortably without taking in lodgers, they are certain to do this; and to accommodate them, they will, in a cottage having three bed-rooms, crowd the family into one room, so as to leave the others vacant for such a purpose. I have known numerous instances of this throughout the counties which I have traversed—families of eight or nine, and sometimes more, being packed close together in one room in a cottage, with two bed rooms, the other room being occupied by lodgers. I have also, as already mentioned, found a lodger occupying the same apartment with the family, in cottages having but one bed room. So long as the necessity exists for making their house a source of profit to them, so long will spare room, if they have much of it at their disposal, be unavailingly bestowed on the labourers and their families.

LABOUR AND THE POOR.

—◆—

THE RURAL DISTRICTS.

[FROM OUR SPECIAL CORRESPONDENT.]

DEVON, SOMERSET, CORNWALL, AND DORSET.

PHYSICAL CONDITION OF THE LABOURER IN DEVON AND SOMERSET.

Letter VI.

In continuation of the subject of my last letter, I now proceed to furnish the reader with a detailed account of what I witnessed in the house accommodation of the labourers in portions of the district of country now under consideration.

Of all the cottages which I inspected, it was in the neighbourhood of Honiton perhaps that I encountered the most wretched specimens. Between that town and the sea stretches a rugged and sequestered district, varying in width from eight to ten miles, which I was advised to traverse, as it might discover to me phases of agricultural life not very generally exhibited along the high roads. Between Exeter and Honiton the country is divided into long and broad valleys, hemmed in by ridges of hills well cultivated to their very summits; but the district in question has a broken appearance, resembling that of a tumultuous sea. The deep valleys are narrow and irregular—the uplands, which are high, sometimes assuming the form of crooked ridges, and at others rising in isolated and conical hills. The land is light and stony, and is cultivated far more extensively than thoroughly. The summits of the hills and ridges are, to a great extent, covered with copsewood, which sometimes stretches down their sides in broad belts into the valleys beneath. The roads are exceedingly uneven, and in some cases almost impracticable. The streams are no longer lazy and turgid, but rush merrily along to the sound of their own music over pebbly channels, clear and pellucid in their waters, as are the more impetuous torrents of the north. They frequently intersect the roads—when they have to be forded, bridges being but rare conveniences in the district. Sometimes, after heavy rains, they render the roads impassable for hours.

You are scarcely a mile from Honiton ere you enter this lonely and sequestered region. Your road leads you now to the hill top, now to the bottom of the valley, and then to the hill top again. The rough and stony track which you pursue is generally flanked by high and crumbling banks, overspread with the ivy, the young oak, the holly, the fern, and the bramble. In short, it is difficult to believe yourself any longer in busy and enterprising England—so sudden and so complete is the transition from one of its main thoroughfares to this lonely and secluded district.

Almost throughout its whole extent the condition of the labourer is one of extreme privation. In parish after parish which I traversed, the evidences of this accumulated upon me. But there was one spot in which the complicated misery which I witnessed seemed to culminate. It was the village and parish of Southleigh.

The parish is one of considerable area, but of very limited population. Indeed, it was difficult to understand where or how the 350 souls inhabiting it were housed; for, with the exception of the small village which it contains, but few cottages of any kind were to be seen in the parish. To the village I directed my footsteps without delay, approaching it from the brow of one of the high hills which encircled it on all sides. The deep glen at the bottom of which it lay was well wooded, and it was not until I was close upon the village that I discovered any traces of its vicinity. First came the grey square tower of the parish church, which peered over the tree tops—then the thin subtle smoke of wood fires mingling with the foliage—and lastly the cottages themselves, with their mud walls and heavily thatched roofs. On descending to the road which leads through the village, I found a woman of about fifty years of age engaged with a pitchfork collecting some straw at the corner of one of the houses. I remarked that the day had been fine—an observation which she seemed to think so commonplace that she scarcely deigned to reply to it. But there was more than this; for both her tone and manner betrayed that she entertained towards me a mingled feeling of suspicion and dislike. I stood looking at her, but she turned her back upon me, and worked all the harder, as if she wished me to understand that the brief interview was over.

"You seem to work very hard," I observed, determined, if possible, to draw her out—"What are you doing that you are so earnest about?"

"Gathering straw," was her categoric reply.

"What are you gathering it for?" I asked her.

"For the pig," said she.

"Do you keep a pig?" was my next query.

"Yes," was all that I got by way of answer.

"What are you going to do with it?" I demanded—"are you going to sell it?"

"We are going to salt it," said she.

I thought her phraseology rather expressive, and ventured upon a smile, at which she did not seem altogether pleased. Resuming my queries, I asked her when she would kill the pig, but to this I received no answer—it apparently occurred to her that she had been altogether too bland and communicative, and so she withdrew once more within herself. "Whose tenant are you?" I asked; on which she turned hurriedly around, and looked at me with a deep scowl, accompanied by a flourish of the pitchfork, which reminded me what vulnerable creatures we are. I shrank back a little, so as to be out of arm's reach of her.

"I meant not to offend you by the question," I added, "I merely wished to know if you were one of Mr. Gordon's tenants."

"I be," said she, in a tone and with a hastiness of manner which showed that I had failed to pacify her. She resumed her work, but, after a short pause, turned round to me and said, "Are you the gen'leman that called on me some time ago?"

"Not I, my good woman," said I; "this is the first time that I have ever seen you."

"Didn't you call on me for the key?" she continued.

"I was never here in my life before," I rejoined, somewhat puzzled at the direction taken by her inquiries.

"Didn't you come for the key, when I refused to yield it up?" she asked, still endeavouring to identify me with a transaction of which I was profoundly ignorant. I reiterated my former denial, which seemed at last to satisfy her; for, leaning on her pitchfork, she exclaimed, with a loud laugh, and a total change of manner, "Good luck! I took you for the attorney's clerk, who was sent here by the squire to get the key."

This explained to me at once the unwelcome nature of my reception. It appeared that, some time ago, a summary process of ejectment had been attempted against her, in which the clerk of a neighbouring attorney played a rather conspicuous part, and which she stoutly resisted, treating the clerk at the same time, according to her own account, to sundry epithets not very flattering to his vanity. From a similar infliction I was only saved by the timely discovery that I was not the identical individual, or another visiting her under similar circumstances. "Excuse me, sir," said she; "it's some time since he has been here, and we so seldom see strange people here that I thought you might be he."

Once established in her confidence, I proceeded to question her about her domestic circumstances, and found her as garrulous and communicative as she had been taciturn and reserved before. Having scraped together an enormous fork-full of straw, she threw it over her shoulder, and informed me that if I wished to learn any more from her, I must follow her to the pig-stye. I had no objection, and did so, ascending for a few steps one of the roads leading up the hill, at the side of which was the residence of the family pig. Having deposited the straw in the stye, and spread it into a comfortable litter for the pig, which she scratched for some time on the back—addressing it, at the same time, in a language which it seemed to understand, but which I didn't—she turned round, leant again upon the fork, and waited to be interrogated.

"Why was the key demanded of you?" I asked her.

"Because we didn't pay no rent," said she. "We didn't pay for a twal'month."

"And why did you not pay?"

"Because the house isn't fit for a pig to live in, let alone a Christian," she replied, with great indignation.

"Can I see the house?" I inquired.

"I'll show you every bit of it, if you just step down," she rejoined; "and if you think it's a place for Christian people to pay rent for, you ought to be a squire yourself."

"But do you think all the squires bad?" I asked her.

"I can tell you who isn't good," she observed, "and I suppose they are all like him."

"Do you intend to pay no rent?" I inquired.

"I have paid it before, and must pay it again, I suppose," she answered.

"How long have you resided here?"

"Twenty years."

"In the same house?"

"Yes," said she, "in this piggery for twenty years."

We had by this time gained the house, but before entering I thought it as well to examine its exterior. It was a cottage, containing, like too many others, but two rooms. The walls were of mud, or rather of what is called "cob"—a kind of mixture of mud and small stones. The roof was of thatch, and had been recently repaired in parts. Each room had but one window; that in the upper room, which was in the gable end of the cottage, being extremely small. On three sides of the house there were great cracks or fissures in the walls, all of which added to its discomforts, and one of which positively endangered its stability. It was in the front of the cottage, near one of the corners, and ran from the thatch to the ground, occasioned by the end wall having fallen considerably from the perpendicular. I asked her if she was not afraid that the house would come down about her ears. She replied to the effect that her apprehensions had been blunted, as they had been excited by the same cause for the last ten years. I then entered the hovel.

Bad and unprepossessing as was its exterior, it did not half prepare me for what I witnessed inside. The chimney stalk was at the side of the door, and its side formed with the wall a small passage, about five feet long, at the end of which was another door, suspended upon one hinge, which opened into the lower apartment. In the recess formed by the other side of the chimney stalk and the opposite wall was the window, so small and so situated that it threw but a shabby twilight into about one-half of the room. The other half was equally lighted when the door was open; but when it was shut it was in such a gloom that it was scarcely possible to discern the objects which it contained. I requested her to leave the door open, that I might see to more advantage, but chiefly—although I did not tell her so—that I might have the benefit of the fresh air, to counteract the sour and sickening smells which were rife within. The ceiling, which was blackened with smoke, was so low that it was only between the small rafters that I could stand erect with my hat on. The fire-place was of an enormous size; but although the day was cold and raw, there was not at the time a spark of fire upon the hearth. There were a few chairs and some tripods, in the shape of stools; about and within the ample fire-place was a bit of log, supported on four rude legs, which formed a kind of bench, on which about three could sit at a time, sheltered by the chimney stalk, in which they sat, from the drafts which pervaded the room in every direction. At one corner was an empty barrel, which answered the purposes of a table, and close to it an old deal chest, over which were two or three shelves full of crockery of all shapes, colours, and devices, and in all stages of fracture. Hard by was a large black-

looking tub, in which there was a quantity of flour which had recently
been sifted from the bran. In the centre of the room was the moiety of
an old round table, at which the family partook of their meals. What
these were will be afterwards mentioned. In the deep recess occupied
by the window sat the eldest daughter of my guide, working hard at
the lace-cushion, taking that position as the one which afforded her
most light in the room. A good deal of the fabric known as Honiton
lace is manufactured here. Some time ago it was understood that the
Queen had given an order for some, and a portion of that prepared
for her Majesty was wrought in the parish of Southleigh. The poor
creatures (women exclusively being thus employed) were quite proud
of their commission. "They tell we that the Queen is to have it as
curtains for her bed," was the information which they frequently conveyed to those inquiring in reference to the subject. The floor of the
hovel was of mud. It had never known the covering of quicklime and
sand, which frequently forms the flooring of the cottages, and which
is to be seen in some of those in the village. Towards the fire-place
it descended so as to form a tolerably deep hole, in which water not
unfrequently collects, and which has been prevented from deepening
still further by a species of rough causeway work with which it is lined.
With this exception, you trod nothing, whilst in the lower room, but
the cold clay which formed the uneven flooring. I hesitated ere I ventured upstairs. The family was not large, as most of the children were
grown up, and were afloat on the world for themselves. But there were
still five at home—the father and mother, a young man of 21 years of
age, a girl of about 18, and another girl of about 13. The five slept
in the room above. In this instance it was more the chamber itself
than its furniture that was at fault. It was wretchedly lighted, and the
room seemed, in places, to be falling in. To ventilation it was an utter
stranger. The crazy floor shook and creaked under me as I paced it.
The bed-room was approached by a few broken steps, which rose to
it out of a dark recess opposite the door, and in which were stowed
away a few pots and pans, some small bundles of faggots, pieces of
broken furniture, and a few implements of labour.

"What do you think of it now?" asked my guide, after I had
emerged into the light and fresh air, "is it fit for a pig to live in?" With
its cracked walls, its clay floor, its imperfect light, and unwholesome
atmosphere, I certainly could not say that it was fit to be the abode
of a human being.

"What rent do you pay?" I asked. "A shilling a week," she replied—a rent for which, in many places, the labourer has a very comfortable home.

The next cottage which I inspected was situated directly opposite the one described. As in that case, the walls were of cob-work, and the roof of thatch. It was one of two cottages which were attached together. The door was in the gable end, which faced the main road. Like that just visited, it had but two apartments, one above and the other below. What struck me before entering was the condition of the window designed to admit light into the lower room. The aperture in the wall was about two feet high and about fifteen inches wide. This was occupied by a leaden window-frame, with small diamond-shaped panes. Some of them were filled with glass, some with brown paper, and others with rags—whilst a large piece of rusty sheet-iron occupied the place of several of them which had been broken. It was difficult to recognize it as a window. Small as it was, only about one half of it was serviceable for the admission of light, the only purpose to which the other half was applied being the exclusion of fresh air. I entered the cottage, and on my eyes becoming accustomed to the twilight within it, I found myself in the presence of five small children and a woman who appeared to be their mother. The floor, as in the other case, was of clay, and the ceiling so low that I had to stoop to walk about. The cottage was, in every way, as wretched in its appearance and accommodation as that which I had just quitted—whilst the general condition of its inmates was much worse than in the other case, seeing that the family was comparatively large, and all the children of so tender an age that they could not work. I asked to be shown up stairs, and groped my way to where I supposed the staircase to be. But instead of a flight of steps, no matter how rude or unsteady, I came in contact with what seemed to be a perpendicular ladder, which led through a hole in the ceiling. On inquiring if this was the only means of communication with the upper apartment, I was informed that it was. It was up and down this that children of two and three years of age had to climb daily, to get to and from their miserable dormitory. The poor woman observed that she was in daily dread of some accident happening, especially to the younger children, in their ascents and descents. It was not an uncommon thing for them to tumble, especially on endeavouring to descend, but hitherto such mishaps had not been attended with any serious consequences, for the clay floor on which they fell was generally moist and soft. As for herself, she did not much care about it, having become accustomed to it; but it was rather a difficult job to go up and down when she had a child at the breast. She had not the means herself of improving her staircase or repairing her window, nor was her landlord disposed to aid her in so doing.

The cottage attached to this had rather a sad story connected with it. It was built of precisely the same materials as its neighbour, and was of about the same dimensions. The end looking upon the hill behind the village had been overgrown with ivy, which had been cut down, as it was supposed that it rendered the cottage damp. The dead wood of the mutilated parasite was still thickly embedded in the wall, as it could not be pulled out without endangering the stability of the edifice. On scanning the wall closely, one could see near the angle of the roof a square hole, in which there was a casement with four panes of glass. The whole window did not look more than fifteen inches square, yet it was all the means by which light was admitted into the upper chamber of the hovel. There was no tenant occupying it at the time, the door being locked—nor is it likely that it will ever be opened again for the admission of another occupant. In the course of a few more years, it will be another cottage blotted from the face of England. Its last occupant had died about a month before. She had been long an invalid, and was removed, shortly before her last struggles, to a cot not far distant, that she might not die alone. About the close of last year, as I was informed by some of the villagers, she was frequently visited by the lady of the vicar of the parish, of both of whom they all spoke in terms of the greatest kindness and affection. Her malady was increasing, and she was then confined to her bed in the upper room of the cottage. On the occasion of her first visit to the invalid, this lady is reported to have said to her, "Betty, do you not feel this room too cold for you?" "Yes," she replied, "I do; but you see there is no glass in the window, and it has been so for a long time." It was as she represented. There was not a single pane in the casement. The temperature without was consequently that within. The wind rushed in whenever there was any stirring; the rain, when it fell, encroached upon the floor, and sometimes upon the very bed; and on stormy winter days, when the snow was driven before the blast, it would enter at the open casement, and form tiny wreaths upon the floor. "And was it allowed to remain open?" I asked my informant. "It would have been, sir, but that the vicar had it glazed at his own expense," was the answer. And who was she whose last sickness was thus aggravated by the cruel discomforts of her home? One who for five-and-twenty years of her life had been a faithful servant to the squire! Her reward, on becoming superannuated in the service, was the liberty to occupy this doomed cottage rent-free. We hear of horses which have served their owners long and faithfully being pensioned off upon the best pastures for life. During my peregrinations through Oxfordshire I was told of the case of one horse which had served its master so long and well that, after it could no longer eat grass, he had it fed on slops, and finally on sugar, to prolong its existence. It died at last in a comfortable stall. But there was no such sympathy in store for poor "Betty" in the day of her extremity. I was anxious to see the room in which this forlorn invalid had lain bedridden for so many months, but I could not do so, as the door was locked, and all entrance prevented. I could, however, see into the lower apartment through the window—it was like the rest, "not fit for a pig, let alone a Christian, to live in."

The next cottage which I entered had a more promising look about it. In the extent of its accommodation it was no better than the others, but it had a hard dry flooring of lime and sand, and was kept clean by a tidy little woman, who was nursing a child on my entering. I found, however, that her means were superior to those of most of her neighbours—her husband being a carpenter, and earning the wages, not of the labourer, but of the artizan.

I crossed the road, and entered another hut, which overlooked the churchyard. It had two apartments below, and but one, I believe, above. The outer of the two lower apartments seemed to be abandoned by the inmates, and looked as if it would have been applied to the purposes of a store-house, had there been anything to store away in it. I passed through it to get to the inner apartment. Everything was grim and black, the ceiling being low, and the floor composed of earth. The water was trickling in different directions about it: and no wonder. The aperture which contained the window was divided into three parts, something like a Venetian window, by two perpendicular pieces of wood, which formed the staple of the casement. There was neither glass nor sash in the middle portion, nor had there been since it was tenanted by its present occupants, which it had been for many years. It was open winter and summer, except when they chose to close it up with some opaque substance, which they seldom did, as they would be thereby deprived of light. One winter it was intensely cold, and they had it boarded up. It remained so, however, but for a very short time, for the board was soon taken down to be burnt as firewood. Immediately below the open window was a cradle, in which an infant was being rocked. It was nothing but a black greasy box, shattered a little on one side, and placed upon a couple of rough rockers. The child was covered by what appeared to be a tattered horse-cloth. Only a few days before, I had inspected a workhouse, where I was shown the apartment which served as a nursery for the children. What a contrast did their comfortable circumstances present to the wretched accommodation of this child of honest and industrious parents! I remained below whilst one of the family went up stairs to show me the state of the ceiling. There was scarcely a plank but seemed to yield under her feet, whilst the seams which extended along the floor at one corner were so broad as to expose to those above everything going on below. The first thing which meets the squire's eye on coming from church is this ruinous hovel with its ever open window. He certainly cannot plead ignorance of the condition of his tenants.

I next visited the house of the blacksmith of the village and clerk of the parish. He was a fine sturdy old man, who had brought up a family of thirteen without ever coming upon the parish. His youngest son, a strapping lad, was working in the smithy along with him. He had got almost all of them well settled in the world, although his difficulty in bringing up so large a family had been greatly increased by the liability of one of his daughters to epileptic fits. His wife was a hale and respectable-looking old dame, who kept his home clean and in order; a circumstance to which alone it owed all the comforts of which it could boast, for in its style and general character, although somewhat larger, it was little better than any of the rest.

My next visit was to a small tenement divided into two dwellings. At one end was a small excrescence, which had the semblance of a shed or wood-house. It had evidently been taken for such by peripatetic bill-stickers, for the door leading into it was plastered over with "posters" of all sizes and characters. It nevertheless formed the antechamber to the dwelling of one of the families occupying the house. On entering I found the floor paved with small stones, after the fashion of a rough and irregular causeway, with a kind of gutter in the centre to let the water run off, for the house lay low and was very damp. Passing through this, which seemed to serve the purposes of a lumber-room, I entered the "day-room" of the family. It was more comfortably furnished than I expected to find it, especially as I had been informed that the tenant had been disabled for some time by rheumatism from working. How a rheumatic patient could expect ever to recover in such a place was to me a mystery, for the earthen floor was quite damp and cold after the rains which had recently fallen. His wife was seated at the lace-cushion by the window, working very industriously, but complaining of her head. Beside her sat a young girl, also with a lace-cushion before her, engaged in making large sprigs, which were to form part of a bridal scarf and veil for some fair lady who was about to be led to the altar. There was still another in the room—an old man, who sat in a corner by the window, sewing a piece of flannel. He was about sixty, but looked older. A few grey hairs still clung to the sides of his head, just above his ears, but all the rest was bald. He had on the top of his head a scar, which was partly hidden by a piece of dirty sticking plaster. He continued his work, but in a most unworkmanlike manner, apparently taking no heed of anything passing around him. I stepped up to him, and asked what he was about, to which he replied that, having nothing to do out of doors, he was employing himself by "doing a bit of tailoring." The whole picture was a curious one: the rheumatic invalid seated by the feeble fire, his wife and daughter working busily over their lace-cushions at the window, and the old man making a waistcoat for himself in a way which plainly showed that "tailoring" was not his vocation. Had the accommodation been better, it would not have been, on the whole, an unpleasing one—but the cottage was one of the worst description, although everything in it in the shape of furniture was neat and clean. The dwelling adjoining it had a better entrance, but the accommodation which it afforded was not a whit better. Here, also, the lace-cushion was in requisition, and the inmates were subject to rheumatism, from the dampness of the floor, which, like that of most of the other houses, was of earth. A part of it looked as if it had been recently under water. On inquiry, I found that it had been so— as it was more or less, indeed, after every heavy rain. In these cases the water was removed by soaking cloths in it, and wringing them dry out of doors. These last-mentioned cottages, with one or two others, occupied the lowest ground covered by the village. Until recently their unwholesomeness and other discomforts were greatly aggravated by a broad stagnant open ditch, which exposed its putrescent contents on the other side of the road. The offensive smells which used to emanate from this hotbed of pestilence were spoken of by the inmates as something incapable of description. "You should have tried them, sir," said a woman who had waxed eloquent on the subject. I told her that I could fancy what they were, and would content myself there-with. Yet, bad and pestiferous as was the malaria engendered by this reeking abomination, it was never removed until the vicar took the matter up. The reader will at once see that in this respect the case of Southleigh is parallel to that of Sutton Courtney. He had the ditch covered over, the filthy volume which used to stagnate in it being now carried off by means of an iron tube sunk a foot or two below the sur-face. In addition to the gain which this has been in point of health, it has been attended with this other advantage, that it has added materi-ally to the width of the road, at a point where more room was wanted, owing to a sharp turn which had to be taken round the end of one of the houses.

After visiting a hovel situated in the midst of some copsewood, a little distance up the slope of the opposite bank, and in which the inmates were obliged, whilst working at the lace-cushion, to place boards under their feet to protect them from the cold wet floor, I be-took myself to the residence of one of the farmers of the neighbour-hood. In this part of Devonshire the number of "small farmers" is very large. This gives rise to many evils, some of which will be alluded to in a subsequent communication. How far they retard the progress of the agricultural labourer may be inferred from the simple fact, that in many cases they are contented with house accommodation little if at all better than that of the labourer who is so badly housed. The per-son in question was one of this class. He was an elderly man, of rough exterior and stern character. During the war, an endeavour was made to force him into the militia, but having no taste for military glory, he put a stop to all the persuasions of the authorities, and to the sugges-tions of patriotism, by chopping off a part of the forefinger of his right hand. This disabled him from manipulating a musket, but it did not prevent him from handling the plough. He has ever since farmed in the neighbourhood on a small scale, in doing which he has amassed a little money. His house was some distance up the hill; but although it might have been well and easily drained, it was scarcely drained at all, for at one end, and partly in front of it, filthy solutions had ac-cumulated to a disgusting extent. They were powerfully impregnated with an infusion of a rotten dung-heap, which supported itself against the gable end of the house. His wife was ill of a mortal disease. She was able to sit up, and was accompanied by her sister, who had come from some distance to see her. They were both seated within the huge chimney stalk, at the back of which burnt a more ample fire than I had seen in any of the other houses. Behind them, and as it were on one side of the stalk, was a window, which lighted up the huge fire-place. On my suggesting that such was hardly the place for an invalid, I was told that it was selected as the most comfortable part of the room. Every now and then a puff of wind would come suddenly down the chimney, and envelop the invalid and her companion in smoke. The house was in no respect better than that of many an agricultural labourer of the class not the most comfortably housed; but it was in some respects superior to most of those in the village below. The lower room had, for instance, two windows, instead of one; its floor was of lime and clay, which kept it hard and dry, and there was a little more room between it and the floor of the upper chamber. It also contained more furniture; that which it had being cleaner and less mutilated than the furniture in the other houses, but in all other respects—in size, in general appearance, in style and design, and in its external accompaniments—it would have been difficult to distinguish it from the rest. It was anything but what one would picture to oneself as an English farmer's home. A little lower down the hill was the residence of another farmer, who cultivated on a somewhat larger scale. It also contained an invalid, a young man, who was just recovering from an acute rheumatic fever. When I entered he was expecting a visit from the clergyman, who also acted the part of physician to his flock. The house was a degree better than that last alluded to. There was a spacious yard in front, surrounded by a number of outhouses. In the midst of it was a filthy pond, surrounded with manure and garbage of every kind, from which proceeded an atmosphere which it weakened one in every joint to inhale. When farmers themselves are contented with such hovels, it is no wonder that they think the agricultural labourer sufficiently well off in his den, or that the landlord—perhaps taking the farmer's notions of comfort as his standard—does nothing toward ameliorating the condition of his humbler tenantry.

For all the hovels described—as well as for others of which they may serve as specimens—rents are paid. In amount the rents vary but little from each other, and they are in general far too high. For the same rent that is paid for these cottages, accommodations on a much better scale are enjoyed by the labourer even in Wiltshire. But few of the cottagers at Southleigh have gardens attached to their houses. Most of them have small field allotments, which are supplied to them by the vicar, at a reasonable rent. In these they raise cabbages and turnips, and, but to a small extent now, potatoes. The failure of the potatoes for several successive years has occasioned the people to lose their former faith in them. They regret, however, not having planted more this year, seeing that the crop has been, generally speaking, both abundant and good, and that they find it difficult to make up for the want of them, turnips being but a poor substitute. The average rent of the cottages is about 50s. a year.

The name of the landlord whose tenantry are so deplorably circumstanced is, as I have already stated, Gordon. It is now many years since he came into possession of the property, which he did by purchase. I was given to understand that there was not a cottage in the parish then which was not in a far better state than it is now. They have been gradually going to wreck and ruin—but little, if any, effort having been made to save them; and all this time, as already stated, the population has been increasing—so much so, indeed, as to require a large addition to be made to the parish church. The cottages have been getting more and more crowded every year, and the whole condition of their inmates more and more wretched. The mansion of the proprietor is about a mile from the village, and is known as Wiscombe Park. For several years after he took possession he resided at the Park—a course which had a very sensible effect upon the employment and comforts of the villagers. But for many years past he has chiefly lived in the neighbourhood of Exeter. His son, however, has recently been residing for some months at the Park, and his presence was of considerable advantage to the poor people. Mr. Gordon has lately revisited Wiscombe; but, should he leave, and his son not re-occupy the house, the condition of the poor will be one of extreme privation during the winter. For some time past, in their hour of difficulty and sickness, they have had none to whom to look for advice and relief but the resident clergyman and his family. The living is but a small one, and it is very hard that the incumbent should be called upon to bear unaided so grave a responsibility and so heavy a burden. I mention this case in all its circumstances, because it is one of the most striking that has presented itself to me, and because it illustrates, though perhaps to an extreme degree, much that is going on in many parts of the country, to alienate the affections of the poor from their social superiors. In Southleigh and its neighbourhood I could trace but too clearly the extent to which this alienation was going on. Mr. Gordon is not the only proprietor in the parish, though he is the principal one, and the village belongs to him. Of none of the parish squires—nor, indeed, of any of the surrounding proprietors—did the villagers speak either with respect or affection. On inquiring into the origin of this hostile feeling, I invariably found that it was traceable to a belief that the proprietors cared not what became of the labourers. Even apart from those considerations of duty and benevolence which should prompt a landlord to bind himself with his people in the strong bonds of a mutual sympathy, the calculations of prudence should suggest the adoption of a humane and considerate line of conduct. I have been astonished at the extent to which I have found Socialist doctrines prevailing amongst the rural poor. They know nothing of Socialism as a distinct political theory, but its principles have made their way amongst them to a considerable extent—their progress being promoted, if it was not originated, by the daily contemplation of their own wretched lot. They contend that they have "a right to live, and to live comfortably, as well as the best of them"—and they begin to reason with themselves that they cannot do this until land is treated not as a property, but as a trust. They have at present no organization or mutual understanding by which they might attempt to carry such doctrines into practice, but they are becoming more and more imbued with these sentiments, and many of them will tell you so.

I cannot say that I witnessed anything in Southleigh absolutely worse than what I have met with elsewhere. But nowhere else have I seen a whole community, although it is but small, in so deplorable a plight. Such instances are most likely to be found in close parishes, where the work of cottage clearance is going on, and in districts which at one time contained a focus of manufacturing activity, but the industry of which has since been paralyzed. This is the case in the neighbourhood of Axminster, as already stated, and in the north of Devon, near the lead mines, which have recently become extinct. They are also occasioned by the sudden growth of a manufacturing or mining interest in the midst of what was formerly a purely agricultural district, causing the sudden concentration of a large population in a spot where the house accommodation for them is limited, and where, from the policy of the proprietors, it is not increased. An extraordinary instance of this I shall have occasion to refer to, when I come to speak of the accommodation afforded to the labourer in some parts of Cornwall. On the other side of Honiton is the parish of Gettiesham. Its condition, as regards the state of the labourers resident in it, is quite a contrast to that of Southleigh. Their houses are better, the situations are more healthy, more is done for drainage and ventilation, and in many cases the rents are more reasonable. In this neighbourhood reside, amongst other proprietors, Mr. Justice Patteson and Mr. Justice Coleridge. The contrast between Gettiesham and Southleigh does not stop here. In the one, the people are badly off—in the other, they are comparatively well off. In the one, they are indebted for the few comforts which they possess to the care and zeal of the clergyman—in the other, they owe their happier lot almost entirely to the sympathy and solicitude of the squires.

But bad as are the tenements usually occupied by the poor, they are not, except in rare cases, quite so revolting in their character, and in the scenes to which they give rise, as are some tenements which have a claim to be regarded in the light of public buildings. These are the parish houses, which are scattered in considerable numbers over the southern and western districts. They are the houses in which the poor were accommodated previously to the erection of the union workhouses. In many cases, since the workhouses came into use, these parish houses have been sold, and the proceeds applied to defraying *pro tanto* the expense of building the workhouses. But in others, the overseers will not part with them, keeping them for the purpose of letting, and thus deriving a profit from them. They are generally let at a lower rent than ordinary cottages, and thus become the resort of those in the most wretched circumstances, who crowd into them by dozens, and fill up almost every crevice of them with lodgers. One of these I saw on the borders of Devonshire and Cornwall, and not far from Launceston. It consisted of two houses, containing between them four rooms. In each room was a family, who used it both night and day; the lower rooms were about twelve feet square; in one of them were a man and his wife and five children; in the other were a man and his wife and eight children; in this latter there were but two beds—the father and mother and two children occupying one, and the other six being huddled together into the remaining bed. They lay "head and foot," as they termed it—that is to say, three with their heads at the top, and three with them at the foot of the bed. The eldest girl was between fifteen and sixteen, and the eldest boy between fourteen and fifteen. The closeness of this room was overpowering. The beds were necessarily large, and occupied most of the floor; indeed, when the whole family was assembled, several of the children were placed upon the beds to keep them out of the way. In this way the beds may be said to have never been cold. How can health be retained or morals preserved under such circumstances as these?

But my space warns me that I must have done. If, in what I have here depicted, I have selected what may be called extreme cases, let it be borne in mind that between the cases so selected and the line of mere comfort there are very many grades of wretchedness and privation. Blame is not solely to attach to such cases as exhibit the extreme of destitution. A labourer's condition may be many degrees above this extreme, and yet be well calculated to justify animadversion and to inspire alarm. I have here said enough to show that the labourers, both in Somerset and Devon, are, taking them as a class, deplorably housed. And so long as they continue to be so, it will be vain for us to expect to raise them in the scale of virtue or intelligence. If we would improve the peasant's morals, we must begin by improving his home.

The Morning Chronicle, Wednesday, November 7, 1849.

To the EDITOR of the MORNING CHRONICLE.

Sir—In your journal of Saturday last, your correspondent, upon the subject of "Labour and the Poor" in the rural districts, asserts that I annually remove, upon my estate in Devonshire, six cottages, thus decreasing the population to the number of forty-two persons in each year, and having for my object the diminution of the parochial burdens. I have found it necessary, during a period of many years, to take down four cottages immediately adjoining my family residence, but I have invariably afforded the occupiers more suitable dwellings. With this exception, upon my property, extending over some thousands of acres, I have never removed a single cottage. Your sense of justice will doubtless induce you to correct an error you have unintentionally been led into.

I am, sir, your obedient servant,

EDW. MARWOOD ELTON.

Brooks's, St. James's, Nov. 5.

The Morning Chronicle, Saturday, November 10, 1849.

LABOUR AND THE POOR.

—◆—

THE RURAL DISTRICTS.

[FROM OUR SPECIAL CORRESPONDENT.]

DEVON, SOMERSET, CORNWALL, AND DORSET.

WAGES AND DIET OF THE LABOURER IN DEVON AND
SOMERSET.

LETTER VII.

As regards wages, my inquiries have been extensive and minute.
The reader will remember that the accident of my being in Thame
when the annual fair was being held there, gave me a good opportunity of comparing the different rates of wages prevailing in the counties of Oxford and Buckingham. I was equally fortunate in South
Devon, stumbling by good luck upon a ploughing match which was
taking place in the neighbourhood of Exmouth. It was a grand gala
day for the whole of the neighbourhood, the match being annually
got up under the auspices of an agricultural association embracing
some half-dozen parishes in the line between Exmouth and Exeter.
A great concourse was collected to witness the exhibition. Farmers
were present in scores from all the parishes interested. Men, women,
and children, from Exmouth and the adjoining villages, were on the
ground in hundreds. The scene was even graced by a number of ladies;
whilst in the medley assembled might also be seen sailors from the
port, and apparently more than one boys' boarding-school, in their
best assortment of broad cloth and linen. The field which was the
scene of the match was by no means a felicitous selection. The usual
object on such occasions is to get a field as uniform as possible in its
surface. This one was far from being so; it stretched along the high
road, descending gently towards the south. At its upper and lower
ends, the surface, stretching back from the road, which was the direction of the furrow, was even and well adapted for the purpose; but the
middle of the field, which was an unusually large one for the district,
was very uneven, putting those who were to plough it at great disadvantage. I remarked to one of the competitors that I was surprised at

the selection, observing that great skill on bad ground might be out-done by little skill having to deal with a more favourable surface. His place was about the middle of the field. He shrugged his shoulders, and in reply observed, "Kissing goes by favour, and so will the prize." Out of some twenty-five furrows, I counted but about five with any pretensions to being straight—and this, too, although each competi-tor had a boy to lead his horses. Some of the most crooked furrows were, however, the best thrown up. After the prize was awarded, the farmers, to the number of about 200, sat down to a hot dinner at two shillings a head—cider included, I believe—in the Globe Inn, Ex-mouth. I bought a ticket and secured a place. The dinner was soon over, and the cloth being removed, toasts and songs became the or-der of the day. I heard much conversation, but little or nothing on the subject of wages. The prevailing topic was the price of corn, and the certain ruin which was impending over them all from free trade. Finding myself very unlikely to obtain much satisfactory information on the subject of wages from the company around me, I descended to the street, and got amongst the "plough boys" and farm labourers of all descriptions and ages, who were congregated in very uproarious as-semblage around the hotel. As they were from the different parishes interested in the match, I was thus afforded a good opportunity of learning the amount of wages, not in a limited locality, but over a pretty extensive district.

I first got into conversation with some boys, dressed in every va-riety of costume, from the smock-frock to a short jacket, and who seemed to be standing guard over some prize mangold wurzel, which were being exhibited in their uncouth proportions to the gaze of the wondering lieges of Exmouth. Every now and then two or three farm-ers would thrust out their heads from the windows above, and look at them with admiration. Having listened for some time to their obser-vations respecting the great event of the day, I interrogated some of the boys in reference to their work, and the remuneration which they received for it. The first to whom I addressed myself was an urchin of twelve in a smock-frock, who told me he did all kinds of work for 2s. 6d. a week. He had commenced work at eight years of age, receiv-ing at first nothing but his "vittles," then 4d., then 6d., and then 1s. in addition thereto. For the last year he had got "handy," and was in receipt of 2s. 6d. a-week, but he no longer received his "vittles" as a perquisite. He was now boarded with his parents, his weekly 2s. 6d. going into the common fund for the family maintenance. A boy beside him, resident in the same parish, and two years his senior, was receiving only 1s. 6d. a-week; and he also was living at home, his mother being a widow with several children, for whose support she was compelled to work herself in the fields. A third was only receiving 1s. 3d. a-week, for which he did duty by driving the horses which dragged the plough. There were several with 6d. a week and their food—but no lodging, and a few with board and lodging, but no wages. The disparity existing in the terms on which they are severally employed was not a disparity between parish and parish, but one which seemed to depend more upon the caprice of the employer than either on the locality, the ability of the boy, or the quality and quantity of the work performed. One farmer gives 2s. 6d. a week to the youthful labourer who does his work no better than another who is receiving but 2s. a week on the adjoining farm. To some extent the wages of even adult labourers depend, as to amount, on the character of their employer— this, however, being the case far more as regards female than male labourers. In different parts of the counties which I have visited I have known women get 8d. a day on some farms for doing work for which 7d. only was paid on the adjoining property. As regards the male labourers however, their wages are more uniform within the bounds of their respective parishes. The disparity in the amount of their wages is more between parish and parish—or between district and district. In conversing with them I found that some had but 7s. whilst others had 8s. a week. I could discover no difference whatever in their work to account for this inequality in their wages. Of two to whom I addressed myself, one had 8s., the other only 7s., although the farms on which they worked were separated only by a brook— but that brook divided two parishes from each other. This capricious inequality characterizes the wages of the labourer throughout almost the whole of the southern districts, from Essex to Cornwall, having existed as between contiguous localities almost from time immemorial, without any very apparent cause either for its establishment or its continuance. But a little reflection will show that, however accidental or arbitrary it may have been in its original institution, there are causes now at work which have a manifest tendency to perpetuate it. Wherever it exists, as between similar districts, it is generally, if not invariably, accompanied by a marked disparity as regards the amount of population. Where wages are low, it is usually found that the population is comparatively abundant, and *vice versa*. I am now, of course, comparing, in this respect, parishes or districts similar to each other, or nearly so, in other respects; for a population which would be scanty in a rich parish or district might be superabundant in a poor one. The density or paucity of population has much to do with the difference in question, for the obvious reason, that the value of labour depends very much upon the amount of the supply of labour at command. There is frequently a greater difference in the amount of population than one would be ready to believe, between two adjoining districts, similarly circumstanced in all other respects. The system of depletion, by the demolition of cottages and other devices which have been resorted to, particularly in close parishes, has mainly contributed to produce this result, and the difference being once established, the law of settlement prevents its removal. The extent to which this affects wages may be appreciated from the fact that it frequently creates a difference of fully 50 per cent. between the rates of wages paid in one and the same county. Here a man is in receipt of 6s. a week for his toil, whilst there he receives 9s.

But although the number of the population—in other words, the amount of labour at command—exercises a very general influence on the rate of wages, there are other causes which occasionally supervene, not simply to modify, but, in some cases, even to counteract its influence. These, when at work, aggravate the evil of a dense, and neutralize the advantage of a thin, population. This is chiefly the case in districts where the land is let, not to a few wealthy and capable tenants, but to a great number of small farmers, who have little or no capital wherewith to work the land properly, and who would not know how to do so could they press the Bank of England into their service. Where such tenants abound, wages are sure to be low and the labourers very ill off, without reference to the question of population. I have been in several parishes in the south of Devonshire which were very scantily peopled, but in which the labourers seemed reduced to the very depths of wretchedness. I almost invariably found that in these many were farmers who were "not fit to be labourers." I have seen specimens of these farmers holding only 30, 40, or 50 acres of land, in reference to whom the expression just quoted was certainly not misapplied. As a class, the least unfavourable feature about them is their want of capital. Their want of enterprise is proverbial, and in ignorance they cannot be surpassed. In common intelligence they are frequently behind some of the labourers whom they precariously employ; whilst, as regards their physical circumstances, as already shown, they are but slightly in advance of them. Their existence is a grievous injury to two classes of men—to the labourers, to whom they pay but the scantiest of wages, and to the better conditioned farmers, whom they compel, by their competition, to pay higher rents for their land. Many landlords cherish them on this account, whilst the more respectable farmers are speculating upon the best means of getting rid of them. At a meeting of farmers in Wiltshire, which I attended, a legislative remedy was discussed, to which I shall in due time advert.

Whatever else, therefore, may affect wages, they are very much influenced by the laws which tend to perpetuate the existing inequalities of population, and by the extent of the holdings in the hands of the employers.

On inquiring more particularly into the rates of wages in the different localities which I visited, I found them in all cases low, and with as great a diversity in point of amount as had been represented to me by the ploughboys at Exmouth. Throughout the Kingsbridge union, which comprises a large portion of the extreme south of Devon, I found 9s. a week to be the average rate. There is more grazing in this neighbourhood than in some of the eastern parts of the county, where wages are much lower, whilst the holdings are, in the main, much larger. Throughout the union, too, the population, as compared with what it is at some points near the borders of Dorset, is thin. The consequence is, that the demand and supply are more equally adjusted, which tends to keep wages up. The farmers likewise are, more or less, men of capital, keeping about the same number of persons in constant employment, and thus preventing the fluctuation which would occur in the rate of remuneration if whole droves of workmen were to be occasionally thrown out of work to compete with each other, as is too often the case in the over populous districts, and in parts where the farmers are destitute of capital. In Kingsbridge union the wages are not only high, as compared with wages elsewhere in Devon—or indeed with the average of wages throughout the county—but they are, or have been, remarkably steady. There has been some talk, however, of reducing them; and 8s. a week is spoken of as the amount at which they are likely to stand before the winter is far advanced.

I have already adverted to the fluctuation which characterizes the wages paid in the line from Exmouth to Exeter. The two rates generally paid are 8s. and 7s. a week. The great bulk of the property in this neighbourhood is part of what is known as the Rolle property, left by the late lord to the second son of the present Lord Clinton. In the other directions around Exeter, I found 7s. a week more prevalent than 8s. Whilst driving from Exeter to Honiton, I inquired of two of my fellow-travellers, who were from different parts of the interior of the country, what the rate of wages might be in their respective localities. Both put them down at "about 7s. a week." I asked if it was possible for men to live on such a pittance. "Not if they have large families," observed one. "At least, one thing is clear, they can't live honestly on it," said the other. I afterwards took the opportunity of asking the driver of the coach, who drove daily between Exeter and Dorchester, and the amount which he named was also 7s. a week. Arrived at Honiton, I inquired for myself, and found scarcely any case in which 8s. were being given. In the parish of Southleigh, already alluded to, and in the conterminous parishes, this was the maximum rate. One woman, whom I questioned, told me that her husband and son had both 7s. a week, but that the work was not steady, so that they could not be said to earn 14s. a week between them for many weeks together. The son was quite a young man, and on my asking her if there was no difference made in the wages paid to married and single men, she informed me that an attempt had been made to get her son to work for less, but that, as he could do a man's work, he had constantly refused to work for less than a man's wages. It was in the neighbourhood of Axminster, and in the north of Devon, near the extinct lead mines, that I found the lowest scale of wages paid. In many cases, in these localities, the labourer was receiving but 6s. a week, and it was apprehended that there would be a very general reduction to that standard. About Axminster two causes co-operated to make the population dense—a good agricultural country, and a manufacturing interest which was at one time lively and flourishing. That interest has since fallen into decay, and hundreds of hands have been thrown upon the surrounding parishes, to compete for work with those who were already feeling the disadvantage of over competition. In the north of Devon, the population was enlarged by the mining operations, which have recently been brought to a close, and the termination of which has flooded the contiguous rural districts with an amount of labour for which there is no adequate demand. Many of those thrown out of work by the closing of the lead mines have wandered up the vale of the Torridge, where their presence has somewhat affected wages. With the exception of the extreme north, where farms are small and farmers but a degree removed from the condition of labourers, wages along the Cornwall boundary of Devonshire are almost as high as in the Kingsbridge union. Taking the whole county, it appears to me

that whilst 7s. 6d. might be too low, 8s. would be too high an average at which to put wages. There is but little difference in this respect
between Devon and Somerset. As in the one, so in the other county,
the wages differ in different localities, but the average will be about
the same. I am here speaking of the average wages now paid—not
what might be the average on the whole year, including the higher
rates paid during harvest. Nor are these higher rates likely very materially to affect the general average, seeing that if more is paid at that
time, multitudes are out of employment altogether during other parts
of the year, or work not from week to week, but from day to day, as
work is furnished them—which reduces their actual weekly receipts
far below the rate per week at which they are precariously employed
only from day to day.

So far, I have not spoken of the wages of women. They are more
generally employed in Somerset than they are in Devon. Indeed, there
are parts of the latter county in which it is rarely that they are seen
at work in the fields. This is the case in the line of country extending
from about Sidmouth to the neighbourhood of Totnes. I not only remarked this myself, but it was mentioned to me by others, who could
not account for it in any way. In the interior of Devon, and along
the Torridge, they are as frequently seen at work as in Somerset. In
that county, however, there is far more work for them of a kind for
which women are more adapted than men—dairy farming being carried on to a much greater extent in Somerset than in Devon. I am
now speaking, however, of labour in the fields. This comprises a variety of occupations, in connection with which cheap female comes in
competition with dearer male labour. Women hoe turnips at a much
less rate than men. A man, however, will do much more in the course
of a day, at this kind of work, than a woman will do. It is also too laborious an occupation for women very generally to engage in. They also
plant and dig potatoes at the proper seasons; they weed the fields, particularly when fresh land is being cleaned preparatory to a crop; they
pick stones from the land and winnow the corn; they plant beans,
and fill, and sometimes drive, the manure carts. These are but specimens of their work, for which they receive, on the average, from 7d.
to 8d. a-day. I have known cases in which less was given, but about
sevenpence-halfpenny may be taken as a fair average of the present
rates. During harvest time they sometimes earn as much as 6s. a week.

Nor have I as yet made any account of the wages paid to the class
of men designated farm servants. There are, in ninety-nine cases out

of a hundred, single men resident on the farm, where they are boarded and lodged. In addition to this they receive from £8 to £10 a year as wages—sometimes higher; but £10 would be a high average of the receipts of this class of labourers. In general their fare is very good—far better, at any rate, than that of the ordinary agricultural labourer. They have generally potatoes or bread, and sometimes both, with warm milk, for breakfast. In some cases a rasher of bacon is added. For dinner they have meat and potatoes, and for supper such cold meat as may have been left at dinner, with potatoes again. Sometimes they have a meat pie for dinner, the cold remains of which will constitute their supper. When they have no cold meat left, they will sup on warm milk and potatoes, or bread. This is, to say the least of it, a substantial bill of fare for the day, and accords with our notions of what a man should eat who has to labour from morning till night and from day to day. They are not in all cases so bountifully provided—much, in this respect, as is the case with wages, depending upon the character or ability, or both, of the employer. But those worst off amongst them are much more favourably situated than the great bulk of those who are best off amongst the agricultural labourers in the ordinary acceptation of the term.

Although I have delayed I had not forgotten to notice a feature with respect to wages peculiar to such of the western and southern counties as are known as the "cider counties." In these counties the labourers generally receive, in addition to their money wages, so much cider per day. This is not confined to men—the women and children employed in the fields also coming in for their cider. In some cases this is compounded for, and a higher rate of wages paid; but in the great majority of cases the money-rate of wages when stated is exclusive of the dole of cider. Sometimes, however, the farmers will include it, and thus mislead the inquirer. Thus, at Exmouth, I was informed by a labourer, who pointed out his employer to me, that his wages were 7s. 6d. a week. A few minutes afterwards I was in conversation with his master, and on inquiring into the rate of wages in his neighbourhood, was told by him that he himself paid 9s. The discrepancy between the two statements staggered me a little, and I mentioned it to him. "Well, to be sure," said he, "I do pay but 7s. 6d. in money, but then he has his three pints of cider a day, which I reckon at 1s. 6d. more." But the farmer always reckons the cider at more than the men do. A disinterested appraiser would, taking into account the rough quality of the cider generally given to the labourer, value the eighteen pints a week which he receives at about 1s. By such statements, those unacquainted with the mode in which things are managed are often led astray. Thus, when a farmer pays so much and cider, he will put the cider into the money account, and leave you to infer, if you like, that the cider is to be put in addition to the whole. Again, when he has compounded with his workman, and pays him a higher rate in consideration of his giving up the cider, he simply mentions the wages, leaving you to find out that they are not accompanied with the usual allowance of the beverage of the county. I have often, for instance, been told by a farmer that he paid 9s. a week. "With cider?" I would ask him. "No," he might say, "that includes the cider," reckoning it at so and so. Or if it were a case in which the cider had been compounded for, he would wait until you asked before he would inform you that it was not given in addition.

But in estimating the condition of the labourer, and that of his family, nothing can be more fallacious than to include this dole of cider as part and parcel of his wages. It has no effect whatever upon the comforts of his family, and cannot therefore be taken into account in considering the extent of their means. In the case of a man working for himself alone, who might find his wages sufficient to enable him to indulge a little during the week, were he inclined to drink cider to some extent, that which is handed to him in the field might be taken into account as so much money, since it might save him so much, provided he were contented with what he got in the field. But even in his case, if he were not disposed to drink, but anxious to save his money, it would be anything but a gain to him. The value of the beverage in money would, in more ways than one, be far better for him, for it would not only enable him to save more, or to procure more substantial aliment, but it might also avert a danger to which he is otherwise exposed—that of encouraging a taste for more cider than he gets, and ultimately for something stronger than cider. In the case of the married man the system is far more objectionable. He does not work for himself alone, having others, and sometimes many others, dependent upon him. He has, therefore, no money to spare out of his scanty wages to indulge a taste for drinking cider, or any other liquor. He has none to spare for such a purpose even when his claim for cider is compounded for by a money payment. And it is hard to compel him to take as part of his wages that which he could not afford to purchase were his earnings paid him in full in money. If he is entitled to 9s., why force him to take 1s. 6d. worth of it in cider, when he could not afford to buy 1s. 6d. worth of cider if the 9s. were all paid him in money? The word "forced" is here not unadvisedly applied, for the great majority of the labourers, particularly the married men, would prefer the cider's worth to the cider itself. The cider's worth would go to enhance the comforts of the family. The cider itself does not and can not. It is, in almost all cases, drunk on the field—in other words, the labourer spends daily about 16 per cent. of his earnings in drink. Whenever it is compounded for, it is for the labourer's benefit that the arrangement is made; and what benefits him in one instance would be advantageous to him in all. The difficulty in the way is chiefly with the farmers, who have an interest in keeping up the mixed system of wages. To some extent it is the truck system, and nothing else. It is equivalent to saying to the labourer, "I will employ you at so much a week, but then I expect you to remember that I keep a cider shop, and that you must buy so much cider from me, at such and such a price, every week"— the price being one which secures to the cider producer a profit at the expense of the cider consumer. It is all nonsense to say that the labourer could not work without his cider. Labourers elsewhere work without it; and why not in Devon or Somerset? Miners are allowed to take nothing with them but water into the mine, although they are dripping wet from morning till night, and their work is as hard, to say the least of it, as that of any labourer on the earth's surface. Besides, if he could not do without it, what would prevent him from buying it? Let him have the value of the cider in money, and let him convert it into cider if he pleases; but give him the chance, at least, of applying it to a better purpose—the enhancement of the comforts of his family. We never think, if we hear of a man engaged in any other kind of work spending regularly a certain proportion of his wages in drink, of including the proportion so spent in the sum available weekly for meeting the necessities of his household; and why should we do so in the case of the farm-labourer in these counties? Let it not be said, then, that the labourer with 7s. 6d. a week, and cider, is in the position of the labourer with 9s. a week without cider. His means of supporting himself and family are to be measured by his money-wages, and by them alone. Taking the two counties in question, I have already stated my opinion that 8s. a week would be too high an average at which to put the money-wages paid throughout them.

The cider given to the women is frequently drunk by themselves— it being sometimes given to their husbands. That given to the boys is almost invariably drunk by them. They get less than a man, but in the same proportion to their strength and wages. It is perhaps in respect to them that the system develops itself in its most pernicious aspect. "I wouldn't work without my cider," said a saucy little imp of about eleven years of age, one of those who surrounded me in Exmouth. By the time they reach maturity they are accomplished drinkers, and this from a necessity of their position. To make them accomplished smokers instead would be equally justifiable. There is no more sense or justice in compelling them to drink cider as part of their wages, than there would be in forcing them to smoke or chew tobacco. If the farmers of the west produced tobacco instead of cider, every labourer would be seen with a cigar in his mouth.

How are the many families dependent upon agricultural labour for their support to subsist during the approaching winter on wages averaging less than 8s. a week? Ask the question of anybody—even of those most likely from their position to be acquainted with the means and contrivances of such families—and they will shrug their shoulders, and tell you that it passes their comprehension.

I have already gone somewhat minutely into the diet and other circumstances of a family living on 8s. a week in Wiltshire. This supersedes the necessity of entering into such an inquiry here. To show, however, how similar, in its miseries, the labourer's lot is in the southern and western districts, I shall once more transfer the reader to the village of Southleigh, and enter with him into one of the cottages. It is neither more nor less than that which I first examined—the abode of my old friend with the pitchfork. She is lighting a few broken faggots at the back of the fire-place, as if preparing for some culinary operation. It will be remembered that her family consists of five—her husband and son and two daughters. The husband earns 7s. a week, *when at work,* and so does the son; the eldest daughter adds something to the family earnings, by means of her lace cushion. But neither of them have constant employment, so that their united earnings will not much exceed the wages of one man continuously employed.

"What are you about?" I ask her.

"Going to get dinner ready," she replies.

"What is it to be?" I continue.

"Some broths," says she.

"Broths! What do you mean by broths?"

"O," says she, "wait, and you'll see."

She thereupon hangs a pot over the fire, half full of water. We wait patiently till it boils. By and bye it begins to simmer, and she drops a little salt into it; then follows a little fat, which she got that morning at the vicar's; and last of all comes a quantity of bread cut up in small cubes, each large enough for a good mouthful. This simple compound is permitted to boil for a minute or two, when it is taken off the fire, and poured into a large dish, and lo! in a trice the family dinner is prepared. It consists of nothing but the "broths." We taste it. It is bread and hot water, little more, for the fat has scarcely flavoured it. They had the same mess in the morning for breakfast, but *without the fat*. It will be repeated at supper time.

"Do you never eat butcher's meat?" I inquire.

"Lord bless you, sir," she replies, "we wouldn't know ourselves if we did. We never have a taste of it, but when we get a bit from the lady (the vicar's lady). Sometimes I get a bone, which I boil, or a bit of mate from her, which I take home in my hand or in my pocket. At other times I get a bit of grease; and but for this we wouldn't taste mate."

"Do you never put anything else in your broth?" I then asked.

"We sometimes put turnips," she answers. "We put turnips almost always when we have no fat."

"But have you no potatoes?"

"No, sir."

"Have you not an allotment?"

"Yes; but we didn't plant no potatoes."

"Why?"

"We were afraid of the disease."

"Do you not find the want of them?"

"Very much."

"How can you keep your pig without them?"

"Well, 'tisn't easy to do it, sir, and I'm afraid we'll be obliged to sell it before Christmas time."

"Have you ever any tea?"

"Sometimes we have a little."

"Do you bake your own bread?"

"Sometimes."

"Have you an oven?"

"No; but there is one in the village at which we all bake. We each give a cake to have our bread fired."

"You buy some of your bread?"

"Yes; the bakers come round with it in carts."

"Do you get your bread cheaper now than before?"

"A good deal."

"Then you are better off now than you were?"

"We would be if wages were as high as before, and we had the potatoes."

"Then, on the whole, you feel yourselves but very little better off?"

"Very little indeed, sir. We can't have bread, no matter how cheap it is, unless we have steady work, and that we haven't even at the present low rate of wages."

When I first entered the village, I met a man a short distance from it engaged in what is called cropping hedges. His daughter, a little girl, had just brought him his dinner. It consisted of nothing but bread and potatoes, and the potatoes were cold. I afterwards saw his wife, and asked her why she did not send him something hot? "Oh," said she, "I have so much to do, that I can't always send him a hot dinner, and my man is not very particular what he eats." This was a fortunate provision of nature on his account. She had her family to look after, and frequently worked out; besides which, her short stock of fuel caused her to boil at once as many potatoes as would serve for several meals.

It would answer no useful purpose to multiply instances of this nature. Those already given serve to demonstrate the general condition of the poor, as regards their diet, where families are large and wages are low. Bread alone, or bread and potatoes—or, where there are no potatoes, bread and turnips or cabbage—form their staple fare, with now and then a little tea, occasionally sweetened with treacle, and perhaps sometimes a little milk for the children. As was said to me by one well acquainted with the circumstances of the poor in these counties, they seldom or never taste meat, but what is given them by the parson, or what they may pick up as "broken meat" in the towns. This is rather a curious distribution of the smiles of fortune, so far as the poor are concerned. They are generally best paid where other circumstances beside their wages conspire to have them best fed. There is a great deal of broken meat in the towns, which goes to the support of the poor—but it is in the neighbourhood of the towns that the labourers are best paid and most able to buy meat. In the more sequestered districts, where they have the lowest wages, they have no such resource as is at the command of the poor in or about the towns.

Such being their condition in so many instances, it would almost seem as if there was but one way to its improvement—and *that* in the descending line. As regards shelter and food, an industrious man is much better off if he pauperizes himself. He has then an airy room, and a clean wholesome bed to lie upon. He has meat at least twice— sometimes thrice—a week, and puddings of a substantial kind, such as suet pudding, when there is no meat. He has also occasionally his soup and his fish, and almost daily his ample supper of bread and cheese. What keeps him from seeking this comparatively comfortable condition? Nothing but the idea of the restraint to which the workhouse discipline subjects him. But if he can get over his aversion to that, his easiest way to improve his condition is to sink the independent man in the pauper. To him independence is privation, whereas pauperism would be comfort.

Fortunately, this extreme privation is not the lot of all. Unmarried men, if they are sober, industrious, and steadily employed, may escape the extremity of suffering to which others are subjected. And so may married men, ere their families have grown numerous, provided their wages are high and their work constant. But with families of three or four—to say nothing of five, six, seven, and eight—it is impossible for the labourers and those dependent upon them to escape the greatest misery, even where wages are highest, and where 10s. 6d., instead of 8s. or 7s. are paid. But, although there are many who, from a variety of circumstances, are not so wretchedly off as those to whom I have alluded, it must be borne in mind that there is an equally large class whose circumstances are correctly illustrated by the cases which I have given. There may be many a labourer, married and single, tolerably well off in Devon and Somerset, but there are multitudes so immersed in the depths of wretchedness, that it is almost impossible to fancy them sinking lower. There are hundreds of families, with four or five children, whose sole dependence is the earnings of the husband—the children being too young and the wife too busy at home to work abroad—their earnings not exceeding 7s. a week. It is on this sad feature of the diversified picture that public attention should be most closely riveted.

On looking into the returns of the Inspector of Prisons in the southern and western district for the year 1847, I find that the average total annual expense on account of each prisoner was £27 9s. 9d. Now, at the rate of 8s. a week, a labourer's wages will amount to £20 16s. in the year, provided his work is constant, which is not always the case. Even if he has none to support but himself, he cannot spend upon himself during the year as much as the public in the district in question spends on each prisoner in gaol. But if he has a wife and five young children to support, the average expenditure on account of each member of his family is about £3 a year—or about the one-ninth part of what is expended on the prisoner. If the whole family were in gaol, instead of living on the £20 16s., to which they are limited out of gaol, the aggregate cost, on their account, to the public would be nearly £200. The expenditure per week on account of each member of a family of seven, under the circumstances supposed, would be about 1s. 1½d.; whereas the actual present weekly outlay upon each pauper in one of the most economically managed workhouses that I have seen—that at Liskeard—is about 2s., exclusive of his proportion of the general expenses of the workhouse. These included, the average would be nearer 4s. than 2s. The 2s. merely include what is expended for his diet and washing. These comparisons are both curious and instructive.

There are many, especially amongst the farmers, who are prone to malign the labourers, and who maintain that the misery so prevalent amongst them is of their own making. There is no doubt but that the privations which they endure are in very many instances aggravated by their own carelessness or misconduct. But it is a calumny to say that their situation would be equally deplorable, no matter what their wages were. I have seen too many instances of prudence, thrift, and comparative comfort to subscribe to such a doctrine—instances few and far between, it is true, in the counties that I have hitherto visited in connection with this inquiry, but which form the rule and not the exception in other districts, where higher wages prevail, and where the well-being of the labourer is attended to by his employer as a matter of paramount duty. In these cases, instead of the extra wages being squandered in drink and licentiousness, leaving the family to pine in wretchedness at home, they are frequently applied to enhancing its comforts and improving its position. In cottages where this is observable I have often seen the extra pairs of shoes for the parents and the children, and in some cases the extra clothing for the Sunday. Let the labourer have but an adequate amount of wages, and he will improve both the condition and the appearance of his family. Persons who think otherwise only fall into the views of those who would make their own gratuitous aspersions of him one of the many reasons which they assign for keeping his remuneration as low as possible.

Labouring men have frequently complained to me of the mode in which the farmers in some districts make use of the position and conduct of young men to affect the general rate of wages. Where the practice of making a distinction as to amount in favour of married men prevails, the highest rate thus paid is often a low one, as compared with the rates paid elsewhere. If young men receive less than married men, the wages of the latter are frequently lowered on the first plausible pretext—the farmers telling them that, as they can get young men to do their work for a given sum, there is no necessity for their employing others at a higher rate. Sooner than be thrown entirely out of work, the married labourers often submit readily to the reduction—which again is made use of to lower still more the wages paid to the single men; so that the former difference is re-established between them, but with this advantage to the farmer, that he is paying less to both. Again, young men, having fewer incentives to steadiness of conduct, frequently abstain from work when they have got a few shillings in their pocket, which are soon spent at the ale-house, when they are impelled to look once more for employment. The farmers, taking their conduct into consideration, tell them that if they have so much money to spend in superfluities, it is clear their wages are too high, and they frequently lower them. So far, few would be inclined to find fault with them. But here again the wages paid to the young man are too often made to affect those paid to the steady, sober, and industrious head of a family. Were his wages to remain stationary, whilst those of the ill-behaved workman were being reduced, no injustice would be done. But the evil is, that when the wages of one class are being reduced, the wages of all are but too apt to go down along with them; and thus it is that many an honest and hard-working man is curtailed in his means of supporting his family, not from his own, but from his neighbour's misconduct.

One of the greatest evils that I find attending the low rate of wages now paid in so many of the rural districts, is the want of a change of clothing for the labourers, both male and female. Most of them wear flannel whilst at work, but few have a change even of that. The consequence is, that they wear the same garment next the skin day and night, although for many hours of the day it may have been soaked with perspiration. I have frequently seen both men and women, whilst at work, perspiring most freely, with their clothes quite wet upon them. It is deemed essential to the health of a miner that he should exchange for a dry suit the clothing with which he comes dripping from the mine. But the field labourer almost invariably permits the garments which have been made wringing wet with perspiration to dry upon his person—and that, too, not merely when he is in exercise, but when he is lying on his bed asleep; for he frequently lies down enveloped in flannel, cold, moist, and clammy, after the day's toil.

Some days since I was conversing with an old man, near Bridge-water, on the subject of wages. He had been a farm-labourer in his youth, but had abandoned the fields for a trade, at which he had made a little competency, which, he remarked, sufficed to keep him out of the workhouse in his old age. He did not speak very charitably of the farmers, whom he characterized as a very selfish and hard-hearted race of men. I observed to him that they justified the present reduced rates of wages by the prevailing low price of corn. He replied that it was not on the side of wages that the shoe really pinched them. He remembered wages high, when corn was about as low as now. "How came they," I asked, "to keep up the wages then?" "I tell you what," said he, "they kept them up, and could afford to do so, because they neither lived in such style nor paid such high rents as they do now."

LABOUR AND THE POOR.

—◆—

THE RURAL DISTRICTS.

[FROM OUR SPECIAL CORRESPONDENT.]

PHYSICAL CONDITION OF THE LABOURER IN CORNWALL.

Letter VIII.

I now proceed, in prosecution of the plan laid down in a former communication, to give a brief account of the physical condition of the labourer in Cornwall. This will include his house accommodation and rent, his wages and diet. The industry of Cornwall is, from its position and resources, of a varied character. It cannot be said to possess any manufactures, in the ordinary acceptation of the term; but from its peculiar maritime facilities, and from its being the extreme and the richest part of the metalliferous peninsula which constitutes the south-west of England, it sustains, along with its agricultural, a large fishing and mining industry. Generally speaking, the various pursuits of agriculture, mining, and fishing are carried on separately from each other; but they are sometimes combined in different ways and degrees—the agriculturist being occasionally the fisher, and the miner being, to some extent, an agriculturist. But it is seldom, if ever, that you find the two pursuits of agriculture and mining combined— the man who is accustomed to drive the plough upon the surface having apparently no inclination to descend below it in quest of a livelihood. Besides, even were he so inclined, his previous habits would by no means fit him for the work. The agricultural labourer is not a very adaptable animal. He may do his own work, but it is with difficulty that you can apply him to anything else. When he engages in fishing, it is only to do the more ordinary parts of the work. He works with, but is not of, the tribe of fishermen. Should he descend into the mine, the chances are that he would never emerge from it. It is a rare sight to see a miner a fisherman. When he is so, it is generally in the pilchard season, when there is a great demand for hands both afloat and ashore. In nine cases out of ten in which you find him thus employed he is a surface, and not an under-ground, man. Indeed, the latter entertains for him the greatest contempt, refusing him a place in the fraternity of miners.

The county of Cornwall is divided into two great slopes, one descending to the Bristol the other to the English Channel. They are separated from each other by a ridge of high land, which, with but few interruptions, traverse the county in the direction of its length. The southern slope has the largest surface, as may be seen from the greater number and magnitude of its streams. It is also, with slight exception, the richest section of the county in an agricultural point of view. It varies greatly, however, in fertility. Perhaps the richest agricultural tract in the whole county is about St. Germains. There the land is tolerably deep, and farming is occasionally prosecuted as a scientific pursuit. In the valleys the land is tolerably heavy and deep, but along the numerous undulations into which the surface is broken, it is light, shallow, and stony. As far on as Liskeard, and in the neighbourhood of Looe and St. Martin's, the soil, although not of the first quality, is well adapted for agricultural purposes. To the north of Liskeard it is very stony and broken, until it reaches the summit of the dividing ridge. Westward from Liskeard, and on to Bodmin, the agricultural tract is prolonged, but becoming less and less fertile every mile. Between Bodmin and St. Austle is a large tract as wild and desolate as Shap Fell, and the only product of which is the fine china clay which is prepared here for the potteries of Stafford and of France. Between St. Austle and Truro the country is generally cultivated; but soon after leaving Truro cultivation ceases, and the traveller finds himself in the midst of that bleak, rocky, and forbidding-looking region, stretching around Redruth, which is the great scene of the mining industry of Cornwall. A smaller proportion of the northern slope is arable than of the southern, and in some parts of it, where the land is cultivated, the tillage is of the lowest order, owing partly to the "hungry" nature of the soil, and partly to the inability of the farmers, who are, in numerous instances, men with small holdings and without capital. Cornwall does not raise much more than half the grain necessary for its own consumption. The deficiency used to be supplied from Ireland, and for the last year or two partly from France. But the comparative failure of the grain crops this season, in that country, has so raised the price of wheat in the French market, that it is not likely that any will come from that quarter this year. At present, the deficiency in Cornwall is chiefly supplied from Sussex, Essex, and Norfolk. Few of the great improvements of the age, as regards intercommunication, have as yet made their way into Cornwall. The stage coach is the only means of transit for travellers, there being no railways but two or three short ones, connecting the different clusters of mines with their nearest seaports. The number of those in Cornwall engaged in, and dependent for their support upon, agricultural labour, was, in 1841, taking the same calculation as in former instances, about 45,000. This is but little more than one-eighth of the whole population, being a small proportion as compared with that exhibited by the other counties considered, in some of which it was about one-third.

In proceeding through Cornwall I found that there was no lack of testimony to the superior condition of the farm labourer in the county. But, as I had over and over again heard this song in places where it had no right to be raised, I determined to examine carefully into every circumstance affecting the labourer's condition ere I concurred in the view which it expressed. If his money rate of wages were to be taken as the sole standard whereby to judge of his comforts, there can be no doubt but that the condition of the labourer in Cornwall would, in the main, be better than that of the same class in any of the counties which I have already visited, and far better than the condition of that class in some of those counties. But there are considerations which enter into the question, as regards the Cornish labourer, which, when taken into account, detract somewhat from the standard indicated by his mere money rate of wages. Still, after having made allowance for such drawbacks as may exist, I am prepared to admit that the Cornish farm labourer is, on the whole, better off than his brethren in either Bucks, Oxford, Berks, Wilts, Somerset, or Devon.

The first point to which I directed my attention was, as in former cases, to the house accommodation of the labourer. I had not long done so before I discovered that in this, at least, there was no ground for the claim of superiority, in respect of condition, preferred for labour in Cornwall. As elsewhere, there were around me abundant evidences of very straitened accommodation for a large and increasing population. The few cottages visible were, in all cases, old and mouldy; in many they had greatly progressed on the road to ruin, and in some were utterly dilapidated. Some of the worst specimens of these miserable tenements may be seen along the high road between Torpoint and Liskeard, and, though at great intervals, in the neighbourhood of almost all the parish roads lying north and south of the main highway. I am now speaking of the purely agricultural portions

of Cornwall, and can assert without hesitation, that the accommodation provided for the labourer in these districts is, on the average, little,
if anything, better than that at his disposal in the adjoining counties.
In extending my observations to other parts of the county, I found
that in many places it was not only plentifully provided with house
accommodation, but that it was thickly strewn with new cottages of a
very superior description, as regards size, design, &c. But these were
invariably to be seen in districts in which not only were mining operations being carried on, but mines had been long established. As in
the character of their industry, so in the accommodation provided for
labour, some of the miners form a striking exception to the rest of the
population of the county. The description of the labourer's domicile
in Devonshire is applicable to his cottage in Cornwall. Nowhere have
I seen, in the latter, such clusters of miserable dwellings, as I have
observed in the former. But there are scattered instances everywhere
of abodes equally dark, damp, unstable, and unwholesome. These are
not confined to the districts more especially entitled to the epithet
of rural. Cornwall is dotted over with small rural towns, every one
of which contains, more or less, an assemblage of tenements which
are unfit to betoken the completion of the first stage in civilization.
Some of them are crowded to a degree perilous to morals and disastrous to health. This arises not only from the want of new, but also
from the destruction of old, cottages. If the clearing system has not
been carried on in Cornwall, the work has been as effectually, if not
as speedily, done by the natural decay of cottages, to save which from
destruction no effort has been made. Take, as an example of what
is to be found in other portions of Cornwall exclusively agricultural,
or nearly so, what has been done in this respect in the parishes of
St. Martin's and Talland. In area, both these parishes are large, and
(with but little exception) they are both entirely under cultivation. A
great deal of labour is annually required for the tillage of so large an
area, and yet but few of the labourers who work in these parishes live
in either of them. They have been gradually driven into the towns
of East and West Looe, where they inhabit the most wretched tenements, looking, in most cases, filthy in the extreme, notwithstanding
the very general cleansing which cottages, here as elsewhere, received
under apprehensions of the cholera. Some of them have taken refuge
in the small fishing town of Polperro, exerting a rather baneful influence upon the morals of the community. They have either been driven
out of their cottages in the neighbourhood, or induced to leave from

the high rents demanded, and have made their way to Polperro, where there appeared to be some room to spare, and where rents are low. A part of Polperro is in the parish of Talland, but lying as it does at one of the extreme points of the parish, the labourers experience the greatest inconvenience in being obliged daily to walk great distances to their work. The bulk of the labourers, employed in the parishes in question, reside in the two Looes and in Polperro; so that some of them have to walk as much as five miles to their work. This involves, in addition to a day's work, a walk of ten miles a day—of itself, in the estimation of many, sufficient exertion for one day. This is certainly one of the greatest hardships to which the poor are subjected from the want of cottages.

As a specimen of how the lower classes in the country districts sometimes live, I mentioned in a former communication the purpose to which a parish-house had been applied on the borders of Devon and Cornwall, and not far from Launceston. Another instance, somewhat similar, has come under my observation in the parish of St. Martin's. The house in question is situated but about half a gunshot from the church and rectory of the parish. It was originally left to the parish, I believe, as a kind of almshouse, which was to give shelter to four aged women, the house having but four rooms, each room being approached by a door from the outside, so as to be independent of each other. The doors leading to the upper rooms are in the gable ends of the house, and are reached by means of dilapidated stone staircases leading to them from the outside. It is now some time since the original purpose of the donor has been departed from, and the house has, for some years back, been let apparently to as many as could crowd into it. It is now as lonely and deserted as if it had never known an occupant. And no wonder. The dread scourge which has desolated so many portions of the land fell with fearful severity upon this unwholesome and over-crowded abode. Cholera entered it and claimed five victims—the rest fled in terror from the plague. The survivors yet occupy a small shed, which was hastily erected for their reception on their abandoning the house of death. No one has since ventured back to it. The windows are broken in, the doors partly dismantled, and on looking through the open casements you can see that fire also has borne its part in the work of destruction. To purify the house, the parish authorities tore down and burnt the partition walls, and the miserable tenement is for the present a wreck. It will not cost much, however, to replace the walls; and it is supposed that ere long the parish will again have its colony of tenants in this parish-house. The reader may form some idea of the manner in which its inmates lived, previous to the visitation of the cholera, from the fact that in one room—so great was the number crowded into it, and so small was the space appropriated to them—the beds, which were three in number (for it served the purposes of bed-room and sitting-room), were piled one above another, like the shelves of a book-case. Such is the domiciliary condition of some at least of the agricultural labourers of England.

In examining into the state of the labourers' cottages, I discovered that as much fault was found by the tenants with the Duchy of Cornwall as with the private proprietors. At many points I was informed that the agents and managers of the duchy exhibit the utmost indifference to the comforts of the tenants, suffering cottages to go to ruin, and listening to no remonstrance in favour of repairs. If this be so, it is unfortunate that such an example should be set by the managers of such a property. For, as regards their domestic comforts, there is nothing from which the labourers suffer so much as from the scarcity of cottages—an evil attended with a multiform disadvantage; for, whilst it compels them to crowd in great numbers into small spaces, it makes them also pay higher rents than they otherwise would do for such accommodation as they have, while it is in too many instances removed inconveniently far from the scene of their labours. If this is repeated, it is because I deem it all important that it should be strongly impressed upon the reader's mind. With such an example set to them, many of the private proprietors of course let their cottages go to wreck, and hundreds of the tenants have complained to me, that whilst they have in vain urged the landlord to grant them necessary repairs, there is no abatement made in the amount of their rents, in consideration of the gradual dilapidation of their houses.

In some parts of Cornwall—such, for instance, as the neighbourhood of Penzance—it is needless to look for decent habitations in the possession of the labourer, so long as the farmers are contented to live in hovels which are below the standard of even a labourer's comfort. In these districts farming is carried on as it were in patchwork—a man leasing perhaps but 40 or 50 acres of land, and having no capital wherewith to work it, as is the case in the neighbourhood of Axminster, in Devonshire. In these districts, however, if the tenement is poor, the rent is generally low. But there are parts of the county in which it would appear that the rents are high in proportion as the cottages are poor. Such is the state of things to be met with in what is generally known as the eastern mining district. Rents are high in all the mining districts; but in the neighbourhood of Liskeard, although the rents are equal to, and in some cases greater than, those in the west, the cottages for which they are paid are, in the main, of a most inferior description. The cottages are, in their dimensions, style, and appearance, such as are to be met with in the exclusively agricultural districts. Indeed, until within the last ten years, the neighbourhood in question was such a district. As soon as mining operations were commenced near Liskeard, a considerable emigration of miners from the westward took place. But as the population of the district increased, there was but little or no increase to the number of cottages. The result will at once suggest itself to every mind. Such cottages as existed were speedily overcrowded, lodgers being taken in every one of them where there was even a crevice to spare. This sudden increase in the demand for house room enhanced the value of house property, and rents were speedily raised—double the amount being paid for one of these cottages that is paid for a similar tenement where no such demand exists. The cottager has thus received no actual benefit, whilst his space has been far more encroached upon than before. Many of them have told me that they are infinitely worse off now in this respect than they were before the influx of miners. They get some money from their lodgers, in addition to their wages, but it all, or nearly all, goes again in the shape of enhanced rents. It is not only in the country parishes that the pressure has been felt, it has also extended itself to the towns. Liskeard itself suffers materially from it. Some of the smaller tenements in Liskeard are crowded to an extent distressing to witness—many of the miners working in the Caradon mines, fully four miles distant, living in the town. This subjects them, in addition to their work, to a walk of eight miles per day; but they are obliged to submit to this, as they cannot find quarters nearer the mines. The houses and villages between the town and the mines are absolutely glutted with people. One case, which may be given in illustration of the state of things in Liskeard, was that of a man and his wife, who had a miner lodging with them, all three occupying the same bedroom at night. On suggesting to the woman that this must be a painful situation to her, she observed that it was, but that they could not help it. They had but two rooms, and neither of them could occupy the lower room. Their rent was high, and they were therefore obliged to keep a lodger, whom they accommodated in the only room at their command, which could be used as a bed-room. Another case was that of a widow, who was in search of a lodger. Her house had but two rooms, the upper of which was her bed-room. I asked her if she intended that her lodger, if she got one, should sleep below. She replied in the negative. I then suggested that the lodger she was in search of was one who would invest himself with a lawful title to the occupancy of her own chamber. She again replied in the negative, and on my looking somewhat puzzled, informed me that it was her own intention to sleep below. The room was so cold and cheerless that she could not offer it to a lodger, yet such was the bed-room which she intended for herself. She said that the arrangement would suit her very well, as the miner would go early to bed, and she would have the lower part of the house to herself. I asked her when she expected him to get up, to which she replied that he was likely to do so at an early hour of the morning, as he had to walk four miles to his work. He would, in short, be up before her hour of rising, which made me suggest to her that, although she might have the lower part of the house to herself at night, she would not be equally favoured in the morning. "Oh, sir," said she, "you mustn't think us so bad as we seem; we're drove often to do what we don't like to do, or we wouldn't have a roof at all to cover us."

I afterwards inspected several of the houses lining the road leading to the workhouse. Some had but one bedroom, but the majority had two. Many of them had been recently cleaned and whitewashed, but most were cheerless and uncomfortable to a degree, some being almost destitute of, and others overcrowded with, furniture. In most there was a lodger, in some two, in others three, and in others, again, four. In all cases, in which there were two rooms, the family crowded into one, to leave the other for the lodgers. In one room three men occupied one bed, but, in general, there were two beds in the lodgers' room, and sometimes both had two occupants. The first I entered was thus situated. I asked the woman what rent she paid. She replied, "four pounds, besides poor rates and gas rates." I then inquired what amount they paid in the shape of poor rates. She told me that they paid several shillings in the course of the year, paying five rates one year; and then added, "they're far better off than we are in the union, although it's we that have to pay for their keep." I had just returned from a visit to the workhouse, and could not gainsay her statement. There was not one of its inmates but was more comfortably circumstanced than she, and yet she was one of the contributors to their support. This is one of the most striking anomalies of our social system—let him remedy it who can.

About a mile from Liskeard, and on the road to the Caradon mines, is the village of Trevecca. That it is but of yesterday is indicated as well by the superior style of its houses, as by the fresh colour of the material used in their construction. It consists of twenty-four houses in twelve detached groups, each group consisting of two residences. The houses, which are all on one side of the road, stand back a little way from the thoroughfare, each having a small patch of ground in front, and about the eighth of an acre attached to it behind. The cottages are two stories high, counting the ground floor as a story; the building material is stone, and the roofs are covered with slate. Altogether the houses look palatial, as compared with the huts of the older villages, or such as are scattered over the face of the county. Nor is their internal accommodation inferior to their external appearance. The two end houses have each five rooms; all the rest have four, two below and two above. The lower rooms are well plastered, and although the beams which support the floor above are exposed, they are clean, with a space of from eight to nine feet between the two floors. They are also well lighted, the windows being large and framed in the ordinary manner, instead of being occupied by the leaden diamond-paned frames so common in the older cottages. The staircase to the bedrooms ascends from the inner rooms, having a good banister, being commodious and of easy ascent. The bed-rooms are large, airy, and well lighted, the walls being plastered both at the sides and over head. Between each house and the back garden is a small paved yard, with accommodation for washing and other conveniences, which should attend every household. At the extremity of the garden, far removed from the house, is a pig-stye for such as may choose to keep a pig. When I visited the village, I found but few doing so, owing to the scarcity and dearness of potatoes—barley being expensive feeding for a pig. So clean, cheerful, and comfortable a scene at once surprised and delighted me, for it was in perfect contrast with the wretched, unwholesome, and straitened accommodation which I had elsewhere but too generally witnessed. On inquiring into the origin of so unexpected a scene, I found that it had been called into existence by the extraordinary demand which had so suddenly arisen in the neighbourhood for cottages. The property on which the village stands belonged to the daughter of one of the most respectable and influential citizens of Liskeard. She projected and executed the undertaking, which has been advantageous to all parties. Some of the tenants are themselves miners, others are not, but take miners as lodgers. Several of them are agricultural labourers, and all of them, before moving into their present abodes, knew what it was to tenant the wretched hovels of the peasantry. Whatever influence the superior style of their domicile may have had upon them, certain it is that, as regards intelligence and their personal habits, they are greatly superior to their class elsewhere. Several of them have told me that they would not return to the holes which they formerly occupied, if they were given them rent free. Their altered circumstances have superinduced an elevation of tone and manner, which it was pleasant to witness, and which were fraught with hope as regards the capacity for improvement of the labouring classes. The snugness of the dwellings, the tidiness of the women, and the cleanliness of the children, all betokened that one of the greatest barriers in the way of improved habits amongst the peasantry is the wretched condition of their dwellings.

There was one drawback, however, to the favourable state of things presented by the village of Trevecca. The great demand for house accommodation, which characterizes the district, caused most of the houses to be overcrowded. In almost all of them, the family slept in one of the bedrooms, the other being given up to lodgers. Most of these latter rooms had two beds in them, and accommodated four people. For 2s. a week each, they get their bed, their washing, their tea at breakfast, and ordinary vegetables at dinner. Some time ago they paid 2s. 6d., when they had as many potatoes as they wished; but now that potatoes are scarce and dear, they are not provided, and the extra 6d. is struck off the week's payment. The lodgers generally take their meals with the family, except when they work during the middle of the day in the mines, in which case they take their dinner along with them. When they dine at home, the dinner sometimes consists of broth, which is made up of vegetables and meat boiled together. The ordinary vegetables, such as cabbage and cauliflower—the latter being very common in Cornwall—and turnips, are supplied by the family; but if any extra vegetable is added, it must be at the expense of the party desiring it. The family contributes but its own quota of the meal, each lodger contributing his. Sometimes a meat pie is made, each party contributing his own share of the contents. I was puzzled how each man could know his own again, but was informed that they did so readily. All this would be very well but for the overcrowding which it superinduces.

In Trevecca, however, the evils of this, in a sanitary point of view, are not so much felt as elsewhere, for the bed-rooms are all large and well ventilated. In a moral point of view, however, it must be equally deteriorating wherever it occurs. But it may be asked, why is the example set by the spirited owner of the village not followed elsewhere, seeing that the demand for houses is yet far from being adequately met? The truth is, that the ratepayers and authorities of the neighbouring parishes are exceedingly jealous of any attempt being made to follow it. They dissuade proprietors from building, lest the mining operations of the neighbourhood should not be permanent. Mining, they say, is quite a new thing in the district, and it may not last. If it declines, a great mischief will have been effected, by extending the number of cottages. There seems, however, to be but little prospect of such a contingency, judging from the appearance of activity displayed at the mines. If anything could arise to bring it about, it would be enhancing the cost of producing copper, which is done by the higher rate of wages paid here than elsewhere to the miners, on account of the high price of their lodgings, and other circumstances, which will be more appropriately alluded to hereafter.

A library, consisting of about 200 volumes, was established in Trevecca. All who had any desire to read having read all the books which they cared for, the library has since been removed to the mines, in the vicinity of which it will pass through the hands of a new set of readers.

The present average rate of wages paid to the agricultural labourer in Cornwall is 9s. a week. This, however, be it remembered, is but the money rate, and by no means indicates the real extent of the labourer's command of the comforts of life. In dealing with the wages of Cornwall, the element of cider has not to be considered, as in Somerset and Devon. The whole of the wages is paid in money, subject, though, perhaps, in different degrees, to some deductions common to other counties. I have already alluded to the comparatively high rent paid by the Cornish labourer, as being, *pro tanto*, a virtual reduction of his wages. But this is not general, the highest rents being charged only in those districts where, from the vicinity of mines, there is a greater demand for, than a supply of, houses. This again, as already explained, only occurs where mines have recently been established, so that it is far from being general. Still, however, in the neighbourhood of all mines, whether long or recently established, rents are somewhat higher than

in the purely agricultural portions of the county. As mining operations are so generally diffused over Cornwall, it therefore happens
that there are but few localities in the county that do not feel the effect
of their vicinity in adding something to the rents. In the agricultural
parishes most distant from them, the rents of cottages are on a level
with those in the adjoining counties. You there, as in Devon, Somerset, or Wilts, meet with cottages, with two or three rooms, rented
at from 40s. to 50s. a year. In these cases the cottagers enjoy their
wages independently of any reduction on this account. In all other
cases, whether the rent be £3, £3 10s., £4, or £4 10s., the abatement
which must be made from the nominal rate of wages is about the same.
Indeed, in many cases where the rents are highest, there is the least
deduction to be made, as they are always highest nearest the mines—
the cottagers having thus a chance of making the difference wholly or
partly up, and sometimes of adding to their means. But a little back
from the mines, where the influence of high rents near them is felt,
without giving the cottagers the same opportunity, the whole of the
difference between the rents which they pay and the ordinary rent of
a cottage may frequently be regarded as so much to be deducted from
their nominal amount of wages. But the most serious deduction is that
which must be made for the high price which they are now paying for
their corn. I have already alluded to the arrangement which has elsewhere, as in Wiltshire, been prevalent—established for the benefit of
the labourer—of letting him have corn for his own consumption at a
fixed price, without any reference to fluctuations in the market value
of grain. So long as the price of grain, notwithstanding its fluctuations, was generally high, the arrangement was advantageous to him;
but now that there is but little prospect of it ever again reaching the
price at which it is sold to him, it is obvious that the labourer must be
injured by its continuance. It falls at present with peculiar severity on
the Cornish labourer. The arrangement here has been, for some time
past, to let the labourer have his grain for 16s. and 8s.—that is to say,
16s. per bushel of wheat, and 8s. per bushel of barley. The Cornish
bushel is double the size of the Winchester, so that, reduced to the
measurement appreciable by a Londoner, the arrangement is to give
the corn at 8s. and 4s. But, to adhere to the Cornish measure, the
present price of the best wheat is about 10s. 6d. a bushel, and it is not
the best wheat that the labourer gets here or elsewhere. The real market value of the quality of grain given to him would be about 9s. Yet
it is for this that he pays 16s. The manner in which the arrangement

operates is this: In Cornwall, but few of the labourers are paid by the week. Some are paid by the fortnight, others by the month. Taking 9s. as the average rate of wages, a man would be entitled to 36s. for four weeks' work. Supposing him to have a family, he would, during that time, consume about three pecks of wheat, and half a bushel of barley to mix with the wheat. On being paid, at the end of the month, the value of these would be deducted from his wages. At the rate which he is obliged to pay, the wheat would come to 12s., and the barley to 4s., in all 16s. He would, therefore, have but 20s. to receive as money wages at the end of the month. The hardship to him is this: Supposing that he was paid his full amount of money wages, and bought his wheat and barley at their real market value, how much of his wages would he have in hand, after he had purchased the necessary quantity for his family's consumption? The wheat, supposing him to purchase the same quality as he receives, would come to 6s. 9d. Making a deduction of but 1s. 6d. from the price of a bushel of barley, he would get his half-bushel for 3s. 3d.; in other words, he would get for 10s. that for which he has now to pay 16s. The difference of 6s. spread over the four weeks makes a difference of 1s. 6d. between his real and his nominal rate of wages for the week. This is but a small sum in the estimation of many, but it is nearly 17 per cent. of the wages of the Cornish labourer, taking them at their nominal amount. To show that it is no trifle to him, he could pay his rent and send three of his children to school by means of the difference which he would gain, but for the arrangement in question. It is obvious, therefore, that when this deduction is made from the nominal rate of wages in Cornwall, the real rate of wages will not be found to range much higher than in Devonshire, where the analogous arrangement is not so hard upon the labourer, and a deduction must be made on account of cider. Sometimes in Cornwall you find the labourer receiving his grain at 14s. and 7s. instead of at 16s. and 8s. This is apt to mislead without inquiry. The farmer does not confer this privilege on his labourer without an equivalent. When the price of grain is lowered to the labourer, his wages are lowered also. I have known cases in which the labourer submitted to a deduction of a shilling a week in consideration of this—that is to say, he submitted to a loss of 4s. per month in consideration of a gain of 2s. 10d. If any one will take the trouble of making the calculation, he will find that this is so. Some of the labourers themselves were not a little astonished at the result when I stated it to them.

Yet, notwithstanding the near approximation of his real rate of wages to the average rate in the adjoining counties, the condition of the labourer in Cornwall is, on the whole, better than that of his class in these counties. This is to be accounted for by the cheapness at which he can supply himself with fish. The most common and the most popular fish in Cornwall is the pilchard. The failure of the potato itself is not more disastrous to the poor of the county than is a failure in the take of pilchards. The average price of them is from 1s. to 1s. 6d. a hundred. This year they have, so far, been very abundant, and have sold as low as 10d. a hundred. After being salted, they are re-tailed at the rate of seven for 2d. Such as can afford to lay in a stock for the year, will salt and lay by from 1,000 to 1,500 pilchards, for the use of a family of five or six. Others, who cannot afford to do this, buy them in greater or less quantities, as they can afford to do so, sometimes paying more for them, and sometimes less. The traveller in Cornwall, whether in the highways or byways, is scarcely ever out of reach of the smell of pilchards undergoing the process of cooking. The whole atmosphere of the county seems odoriferous with pilchards. As I now write, in the principal hotel in Redruth, the whole house is pervaded with the odour of this favourite fish. They may not be as strengthening as animal food, but they form a nutritious item in the Cornish labourer's diet, which is almost entirely wanting in that of the poor of the neighbouring counties. The potato, when abundant, is the favourite vegetable taken with the pilchard. In the absence of the potato it is eaten with bread. When used with the former, the pilchard and the potato are boiled together. Sometimes the potatoes are mashed and baked before the fire, with the pilchards on the top of them, which diffuse their oil through them, and give them a strong flavour. It is seldom that the pilchard constitutes an ingredient of the "pasty," so commonly met with as entering into the labourer's diet in Cornwall. The mackerel frequently does, which can also be procured very cheaply during certain seasons of the year. Generally speaking, the "pasties" consist of potatoes and bits of meat, more frequently salt pork, covered with a rather tough crust made of flour, and some-times of flour and barley meal mixed together. In the absence of the potato, the turnip constitutes one of the internal ingredients of the pasty. Sometimes it is merely a mass of dough, lightened and sweet-ened a little by a few raisins or currants. It is few that can afford to have them frequently with meat. They are generally made for the labourer himself, his family contenting themselves with lighter and more frugal fare. "This is John's dinner," said an elderly woman to me with whom I was one day conversing in her own house, putting at the same time a large pasty into my hand. "What does this contain?" I inquired. "Potatoes and pork," she replied. "Will John eat this at a meal?" I asked, for the pasty was large and weighed heavily. "Aye, and think nothing of it," she answered, astonished at the question. I could not avoid congratulating John in his absence on the extent of his appetite and the excellence of his digestion. The family in this case consisted of only the father and mother, and one son, who was grown up, but was seldom at home. When at home he occupied the same bed-room with his parents. The wife generally contented herself with pilchards, reserving such scraps of beef and pork as she could procure for her husband. It is only in such cases that the labourer in Cornwall is so nutritiously fed. When his work is steady and his family small, he himself may have a moderate allowance of animal food, the rest of his household feeding on fish. When his family is tolerably large, or his work is not very steady, they may all have to confine themselves to fish; but when his family is very large, or very *long*—as they term it here—it is not always that they can all get even fish, although his work should be steady. There is many a labouring family in Cornwall nearly as ill off, in a dietary point of view, as some of those in Somerset or Devon.

It will have been seen that the maximum rate of wages in Devon is the average rate in Cornwall. But, as in other counties, a reduction of wages is very generally talked of in this. The farmers are grumbling on all hands, and complain bitterly of their fate, in being obliged by the low prices of corn to curtail the comforts of those for whom they affect a very praiseworthy extent of sympathy. Not a word is said of lowering the rate at which they dispose of their corn to the labourer. They forget that he is paying them for inferior grain at the rate of 64s. a quarter, when the best wheat is selling in the market at 42s. They could materially add to the labourer's comforts in this county by permitting him to buy his corn at the market price. At all events, if they lower his wages they should in justice rid him of the very disadvantageous arrangement from which he now suffers. But it is not a reduction of wages that they contemplate immediately so much as a reduction of employment. They will begin to economise, not by reducing the wages of those kept at work, but by discharging from work many that are now employed. The blow will fall first upon such as are not altogether able-bodied. A great many of them, indeed, have already been discharged, as the increase in the number of applications for relief can testify. The applications for relief, at the Liskeard union, are now about ten to one as compared with what they were a few weeks ago. Amongst the applicants, however, there have been no able-bodied men. The farmers are in hopes of being able to keep them employed—in order to do which they must discharge, as they say, some of those not able-bodied, reduce the wages of others who may be kept employed, and lastly, if necessary, lower the wages of the able-bodied themselves.

I have put the average wages of the day labourer in Cornwall at 9s. a week. In some parishes, such as that of Linkinhorn, I found 8s. paid. But then some compensation was made the labourer by having his corn given to him at a somewhat lower price. Throughout the comparatively rich agricultural district around Truro, I found 10s. a week a very common rate. On this the labourer might live with some comfort, provided his family were small and his rent as reasonable as it is in Devonshire and elsewhere. But, unfortunately, there is about Truro a great scarcity of cottages in the outlying parishes. The consequence is, that the labourers have to herd together to a great extent in the town, paying £4, and sometimes £5 for a house. This also subjects them to the cruel necessity of a long and fatiguing walk, both before and after their day's work. One man told me that he had been working for some time on a farm near Lord Falmouth's residence, upwards of three miles from Truro. He had not been steadily employed during that time, but was paid at the rate of 10s. a week for his work. He had a family of eight, including himself and wife, to support, and had also to pay £4 for his house, which had only three rooms. He told me, that for the last week they had but a pound and a half of animal food for the eight of them. I asked him what it was, to which he replied that it was some fat mutton, with which they flavoured their potatoes.

"Have you a good supply of potatoes?" I asked him.

"We have to buy all we eat," he answered. "We could not live on turnips and barley alone."

"Why did you not plant some?" I inquired.

"Because I gave up the little ground I had," said he.

"And why did you give it up?"

"Because the potatoes have failed so."

"But they have not failed so badly this year. If you had held your land, and planted some, you might now have had a good winter's supply for your family."

"That's all very well," he replied; "but when a poor man comes to pay a shilling a yard (twelve feet square) for ground, and gets nothing from it for two or three years, he's very likely to lose heart, and throw it up. I did, and so have many more."

"You have fish occasionally?"

"Yes; but we can't often afford it."

"Then what is your chief diet?"

"Bread (frequently barley), potatoes, and turnips. There's my dinner to-day, sir," he continued, breaking a pasty in two, which he took from his pocket. The tough, black crust enclosed a quantity of watery-looking turnips.

"And can you do a day's work on that?" I asked him.

"Such as it is, sir, I can," he observed; "but it isn't such a day's work as a man could do on meat."

On the whole, whilst the house accommodation of the labourer in Cornwall is little, if at all, superior to that in the neighbouring counties, his condition otherwise is a little, though very little, better; for after making all the deductions which must be made from his higher nominal rate of wages, there are circumstances connected with his case, such as his usually cheap and plentiful supply of fish, which place him in a somewhat better position, as regards diet, at least, than his brethren in the counties previously considered.

LABOUR AND THE POOR.

---◆---

THE RURAL DISTRICTS.

[FROM OUR SPECIAL CORRESPONDENT.]

CONDITION AND PROSPECTS OF THE AGRICULTURAL LABOURER IN CORNWALL.

Letter IX.

The Duke of Cleveland and the Dowager Lady Sandwich are the joint owners of considerable property in the county of Cornwall. One of the estates subject to this joint ownership is a small one, scarcely comprising 600 acres, situated in the parish of St. Martin's, near Looe. The property lies in a long irregular strip, stretching back from the sea to the estate of Morval, belonging to Mr. Buller, which it touches in one part, and to a portion of the "Duchy property," which it adjoins in another. Although of such limited extent, it is cut up into a number of small farms, which are in the possession of tenants destitute alike of capital, enterprise, and skill. Having reason to believe that the circumstances of the labourer on this property would form a not inapt illustration of his average condition throughout the greater part of Cornwall, particularly in those districts in which "small farming" is prevalent, I inspected, in addition to some of the farm-houses, every cottage upon the estate. I now proceed to state the results, and it may be that the proprietors themselves will be as much astonished at what I shall relate as will the public in general; for I am inclined to believe that they are completely ignorant of the condition of their property in the parish in question. Indeed, on inquiry of one long resident in the neighbourhood, if the Duke of Cleveland had ever visited it, I was informed that whilst Earl of Darlington he did once get as far as *the borough of Saltash*. "Did he come as far as St. Martin's?" I asked. "I do not believe that he has ever seen an acre of his *property here*," was the reply.

Let me here premise, that portions of the estate are in the occupancy of *"lessees for lives"*—a general system in Cornwall; whilst other portions are what is called *"in hand"*—that is to say, the proprietors are directly receiving the rack-rent for them. For the circumstances of the portions leased on lives they may not be wholly answerable, but for the state of the farms *in hand* they are directly and solely responsible. I do not select this estate, or even this parish, as affording the type of the best or the worst tenements in Cornwall. The estate is, as regards management, an average one, in a parish which, as regards the condition of the labourer, may be taken as an average one in the county. Let me also state that on leases for three lives, granted in consideration of a "fine" and a reserved nominal rent, harvest journey, heriot on death, &c., much property in Cornwall is still held.

As introductory to a description of the circumstances of the labourers on the estate, I shall first briefly advert to those of some of the farmers who cultivate it. I was kindly directed in my inquiries by the rector of the parish, the Rev. Mr. Farwell, without whose aid it would not have been easy for me to have accomplished my object.

The tenements to which we first directed our footsteps consisted of a group known by the designation of Barbican. There were in all four dwellings, with a considerable number of out-houses attached to them. A spot more favourably situated for drainage and health can scarcely be conceived, forming part, as it does, of a rather steep declivity, looking towards the sea. Indeed, there is not a house on the estate of which the same cannot be said, the broken and undulating surface of the district being replete with airy situations, and affording opportunities for drainage denied to the residents on the marshy plain. The houses in question were all built of the small slaty stone so commonly met with in Cornish architecture. In each case the walls had lost their original colour, being more or less covered with that peculiar mossy vegetation which betokens the prevalence of moisture in the climate. They were all *thatched* (the usual covering of dwellings in Cornwall remote from the slate districts), and with the exception of one, the largest of the group, which was being kept up for a purpose to which I shall presently advert, they were in a state of progressive dilapidation.

The first house which we entered was in the occupancy of a farmer of the name of Thoms. It had been a farm-house almost from time immemorial. The tenant is a man between fifty and sixty years of age. He cultivates fifty acres of ground, for which he pays a yearly rental of £60. He holds directly of the lord. He has held the farm for the last six years, having, up to that time, been himself a labourer, at 9s. a-week, with the previous occupier. He was labouring under a severe attack of asthma when I saw him, of which, he said, he could not get rid. The house was not exactly open to the weather, but it was full of drafts, the doors being loose and crazy. They were about to be replaced by new doors, which was all in the shape of repair which the house had received for years, or which it was likely ever to receive. It was, in fact, doomed, and the repair of the doors would not tend to perpetuate the existence of the shell, which was giving way in all directions, and to support which nothing was done. There was but one tenantable room below, which was occupied by the family, consisting of the farmer, his wife, and daughter, and a boy or two at service. When we entered, dinner was on the table, consisting of some broth, with a little meat in it, several large slices of boiled turnips, and some black-looking "suety" puddings, to be eaten with the meat. The flooring was tolerably good, and the walls and ceiling were whitewashed, but the latter was so low that I could scarcely stand upright. In a small recess leading from the room were pots, pans, pieces of bacon, washing tubs, fire-wood, &c.; whilst a hole leading off that again was made sacred to the purposes of a dairy. In the roof, up stairs, there were two sleeping rooms. On the other side of the small passage was another room, covered above by the roof, which was full of lumber and farm implements of the simplest description. The walls of this apartment leant at almost all angles from the perpendicular, and in some places appeared very unsafe. The coarse plaster had long since peeled off from the greater part of them. Directly over the contracted passage the ceiling bulged downwards, and was so frail that, in drawing our attention to it, the farmer raised it to its proper position with his hand. There was no drainage about the house, and filth had accumulated on all sides, the smells proceeding from which were as varied as they were offensive. Such are the circumstances, not of a labourer on this property, but of one of the employers of labour. "Like master, like man," is a proverb. What are we to expect of the employed, when the employer himself is in a worse condition than that in which the employed should be? I asked if he gave steady work, to which he replied that he did not. And why? Simply because he had not always the money wherewith to pay for it. He had no capital whatever on which to come and go. The farm was, consequently, but half tilled, the occupier scraping sufficient out of it to enable him to pay a higher rent than the average rent of the parish, and to remove himself but one degree from starvation.

Contiguous to that just described was another farm-house. It formed, with a barn, one side of a court-yard, of which a low stable or two, with some other outhouses, formed the others. The court-yard was about 25 feet wide, and from 70 to 80 feet long. The whole of it, up to the very walls which inclosed it, was covered with straw, which was rapidly decomposing into manure. In some places it was wet and discoloured, in others it was drier and fresher, and we sunk up to the knees in it in making towards the door. By and bye it would all become manure, when the front of the dwelling-house, which looked upon the court, would form one side of an immense dung heap. The fermenting mass would then underlie the windows, and partially block up the doorway. This was only what it did year after year. On coming suddenly in sight of this scene, I could scarcely believe that I was looking upon the habitation of a British farmer. The only living occupants of the courtyard, visible at the time, were three donkeys, several fowls, and a couple of pigs, who all seemed to be living amicably together on the socialist principle of a community of goods. As we made for the door—now through sheer muck, and then through the drier straw—one of the pigs projected itself half way in, and gave several grunts, as if announcing our arrival. It then made way for us to pass, and we entered the tenement. It contained four rooms, two below and two above. On the left of the doorway was a very small sitting room, with a deal floor, a step in advance, certainly, of the clay or the flag-stone. On the right was a much larger apartment, which, it was obvious, served the purpose of kitchen, dining room, and sitting room for the family, on all ordinary occasions. The ceiling, as in the other case, was extremely low and perfectly blackened with smoke. The rough damp floor was composed of flags of almost every size and shape. There was but one window in the room, which was small, and admitted into it a kind of twilight. The family at one time numbered fourteen, but it had since been reduced to four, some being married, and others out at service. There were but two children left at home, a son and daughter, both grown up. The daughter was repairing some garment with her needle, the son, in his smock-frock, stepped in from the barn to see what we were about. The house and farm had been occupied by the same family for about thirty years. The present term would expire in about eighteen months, and the tenant was doubtful if he would continue his occupancy, even were it in his power to do so. During the whole time that he had occupied it, the house had undergone little or no repair. Its whole aspect betokened that it was fast crumbling to decay. The sinking wall was bending with its weight; the window-caps were of wood, so old and rotten that it almost powdered on being touched. We stepped into the barn. It was a small, but naked and desolate-looking place. The farmer himself was there, engaged with a labourer in threshing barley. "You're not too well off for accommodation here," I remarked to him. "Indeed, sir," he observed, "it is not fair play to good grain to thresh it out in such a place." At the end of the house was a pig-stye, in which, I was told, was a "prime pig," whilst opposite it, on the other side of the court-yard, were the stables, which were small and filthy. Between the pig-stye, the stables, and the dung heap, which covered the court-yard, the reader may imagine what the atmosphere was which the inmates of the house breathed.

On the opposite side of the road was a third farm-house, larger than either of the others, but built of similar material, and in the same style, and looking as green, mouldy, and unwholesome as any of them. It gave token, however, of being kept in repair, and such was really the case—the intention being, when the present terms shall have expired, to throw several small farms into one, and keep *this* as the only farm-house upon it. This may be sound policy; for the larger the farms, provided they are not made too large, the better. But whilst this house is to be kept in repair, the others, it appears, are to be left to go to ruin. If several small farms are to be thrown into one, the object will be to improve the tillage and increase the yield of the land. But to do this a greater amount of labour, steadily employed, must be applied to the land. But if such is to be the case, where are the labourers to live? There will be no accommodation left for them on the large farm in contemplation. They will have to live in Looe, not only off the farm, but also out of the parish.

Satisfied with these specimens of farm-houses on this property, I next directed my attention to the cottages of the labourers. The last house of the group alluded to was in the occupancy of a labourer. It was the smallest and shabbiest of the group, but it was once a farm-house, although it is no longer so. On stepping over the filthy gutter which intervened between it and the road, and opening the outer door, we found ourselves in a somewhat spacious passage, one side of which was formed by the end wall of the house, and the floor of which was composed of a species of guttered causeway. This passage ran from the front to the back of the house. At the back end, and directly opposite the door, was a staircase, which led to the upper apartments, of which there were two. On the left of the passage was a door in a wooden partition, which we opened, and which led into the day room of the family. To gain this apartment we had to descend three steps. The floor was roughly flagged, and slightly sprinkled with sand. But it was moist, cold, and clammy. On our entering, we discovered the family at dinner. The family consisted of but four individuals—the labourer and his wife, a grown-up girl, and a boy of about eleven. The first two rose on our entering, but the others remained at table, ravenously consuming what was before them, which was a concretion, in the shape of soup, of bread and turnips boiled in water, flavoured with a little suet. I asked the boy if he could read. He replied, "No," with the spoon so far down his throat that he could scarcely articulate. I then inquired if he knew his letters; whereupon I was told that he could recognise some of them. I expressed my surprise that a boy of that age should be so ignorant, and a school hard by; but I was assured that he was by far "too handy to send to school." The room was better provided with light than most of the labourers' cottages, the window being unusually large for a house of the kind. The occupant worked steadily on the farm, and had his house rent-free—a nominal privilege, however, as a deduction was, in consideration of it, made from his wages. On complaining of the smells which pervaded the house, I was told that they came from the back premises. My friend entered the passage, and opened the back door, which was under the staircase. I have already said that the family-room was three steps under the passage. Behind the house the ground abruptly rose for several feet above the passage. About five feet above it, and but a few yards back, was the pig-stye. Close to it was a stable, and hard by a large dung heap, all close to the house, at an elevation of almost eight feet above the sitting-room, and about the level of the bedrooms. Immediately below the pig-stye, and between it and the house, was a large pool, full almost to overflowing with filthy and stagnant water. There was no drain connected with it, and it was never empty. The blast of pestilential air which entered the house, on the back-door being opened, was almost enough to knock down one who was unaccustomed to it. I asked the man how he could tolerate such a nuisance, and all the answer I got was that it was the "leakage of the stye and stable." This completed the group, each dwelling and outhouse of which was not only surrounded, but imbedded, in filth, although the opportunities for drainage were most ample. The road which passed between them was discoloured, whenever it rained, with the filthy infusions which came trickling from the fermenting abominations, which rested against their very walls.

The next point to which my attention was directed was the neighbourhood of the Manor House of Hay. The house is a long and straggling building, far advanced towards decay, and is now occupied by one of the lord's lessees on lives. In its external accompaniments it is no better off than the tenements just described. It is equally wanting in drainage, and equally beset with pestiferous accumulations. At one end of it was an enormous heap of that which, as regards effluvia, is the worst of all the manures, viz., decomposing seaweed. It had lain for some time fermenting and putrefying, and, as we approached the house, the whole atmosphere was impregnated with its pent-up odours, which were let loose by a boy who had just disturbed the mass, and was loading some of it into a cart. The worst of it was, that the manor-house was not the only dwelling which was in close proximity to this nuisance. Directly opposite were two cottages, one of which was inhabited by an old soldier, who officiated as clerk of the parish. He lived in it alone, and had occupied it for thirty years. It was small, dark, and ill-ventilated, and was sadly in want of repair. He held it, not direct of the lord, but of one of his lessees. The thatch was so rotten, that in some places he had put up pieces of matting to prevent it dropping bit by bit upon the floor. On one or two occasions a little new thatch had been put on the outside, but the whole had never been thoroughly repaired. The house was but a poor one when he first took it, but it had since been getting worse and worse every year, and must soon go completely to ruin. He was a pretty old man, but he scarcely thought it would last even his time. But they were all going the same way, he said, and in the course of a few years there would be but few left in the parish. This, as it appeared to him, was what the lords seemed anxious for. Generation after generation, the peasantry were being driven into the towns, and in a few years but few would be left upon the farms.

Descending the hill, we came to the other cottage, which was on the same side of the road, and immediately below this house. But, stretching from the one to the other was one succession of filth of all kinds, which not only went up to the walls of the houses, but here and there encroached upon the road. In fact, the whole of the wide space between the cottages and the manor house, comprehending the road, had the appearance of one great stable-yard, which was seldom cleaned, and never thoroughly so. After a little rain it would have been impossible to have entered any of the cottages without having the feet besmeared with something worse than mud. At no time of the year, not even in the coldest weather, was the atmosphere around these dwellings free from pestilential effluvia. On entering the second cottage I was surprised to find that which was so filthy without so neat and tidy within. The accommodation was very scanty, and the light insufficient, but the flag floor was white from scrubbing, and the little furniture displayed was scrupulously clean, and neatly arranged. A neat, tidy, and thrifty little woman presided over the house, and explained it all. I asked her why she did not get the outside cleaned up a little? She replied that she had often endeavoured to do so, but that, although she was equal to the task of keeping the interior in order, she could not prevent them from accumulating manure all about, nor could she dig the drains, which were absolutely necessary for the purification of the place. I asked her if the smell was always as offensive as then? She said it was generally very bad, but that, fortunately, in summer, when it would be worst, the manure was carried off, more or less, to be put upon the fields. It is almost a universal practice in Cornwall to place straw upon the roads to the farmsteads, so as to be worked into what they call "dressing," which is finally scraped up and carted to the field as manure. That it is of small value after being thus prepared and well washed by Cornish rain may readily be imagined.

About a stone's throw below this group was another cluster of houses, with but one dwelling-house amongst them. It seemed that the lower down the hill we got the worse became the character of the tenements. This last group consisted of a stable, a barn, a species of shed in which a cart might be put, and a cottage. This last stood alone, the stable-yard intervening between it and the houses. On leaving the road to approach this group, we had to pick our steps through a compound of mud and dung, collected in a very soluble state about the gate. We had then to encounter the filth of the stable, of which it was difficult for us to make the detour. We then gained a springy dung heap, composed partly of straw and partly of seaweed. This brought us close to one angle of the cottage, which we had to turn ere we found the door. Before doing so, however, our ears were saluted with the disagreeable chorus of a child screaming at the highest pitch of its voice, and a woman scolding in a tone betokening both impatience and passion. On our suddenly appearing, the child stopped crying, whilst the woman endeavoured, but unsuccessfully, to moderate her wrath. The poor child was bare about the neck and shoulders, which were crimsoned all over from the flagellation which it had received. It had on its feet shoes that might have fitted the mother, but it had no stockings, and its little legs were bare up to the knees, if such a term can be used of legs literally encrusted with filth. It is a positive fact that they were so covered with dirt that you could not, from the ankle to the knee, discover the colour of the skin. Nor was this the filth of a day. The incrustation was the growth of weeks. It was as we saw it that the poor child lay down at night and arose in the morning.

To get into the house we had to descend a little to the door, and had then to go down a step to gain the room within. There was no passage or inner door, that which we entered opening at once into one of the gloomiest dens that I had yet witnessed. The floor was half clay, half flag, and near the door was a little puddle, caused by the water oozing in from without. There was but one window, and that of the most miserable description, the light being deficient, although the door was wide open. The floor was besmeared with turnip-peelings and other things equally out of place. The miserable furniture, of which there was but little, was black and greasy looking, like the ceiling. There was not a chair in the room which she could offer us to sit down upon. There was a small bench fixed to the wall, before which was a table, on the other side of which was another bench; but everything—table, benches, and all—was damp and clammy. There were three other children in the room when we entered it. One was a boy about nine years old, who nursed a child on his knee; the other a little girl, considerably younger. Both the boy and girl were seated, each on a little black box turned upon end. Neither of them rose or moved a muscle as we entered, but they gazed upon us with a stolidity which it was painful to witness. I soon ascertained that the boy did not even know the letters of the alphabet; but before leaving my friend got a promise from the mother to send him immediately to school, which was a little more than a mile distant. The woman's name was Mutton. I asked her what rent she paid for the house, to which she replied that they had it rent free, her husband having steady work on the farm. But, as in the case already mentioned, the abatement of rent was made good by the reduction of wages. Altogether, as I proceeded, I thought even Southleigh outdone. I cannot say that the cottages were in themselves worse than those of Southleigh; but, as regards external accompaniments, the tenements on the property of Mr. Gordon were clean and decent as compared with those on this remote estate of the Duke of Cleveland.

We then directed our steps more inland, and the next cottage which we came to adjoined the National School of the parish. As compared with those we had seen, it had a cleanly and cheerful appearance, from the quantity of whitewash with which its walls were covered. The upper half of the chimney, however, seemed to be parting company with the roof, and was apparently only kept from tumbling by the ivy, which bound it to the house. The cottage had but two rooms, one above and the other below—the upper one being, as usual, the sleeping room. It had two beds in it, one of which was occupied by the son, a young man, when at home, and who, as I afterwards ascertained, was the father of an illegitimate child by one of the girls of the parish. There had at one time been a large family in this room, but they were now scattered. The rent paid for the cottage, with a little piece of ground attached, was 1s. a week. It was rated to the poor at 30s. per annum. Mrs. Mutchmore, for that was the woman's name, showed me the receipt for the last quarter's rate. It amounted to 6d., the rate being one of 4d. in the pound. At the end of the house was a pig-stye, with a "brave pig" in it, to exhibit which Mr. Mutchmore opened the door of the stye. But the smell made us recoil from the sight. He smiled and shut the door again, and I dare say thought us rather delicate. He had been for months a victim to the influenza, under which he was then labouring, and of which he said he could not get rid. It sometimes kept him for weeks at a time from work. When employed, his wages were 9s. a week.

From this we crossed some fields to a place called Coombe. Here I found two houses under one roof, tenanted by two different families. It had, in all, five rooms—two below and three above. There was one door in front, and another behind. The family which occupied one end of the house was named Martin, that occupying the other, Hawkins. The front door entered the room occupied by the Martins, the back door that occupied by the Hawkinses. If the Hawkinses wished to gain their own room from the front, they had to pass through the Martins' room, and if the Martins wanted to use the back door, they had to go through the Hawkinses' room. The two rooms communicated with each other by means of a door in the partition wall. There was but one staircase common to both, and that was in the room occupied by the Martins, which was by far the larger of the two. Having thus to use so many things in common, it was highly essential that they should agree better than neighbours generally do. As in the other cases, the house was on the side of a hill, but there was no drainage. There was much want of it, however, for immediately above and in front of the house was the usual accumulation of manure and garbage so common in these parts. Whenever it rained heavily the base of the house was temporarily flooded outside, as was evident from a kind of high-water mark, which might be traced along the stones, indicating the line to which the water and filth rose on such occasions. The number of inmates was not large, considering the room. The Martins numbered five in all; the Hawkinses the same. It was their distribution which was objectionable, as regards their sleeping accommodations. The parents of each family occupied a room by themselves; the children of both families slept together in another. The Martins had one boy, about ten years old, and two girls, one nine and the other seven. The Hawkinses had two daughters, one about sixteen and the other much younger. The elder had been out at service, in a common lodging-house in Liskeard, and became pregnant by one of the miners. She went home to be confined, and her child was born under her father's roof. It is with her and with her child that the rest of the children of both families sleep. What can be expected from such an association?

It was not until some time after we got into Mrs. Martin's room that we could discern distinctly all the objects which it contained. There were two windows in it, but they were small. As regards ventilation they were useless, for they did not open, which is the case generally with these cottages. Her husband was a labourer, and earned his 9s. a week, with liberty to buy his corn at the market price, as he was not steadily employed on any particular farm. They were thus enabled occasionally to buy a piece of mutton, and always killed their pig at Christmas. As to dietary, therefore, they were not so ill off as some of their neighbours. The same may be said of the Hawkinses. Their room was miserably small, over-crowded with furniture, and dirty as compared with the other. It was about sixteen feet long, and about ten wide, and was very dark, except when the door was open. After inspecting the back premises, I re-entered the house, and found a young girl along with Mrs. Hawkins. I inquired if that was her daughter, and was somewhat surprised on her informing me that it was, and that it was the one that had the child. She curtseyed, as if confirming her mother's statement. I could scarcely credit that one who appeared to be yet but a child herself should be a mother. Not a blush rose to her cheek, and neither mother nor daughter seemed to be oppressed with any sense of shame. This is the worst feature of all, in cases of this kind, in the country districts. I asked her who supported the child, to which she replied that they had to do so themselves. She also informed me that she had tried to affiliate the child upon one of the miners, but that as they never had been seen together she did not succeed in the attempt. This was told me with the utmost *nonchalance* and composure. Yet she was, night after night, the companion of her younger sister and of Mrs. Martin's children.

I went up stairs, accompanied by Mrs. Hawkins. The floor of the middle room was rough and splintered, and appeared to be giving way. In one place it bent and creaked under my weight. She observed to me that people in their circumstances must not be particular. She then showed me her own bed-room. The thatch projected through the woodwork above, and at the angle of the roof there were several gaping rents, through which daylight was visible, and through which, when it was wet, the rain fell in streams upon the floor at the foot of the bed. Her husband, also, is troubled with an influenza, of which he cannot get rid, and no wonder. The door was not large enough to fill the doorway; but, although it could not keep out the wind, it served to keep out the cat, which she appeared to think its main object. She frequently worked in the fields, picking stones and weeding in autumn time, and hoeing "turmots" (*Anglicé,* turnips) in the spring. For this she got 6d. a day, unless she hoed by the piece, when, by working from early morning to late at night, she might earn a shilling.

As we pursued our way through the fields in quest of other cottages, we met Mrs. Martin hurrying homewards, with her two daughters by her side. The younger child was not more than seven. She was a delicate, shrinking child, small for her age, and her large blue eyes gleamed with a degree of intelligence which seemed precocious. She had an extraordinary memory, could read well, and use her needle adroitly, which was evident from her sampler, which she carried in her hand, for she was on her way home from school. Yet this sweet and intelligent child is one of those condemned to breathe the contaminated moral atmosphere of her home, sleeping in the same room, if not in the same bed, with the guilty and shameless associate of the miners of Liskeard. Poor little Susan! Would that opulent benevolence would snatch her from at least a doubtful fate!

Having passed through several fields, we came to another group of houses known by the name of Tregoad. The principal residence of the group was a farm-house, being decidedly the best of its class on the property. It owed all its comfort, however, to some additions which had been recently made to it. Back of it were a number of out-houses enclosing the farm-yard, or, as it is called in the rural nomenclature of Cornwall, the "town place." A little in front was a cottage more than half gone to ruin. It was larger than cottages usually are, and was at one time a farm-house itself; a long chimney stalk rose in front of the house, close to one side of the door, to nearly the height of the house. Here again the ivy appeared of essential service, for nothing else seemed to support the chimney, which inclined over the door several degrees from the perpendicular. I asked the inmates if they were not afraid of their lives, but they seemed quite at ease, saying that it had "been that way" ever since they could remember. And that way it will remain, until some fine morning it tumbles through the roof. A rougher flag-floor than that of the narrow passage-way of this hut I never saw. It was full of holes, each of which would have held at least half a gallon of water. On the right hand side was a miserable, naked-looking apartment, to gain which you had to descend a step or two. It was a shoemaker's shop, or rather that of a cobbler, for he had not a new shoe in his store, although there were several old ones lying about in various stages of decomposition and repair. Nor did he seem to have any new leather, his stock of material apparently consisting of bits of old harness, which were strewn about the floor. For the wretched room in which he worked he paid 6d. a week, a sum which, it seemed to me, would have been sufficient to buy out his entire stock-in-trade, together with the goodwill of the business. On the left was the common room of the family, which was that of an agricultural labourer. There were two rooms up stairs, the flooring of which was rather unsafe, judging from that part of it which was over the passage, and which was only kept from giving way by a rude and temporary expedient. These expedients are resorted to until the whole fabric is ready to crumble to pieces, when decay is left to do its work. They only serve to make it barely tenantable as long as it stands, but do not absolutely retard the day of its final ruin.

We next passed through a turnip field, to another group, called Pethick. In doing so, we met a little boy, relieving two donkeys of their panniers, with which he had been "driving turnips" all day.

"Do you work with Mr. Rosevere?" I inquired.

"I be working with him," said he.

"Do you get any wages?"

"I get six-and-twenty shillings a year," he answered.

"Anything more?" I asked.

"I get my mate," said he.

"Can you read?"

"No."

"Do you know your letters?"

"I do some on 'em."

"Do you go to school?"

"No."

"Did you ever go?"

"Yes."

"Did you ever go to Sunday-school?"

"Yes."

"Do you now?"

"I haven't gone," he replied, "since the things have laid in." My friend fortunately understood Cornish, and interpreted this for me. The boy had not gone to Sunday-school since the arrival of the season when the cattle were housed.

The situation of Pethick was preferable to that of either Coombe or Hay. But its superiority went little or no further. It consisted of three cottages, with a barn and several outhouses, the whole being divided into three groups, and enclosing nearly three sides of a tolerably large square. The whole assemblage had a green and mouldy look about it; and the small stone of which the walls were composed crumbled almost to the touch. Each house was thatched, the thatch being in most cases covered with vegetation, denoting its age and the long absence of repair. On turning the first that we encountered, to get into the enclosed space, we had, as usual, to make our way through a quantity of mud and manure, which were left from year to year to fraternize together. About twenty feet from this cottage was a huge puddle, which seemed to be the common receptacle for all the filth of the group. Its thick putrid contents were covered with a slime, which reflected, whenever the sun shone upon it, all the tints of what is known in Cornwall as peacock ore. In the first cottage I entered were a lame woman and a male invalid. It had four rooms, two below and as many above. The outer door opened directly into one of the lower rooms, which served as a lumber room. In order to divide this from the part of the cottage used as a dwelling, a partition was run from the left side of the door, which formed a passage with the wall of the inner room, which was on the right. The partition was a kind of rough frame of wood, filled up with wisps of straw. It did not rise to the ceiling, nor did it extend farther back than the door on the right, leading to the inner-room. You could, therefore, go round it into the lumber-room. I did so, and was fain to retreat, for the smell which I encountered was offensive to the last degree. But the inmates seemed insensible to it. The whole foundation of the house appeared to be rotten from the filthy solutions in which it was constantly immersed. The family had once been large, but it had gradually dwindled away, the mother informing me that some of the children had gone off to service, whilst as to others she had "buried them." Her own lameness had been occasioned by a cold which she caught whilst "lying-in with her last child." She was then living at Looe, in a house which was sometimes encroached upon by a high tide. It happened to be so in her hour of trial, and from the effects of the cold which she then caught she never fairly recovered.

Attached to this was another cottage, beyond which, and in the same line, was a barn. We had to cross a gutter in front of the door of this second cottage, to gain the threshold, which gutter also passed the entrance to that just alluded to. On the upper side of the door of the second cottage—for the whole row was on a slight declivity—was a putrescent dung heap, kept from falling across the entrance by a stone slab turned on edge. It was the compound essence of this filthy accumulation that trickled in the gutter, which slowly emptied itself into the reeking and fermenting pool already alluded to. This cottage was closed, the family being from home. The family consisted of a labouring man, about thirty, his wife, and one child. He had had an illegitimate child since his marriage, for which he was paying a shilling a week out of his wages, which were 9s. We shortly afterwards met him, and on my inquiring what kind of a house he had, he replied that it was a "bravish house," by which he meant that it was tolerably good. I had looked in at the window, and found it dark, dingy, and disgustingly filthy.

There was still another cottage in the group. It had two rooms, and was inhabited by a couple tolerably advanced in life. Their family had been long since scattered, the woman told me. Three of her sons were in the navy, and one in the army. I thought that she had done something for her country, and that it was high time that her country did something for her and others in similar circumstances. They had the house rent-free, with about twenty-yards of potato ground (a yard being twelve feet square, and rented at 1s.), and 6s. 6d. as wages, with their corn at 12s. and 6s. All this made their wages very nearly equal to 9s. a week.

These, as I have described them, are all the houses on the property in question. Are the proprietors aware of their condition? We concluded our rounds, which occupied two entire days, by an inspection of a couple of cottages on a small property in the neighbourhood, owned by a Mr. Tuckett, a resident of Plymouth. Externally, they bore marks of comfort and even neatness; for they were faultlessly whitewashed. Their accommodation, however, was very limited, the first that I entered having only two rooms. The upper one was the sleeping room. The thatch, which was visible between the rafters, was almost covered with cobwebs. I asked Mrs. Simmons, for such was the name of the wife of the tenant, who was himself a gardener, receiving pretty constantly employment from the rector, why she did not keep the roof cleaner? She replied that she was afraid to disturb the cobwebs, lest she should bring down the thatch. The fact was, that the latter was so rotten that it powdered to the touch. I tried it at one point with a broom; and on brushing away a cobweb or two, the rotten thatch came with them in dust. Yet, for a house so circumstanced, and with accommodation so straitened, she paid no less than £4 a-year.

The house was much infested with rats, which increased in numbers, despite all the cats, traps, and other appliances for rat killing in the neighbourhood. Different members of the family had been aroused from their slumbers by being bitten by them. As we entered, a girl was seated in one corner of the room, sewing; she soon rose and left. "Is that your daughter?" I asked. "No; but she soon will be," was the answer. My friend looked surprised, and the woman continued:— "I did not like it at first, sir; but then, you know, she's so handy with her needle." The girl had borne a child to the son of Mr. and Mrs. Mutchmore, the young man who, when at home, as already described, occupied the same room with his parents. She was now about to marry the son of Mrs. Simmons, and her chief merit in the eyes of her mother-in-law was that she was "handy with her needle!"

I afterwards inspected some cottages on the estate of Morval, in the parish of the same name. The estate is the property of Mr. Buller, a resident proprietor. The benefit of his presence amongst them is perceptible in the superior condition of his tenantry. Their houses are built in the same style as, and have, generally speaking, no greater accommodation than, those described. But they are not permitted to become so ruinous, nor are their external accompaniments so filthy, unwholesome, and indecent.

The property I have before described is, as regards the condition of the cottages, but too true a type of many properties in many parishes contiguous to it. I have already said, that I did not select it for description as a specimen of the best or the worst parishes in the county. There are many parishes superior to it, as regards the accommodation of the poor, but there are also many much worse. Take, for instance, the adjoining parish of Talland, and the few cottages which remain in it are even inferior to those in St. Martin's. In fact, they are so wretched, and the rents so high, that their occupants are fast disappearing from the country, and seeking shelter in the towns of Looe and Polperro, to the great inconvenience of themselves, and to the detriment, both physical and moral, of these small communities. Take, again, the parish of Linkinhorn, a little back from Liskeard, where, whilst they are equally bad, the rents are high, and the cottages far more overcrowded. Or take the Duchy property, adjoining the estate described, and the type holds equally good. Going eastward, in the direction of St. Germans, you have a repetition, at almost every step you take, of the same physical wretchedness, accompanied by the moral degradation which is its necessary consequence. Along the high roads even, you will see specimens of cottages as bad as those described. Half way between Torpoint and Liskeard are wretched specimens to be met with. The same between Liskeard and Bodmin, and along the line between Bodmin and Fowey. Due west of Bodmin, and to the north of the dreary district of the China clay-pits, are many of the same description. The wild heathy district whence the China clay is extracted is strewn with them. They abound near St. Austle, Grampound, and Truro, and, with the exception of the cottages more recently built, are to be found all over the region known as the central mining district, the focus of which is Redruth. They dot the uplands that sweep around Mount's Bay, and come close to the very suburbs of Penzance. In this district it is difficult sometimes to distinguish between the wretched hovel called a farm-house and the miserable domicile of the labourer. Westward of Penzance, and on to the Land's End, it is the same. But it is along the north coast of Cornwall that the domiciliary condition of the labourer reaches its lowest point of wretchedness. If you take the line from Sennen, the first and last town in England, to Hartland Point, the majority of the cottages inhabited by the labourer are in a worse state than even those on the property described. It is in the neighbourhood of the extinct lead mines, and near the ruined fishing villages of the north, that the most miserable specimens are to be found. If any one wishes to acquaint himself with the real extent of the physical misery under which human beings can exist, let him go and visit St. Agnes, the vicinity of Tintagel, and more particularly the wretched town of Port Isaac.

But overlooking, for the moment, such as are better, as well as such as are worse off, the specimens which I have given may be taken as the average house accommodation of the 45,000 people who in Cornwall either labour themselves in the fields, or are dependent on such labour for support.

The tourist in the Highlands will meet between Loch Lomond and Glencoe with a lovely little loch, on a small wooded point projecting into which the Marquess of Breadalbane has built a shooting-box. Behind the house, and some distance up the hill, is the handsome residence of his lordship's hounds. It is a neat little building, erected in the Elizabethan style, kept dry and warm, and covered with slate. The tenants in St. Martin's would scarcely know themselves if they were lodged in tenements like the Marquess of Breadalbane's dog-kennel.

It was whilst making my tour of inspection amongst the Duke of Cleveland's cottages that I had a long conversation respecting them with one of the oldest residents of the parish, who has himself been a farm labourer for fifty-six years of his life. His name was Alexander Lee. He was in his sixty-fourth year, and had gone to work when he was eight years old. I met him on the road, riding a small pony, on which he sat with both his legs on one side, for he had recently lost the use of them. He described the house accommodation of the poor many years ago to have been bad enough, but he thought that it was getting worse and worse every year, although he admitted that their general condition was improving. As a specimen of what was the case twenty-five years ago, he very coolly informed me that he, his wife, and five children occupied the same bed-room, at the time there were also in it two women about to be delivered of illegitimate children. They were delivered in that room, and remained for some time afterwards in it, the whole number occupying the room being then eleven. When the women and children were gone, two men took their places. On my expressing my surprise that he could submit to such a state of things, he simply remarked that they were then glad, as now, to do many things that they didn't like for a "bit of money." I asked him in what respect he thought the condition of the labourer better than it was formerly. He said that he thought it improved as regarded his diet and clothing. Whilst wages had declined but little, the price of most things had gone greatly down. Formerly, when the farmers got high prices for corn, the labourer had to pay a high duty on salt—a serious consideration with him if he contemplated keeping a pig for his own use. He had also to pay double, and sometimes treble, what he now paid for bread. He scarcely ever saw tea then, and never tasted sugar, although it was but little of either that he saw or tasted yet. Besides, there prevailed shortly after the war a very pernicious practice of determining the amount of wages by the extent of a man's family. For instance, if a man had nine children, he might get 9s. a week, whereas if he had but four he might be offered 7s. a week. The point was not whether he could do his work, but how many mouths he had to feed. Not only did this encourage men to marry early, but it was generally to the halest men that the lowest wages were proffered. And, according to my informant, a man with four has more need of good wages than a man with nine children. "We never count a man's family more than four, sir," said he. "But why not more than four, if he has nine?" "O, because by the time he has four one at least is in most cases ready to go to work, and as he has more some of the rest get hardy and earn something." He proceeded to say that the young men with small families, and those without any incumbrance did not long submit to so unreasonable a discrimination, most of them emigrating to America. "Some of the best workmen of this parish, sir, went off to America, and they are doing so yet, and will be ready, in case of a war, to come agin us." He thought that if a man could have steady wages at 9s. a-week, he would be well off, even if he had some children. That would enable him, he said, in a fortnight, to get about 2s. in advance of his "grist," which is his monthly allowance of corn. I have already shown that that monthly allowance, when the corn is given at 16s., and 8s., would come to 16s. He would get this corn within the first fortnight, when a fortnight's wages would be paid him. Deducting the price of the corn, he would have 2s. over of that fortnight's wages, and the whole of the remaining fortnight's earnings would come to him in money. Such was, in his estimation, the essential condition to a labourer getting comfortably along. If, at the end of the first fortnight of every month, he found himself 2s. in advance of his "grist," he had no good reason to complain.

I shortly afterwards met another working man on the high-road to Looe. He was employed in the town of Looe, having abandoned the fields. His wages when at work were 2s. a day, but then his employment was not regular. Taking the average of the year, he did not regard himself as any better off than a farm labourer with steady work at 1s. 6d. a day. He very much feared that that rate could not be paid to the farm labourer long.

"Can the farmers afford to keep it up?" I asked.

"They can't, sir, the way they're going on."

"What are they doing?"

"They're not doing nothing," he replied. "Instead of trying harder to make a good thing of it, they're doing less than they used to do. You don't see no dungheaps nor no burning of lime in the fields now, as before. It's dressin' they want. If they don't dress, they can't expect no returns, and they don't dress enough. They think that a pinch of guano will do for a good dressin', but they're mistaken; and if they don't take care, they'll all go to the wall. I tell you what it is, if they don't dress the land more, they'll all have to scat."

I was here once more indebted to my friend's knowledge of languages, "scat" being the Cornish for "fail."

LABOUR AND THE POOR.

———◆———

THE RURAL DISTRICTS.

[FROM OUR SPECIAL CORRESPONDENT.]

THE FISHERIES AND THE FISHERS OF CORNWALL.

LETTER X.

Although, strictly speaking, not falling within the compass of an inquiry into the condition of the agricultural labourer, I propose, before quitting Cornwall, to give a brief account of its fishing and mining interests, and of those employed in connection with them; as, otherwise, the sketch of the industry of the county would be incomplete, seeing that it cannot with propriety be classed either with the Manufacturing or the Metropolitan Districts. In doing so, I shall first consider the fisheries of the county, and the circumstances of those engaged in them.

Cornwall was celebrated for its mineral wealth long before it attained any very great celebrity in connection with its fisheries. For the last three centuries, however, the latter have been plied with unwearied assiduity and varying success. This, like all the other great branches of our industry, was, early after developing itself, taken under the fostering care of the Legislature; but it may be reasonably doubted, looking back at its legislative history, whether the interest sought to be thus advanced was not more injured than benefited by the interference. To this day the fishing of the county is strictly regulated by Parliamentary enactment; but the regulations to which it is now subjected have reference more to the practice of fishing itself than to the trade in fish, in its economical aspect.

The chief fisheries of the south and west of England are undoubtedly those of Cornwall. The only two ports on the English Channel which can at all compete, as fishing stations, with the Cornish ports, are Brighton and Plymouth. The fishermen of Sussex, Devon, and Cornwall, all sweep the entire Channel for fish—the Brighton and Plymouth boats being sometimes seen on the Cornish coasts, and the Cornish boats far more frequently seen off the shores of Devon and Sussex. The most hardy, adventurous, and scientific fishers of the south are those of Cornwall. They do not confine themselves to their own stations, but proceed to great distances in prosecution of their vocation—the Brighton fishermen, perhaps, coming next to them in hardihood and adventure. They not only frequently proceed more than thirty miles to sea in quest of fish, but they compete even with the Irish fishers on their own coasts, and have been known to pass through the Caledonian Canal, and descend the east coast of Scotland and England in pursuit of the herring.

But a short time ago the fisheries of Cornwall embraced the entire coast of the county, and extended in an unbroken line from Lundi Island, round the Land's End, to the Rame Head. But this is no longer the case, the fishing interest of the north coast having become almost extinct from the uncertain movements and capricious habits of the fish. As on all other points of the coast of the United Kingdom, where fishing is plied as a distinct vocation, the habits of the shoals of fish which annually visit the shores of Cornwall have greatly changed within the memory of living man. But a few years ago the pilchard used regularly to ascend the Bristol Channel as far as Lundi Island, whence they would strike off towards Milford, and thence across St. George's Channel in the direction of Waterford. But, for some time past, they have shown no preference for the estuary of the Severn, seldom ascending now much higher than St. Ives, and striking thence across to the Welsh and Irish coasts as before. The consequence has been the ruin of the small fishing communities which extended from St. Ives to Lundi Island. Some of them yet exhibit faint symptoms of fitful and galvanic life, but most of them are perfect wrecks—the ruin entailed upon them having been not only disastrous to themselves, but also most injurious to the interests of the agricultural labourer in the immediate vicinity of each. The fisheries of Cornwall may, therefore, now be regarded as confined to that portion of the coast which extends from the Rame Head, round the Land's End, to St. Ives—that is to say, to the whole southern, and a small part of the northern, coast of the county. St. Ives is now the chief fishing station on the north, and Mount's Bay that on the south. On this latter coast there are many other stations, differing from each other in magnitude and importance—such as Falmouth, Mevagissy, Charlestown, Towey, Polperro, and Looe. Along the shore of Mount's Bay, which stretches from the Lizard Point nearly to the Land's End, are several fishing communities, the chief of which are Newlyn and Mousehole. They are all, however, comprehended under the common designation of the Mount's Bay fisheries.

Cod, hake, ling, and congor are caught in considerable quantities off the Cornish coast, but the mackerel and the pilchard are the great source of the fishing industry of the county. Although these are the chief products of the fisheries of Cornwall, they are not the sole objects of a Cornish fisherman's exertions. When he cannot fish on his own coast for the fish frequenting it, he is off to the Irish, and sometimes to the Scotch coast, in search of the herring. The herring fishing, therefore, although the herring is not strictly a Cornish fish, must be included in the annual routine of a Cornish fisherman's vocation.

There are three kinds of fishing practised in Cornwall—the drift-net fishing, the seine or sean fishing, and that by hook and line. Both mackerel and pilchard are caught by the drift nets, whilst pilchard alone is generally the object of the seine fishing. When the hook and line are used, it is cod, hake, ling, or whiting that is generally caught. For each species of fishing a distinct set of boats is used. The longest and best boats are those employed in the drift-net fishing, the smallest are those used for that by hook and line, seine fishing being carried on by an intermediate class of boats. The hook and line fishing is generally abandoned to men with but little capital, or to those who are unfitted for the other and more arduous branches of the calling. The hook and line, too, are not unfrequently resorted to by the drift-net fishermen, when, from the absence of the pilchard or mackerel, or other unfavourable circumstances, but few fish are meshed in the nets.

In order that the reader may properly understand the life and labours of a Cornish fisherman, I shall now—having taken, as it were, a bird's-eye view of the fisheries and of the modes in which they are plied—describe it briefly to him, commencing with the month of January and ending with that of December.

The fish which, earliest in the year, engages the fisherman's attention is the mackerel, which, in its annual migrations, comes first within the rather wide scene of his operations in the month of January. But before following him to his first fishing-ground for the season, it may be as well here to describe his boat, and the other appliances of his calling.

The boats employed for the capture of the mackerel are the drift-net boats already alluded to. They are the largest, the most commodious, and the best built of the fishing fleet of Cornwall. From a slight peculiarity in their build, and their close resemblance to each other, they are generally at once recognised whenever they appear off the coast. This is more especially the case with the Mount's Bay boats, which have so strong a family likeness pervading them as to render it next to impossible to mistake them. They are great pets, not only with their owners, but also with those who join in the adventure and man them. A Mount's Bay fisherman will wax as eloquent on the good points of his boat as a huntsman will on the virtues of his horse. The total number of boats connected with the fisheries of Mount's Bay is from 250 to 300; nine-tenths of which may be taken as engaged in the drift-net fishing. They are chiefly built of oak, sometimes of elm, and average from 20 to 22 tons burden. The drift-net boats are divided into two classes, determined by their dimensions and capacity. The first class boats have a length of keel of from 30 to 35 feet, and a breadth of beam of from 7 to 12 feet. They are sharp at both ends, but are generally very wide at midships. The ballast, which is usually of stone, is stowed away beneath a low deck, or rather a kind of flooring for the boat. The Mount's Bay boats are now almost all partially decked, having a cabin both fore and aft, in which the men can eat and sleep, and a covered chamber between the masts, in which the nets are stowed away until they are called into use. Some of them, by simply covering a large hatchway in the middle, can be rendered full-decked at once in case of necessity, which is a great safeguard to them in rough weather. It is not many years since the fisherman's lot was less comfortable on board his boat than it is now. A short time ago, but few of them were provided with any cabin at all. The men were then subject to very great privations, from their constant exposure to the weather. With the exception of the sail or the tarpaulin, in which they might wrap themselves, they had no shelter whatever from the wind and rain. In Mount's Bay this has been rectified; but the improvement has not very generally extended itself. The smaller boats used at other fishing stations, such as Mevagissy, Looe, and Polperro, are very seldom even partially decked. The fishermen of these places are therefore subjected to much greater privations than their more fortunate, because more provident, brethren of the west. In some of the boats provided with cabins there are fixed berths for the men to sleep in; whilst in others the cabins are sufficiently large to admit of the hanging of hammocks. Considering his frequent and long exposures to the weather, especially during the winter fisheries, a great step towards the preservation of his health and the general amelioration of his lot has been taken, in simply providing him with a covering to shelter him whilst he sleeps. The boats have generally two masts—a fore and mizen mast. Their sails consist of a fore and mizen lug sail, two top sails, a jib and fore sail. Their sails are very large, some of them containing from 130 to 150 yards of canvas. By carrying several sets of sails they are provided against ordinary accidents. When in trim for sea their draft is about two feet more astern than at the bow. They generally draw about five feet aft, and not more than three in front. In building these boats every effort is made to endow them with good sailing attributes. As a general rule they sail best on a wind. The fishermen have an important object to secure in having them constructed to sail well, particularly in the summer time, when it is especially necessary to get the fish caught early to market, as any great delay would impair their freshness, and materially lower their value. The model of his boat is therefore always a matter of great solicitude to the fisherman. In addition to this, with a view to speed, he resorts in Mount's Bay to a practice not very generally known or imitated in the other fishing ports of the country. When he overhauls his boat for a change of fishing, he besmears the bottom with a coating of blacklead, which, he believes, preserves unimpaired its sailing powers, by preventing the rapid accumulation of seaweed and dirt on her hull, which would otherwise take place and clog her speed. The boats differ in price according to their class. For boats of the same class, however, the same price is generally paid. A first-class boat will cost, ready for sea, about £180. The price of a second-class one is about £120. This is, of course, in both cases, exclusive of nets and other appliances. But as a man may save money by buying the cloth for his coat, so may a fisherman by buying the wood for his boat, particularly if he can give ready cash for his materials. In that case he might get a first-class boat, ready for sea, for £140, the hull alone costing about £80. But, of course, if he gets credit, which is generally the case, and orders his boat without himself providing the materials, the prices first mentioned are those which he will have to pay, according to its class. The boats are owned in different ways. A few of the wealthier fishermen have a couple of them, but the majority have only one. In some cases the boat is subject to a joint ownership; two, three, or four, as the case may be, having an interest in her. In other cases the boat may belong to one or more parties, whilst the nets, &c., appertain to others. There are others, again, who have no share either in the boats or nets, their only capital being their labour. A boat's crew may thus consist of the owner or owners of the boat, the owner or owners of the nets, and those who have only their labour to bring to the adventure, which is thus a species of co-partnery for the time being, each partner's share of the proceeds being determined, of course, by the amount of his interest. But the possession of the boat, whether owned by one or more, is only half the battle. Other and equally expensive appliances are necessary, which I shall now proceed to explain.

The boat is, of course, imperfect without its complement of nets. These, as already seen, are not always the property of the owner or owners of the boat, for the boat and nets may belong to different individuals, or sets of individuals. This is often the case, the nets being so expensive that it requires a fisherman to be a man of some considerable capital to have both boat and nets exclusively his own. A few have not only one but two boats, with their full complement of nets.

The nets used by the Mount's Bay fishermen are generally made in the port whence the boat sails. Sometimes the men themselves, when they have nothing else to do, employ themselves in constructing them; but this is a task which is generally left to the women and children to perform. The twine of which the nets are made is, in almost all cases, procured at Bridport, in Dorsetshire. In general it is very soft, but not fine. The fisherman receives it in what are called "parcels," each parcel containing twelve large skeins, for which he pays about 13s.; the price, however, depending to some extent on the nature of the transaction, as to whether it is a cash or a credit one. The nets are made, as it were, in sections. It requires seven parcels of twine to make a pilchard or herring net. Four of the smallest sections, when put together, form a net which usually goes under the designation of a piece-of-four. A complete net, as actually used in fishing, for a first-class boat, consists of fifteen of these pieces-of-four. The makers of the nets are generally termed by the fishermen the "breeders." As they come from the breeder's hands each piece-of-four is from fifty to sixty fathoms long, but they have afterwards to undergo an operation to prepare them for service, which causes them to shrink considerably. In addition to this, they are, when actually used, so put upon the "head ropes," that their length is diminished to about 36 or 38 fathoms. In depth the nets vary from 13 to 15 score meshes, there being about ten meshes to each foot, which will make them from 26 to 30 feet deep. A set of nets therefore, in actual fishing order, would in length extend to about 600 fathoms, or somewhat more than two-thirds of a mile. In general the nets are "home made"—that is to say, at the house of the fisherman for whom they are made. The wages given for making them are very low, which chiefly prevents the men, even when they have spare time on their hands, from frequently employing themselves in their construction. Sometimes they are made by the wife or daughters of the fisherman, when, of course, the wages which would otherwise be paid for them are saved. At other times girls and children are hired for the purpose. A girl, if she works early and late, can work off about two skeins a day. In doing so her fingers fly about as nimbly as do those of a lace worker over her cushion. Her remuneration is one shilling a week and her food. Sometimes, however, the nets are "put out" to be made, when the "breeder" gets £1 per net, in which case food is not included. When the work is thus given out by the piece, as many as three skeins a day are sometimes worked up; but this requires extraordinary exertions, which could not be long continued. The entire cost of a piece-of-four is about £8. The twine alone costs about £4 11s. There is then the cost of making and of barking, and the expense of the cork and head ropes required. A complete net therefore, consisting of fifteen pieces-of-four, will cost about £120. The same nets are generally used both for the pilchard and the herring fishing, but some boats are provided with different sets of nets for each. For herring, the law requires a larger mesh than for pilchard fishing. When there is but one set of nets for the two fisheries, the mesh is generally the smallest allowed by law for the capture of the herring. Of this mesh there are about ten and a half to the foot. This, which is the smallest for herring, is about the largest mesh used for the pilchard. The consequence therefore of having but one set of nets is, that some loss is experienced in both fisheries, for whilst the larger herrings do not get meshed, the smaller pilchards escape through the meshes. Until recently, the fisherman was subjected to a large yearly outlay for barking his nets. To preserve them from decay, and keep them in good working order, they were generally barked four times a year. The barking of a set of nets for the season then cost the fisherman about £11 4s. In addition to this, the process entailed upon him, on the average, a loss of from four to six days' fishing. But by the use of catechu instead of oak bark, a saving, both as to time and money, has been effected. The nets are now overhauled but twice a year, at a cost of about £1 each time. It is strange that, notwithstanding this great saving, the oak bark should still be used at many of the fishing stations. At Mount's Bay it is now universally superseded by the catechu, which was at first looked upon, even there, with some suspicion—so slow is the progress of improvement, even when men's interests would be directly subserved by advancing it. The length of time for which a set of nets will last depends upon a variety of circumstances. If the twine is good, and they are well barked, and kept carefully dry when not in use, they will last for a considerable time. Their endurance greatly depends, too, upon their owner's success in fishing. If that is great and constant, his nets will all the more often require repair, as well as more frequently require to be renewed. They generally last, however, from four to seven years.

The nets are not in all cases made at the stations where they are used. But few, for instance, are made either at Looe, Polperro, Fowey, Charlestown, or Mevagissy. This is to be regretted, for the sake of these communities themselves, inasmuch as they swarm with idlers, who might be thus usefully employed. But they prefer getting their nets ready-made from Bridport. The women and children have thus little or no employment wherewith to fill up the time on their hands.

I have hitherto spoken only of the nets used for the capture of pilchard and herring. But the observations made with respect to them apply, with but few exceptions, to the mackerel nets. These are generally longer, when in actual use, than the herring or pilchard nets. A complete set for a first-class boat generally consists of twenty-eight pieces-of-four—each piece-of-four, when fit for use, measuring about thirty-two fathoms in length, and about three in depth. A mackerel net will thus be about a mile long. The mesh, when the net comes from the "breeder's" hands, is about an inch-and-a-half in size, but it is reduced to nearly an inch-and-a-quarter by the use of the catechu. These nets last about the same length of time as the other; although, from the frequency with which they are in use, they require more constant repair.

The seine nets are made with a much smaller mesh than either of the nets alluded to. The reason of this will be obvious when the process of seine-fishing comes to be described.

Being prepared with all the appliances of his craft, it is now time to follow the fisherman in pursuit of his prey. The mackerel first calls him from his home, and it is often the last fish to engage him during the year. This fish is on the Cornish coast, more or less, throughout the whole year, but as it frequently varies its position, the fisherman must dance attendance upon it at different points of the coast. During the winter months, the course of the mackerel is generally up the Channel, which they sometimes ascend as far as Brighton, and more frequently as far as the Isle of Wight. But, as a general rule, they do not ascend in great masses much beyond the Devonshire coasts. Until the advance of spring they keep in deep water, at a considerable distance from the shore; as spring approaches, they change their course, and tend towards the westward, in doing which they come nearer the shore, and rise to the surface. It is then that the fisherman deems it time to commence his operations.

As at this period they are to be found in the greatest quantity on the coast of Devon, the Cornish boats sail eastward to Plymouth, where they meet the Brighton boats, which hie westward to the same point. They annually meet at their common rendezvous, Plymouth Sound, about the end of January. The Cornish boats, particularly those from Mount's Bay, are generally first on the ground ready for action. Both they and the Brighton boats are frequently at work before the Plymouth fishermen themselves are ready to begin. It often happens, therefore, that the Plymouth market is for some time supplied by the Brighton and Cornish boats. It is seldom that any preparations are now made for the spring mackerel fishing until some time in January, although the Mount's Bay boats have been known to be off for Plymouth before Christmas.

There are three mackerel seasons throughout the year—the spring, summer, and autumnal seasons. In prosecuting the spring and autumnal fisheries the drift nets only are used. During the summer months, when the fish approach the shore, and get into shallow water to deposit their spawn, they are caught in considerable quantities by the seine. But this fishing is very irregular. The mackerel is also sometimes caught by the hook and line, but in such small quantities as scarcely to entitle this mode of capture to be regarded as a distinct branch of the fishing of the county.

By far the most important branch of the mackerel fishing is that carried on with drift-nets. The seine fishing is limited in duration, and so frequently fails, that it is to the drift-nets the different markets of the south-west have chiefly to look for their supplies.

The number of boats in Mount's Bay that engage in the mackerel fishing is from 150 to 200. After having been thoroughly overhauled during the previous December, they are afloat and ready for action early in January. Nothing can be finer than the sight of the Mount's Bay fishing fleet when equipped and ready for sea. The number of hands to a boat does not vary much, although there is considerable variety as regards their ages and capacities. Some boats have seven men and a boy on board; others carry seven men without the boy; and others again but seven in all, including a boy. In most of them a boy is to be found, who, although he may take no active part in the fishing, is nevertheless exceedingly useful on board for many purposes, cooking included. He is thus early inured to the undoubted hardships of the life which, in all probability, he will ever afterwards follow. The men go on board well and warmly clad, and frequently with a complete change of dress. His enormous boots form an expensive as well as a prominent item in the fisherman's attire. The poor fellows have generally their names marked upon the breast of their Jersey jackets, so that they may be recognised in case of any casualty. It is but a short time since some were washed ashore at Polperro who could only have been thus identified by their friends. I asked my informant if they lost many at that port? "No," said he, "they're seldom lost; they're generally washed up some time or other at the point there."

The men never take spirits nor even malt liquor on board with them. Their commissariat generally consists of bread, sometimes potatoes, tea, and coffee, a little salt meat, and a supply of fresh water. Thus provided, they set off in January in their small but seaworthy craft for the mackerel fishing off Plymouth Sound.

They generally manage to arrive at the fishing ground a little before sunset. At sunset the boats are permitted to drive or float, as it were, at random, during which time the nets are being heaved overboard, generally from the right quarter of the boat, the object being, if possible, to throw them across the tide. The nets all overboard, soon assume a perpendicular position in the water, the whole being kept close to the surface by the large and buoyant corks attached to their upper edge. It is different in the pilchard fishing, the nets being suffered to drop some distance below the surface, but still hanging perpendicularly in the water. When the nets are all let out, the drift rope, attached to the head of them, is given out for some length, after which it is carried forward, and secured to the bow of the boat, which thus rides to the nets as if at anchor, and keeps them constantly on the stretch. Things being in this state, the men proceed to prepare their supper. As they always carry a portable cooking apparatus, they have hot tea or coffee always for breakfast and supper, and, such as choose, for dinner also. This, with bread, salt meat, and fresh fish, forms their chief fare. They renew their stock of provisions every time that it is necessary to do so, when they are ashore disposing of their fish. Supper being over, the first watch is set for the night, the rest of the crew retiring to rest. At midnight they are called up, and if the watch can report symptoms of a good "take," the nets are then hauled in. If not, the first watch retires to sleep, leaving the second on duty till four o'clock in the morning, when they are called, and the nets almost invariably hauled in. This is done by moving the drift-rope to the right quarter, over which the nets are hauled. If the fish caught are in moderate quantity, they are taken out of the net as it is being drawn; if in great quantity, and the fishing is near the shore, the fish are left in the meshes, and the net drawn as soon as possible, lest it should ground. The fish are, in this case, detached from the net when the boat gets ashore. When the demand for fish is great in Plymouth, and the price consequently good, the boats may not come ashore for a week or more at a time, the price paid being sufficient to induce others to visit them in light sailing trauls, who purchase their fish from them, and sell them ashore. About Mount's Bay it is customary for the boats to land every morning with their fish, which is disposed of to the "jowsters"—a set of middlemen, as it were, between the producers and consumers—who transmit the fish to Bristol, or hawk them about the country in carts. These hawkers, or jowsters, visit almost all the fishing ports, coming frequently all the way from Launceston to Polperro and Looe to purchase fish. Saturday is the only working-day on which they do not make their appearance, when fish is exceedingly cheap at the ports, whiting frequently selling for a halfpenny a pound. When the fishing is being carried on off the Scilly Islands, or in St. George's Channel, and the daily access to market is rendered impossible, another plan is hit upon for the disposal of the fish. Eight or nine boats then act in concert, one being made the messenger for all the rest, and conveying the fish of all to market. The boats take this duty in rotation. The period of their absence depends upon the distance of the market, but it varies from two to four days. The boat which is thus absent disposing of the fish, is entitled on its return to an equal share of what the others have caught in the meantime. Sometimes, on reaching a market, the messenger boat finds it overstocked, in which case another market is if possible sought without delay; when reached, it also may be found overstocked, or by the time it is reached the fish may be unfit for sale, and has to be thrown away. This is not, during some seasons, an unfrequent occurrence.

The division of profits is generally made as follows:—One-seventh of the proceeds is laid aside for the boat; the remainder is divided into two equal parts, one of which is appropriated to the nets, the other being divided amongst the men, share and share alike. If there is a boy on board he is entitled to half a man's share. If the owner of the boat, or of the nets, is on board, he is entitled to his share as one of the crew, in addition to what is appropriated to the boat or nets. This appropriation is made with a view to keeping them in working order, and of returning a fair per centage upon their original cost.

The mackerel fishing is liable to great fluctuations, its success depending upon a great variety of circumstances. Sometimes, for instance, the fish may pass up or down near mid channel, at other times near shore, sometimes near the surface, and at others in deep water. It may thus be that the fishing may be plied for days with discouraging results, owing to ignorance of the position of the fish. Sometimes a very slight change of position makes all the difference in this respect.

The mackerel fishing off Plymouth Sound lasts for about six weeks, the fish taking then a westerly direction. They are pursued by the Cornish boats, particularly those of Mount's Bay, off which the fishing is pursued with great industry for about six weeks more.

Formerly a lull used to take place from about the middle of May to the middle of July, in the active routine of a fisherman's life. To the great bulk of the drift-net men this time was wholly lost, the only fishing which could be plied, and that for only part of the time, being the precarious one of seining the mackerel, and few of them having any interest in seines. But now this is all changed, and the two months which used to be lost are at present to the fisherman the most active, adventurous, and sometimes the most profitable of the year. As soon as the mackerel fishing is over for the spring and summer, he begins to prepare for the herring fishing. In doing so the nets are closely looked to and repaired, and the boat is thoroughly overhauled; for in prosecuting this branch of his vocation he has to change the scene, and frequently goes to a great distance. About the middle of June all is prepared, and the great bulk of the Mount's Bay boats repair to the Irish Sea and the north coast of Ireland; most of them make Howth their headquarters. The herring fishery thus prosecuted is not so much a Cornish fishery, as an occupation for Cornish fishermen—and that, too, at a period of the year when they would not otherwise be employed. The value of this adventurous episode in the annual routine of their exertions may be inferred from the fact that they have sometimes carried back with them from seven to ten thousand pounds into Mount's Bay alone. This I had from a gentleman well known in Cornwall, and connected with a bank through which most of the money passed. It was about 1820 that Cornwall sent its first fishing expedition to the Irish coast. So encouraging were the results of the first experiment, that it has since been repeated every year, and is now as much looked upon as part and parcel of the work of the year as is the fishing off the coast. I have already intimated that they have been known to ascend the Scottish coast, and go through the Caledonian Canal to the German Ocean, fish down the whole of the east coast, and return home by the Straits of Dover and the English Channel. But the Irish Sea is the chief scene of their labours during this portion of the year. During their stay there they supply the English, Irish, and Welsh markets bordering upon that sea. When the weather is good the Irish boats compete with them; but they laugh when they tell you that whenever the weather is bad they have the fishing all to themselves. The fishermen do not all go to the herring fishing. The old and the very young stay at home, as do such as are indolently disposed. They generally, however, ply the hook and line fishing in the absence of their fellows.

About the end of July the absent fishing fleet re-appears off the Cornish coast. The fishermen return, not to leisure or recreation, but to ply their vocation against a new prey. About the period named commences the early pilchard fishing for the year. The pilchard fishing is a momentous event in Cornwall, the pilchard season being, in fact, the turning point of the Cornish year. From that time up to the beginning of September, the whole coast, from St. Ives to the Rame Head, is in a state of excitement and activity. Extra hands are called into requisition, and whilst some abandon the fields, others quit the mines, to lend their aid, and to lay in for their own and their family's consumption a stock of this favourite and useful fish for the year. So much do the comforts of all the labouring classes depend upon a successful capture of pilchards, that an unproductive season is nearly as disastrous as a deficient harvest would be.

Like the mackerel, the pilchard is caught both by the drift-net and the seine. The description given of the process by which the former is captured will apply to the latter—bearing in mind that the boats have, generally speaking, fewer hands in fishing for pilchards, that the nets are shorter, and that they do not, like the mackerel nets, swim on the surface, but drop some distance below it, being prevented from going to the bottom by buoys attached by short cords to the head ropes.

I may here mention, however, that when the nets are thrown, they are so attached to the head ropes as to have a drawn appearance—a device which enables them to bear the pressure better when they have a plentiful take of fish. Were they extended at their full length a heavy catch might break them, when great portions of them would be lost.

Having frequently spoken of the seine fishing, I now proceed to describe it. There is but very little of it now carried on in Mount's Bay, or indeed at any point on the southern coast of the county. There are still a few seines at Newlyn and other stations on the bay; but there are now none at Mousehole, the next fishing village in point of size and importance to Newlyn itself. The chief seat of the seine fishing is St. Ives, on the opposite coast, at which place drift-net fishing is pursued, but to a very limited extent.

Seine differs from drift-net fishing in this, that it is pursued during the day, and almost invariably near the shore and in shallow water. It also differs from it as regards the whole *modus operandi*. To work a seine three boats are required. The first and largest is called the seine boat, and carries the stop seine. It is generally manned by a crew of nine, six of whom are to row, two to shoot the seine, and one called the bow man, on whom the course of the boat depends. The second boat, a smaller one, is called the "volger," or follower, and carries the tuck seine. The third is the "lurker," the smallest of the three, and is chiefly occupied by a functionary called the "huer," and some boys. The whole number of hands usually employed to work a seine is about fifteen, in addition to the boys. The stop seine is of various lengths, being generally from 250 to 300 fathoms. Its depth is from 13 to 16 fathoms. Its meshes are much smaller than those of the drift-nets, the object being to enclose the fish without meshing them. The seine net has a line of head ropes, to which are attached corks and other buoys, to keep its upper edge near the surface. To the lower edge are attached innumerable small pieces of lead, which bear it down and keep it close to the ground, the object being to shoot the seine in shallow water with a clear bottom. The "tuck" is a similar net, but of smaller dimensions; its mesh is of the same size as that of the seine, but it has in the middle a hollow bag, as it were, into which the fish go when the process of tucking is going on. These nets are very expensive, costing about £300. The boats, with everything complete for seine fishing, will cost from £800 to £1,000. It is obvious therefore that none but considerable capitalists can engage in this species of fishing; indeed, almost the whole seine fishing of Cornwall is in the hands of a few wealthy capitalists, the smaller capitalists confining themselves to the deep sea, or drift-net fishing. The seine fishing is usually pursued from sunrise to sunset, the seines, however, being generally shot in the afternoon. The boats having taken their station, remain at anchor waiting for a signal from the huer. The business of this functionary is to take his station on an eminence within sight, and watch for the fish. As soon as he sees them he holds up both hands, in each of which there is generally a bunch of furze, so that the movement can be more distinctly seen. Each seine has its own huer, and the object of the lurker is chiefly to attend upon him if necessary. As soon as this is observed, all is got ready for action on board the little squadron, the huer then indicating, by waving his right or left hand, on which side the fish is to be found. If he is doubtful as to whether there is fish or not, there are signals by which he can send the volger or lurker to reconnoitre in any particular spot. The signal that there is fish being given, the boats weigh anchor and prepare to shoot. The operation of shooting is preceded by another signal, which, being given, the stop seine is thrown overboard, and the two shooters have it all given out in about five minutes. The huer remains at his post giving signals until, by the movement of the boats, the ends of the seine are brought together, by which means the fish are enclosed, and, whilst they do not get meshed, cannot escape. The huer is then taken on board by the lurker, and gives further orders for the management of the seine. The seine is then secured by several anchors, according to the strength of the tide, and the next operation is deferred until low water, or nearly so. That operation is "tucking," and is conducted as follows:—The volger passes over the corks of the seine-net at anchor, and takes up a position in the enclosed space. The tuck-net is then attached to the upper edge of the seine-net, after which the lower edge of it is drawn up, and a quantity of the fish enclosed are caught in the bag or "bunt" of the tuck. The fish is then lifted by "flaskets" into the boats and sent ashore. There they are put into what are called "corvals," in which they are carried by the women to the cellars where they are to be salted. A corval holds about 360 fish, for carrying which a woman gets 1d. or 2d., according to the distance. The wages of the cellar-women, who salt the fish, are about 3d. per hour, in which time they can lay down a great many in salt. Seine fishing is too precarious in its results for the men engaged in it to take their chance of the adventure and share in its profits, they are therefore invariably employed at fixed wages; the ordinary men receive, on the average, 10s. a week; the seine shooters

12s.; the master seiner has generally 15s.; and the huer one guinea per week. In addition to his wages, the huer claims one seventeenth of the whole fish caught. Sixpence per hogshead is also divided between the two seine-shooters and the bowman, the seine-shooters getting 2½d. each, and the bowman the remaining penny. With the exception of these and the master-seiner, the rest of the crew may be, and generally are, landsmen.

During all this time the deep-sea fishers are capturing the pilchards with their drift-nets, and are chiefly instrumental in supplying the home market. The fish caught by the seines are mostly cured for exportation, large quantities of them being sent to the Mediterranean, particularly to Naples and other parts of Italy, where they are largely consumed during Lent. It is thus that a favourite toast with the fishermen is "Long life to the Pope and death to thousands." The thousands, of course, apply to the fish. On my asking one of the fishers why he drank long life to the Pope?

"It would be a bad thing," said he, "if some wasn't to think fish necessary to salvation on a Friday."

The value of the pilchard fishery may be inferred from the following statement, showing the extent to which it was exported during each of the years from 1833 to 1846 inclusive:—

Year.	Hhds.	Year.	Hhds.	Year.	Hhds.
1833 ...	9,924	... 1838 ...	7,627	... 1843 ...	8,820
1834 ...	25,034	... 1839 ...	12,824	... 1844 ...	13,959
1835 ...	23,314	... 1840 ...	23,310	... 1845 ...	29,986
1836 ...	18,718	... 1841 ...	9,605	... 1846 ...	34,350
1837 ...	15,384	... 1842 ...	20,714		

It will be seen that the fluctuation in the quantity exported has been very great from year to year. The price has fluctuated to an equal extent during the same period—having ranged from 33s. to 60s. for winter, and from 35s. to 70s. for summer fish.

The early pilchard season is scarcely closed when preparations are made for the autumnal mackerel fishing. This is generally at its height during the month of October, when the largest and the finest mackerel are caught. It is immediately followed by the late pilchard season in November, which sometimes extends into the following month. But, generally speaking, there is a complete cessation from fishing during the month of December. But even then there is no rest for the fishermen, for this is the time when their chief repairs are effected.

The boats are thoroughly overhauled, and the nets carefully inspected, foot by foot, and by the advent of the new year all is prepared for the same routine of busy and adventurous occupation as has marked the year which has closed.

From this hurried account of the life and occupation of the Cornish fisherman, this, at least, will be obvious, that in the main he enjoys the advantages of continued employment. This is more particularly the case in connection with the deep-sea fishing, which is generally plied by those who combine the capitalist, on a small scale, with the fisherman. The seine fishing affords neither such steady nor such lucrative employment to the great bulk of those engaged in it. It is confined to a particular season of the year, and that not of very long duration. Whilst it lasts it calls into requisition the labour of a great many extra hands, which flock from the interior to the coast. So far as these are concerned, however, the pilchard fishing has this advantage, that it is most active just before and after harvest, thus giving employment, at good wages, to many on shore whose employment would be otherwise precarious, and whose wages would be low and fitful.

It follows, from the constant nature of their employment, that the fishermen are comparatively well off as a class. To the great majority of them the whole year is more or less profitable. They are not in the position of the ordinary agricultural labourer, who may be employed to-day at wages insufficient for his own and his family's comfort, whilst to-morrow he may be entirely out of work, without a penny wherewith to buy bread for his children. There are few pursuits more liable to fluctuation than that of fishing. It may be profitable to-day and profitless to-morrow; but it has this advantage, that it is sometimes highly profitable, enabling the provident man to provide to some extent against the contingency of profitless adventures. Not so, however, with the agricultural labourer. At the best, his work for the day brings him but a sufficiency for the day. He has no surplus, and can make no accumulation as a resource against a temporary failure of work. The fisherman need never be out of work, though at times his work is profitless. For this, however, he may be prepared; but the agricultural labourer depends upon the continuity of his employment, not only for his comforts, but for the barest necessaries of life.

Although the fishermen are comparatively well off as a class, they are not all equally so. They are divisible into three classes—those owning the boats, or the boats and nets; those owning the nets alone; and those having only their labour to bring to the work. These classes differ in their relative proportions at different points of the coast. Those who own the boats and nets, or the boats or nets separately, are the capitalists of their calling. When the fishing is at all prosperous they make a good thing of it, by the appropriations made at the division of the spoils to the boats and nets. You can almost always distinguish a fisherman thus situated by his generally healthy look, and the superior style of his house, family, and dress. His profits may frequently be discouragingly small, but a season must be very unfavourable indeed to reduce him to very straitened circumstances. The loss of a boat or of a net may ruin him, and reduce him to the condition of the lowest class of his calling. The nets are sometimes destroyed by an over-take of fish; at other times they are cut, particularly the mackerel nets, which swim on the surface, by vessels passing to and fro in the Channel. The lowest grade of fishermen are no strangers to privation. It is seldom that they can command much beyond the necessaries of life, and not always even these. After the seventh, and sometimes only the eighth, is laid by for the boat, they get only their share of the moiety which remains, the other moiety going to the nets. Their earnings are neither large nor regular, although their work is tolerably continuous. In addition to this, they have to submit to great extortion in their purchases of such necessaries as tea, coffee, and sugar. They cannot afford to go to Penzance, and buy in quantities of the retail dealers there, thus paying but one retail profit. They purchase in small quantities, from an inferior set of dealers, who charge their own profit over and above the retail profit in Penzance, the poor consumer thus paying two retail profits instead of one. This is one of the penalties of being poor. Poverty is at every disadvantage. This of itself is sufficient to account for the scanty command which this class of fishermen have, even in the best of seasons, of the comforts of life. They are a more emaciated and sickly-looking, whilst they are a less spirited, set of men than their more fortunate brethren, possessed of a little capital in the shape of boats or nets.

For the last few seasons, all classes of fishermen have been, more or less, in a depressed condition. Not that the fishing has been unfavourable, or the prices very unremunerative. The great cause of the depression of all, and of the privation which has overtaken the lowest class of them, is the failure of the potato. This has been a great blow to the fishermen. Some of them used to raise their own potatoes, but the great bulk purchase them. But few have raised any this year, and fewer still are able to buy them at their present price. Independently of their cheapness when abundant, the potato is the best accompaniment to the pilchard, which forms the staple of the fishermen's food. They will only eat bread to it when potatoes are not to be had. When they do eat bread, that of which they are most fond is the barley-bread, which they bake in the form of a loaf. Indeed this is general throughout Cornwall, barley-bread being consumed by the fishers, miners, and agricultural labourers. The labourers of Devon and Somerset would turn up their noses at it. Nothing but the finest flour will satisfy them. Yet the barley-bread is both sweet and nourishing. I have frequently tasted it, and found it excellent. It has the additional recommendation of being comparatively cheap. When the potato is used with the pilchard they are boiled together, or the potato is mashed and then baked before the fire with the pilchard over it. The oil of the fish is thus diffused through the potatoes, and strongly flavours them. When bread is used, it is a common practice, after the pilchard is cooked, to squeeze it between two pieces of bread. It thus gives out its oil, with which the bread becomes well saturated. The pilchard is a very fat and oily little fish. Naturalists may tell us that it is not exactly a herring, but it looks amazingly like one. It also greatly resembles the herring both in taste and flavour—both, however, being somewhat stronger than those of the herring. To those accustomed to pilchard—and what Cornishman is not?—the herring appears a dry and tasteless fish. It is a great favourite because it is strong and tasty, and generally very cheap. It is also liked in families, because, at a meal, each member of the family has generally his own fish. This prevents the squabbling which sometimes takes place over a larger fish, which has to be divided.

There was, perhaps, no district in England on which the loss of the potato fell with greater severity than on Cornwall; yet, when the distress was at its greatest height, the sufferers could not be prevailed upon to eat Indian-corn bread. They seemed to be utterly ignorant of its very nature, their aversion to it having a no more respectable origin than a groundless prejudice.

This season there are many of the lowest grade of fishermen and their families in the deepest distress. Numerous instances of extreme privation came under my notice in the smaller fishing ports. At Mount's Bay, the proportion of this class is smaller, as regards the whole number, than elsewhere. The distress is greatest where there are families of very young children, or where the families are large, and consist mainly, or wholly, of girls. Some most painful instances of privation, under these circumstances, came under my observation at Looe and Polperro.

Much privation is, of course, averted from the door of the fisher-man by his great command of fish. The practice is to salt such fish as cannot readily be disposed of on coming ashore. Pilchards, cod, ling, and hake are thus salted, either for sale, should any demand arise, or for the use of the family during the season. The curing houses, where the fish are dried and salted, are to be seen dotting the hill sides in the neighbourhood of all the fishing ports. They present a singular appear-ance against the dark hill sides, overhanging such places as Mevagissy and Polperro.

When the boys are active, too, it often happens, even before they are old enough to be taken to sea, that they cost little or nothing to their parents, so far as their diet is concerned, especially during the busier parts of the fishing season. When a boat goes out for pilchards, it frequently occurs that it brings to shore a quantity of other fish. Of this other fish neither the boats nor nets get any share, the whole being divided amongst the men. On coming ashore they pick the best of them for their own use, and leave the rest to such boys as will, in consideration thereof, clean out the boat. They light a fire, and cook the fish themselves. At Polperro they cook them at some lime-kilns in the neighbourhood, digging up a few potatoes, perhaps, from a neighbouring field, to eat along with them. They often, in the same way, procure large cray and unsaleable shell-fish, which they cook and eat, without making their appearance at home until bed time.

Again, the privation to which many are subjected is to a great extent attributable to themselves. Some suffer as the consequence of their improvidence and bad habits; others, from being very inexpert at their vocation. Two boats may fish close to each other, one of which may return laden, and the other empty. So much depends on the fish-ermen.

I am told, by one well acquainted with the lives, habits, and neces-sities of the fishermen, that they cannot live at all comfortably under 13s. a week. It is not easy to get at the exact number employed in the Cornish fisheries. About Mount's Bay alone there are fully 1,500 men and boys so employed. In order that they should live comfortably it is necessary that they should land each year about £50,000 worth of fish. Of this sum, £36,000 should go for wages, and the remaining £14,000 for repairs. It is extremely difficult to get at a fisherman's earnings, as it is only the seine fishers who have fixed wages. But, taking one year with another, they are supposed to amount to from 10s. to 13s. per week. This is of course applicable only to the lowest grade of fishers—the others earning much more if the season is at all prosperous.

As regards the house accommodation of the fisherman there is the same difference to be observed as there is in reference to his wages. The lowest grade are the worst housed; and at some points, such as Looe and Mevagissy, their habitations are of the most straitened and filthy description. There are tenements in West Looe and Mevagissy that may well vie with the cellars of Leeds, or the attics of Rosemary-lane. The same observation might at one time have applied to Polperro, which, when I visited it, was remarkably clean. The whole town had been whitewashed externally, and the floors in almost every house were kept sanded and clean. The rooms were well ventilated, and everything had a neat and tidy appearance about it. Some tenements were, indeed, squalid and miserable enough, but the description here given applies to the great bulk of the town. Polperro has been rewarded for its cleanliness, for it has escaped the visitation of the cholera. So much cannot be said of Mevagissy. This place also underwent a general cleaning, but no sooner was its purification effected than the inhabitants relapsed into their former habits of filthiness, and now almost every trace of cleanliness is gone. Here the cholera fell with terrible severity. The people of Mevagissy form, in many respects, a marked exception to those of most of the other fishing towns. The inhabitants of the neighbouring districts stand in dread of them, and hold no communication with them beyond such as is absolutely necessary. At St. Ives there is also much domiciliary wretchedness, but the greatest misery in this respect is to be found in the decaying fishing stations to the north-east of that town. At Mount's Bay they are better off. In Newlyn and Mousehole, the two largest villages, the bulk of the houses are comparatively good. They are not so crowded as elsewhere, and have all at least two bedrooms. They have also two rooms below, one of which, unless the occupant has a covered place behind, is used as a cellar, where fish are cured and salted. A fisherman's house is not complete without his cellar. If he has not one under his roof, he must hire one elsewhere. The evil of filthy and over-crowded dwellings is much enhanced in some of the fishing villages by the number of agricultural labourers who, by the clearing system, are driven into them from the circumjacent rural parishes. The rent of a house averages about £4.

The better class of fishermen, and the provident of all classes, have clothing for shore and clothing for sea. That for shore is used when they are at work on land, in addition to which they have generally a Sunday suit.

Whenever butcher meat figures in their diet, it is almost invariably fresh. They eat too much salt fish to have any relish for salt meat.

The diseases to which they are liable are mostly of an inflammatory character. They are also frequently subject to cataract, from exposure combined with much straining of the sight.

When I visited Newlyn and Mousehole (*Cornicè*, Mouzle), I found the fishermen standing about in groups, evidently discussing some point interesting to them all. On reaching Mousehole, I inquired what it was, and was informed that they were waiting in momentary expectation of getting news of the approach of the late pilchards. They were waiting, one of them told me, to hear of the "north coasters:" these being neither more nor less than the pilchards, which, descending from St. George's Channel, strike, about this time of year, the coast of Cornwall. Within the memory of living man it is only since 1819 that they have been in the habit of coming from this quarter. Some of the oldest fishermen remember hearing their fathers say that they knew them to do so. They were rather late of making their appearance this year, and some anxiety was felt on their account. Scouts were daily running from St. Ives to Mount's Bay, bringing tidings concerning them. It is at St. Ives they first touch, after which they turn the Land's End and enter the Bay. If they have not made their appearance by this time the late pilchard fishing will be a failure for the year. This will be a serious misfortune.

Although but a mile and a half apart from each other, there is a great difference between the character and habits of the people of Mousehole and those of Newlyn. There is much more recklessness in the latter than in the former. The men of Newlyn do not drink on board, but they drink a good deal on shore. A tipsy man is scarcely ever seen in Mousehole. This great reform is the work of the last few years. There were formerly five public-houses in the village, and now, although it has a population of about 1,500, it does not afford suffi-cient custom to support even one. The habits of the people are in all respects superior to those of Newlyn. No fisherman from Mousehole will take to the sea on a Sunday. Every one of them attends some place of worship or other on that day. They are generally Methodists.

They are also very well educated, considering their circumstances. The village school is a very efficient one.

As indicative of their energy, I may here mention that the fishermen of Mousehole have, at a cost of £1,400, built for themselves a pier, which, with the breakwater built many years ago by the Government, forms their little harbour. To construct it they raised £1,200 on their own joint bond, which they are paying off by instalments, each boat being put under a yearly contribution for the purpose. But their harbour is far too small, and they are very anxious that the Government should aid them in enlarging it. The assistance of Government might be much worse bestowed.

On the whole, therefore, although considerable distress at present prevails amongst a portion of this laborious, adventurous, and deserving class of men, their privations are seldom so severe or so long continued as are those of the agricultural labourer. Nor is there a class— not even the lowest grade of fishermen—the members of which, by ordinary care, activity, and providence, may not place themselves in a far better position than that of the labourer in the fields.

LABOUR AND THE POOR.

—◆—

THE RURAL DISTRICTS.

[FROM OUR SPECIAL CORRESPONDENT.]

THE MINES AND MINERS OF CORNWALL.

LETTER XI.

Long before Roman, Dane, Saxon, or Norman put his foot as a conqueror on British ground, Cornwall was both known and frequented for its mineral wealth. The earliest celebrity which the county seems to have attained in this respect was for its tin; but subsequent mining operations have proved it to be also rich in copper and lead. It likewise possesses iron, but not in very great quantity; whilst silver is found to a small extent in the lead mines. For many centuries the tin produced in Cornwall was extracted from mere diluvial ores, or superficial deposits, it being only within a period comparatively recent that the system of mining was commenced which has since developed itself on so stupendous a scale. The county was long known for its tin ere copper was extracted from it to any extent. But although this branch of the mining industry of Cornwall was the most recently developed, it is now the most extensive of all, the copper mines being the most numerous, and employing the greatest number of hands in the county.

The ores of Cornwall, whether of tin, copper, or lead, are found in veins. These veins are called lodes. They run in very irregular lines, varying greatly in width, but all resembling each other in this respect, that no limit can be assigned to their depth. The two great features in the geological structure of the county are the granite and the slate stone. In the granite the tin is generally found—in the slate stone the lead; and the copper usually at or near the junction of the two. In parts, these different ores are found by themselves, in other places they are mingled together. Thus, from a particular lode copper, tin, or lead only may be extracted—or copper, tin, and lead may be found in different proportions together. Copper and tin are frequently found in one and the same lode; and when they are not so, the different lodes in which they may lie are sometimes so close to each other as to be within the bounds of one and the same mine; so that whilst one shaft of a mine may descend into a copper, that contiguous to it may penetrate a tin lode. It is thus that many of the mines, particularly in the west, are worked both for copper and tin.

The mining interest of Cornwall is, beyond all question, the most important in the whole county. The number of people employed in and about the mines, including surface and underground workers, was, in 1841, upwards of 27,000. On a calculation similar to those made on former occasions with respect to the number of persons dependent for support upon agricultural labour in particular districts, this would give about 87,000 persons as the number dependent upon mining operations for their subsistence. The importance of the mining interest will be appreciated when it is considered that it supports nearly double the number of people maintained by agricultural labour in Cornwall. It is next to impossible to get at the number at present occupied in and about the mines; yet there is reason to believe that, though the population of Cornwall will show an increase of nearly 40,000 within the ten years from 1841 to 1851, the number of those employed in and about the mines, and dependent on such employment, will not exhibit any very great increase. Indeed, but for the recent opening of the mines in the neighbourhood of Liskeard, and the activity with which mining operations are there at present pursued, the probability is that their number would have decreased.

In regard to mining, Cornwall is divided into three great districts—the western, the midland, and the eastern. The western comprehends the parish of St. Just and its neighbourhood. The midland has a larger range, extending from Hayle on the east, to the parish of St. Blazey, near Fowey, on the west. Fully one-half of this district is wild, uneven, and bleak, and scarcely adaptable for the lowest agricultural purposes. Its chief *foci* are St. Agnes, Camborne, Redruth, and St. Austle. The eastern district comprehends the mines in the neighbourhood of Liskeard, and those at Callington, on the borders of Devon. In all these districts, copper, tin, and lead abound in varying proportions, the copper being generally in the greatest quantity, except, perhaps, in the neighbourhood of St. Austle. Lead mines are worked to a limited extent in the neighbourhood of Liskeard; the chief mining operations in that quarter, however, being confined to copper.

As the main object of the present inquiry is to ascertain the condition and prospects of the labourer, I shall confine myself to a brief account of the practical working of the mines, with a view to the elucidation of the miner's duties, and of the different circumstances which more or less affect his lot and fortunes. Before doing so, it will be as well to premise that the term miner exclusively applies to those actually working in the mines—the capitalists, or those employing the miner, being known as the adventurers. Each mine is owned by a company of adventurers, the capital being divided into shares, which are marketable and transferable like those of a railway company.

To explain the process of mining, it is advisable to begin with the beginning—in other words, to follow a mine from its first establishment, until it is in complete and active operation.

The lodes generally manifest themselves, more or less, on the surface. But, even when the indications of ore are greatest, it requires a practised eye to distinguish them, for frequently the richest ores give the least token of their presence to the inexperienced observer. When there is reason to believe that a lode worth trying exists in a place not hitherto worked, a set of adventurers form themselves into a company for the purpose of working it. In doing so their first business is to apply to the lord of the soil for a licence to work the lode for a given time—sometimes for six months, but generally a year—upon trial; the lord to receive a specified proportion, usually one-fifteenth, of the ore which may be raised during the period of the licence. The lord also comes under an obligation, should the adventurers at the expiration of the licence be disposed to continue the working of the mine, to lease it to them for a certain number of years, generally upon the same terms as those of the licence, so far as his share of the proceeds is concerned. Should the project prove a failure, it may be abandoned at any time before the expiration of the licence. This mode of paying the lord his dues is objected to by many, on the ground that it frequently operates harshly upon the adventurers. They urge that however much the mine may be losing, the lord is always sure of a profit. Thus, if £15,000 worth of ore is raised and disposed of, it may cost the adventurers £15,000 to raise it. If in that case they paid the lord his fifteenth, the company would lose £1,000, instead of making a profit. But this would be equally the case were the lord, instead of his share of the proceeds of the mine, to receive a fixed money rent from the adventurers. Thus, if the fixed rent were £2,000, and the produce worth £15,000, as in the case supposed, the loss to the adventurers would be £2,000, instead of £1,000. It is quite true that, by the present arrangement, the lord is always sure of a profit, because he runs no risk; but that profit, like the profit of the adventurers, fluctuates with the price of copper, and when the price is low, the present bears upon them more lightly than any other arrangement would do.

The course here mentioned is that which is pursued when it is in contemplation to open up an entirely new mine. But it frequently happens that a new mine is opened within bounds already set out to a company of adventurers, and within which they are already working a mine. In such case no new licence is, of course, required. When a new mine is thus opened, the way is generally led by a party of miners, who undertake to try on the "tribute system," which will be immediately explained, either what they believe to be a fresh lode, or a portion of the lode already worked, but which the existing operations are not likely to reach. In the latter case the result, if the experiment is successful, is generally the sinking of some new shafts, which are soon connected with the existing works, whereby the scope of the existing mine is only enlarged. But whether an entirely new mine is to be opened, or the range of an existing mine is only to be enlarged, the operations commence by the sinking of shafts, and the construction of levels; these must be done ere the mine is in workable condition. And this brings us at once in contact with the actual work of the miner.

The miners are divided into two great classes—the surface and the under-ground men. The latter are by far the most numerous, being fully 3 to 1, as compared with the former. The under-ground men are again divided into two separate classes, known, in mining phraseology, as the "Tutmen" and "Tributers."

The tutmen are those who do "tut" work, which is neither more nor less than simple excavation. In commencing a mine, therefore, the tutmen are the first called into requisition. They sink the shaft and run the levels—all the ore which may chance to be raised during the process belonging exclusively to the adventurers, always with the exception of the lord's dues. The work is given out by the fathom; it is regularly bid for, and the parties offering to do it for the lowest price secure the work. It generally happens, however, that one of the captains of the mine ascertains beforehand, as far as can be, the nature of the work, and sets his own price upon it—the price at which it is taken seldom varying much from the captain's price. Both tut and tribute work are usually taken by what is called a "party;" the party, in both cases, consisting of several individuals, their number varying according to circumstances. The party is divided into gangs, which relieve each other in rotation. There are three gangs to a tut party, each gang working eight hours at a time, the whole 24 hours being thus turned to account. The gangs employed in tut work are strictly required to relieve each other at the proper time. As their work is chiefly preliminary to the real business of mining, it is of course the object of those who employ them to have it done as speedily as possible. Nor are the interests of the tutmen themselves interfered with by this—for, as their work is piece-work, the sooner they get through it the better. A greater degree of discretion is generally given to the tributers, as to how long they may work, and when they may relieve each other—it being supposed that they have sufficient inducement to diligence in the share which they have in the proceeds of their own operations. At the poorer mines tut work is generally confined to ground which is not metallic, tribute work having reference invariably to metallic ground. At times, however, tut work embraces ground which is metallic—but this is always in the richer mines. When the ore is known to be good, it is raised at so much per fathom, in which case it all belongs to the adventurers. It is generally work of a more speculative kind that is set on the tribute system; and it is because in the poorer mines all the work is of this kind, that the whole of the ore is raised on that system. But even when it is raised on the other system, that is to say by tut work, it is not unusual to give the men employed a small interest in the ore produced. This is done in order to make it their interest not to waste or spoil the ore.

The work of the tutman is, as already said, that of simple excavation, at so much per fathom. He bids for it with a real or presumed knowledge of the nature of the ground to be worked—the same knowledge being possessed, or presumed to be possessed, by the captain assigning him the work. Miscalculations in this respect are not unfrequently made, which are in their results sometimes in favour of, and at others against, the tutman. Although their work has not so much the character of a gambling transaction about it as has that of the tributers, still it is not entirely free from that objection. He may bid for work, and it may be assigned to him, on the supposition that the ground is hard and difficult to be operated upon—or the same may be done on the contrary supposition. In the one case it may be found, after a little trial, much easier, and in the other much more difficult to work, than was anticipated. Thus, by the chance of his work, he may be a gainer to some extent, or a severe sufferer. Thus, after taking work which appears easy at a comparatively low price per fathom, he may, after penetrating for some distance through disintegrated granite, which is easily removed, or soft clay, come to a hard mass of granite, which opposes a serious obstacle to his progress. This the tutman calls a "pebble," and it is a serious question with the party on discovering it, whether they will change their course to avoid it, if possible, or dash right through it, in the hope that it does not extend to any great depth. There is risk in either case, as the time lost, and the expense incurred, in attempting to turn or avoid it, may be much greater than was anticipated. Nor is it always that it can be avoided at any cost. Then, again, if they attempt to go through it, their hopes may be disappointed, as its depth may be very great. Sometimes, after going through it for some distance, they give it up in despair, and attempt to turn it, which they find, to their mortification, after having lost so much labour, that they can rarely do. When the work goes thus against the tutman, he very soon complains, and if his complaint is well grounded, a favourable modification is generally effected in the arrangement between him and his employers.

The undertaking of the tutman is to bring to the surface so much matter, whether ore or "stuff," or both together, at so much per fathom. To fulfil it, he requires the use of machinery to raise the matter excavated to the surface. That which he thus employs is, of course, the machinery on the spot, adapted for the purpose and appertaining to the mine. For this he is usually charged at the rate of 14s. a fathom, which is so much to be deducted from his earnings. There are other deductions also to be made, but as these are common to both tributers and tutmen, their explanation will be deferred for the present.

The first work with which the tutman grapples is, of course, the sinking of the shaft. The object is, if possible, to have the shaft perpendicular. Such a shaft is not only the most convenient, but it is also attended with the least expense in the future working of the mine. But much in this respect depends upon what is called the "underlie" of the lode. It is very seldom that the lode is perpendicular, its inclination being, as it proceeds downwards, generally to the north. If the underlie is not great, the shaft may to a considerable distance follow the lode. If it is great, the shaft descends, not in one continuous line, but, as it were, by a succession of steps. It will be sunk perpendicularly by several fathoms at a time, the lode all the time diverging from it to the northward. At certain distances halts are made, and horizontal courses run in the direction of the lode, until it is again struck. Each time the lode is struck the shaft is sunk again, the lode to be reached again by a horizontal course as before. As the shaft is being sunk, the levels are being constructed. It is necessary that the reader should comprehend what these are, as on his doing so will greatly depend his comprehension of the operations which follow. To enable him the more readily to understand the internal arrangements of the mine, let us suppose both the lode and the shaft to be perpendicular.

The lode, be it remembered, is neither more nor less than a crevice or fissure in the granite or in the slate, or at the junction of the two, varying in width and generally running from east to west. This crevice is usually filled with disintegrated granite, clay, or other soft matter, interspersed with which is the metal. Were the lode perpendicular, the shaft, in following it downwards, would be perpendicular also. The shaft is usually in the form of a parallelogram, about five or six feet wide, and about double that in length. The sides are almost invariably secured with woodwork, so as to prevent them from falling in. Down the middle, and dividing the parallelogram, as it were, into two squares, runs a strong wooden partition, which in reality makes two shafts of it. One is for the raising of the ore and rubbish; the other is that by which the miners have access to and egress from the mine. The levels are parallel courses, which diverge on either side from the shaft, and follow horizontally the course of the lode. These courses are at different distances from each other, but, generally speaking, they are not more than ten fathoms apart. Thus, after the shaft is sunk a certain distance, the first level will be run—in other words, a horizontal passage will be cut from either side of the shaft, following the direction of the lode. The height of this passage is usually from five to six feet. It is also commonly three feet wide, so as to give room for the operations to be conducted within it. This is its width, however narrow the lode may be; nor is it frequently made any wider, even when the lode is wider, unless the lode is sufficiently rich to warrant its being made so. There is no limit to the length of the passage or canal, but such as may be set to it by the superficial bounds of the mine. The shaft is then sunk, say for ten fathoms more, when similar levels are constructed, directly under those alluded to. This operation may be repeated so long as the mine continues sufficiently wealthy to induce the adventurers to keep sinking the shaft and constructing new levels. Some mines have attained a depth of 300 fathoms, so that they have about thirty different sets of levels, all ranging one beneath the other.

When a new level is wanted, the shaft is first sunk to the proper depth, when the level is opened up. The *rationale* of a mine under these circumstances would be neither more nor less than a perpendicular hole sunk in the lode, with a series of horizontal holes projecting into it, at regular distances from each other, from either side of, or at right angles to, the perpendicular one. It is obvious that, when the lode is not perpendicular, which is usually the case, and the shaft, instead of being continuous, descends, as it were, by steps, the levels, instead of being directly under each other, will be below, but a little to the side of each other—the distance to which they will be to the side of each other depending upon the inclination or underlie of the lode. Thus, if the lode underlies to the northward, each successive level will be more to the northward than those above it, and less so than those below. Generally speaking, instead of the shaft following the levels, and so being broken into different sections, it is sunk perpendicularly, being accessible to the different levels by means of horizontal curves connecting them together.

When the mine is extensive it is usual to sink several shafts. Thus, at the Carn-Brea mine, which has a superficial extent of a mile and a half in length, and about three-quarters of a mile in width, there are from 20 to 30 shafts. Other mines have even more than this. These shafts are often situated along the line of the lode, and are constructed to facilitate the operations of the mine, which would be much impeded were there but one outlet, when the levels have been pitched far back. When several shafts are thus situated the levels extending from one will run into those extending from another, so that the different levels will thus have the advantage of more than one outlet. Several shafts are sometimes sunk when the mine is very deep and the underlie considerable, not in the direction of the lode, but in that of the underlie, so as to perforate the body of the lode at different points. These are mainly intended to facilitate operations in the lower levels, which would otherwise be too far removed from the outlets of the mine. When the mine is deep and the shafts are far apart, the levels are here and there connected with each other by what are called "winzes." A winze is a cutting extending from one level to another, and when perpendicular, which is not always the case, is just like the section of a shaft extending between level and level. This has the double object of facilitating the communication between the different levels, and of improving the ventilation of the mine. Sometimes, despite the presence of numerous winzes, the circulation of air is so imperfect in a mine, that boys are employed below in working machines which increase the current.

The description of the internal economy of a mine would be incomplete without an allusion to what is known as the adit level. This is found in mines which are situated on the side of a declivity, and its chief object is to prevent the necessity of having to raise the water pumped from the mine to the very top of the shaft. The adit level may be the first, second, or third level of a mine, counting from the top, the depth at which it is run depending partly upon the depth of the valley upon which it opens, and partly upon the nature of the portion of the mine above it, as to whether it is wet or dry. Thus, if a mine is situated on the side of a valley, and the shaft is sunk about 100 feet above the lowest level of the valley near the mine, the adit level may be run out into the valley about 90 or 100 feet down. Through this the water will escape, and the expense of raising it to the top will be saved. The adit level is also useful as an auxiliary to ventilation.

These observations apply equally to copper, lead, and tin mines; and everything here described is necessary to be done before the mine is in working order. And all this is exclusively the work of the tutmen. It does not necessarily follow that ore has been raised during the operations, although considerable quantities are sometimes brought to the surface in sinking the shafts and running the levels. It is not until these are completed that the real work of mining begins. The levels are then taken possession of by those whose business it is to produce the ore. When the lode is very rich, the tutmen, as already explained, are engaged to work it at so much per fathom. But the production of the ore is generally the work of the tribute man, who is after all the real miner.

From the explanation here given, it will have occurred to the reader that between every two levels on either side of the shaft a deep belt of the lode intervenes. Thus, between the surface and the first level there is such a belt, as also between the first and second levels, &c. That between the first level and the surface is seldom worked to any great extent, but the others are, according to the richness and quality. These intervening belts are, in the jargon of the miners, called "pitches," and it is by the pitch that the work is set.

Each mine has its own regular setting days, and the process of setting is as follows. At the proper time and place the tributers and the captains of the mine meet together. I may here explain that the captains are invariably men who have risen from the rank of miners.

It is their duty to set and superintend the work, to do both of which properly they must frequently descend into the mine. There are three or more of them, according to the extent of the mine, and one or more of them are invariably below. The setting is a species of auction, the captains being the auctioneers, the miners the bidders, and the pitches the subject-matter of the transaction. Since the previous setting-day more pitches may have been opened, either by the further sinking of the shafts and the construction of additional levels, or by the extension of the levels already existing. It frequently happens, too, that pitches already partially worked but abandoned may be offered. In such cases they may be taken by different parties, or by the same parties at a higher rate. Both miners and captains are supposed to have a knowledge of the quality of the pitches, and it is upon this knowledge that they proceed to business. The pitches are put up, one after another, not to the highest, but to the lowest bidder. There are maps of each mine, and the pitches, levels, shafts, and winzes, are all as well known to the parties concerned as are their streets to the denizens of a town. Pitch so and so is put up, and the bidding commences. The offer, on the part of the captains, is to set the lode to the party that will work it for the smallest share of the proceeds. This explains the position of the tributer, and the character of his work. He does not work for fixed wages, or for so much per fathom, but becomes, *quoad* the portion of the mine which he engages to work, a partner, as it were, in its profits and losses. The share in consideration of which he will work a pitch depends upon his belief as to the quality of the lode at that particular point. Thus he will offer to work a rich pitch for 5s. in the pound—that is to say, for 5s. out of every pound's worth of ore which he may raise to the surface. This is called his tribute. To work a poor pitch, however, which yields but little ore to a great deal of labour, he may ask as high as 13s. in the pound. Sometimes he will work at a lower rate than 5s., but when the ore is so rich as to tempt him to go much lower than that, the adventurers generally give it out on tut by the fathom, retaining all the produce to themselves. Between 4s. and 13s. in the pound is the range at which the tribute man generally works. It is seldom that there is any indiscriminate bidding, or any great scramble at the settings. Men who have obtained a footing in the mine have generally the preference over strangers. The captain has generally his price for each pitch, and if it is a new setting for the same pitch, he usually offers it to the party who have already worked it. If they take it, the matter so far is at an end; if not, it is then put up, and the lowest bidders, before a stone which is thrown up falls to the ground, receive the work.

The pitches are set for two months at a time, an arrangement advantageous to all parties; for if the tributers find a pitch poorer than they anticipated, they are not obliged to work it for a greater length of time—whereas, if it turns out much richer than was expected, the adventurers will be enabled, at the end of that period, to secure their fair share of the produce. The tributers have this further advantage, that, should they find the pitch very poor, they may throw it up at the end of a month, although they have taken it for two; and in such a case it may be reset to them at a higher rate.

I have already intimated that, in setting the pitches and giving out tutwork, a preference is usually given to those who have been established in the mine, provided they are disposed to take the work at or near the captain's price. This preference has given rise to the practice of taking "farthing pitches," as they are sometimes called—that is to say, taking a pitch at the low and merely nominal tribute of a farthing in the pound. The object of doing so is simply to get established in the mine. At the next setting those parties will be on the same footing as those who preceded them in the mine. But advantageous as this appears to be to the adventurers, it is not in reality so. Beyond getting established in the mine, the men have no inducement to work, their tribute being merely nominal. The consequence is that they waste their time, doing little or no work whilst below, to the obvious detriment of the adventurers. This is now so clearly seen, that in most mines the system of farthing pitches has been discontinued, the adventurers having been all the more inclined to depart from it, from the umbrage which it frequently gave to those who had been long in their employment.

When a pitch is set, it is marked down in the books of the mine as set to such and such a party. Their names or marks are all subscribed to the notification. The party varies in number, according to the nature of the pitch, and the quantity of labour which will have to be expended upon it. Sometimes the party does not exceed four, at other times it consists of six or eight, and occasionally extends to twelve.

The share of the tributer is determined as to its amount by the value of the ore when ready for market. He has, therefore, not only to extract it from the lode, but also to prepare it for market. This is done on the surface by those whom he employs for the purpose. At every mine there is a large number of surface workers, amongst whom may be seen some men, but the majority of whom are women and boys. They constitute from one-fifth to one-fourth of the whole number employed in and about the mine. These surface workers are almost all in the pay of the tributers or underground men. It is their business to take the ore as it comes from the shaft, to have it stamped, cleaned, and washed, and prepared for the smelters. The larger masses are broken with hammers, generally by women, until the whole pile is in pieces about the size of a large egg. If the ore is very rich, it is then carried to the rollers, between which it is crushed. It is then ready for market. This applies only to the copper ore, which is considered good if it has from 10 to 15 per cent. of metal in it. The preparation of the tin ore is very different. It often comes to the surface with no more than 6 per cent. of metal in it. But before it is ready for market and in a state fit to be received by the smelters, it has to be "worked up" until it contains 75 per cent. of metal; in other words, the great bulk of the dross must be got rid of. The ore is first taken to the stamps. These are perpendicular beams of wood, set in frames, each beam being shod at its lower end with a large and heavy mass of iron. In one stamping-machine there may be a great number of these beams. They are raised alternately by a cogged cylinder driven by the steam-engine, and fall with great weight upon the rough ore, which is placed below them, and which they grind very fine. The ore when placed below them is immersed in a stream of water, whose only outlets are fine wire sieves, close to the lower end of each stamper. Through these sieves the water is forced with great violence, carrying out with it such parts of the ore as have been sufficiently crushed to pass through. Such as is not small enough remains below the stamper until it becomes so. As the crushed ore passes from the stamper it is carried by the water to beds, which slightly decline towards one end. The best part of the ore sinks immediately at the upper end of these beds, the dross not sinking until it reaches the lower end. This dross still containing some metal is again washed, by being divided into other beds similarly situated, and the process is resumed until little but dross remains. In this way the tin ore is worked up to the requisite quality of 75 per cent. When the copper ore is not very rich, it also is put under stamps, and undergoes the process of washing. There are other operations, such as "jigging," &c., all having in view the preparation of the ore for market. It is when sold, after it has been so prepared, that the tributer's earnings are determined, in ascertaining the net amount of which he has of course to deduct the wages of those employed by him on the surface for the preparation of the ore. Nor is this the only deduction which has to be made, as will be presently seen. The tin ore is not thus prepared at his cost, being generally bought of him at the top of the shaft, the adventurers working it up to the requisite point.

Breaking Copper Ore—Cornwall

Before considering the miner's wages, it will be as well to see him at work. To do so, if the reader will accompany me, we will descend a shaft together.

The mines are not all equally wet, but no one can expect to penetrate very far into a mine and emerge dry from it. We have, therefore, to go to the "shifting-room," and attire ourselves in a miner's garb. It consists of a suit of thick flannel, with a stout coat over it, heavy shoes for the feet, and a hat generally made strong enough to "bear a good knock." We must also provide ourselves each with a candle. The candle is stuck into a piece of clay, which again is stuck upon the hat, which is of the "wide-awake" shape. Thus equipped we descend the ladders. As we approach the shaft, we perceive a steam rising from it. This, we are informed, is the breath of the men at work below. The very mine itself seems to breathe. There are, at least, 600 men at work beneath our feet, at various depths, some 100, some 500, and others 1,600 feet. The ladder is very narrow, with iron bars, and is well nigh perpendicular. The bars are moist and greasy from the men passing frequently up and down, which makes us cling all the more firmly, considering the unknown depth of the shaft, and the almost perpendicular position of our means of descent. We bid adieu to daylight almost by the time we have reached the first level. There is no one at work in it, so we descend to the second. We pass it and several others until at length we reach the seventh level. We are then about 400 feet under ground, a sufficient depth to bury St. Paul's. We take the level to our right, and pursue it until we reach the men at their work. There is a tramroad along the level, for "running the stuff" to the shaft, so that it can be raised to the surface. In some of the smaller mines this is done by boys with wheelbarrows, which, with the exception of working the ventilating machines, is the only purpose to which boys are put below. We proceed about 100 feet in a horizontal course, when we come upon the miners. When they take a pitch, they generally work it *up*, not *down*—that is to say, the men working from the seventh level work up towards the sixth, not down towards the eighth. Their object is to follow the lode and extract the ore from it, disturbing as little of the non-metallic ground as possible. When the lode is wide enough, they work nothing but the lode, leaving the matter on either side untouched. A miner will thus work in a lode only 18 inches wide; but if it is narrower than that, he has to clear away some of the "country"—which is removing a sufficient quantity of the granite, slate, stone, or other substance which may envelop the lode, to enable him to follow it. Those upon whom we have come are engaged at this work. They are preparing to clear away the granite by blasting it. The hole for the powder is made with a "borer," held by one whilst the other strikes it with a large sledge hammer. The latter is in a state of profuse perspiration, whilst the other is shivering with cold. They are both completely wet, as indeed we are ourselves. The man with the hammer has nothing on but his flannel trowsers. The beatings of his heart, which are quick and strong, strike painfully upon the ear. He seems to be galloping through life—and so he is, for the miner is generally but a short liver. We leave this part of the level, and take that on the other side of the shaft, which we follow for a considerable distance, until we come to a hole, through which we have to crawl on all fours. We then find ourselves at the bottom of a winze, which we pass, and pursue the level. The men have worked up for a considerable distance, making stages for themselves as they rise into the lode. The ore is carefully separated from the stuff, and is carried over the tramway to the shaft. Such is the merest outline of the work which the mine exhibits. Space will not permit me to go into details here. We return again to the surface. But to climb a series of perpendicular ladders, reaching as high as St. Paul's, is no joke. We take about half an hour to do it, resting at the different levels as we ascend. We arrive at the top utterly exhausted, and thankful that we have emerged again into daylight.

Such is the position, and such are the circumstances of the miners when at work. They generally relieve each other every eight hours, each gang working eight out of the twenty-four. Their tools are chiefly the sledge, the borer, and the pick, with the last of which they remove the dislodged granite and other stuff which do not require blasting. I one day overtook a tributer making for one of the mines near Redruth. He told me that he worked in the 300 fathom level—that is to say 1,800 feet below the surface. His engagement was to be on the ladders by six in the morning, and he emerged from the mine about five in the afternoon. Nearly two hours were spent in descending and ascending the ladders. At this period of the year, with the exception of the Sundays, his life is one perpetual night. The temperature was so high in his level, that they all worked naked, ascending, every hour or so, to several fathoms above them, to dip themselves in some pools, which were comparatively cool. He was a tributer, and the tributers look with as great contempt upon the tutmen, as the tutmen do upon the surface labourers. Indeed a tributer will be on the point of starvation before he will take tutwork. Some mines, like the Carn-Brea mine, employ about 1,200 people; others more. The Caradon and other mines which have recently sprung up in the neighbourhood of Liskeard afford subsistence to about 10,000 people, including the miners and their families.

It is not very easy to get at the earnings of a miner. The wages of the surface-workers are fixed and known, but the earnings of the underground workers depend as to amount upon so many circumstances, that it is difficult to ascertain them. Throughout the midland mining district, particularly around Redruth, which is the centre of the most extensive mining district in the county, they have been receiving for some time past from 45s. to 50s. a month. At the Caradon mines the earnings are, on the average, about 10s. per month higher than those in the west. When these mines were established a large migration of miners took place from the west, for whom no adequate house accommodation has since been provided. They are thus not only compelled to huddle together in large numbers, but they have also to pay very

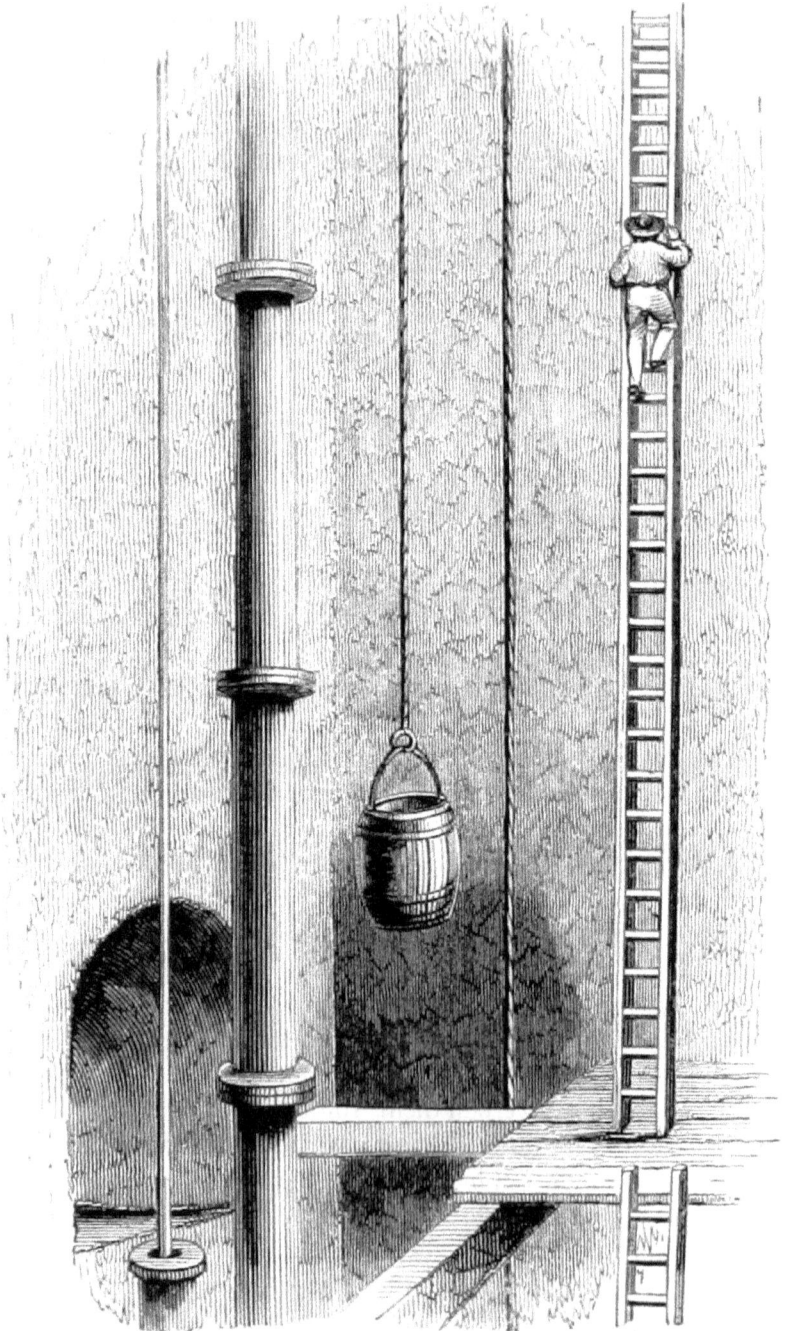

Descending a Cornish Mine

high for the wretched accommodation afforded them. Many of them have left their families in the west, and cannot remove them, owing to the scarcity of cottages near Liskeard. They are consequently saddled with the expense of two establishments. In addition to this they have not the advantage of allotments of ground, so common in the west, in cultivating which they could employ their leisure time, of which the miner has a great deal. All these disadvantages have necessitated a higher scale of wages in the east than in the west.

The wages, or earnings, are paid once a month; but, to keep the miners and their families going, a portion is paid on account once a fortnight. This is called their "subsist," or more commonly "stist." This is objected to by some, as tending to make men lazy. Where the farthing-pitch system is in vogue, it works very badly. In such case the men are not entitled to anything till the end of the first two months, and they do not get their subsist until a fortnight before the day on which they are entitled to their earnings. The consequence is, that they work for six weeks without receiving anything. They are thus driven by their circumstances to go into debt with the retail dealers for the necessaries of life. Once in debt, it is very difficult for them to get out of it, and reckless habits frequently supervene. The wages paid to the surface workers are 8d. a day to women, and from 4d. to 6d. a day to boys and girls. At Caradon the women had, a short time ago, 1s. 3d. a day, but their wages have since been reduced to 1s.

Connected with almost every mine is a sick club, or benefit society of some kind or other. For the payment of 6d. a week to the club, a miner, when ill, or labouring under the consequences of an accident, has the benefit of good medical attendance. If he pays 1s. 3d. a week, he is entitled to such attendance for his family as well as himself, in addition to which he gets a certain weekly allowance, if he is detained from work by illness or an accident. The miners have no option as regards these clubs, the adventurers requiring them to join them. Indeed, a deduction on this account is made from their earnings. There is also a forge attached to each mine, at which the tools used by the miners are sharpened and repaired. For such work as they may have had done at the forge a deduction is also made on pay day. There is likewise the barber of the mine, who shaves the men, another deduction being made on this account. Further deductions are made for the candles, gunpowder, and so forth, which they may use when at work below. The number and variety of their deductions may be taken from the following list, which I find in an account now before me:—Subsist and barber, doctor and club, candles, powder, hilts, fuse, rope, cans, nails, shovels, locks, paper, barrows, canvass, smith cost, trimming, wheeling, dressing and labour, tonnage, tramming down, stems, and spales.

One of the greatest evils attending the employment of the miner is the speculative character which it assumes. His whole life is spent in a species of gambling. If his "take," as he calls the proceeds of his pitch, is good, he may make £100 in a month; but if he has a series of bad takes, he may work for months without earning anything—nay, more than this, he may all the time be getting in debt, not only with tradesmen, but with the adventurers, for the supply of such articles as he uses in mining, and the value of which is deducted from his earnings. It is the fitful character of his earnings that justifies the remark made to me by one very competent to decide, that where one hears of a tributer having 14s. or 15s. a week, it is seldom that he can be put down as so well off as an agricultural labourer with constant work at 10s. When men get inured to it they cling with tenacity to a life of excitement, and such is the life of the tributer. Considering its many disadvantages—the length of time for which it may be worse than unremunerative, and the inroads which it makes upon health—the wonder is that it is pursued at all. The counterbalancing element to all these acknowledged drawbacks, in the tributer's mind, is the great gain that is sometimes made. The circumstances under which the miners thus earn and receive their money impart a general recklessness to their character. Some of them have sufficient forethought and self-control to lay by in their day of prosperity what enables them to meet without difficulty a series of unlucky adventures. But the bulk of them are too apt to spend their money as fast as they get it—sometimes revelling in abundance, and at others suffering the very extreme of privation. As a class, they would be much better off if regular and fixed wages could be given them; but, owing to the difficulties attending the supervision of work in the mines, such a course is deemed impracticable.

The captains must be shrewd, active men, well acquainted with the practice of mining, for the miners are sometimes inclined to be lazy, and at others to play tricks. The amount of work done by the tutman is generally easily ascertained by the quantity of stuff brought to the surface. But if he is not well watched, he is apt to pretend that the ground offers more impediments than were anticipated, with a view to a favourable modification of his bargain. The tributers are also prone to make very unfavourable representations of their pitches, in order, if possible, to raise the amount of their tribute. Thus, they will send to the surface the poorest part of the lode, representing it as the best, as evidence that their complaint is well grounded. To counteract such devices the captains must be constantly on the look out. There is a trick called "kitting," to which the tributers sometimes resort. When a pitch supposed to be bad is taken at a high rate of tribute, say 13s., and one supposed to be good at a low rate, say 5s., they are apt to transfer a portion of the ore of the rich pitch to the poor one, when it is sent to the surface, as coming from the poor pitch, and the high rate of tribute, instead of the low rate, is paid upon it. The gain by this is divided amongst those concerned in the imposition.

The house accommodation of the miners is, generally speaking, of a very inferior description. It is worse in the eastern mining districts than in those of the west. In the extreme east, the evil is being partially remedied by the liberal policy pursued on the Bedford estates. Until lately, it was not generally supposed that there was much overcrowding in the midland districts. But many startling revelations in respect to this have recently been made by the house-to-house visitation of the different local boards of health. Taking Redruth as a centre, and describing around it a circle with a radius of five miles, there will be found a larger proportion of good cottages amongst the tenements occupied by the miners than elsewhere in the county. Many of these, generally the best of them, have been built by the miners themselves—that is to say, by such of them as have been provident enough to save money for the purpose. The worst tenements in this district are the older cottages, which can be easily distinguished from the others by their mouldy walls, small windows, and thatched roofs. Many of the modern cottages are well built, being two stories high and well lighted. They are usually covered with slate. Their position, too, is better selected, with a view to health, than has been that of the older cottages. But the advantages of room and good position are in too many instances counterbalanced by the numbers which crowd into the best of the cottages as well as the worst. I was told by a member of the local board of health for Camborne that he knew of a case in which fourteen slept in one room, some of them being members of the family, and the rest lodgers in the house. On my asking him how many beds they had to sleep on, his reply was that "the room was all bed." The rent generally paid for a cottage is from £3 to £4, exclusive of potato ground. Such as build for themselves can procure a good stone cottage, with four rooms, for from £40 to £50. They have generally a piece of ground attached to it, to occupy them during their spare time. Many such houses have been built by the miners in the neighbourhood of Penzance. Of these, numbers are now deserted and tenantless, their owners having emigrated, some with and others without their families. So anxious were the men to get away, that they have in many cases left the houses which they themselves have put up at their own sole cost.

The miners, as a class, sacrifice, to a great extent, their domestic comforts to their inordinate love of dress. This failing has long characterized them, but within the last few years it has greatly increased. The increase is attributable to the greater ease with which they now procure the materials for dress—"tallymen," or peripatetic dealers, perambulating the country in all directions, selling to them goods at high prices, but taking payment by weekly or monthly instalments. To see the miners, both men and women, at church on a Sunday, or enjoying themselves at a fair at Redruth, one would not suppose that there was much distress of any kind amongst them. Most of the men are attired in fine broad cloth, whilst the women parade their finery. But many who come out covered with broad cloth, or arrayed in flaunting flounces, emerge from holes and dens more resembling pig-styes than human abodes.

I was not prepared to find the diet of the miner so poor as it generally is. I have seen many instances, in all the mining districts of Cornwall, of families living in great comfort, having a good and spacious house to live in, and a sufficiency of nourishing food to consume. The children, too, in such cases, are generally sent regularly to school. But, in all these cases, I found that the husband was a prudent saving man, who kept his small account at the savings bank, and that the wife was a good manager, thrifty, and attentive to her household duties. Much depends upon management. Some families get on very comfortably on 50s. a month, with which others cannot manage to escape great privation. The love of dress greatly affects the miner's diet. This is frequently but a coarse unleavened paste, with, perhaps, a few pieces of turnip, or an apple or two enveloped in it. Sometimes he has neither the turnip nor the apple in it, having nothing but the heavy paste to eat. Occasionally it is sweetened with a few raisins or currants. Numbers of them seldom taste meat; indeed, many have told me that they have been for weeks together without partaking of it. In many such cases, however, their own improvidence is chiefly to blame. Such as work under ground during the day take their pasties with them to the mines. If they are at work not far from the surface, they ascend about the dinner hour, and have the pasties heated for them at the forge. When they are too far below to do this they eat them cold. The surface workers have half an hour generally allowed them for dinner. Those underground eat when they please.

As has been shown to have been the case with the fisher, the loss of the potato has also been a great blow to the miner. Whether a tutman or a tributer, he generally works but about eight hours a day, and has thus a great deal of spare time on hand. It is, in more respects than one, of the utmost importance that this spare time should be well employed. So long as the potato succeeded, the spare time of the miner was, in perhaps the majority of instances, well employed. If he had not a garden attached to his house, he generally rented a piece of ground, which he applied to the production of potatoes and other vegetables. These holdings varied from an acre to two or three acres of land, and were generally leased to him for three lives. In some districts, where the land had not been cultivated before, he would have a piece of waste land and enclose it, and thus reduce it to cultivation. A great deal of the surface of Cornwall has been thus reclaimed, and a large proportion of Lord Falmouth's present rental is derived from land originally reduced by the miner. The miner was thus always secure of a good supply of potatoes and other vegetables, for the climate of Cornwall is admirably adapted for the production of vegetables of almost all kinds. The quantity of potatoes which he produced was frequently not only sufficient for the consumption of his family, but also for the feeding of one or two pigs. When he killed his pig, which he generally did about Christmas, he would sell enough of it to enable him to buy another young pig or two, sufficient being still left to supply some animal food to his family. When he killed two pigs, which was not unusual, he would sell enough to enable him not only to buy two other young pigs for the succeeding year, but also to pay the rent of his plot of ground, so that the remainder of the pork, and the potatoes and other vegetables which he had for the use of his family, were all so much clear profit to him. The extent to which this enhanced both his own and his family's comforts may be easily imagined. In addition to the employment of his own spare time, it also gave employment to his wife and children. The chief advantage of this was, that, in many cases, it enabled the parents to send the children for some part of the day to school. But it was also advantageous to the adventurers and the public. The miner, when certain of a sufficient supply of potatoes and other vegetables to fall back upon, in case of a temporary suspension of his money receipts, was far more adventurous in prosecuting the discovery of new lodes. A very high rate of tribute is generally given in such cases, and miners have frequently thus realized their luckiest adventures. If, for instance, a miner had reason to believe that, in a certain place not yet worked, a lode existed which would pay for the working, he would offer to try his luck, at a tribute of, perhaps, 13s. in the pound. If his judgment was correct, for the month or two for which the arrangement lasted he would realize considerable profits, and establish for himself a claim to constant employment in the lode which by his enterprise and acumen he might thus add to those already worked by the adventurers. If he failed, he lost his time and his trouble; but still he was not destitute, inasmuch as he had his potatoes and other vegetables, and his pig or pigs, to fall back upon. He was not thus absolutely dependent from month to month for subsistence upon his money wages, as he is too generally at present. It is this dependence that prevents him now from taking his chance in this way, for, in the majority of cases, if he were to run the risk and fail, he would be rendered absolutely destitute by the loss of his time and the stoppage of his wages. It would be erroneous to suppose that the cultivation of the potato has been altogether abandoned. The prospect of its again succeeding, is likely to restore confidence in it, and it is probable that, in the course of a year or two, its cultivation will be as successful, and its consumption as great in Cornwall, as it has heretofore been. This will effect great changes for the better in the condition of the miner and his family.

I was so unfortunate as to stumble upon St. Just when all work was suspended in the parish. This I regretted, as I was anxious to witness the operations carried on in the stupendous mines situated in this district, whose shafts, as it were, overhang the sea, and whose levels project far beneath it. The annual feast of the patron saint of the parish was being observed when I visited it. This ceremony is common to all the western parishes of Cornwall. In this instance it commenced on the Sunday, when the religious part of the ceremony was performed. For the three following days the parish was the scene of a miniature carnival. From 75 to 100 bullocks were slain for the occasion, which gave about 5 lbs. of meat for every person—man, woman, and child— in the parish. Of course, during these days no work was done. Thursday would also be a *dies non*. On Friday some would return to work, but the great bulk would make a week of it. After this, the parish would return to labour and sobriety, and think no more of the saint until the next return of his festival.

The miners are by no means a long-lived class of men. Their employment is such that the strongest constitution will, ere long, feel its pernicious influence, and break down before it. There are diseases peculiar to their work, which only a small proportion of the miners escape, provided they continue at it for several years. The two great exciting causes of disease are impure air and climbing the ladders. The miners when at work have occasionally to encounter all kinds of pernicious gases; but those most frequently met with are carbonic acid, sulphuretted hydrogen, and carburetted hydrogen. The first is the invariable product of respiration and combustion. Sometimes as many as 600 people will be at work at one and the same time in one and the same mine. The respiration of so many in a mine, never too well ventilated, must soon contaminate the atmosphere. Many mines, too, be it remembered, are never without large numbers of people in them. The quantity of gunpowder used is also another means of rendering the atmosphere impure. There are two atmospheres which the miners dread—the "cold damps" and the "poor airs." Of the latter there is a modification known as the "hot poor air." They are constantly wet whilst at their work, and subject to great and sudden changes of temperature. At one moment they may be in a profuse perspiration, and at another subjected to a cold and chilling draught of air. From all these causes they are extremely liable to impaired respiration and fatal diseases of the chest. You can almost tell how long a miner has worked under ground from his pale and emaciated look. Some of them attain a green old age, but these are almost invariably such as have abandoned their under-ground employment after adhering to it for years. If they pursue it for fifteen or twenty years, the chances are that their average life will not much exceed thirty-eight years. Even without the impure atmosphere of the mines, the climbing of the ladders would of itself be sufficient to superinduce serious disorders of the heart and chest. The heart is in a state of high palpitation when the miner reaches the top of the shaft, whilst the lungs are in violent exercise. It is no wonder, seeing that sometimes they have to climb ladders four times the height of St. Paul's. Dilatation of the bronchial tubes is a disease very common to them. In some mines machines have been invented to supersede the necessity of this laborious mode of descending into and ascending from the mines. These machines, however, can only be used in perpendicular shafts. The want of space prevents me from here describing them. The miners are also liable to many accidents. They seldom fall down the shafts, most of the accidents which happen being the result of careless blasting. These are now greatly provided against by the use of the patent safety fuse.

The present generation of miners are deplorably deficient in education. The number of those who can read or write is very small. But few of the rising generation attend any school but the Sunday school; and a large proportion do not attend even that. There are schools enough in the neighbourhood of the mines; but the children are in most cases put to work as soon as they are able to earn anything. At the Caradon mines I was informed that not one-half of the children could write, whilst not much more than four-fifths of them could read, even imperfectly.

The mining population of Cornwall is generally of the Methodist persuasion. In many of the mines the captains are their preachers. Many of themselves are office-bearers in their respective churches, which has a great effect in keeping the whole body in order. They attend church very regularly. I regret, however, to say that I did not hear the best account of the morals of the miners. Early marriages are very common with them. The number of petty crimes is very great, particularly in the west, but fluctuates very much. It is generally greatest after orgies such as I witnessed at St. Just.

I have been compelled, by want of space, to hurry over much on which I could have greatly enlarged. There are other topics—such as the "ticketing system," by which the ore is disposed of to the smelters—to which I might have adverted, had space permitted, bearing as they do, more or less, upon the condition of the labourer in the mines. But I must postpone these for the present.

On the whole, I do not regard the condition of the miner as so good as that of the fisherman. The fitful nature of his earnings, and the gambling tendencies of his employment, beget, in too many instances, reckless and extravagant habits, which reduce him, as regards physical comfort, to the level of the agricultural labourer, although his yearly receipts may be double those of the man employed in the fields.

Although not exactly miners, I cannot conclude this letter without a passing allusion to the workers in the china-clay pits between Bodmin and St. Austle. The clay, which they extract from the wild district between these two points, is disintegrated granite. They procure it by washing from the pits, and send it off to the potteries in blocks as white as snow. The streams of the district are of the colour of milk, from the washings which flow into them. As a class, the people who prepare the clay are not well off. They are a cleanly set, but their wages are generally low; whilst the house accommodation of two-thirds of them may be inferred from their miserable huts, which the traveller perceives strewn over the heathy plain.

The Morning Chronicle, Saturday, November 24, 1849.

PRICES AND WAGES.

———◆———

To the EDITOR of the MORNING CHRONICLE.

Sir—I earnestly wish that all who still, against all facts and reason, believe that wages rise and fall with prices, would attend to the following statement in the interesting communication on Labour and the Poor, in your paper of Saturday:—

"I asked him (a Cornish labourer) in what respect he thought the condition of the labourer better than it was formerly? He said that he thought it improved as regarded his diet and clothing. While wages had declined but little, the price of most things had gone greatly down. Formerly, when the farmers had got high prices for corn, the labourer had to pay a high duty on salt—a serious consideration with him, if he contemplated keeping a pig for his own use. He had also to pay double and sometimes treble what he now paid for bread."

Here is a simple but important announcement. I should like to ask, what are we to think of the conduct of those who prevented this poor man from making the most of his labour? Who compelled him to take less food for it than he might have fairly got? And who thus heightened their rents at his cost? All that I can say in excuse of them is, that they were not guilty of *intentional* robbery. They laboured under the amazing hallucination that they were benefiting him and such as him. Their conduct, however, if not intentionally, was yet essentially robbery and murder.

The case cited by your Correspondent is just one proof of the undeniable truth that the late great fall of prices has been attended by no proportionate fall of wages, which are, therefore, able to procure to the labouring man a bountifully increased share of the blessings of nature and providence. That this is the case within my own sphere of observation is too plain to be doubted. I have the charge of an entirely rural parish, the whole working population of which seem most grateful to God for the change in their condition made by Free-trade. That change simply is, that while their wages are the same as before, provisions are immensely cheaper. There is never a day that I do not both hear and give cordial congratulations on this result. I do not say that agricultural capitalists are entirely reconciled to it. I am sorry that they are not. They have been accustomed to artificial, excessive, and unjust prices, which they reluctantly lose. I would beseech them, however, to reflect that they pay no more for British manufactures than their fair worth in the market of the world, and that therefore they ought, with a good grace, to submit to sell their corn on the same terms. Exacting a higher price, they inflict an injustice on purchasers.

I enclose my card, and am, sir, your obedient servant,

A PARISH CLERGYMAN.

The Morning Chronicle, Monday, November 26, 1849.

At the request of several correspondents, we add that Post-office orders may be addressed to Mr. David Jones, *Morning Chronicle* Office, 332, Strand.

The Morning Chronicle, Tuesday, November 27, 1849.

To THE EDITOR OF THE MORNING CHRONICLE.

SIR—In accordance with my request that you would mention a name in which Post-office orders might be filled up by those at a distance, disposed to send contributions in aid of your benevolent and meritorious exertions on behalf of "Labour and the Poor," I now enclose an order for 5*l.*, filled up in the name pointed out.

I have taken in *The Morning Chronicle* as my daily paper for many years; although my views on all subjects are not in perfect unison with those I find there; this is not necessary, or to be expected; for when we embark on the *mare magnum* of politics or political economy, collision of opinion tends to ultimate good by eliciting truth. Happily, however, on the subject under consideration, there cannot be two opinions where the heart is in the right place. The good feeling and kind sympathy of your Commissioner will vibrate through the length and breadth of the land, as already appears from the numerous letters of approbation and contribution daily filling your columns. This subject should not be viewed only through the medium of benevolence, but, as hinted in your paper, we should not lose sight of the troublesome consequences that may arise out of the extension and continuance of sufferings so properly alluded to by your Correspondent.

Those who are surrounded with the comforts and superfluities of life will learn from your columns the masses who are suffering under the pressure of opposite circumstances, and the risk of pushing them on to despondency or despair. A people may be long kept in ignorance and darkness, but once let the light in upon them and they cannot be brought back to the same state. I rejoice to observe, from the numerous communications in your paper, that the subject is exciting a lively interest in all directions.

The enclosed Post-office order for 5*l.* I wish placed in the hands of your compassionate Commissioner, to be distributed at his discretion, when wending his weary way among the dwellings of the destitute and helpless—like the good Samaritan, pouring in oil and wine, while priests and Levites pass by on the other side.

I have been struck by a statement made by your Commissioner, in one of his letters, of the miserable weekly pittance of salt butter, a prime necessary of life with the poor, which a rural labourer could afford his family. On this article there is a duty of ten shillings a hundredweight: the cost of such as is used by the poor may be about fifty or sixty shillings. There is also a heavy duty on cheese. By such unjust and oppressive taxation on the immediate necessaries of life, the price of the subsistence of the poor is enhanced, so that they can scarcely keep themselves in life; and we thereby increase the intolerable and constantly-accumulating burden of the poor-rates. Again, Government have very properly been expending large sums on boards of health and sanitary commissions, for investigating the causes, and for suggesting measures to prevent or alleviate the desolating ravages of such epidemic and contagious diseases as cholera and typhus fever. The chief result of their reports is the recommendation of cleanliness of every description, both personal and domestic; and yet we have a heavy tax on soap of 14s. a hundredweight—fully a third of the present price, the principal agent of domestic and personal cleanliness. This tax, then, being the enemy of cleanliness, is the ally of epidemic and infectious diseases. No Chancellor of the Exchequer will venture to say the resources of the country are so exhausted that no substitute (if any is necessary) can be found. As the protection of property is a main cause of our expenditure, in fairness it ought to bear the chief burden.

I am, sir, yours,

GEORGE M^cCALLUM.

India-street, Edinburgh, Nov. 24.

LABOUR AND THE POOR.

—◆—

THE RURAL DISTRICTS.

[FROM OUR SPECIAL CORRESPONDENT.]

CONDITION OF THE LABOURER IN DORSET.

Letter XII.

Dorset has a bad name as regards the condition of the labourer. Whether or not it deserves its unenviable pre-eminence in this respect, the reader may be able to judge from what follows:—

In prosecuting my inquiries in this county, I selected three different centres of observation—Wareham, Blandford, and Shaftesbury. I chose the first because, the district around it not being exclusively agricultural, wages are materially affected by the presence of other occupations, which give rise to a considerable demand for labour. The second I took as being the centre of a purely agricultural region, where the rural labourer might be seen in what may be regarded as his normal condition; and the third, as being not only contiguous to an agricultural district, but also on the borders of Wiltshire, with which county I was anxious to compare Dorset, as I have frequently been told that "bad as we are here, we are not quite so bad as they are in Wilts."

The district extending for many miles around Wareham is of a very varied character. To the eastward it has the large and irregular sheet of water known as Poole Harbour, whilst in all other directions it is surrounded with heath. In some directions the waste extends much further than in others. Westward, towards Dorchester, and along the line of railway, it is only here and there broken by arable tracts. Towards Bere, it extends in a north-westerly direction to a depth of fully five miles. Due north, on the way to Blandford, it is sooner penetrated and left behind; whilst towards Wimborne, in the north-east, it extends, with but little interruption, to the borders of the county. Going to the south from Wareham, the heath, which is here very boggy, extends nearly to Corfe Castle, a distance of about four miles—the belt of land intervening between the latter place and the sea being more or less arable, and in some places highly cultivated.

Taking a radius of about eight miles, and describing therewith a circle round Wareham as a centre, the greater portion of the tract embraced within the circumference would be water and waste.

In a district poor as this is, in an agricultural point of view, it might naturally be supposed that wages were low, and that the condition of the labourer was wretched in an equal degree. But such is not the case, wages in the district in question being comparatively high, and the physical condition of the labourer, in some respects, superior to what it is in the more purely agricultural tracts of the county. This is accounted for by the fact that there are other outlets for labour than the farms in the neighbourhood of Wareham.

The chief of these is to be found in the clay-pits, which lie immediately south of the town. These give rise to some trade on the Frome, between Wareham and Poole, affording occupation to a considerable number of bargemen. There are also the stone quarries at Swanage, which act as an outlet, whilst numbers find employment in connection with the improvements which are being effected by Lord Eldon in the neighbourhood of Encombe.

The largest clay works in the kingdom are to be found here. They are in the hands of three different firms, the chief of which is that of the Messrs. Pike, and they give employment to from four to five hundred men. The clay extracted is of a totally different character from that produced by the China clay pits between Bodmin and St. Austle, in Cornwall. It is coarse, as compared with that; being such as is used in the manufacture of common stoneware. It is not worked previously to exportation to the potteries, being sent thither in bulk, just as it is extracted from the pits. The property on which the clay veins are found belongs chiefly to Lord Rivers and Mr. Calcraft, formerly member for the county. When a vein of clay is discovered, the parties wishing to work it obtain a lease of the ground from the proprietor, to whom a certain rent is guaranteed. In consideration of this rent, however, the lessees are not permitted to extract beyond a certain maximum amount of clay. If they do extract more during the year, the land is entitled to a tribute of 2s. per ton upon the excess.

The lease being obtained, the first thing to be done towards the working of the vein is the removal of the "heading"—which designation is applied to the superincumbent stratum of earth or gravel. This is done by a "party" of excavators, who engage to remove it at so much for the cubic yard. Sometimes the clay is but a few feet beneath the surface, at others it may be upwards of a hundred. Other things being equal, the deeper it is, the adventure is, of course, all the less profitable. Some veins, which are near the surface, lie parallel to it, and are easily worked. Others, although near the surface at one end, dip so rapidly that the expense of working them causes them sometimes to be abandoned before they are exhausted.

The heading being removed, the vein is ready for working, which is also done by parties, each party consisting of 6, 7, 8, or more individuals. They work together, their engagement being to extract the clay at so much per cubic yard. They can thus earn less or more during the week, according to their diligence and industry. The work is such as to require those engaging in it to be strong and healthy men. The clay is, as it were, quarried out of the pits. The instrument chiefly employed to detach it in blocks from the mass, is a narrow but heavy spade, weighing from 17 to 20 lbs. The men stand almost erect as they strike the spade into the clay, which they thus cut into strips, about a foot wide, to the depth of the blade of the spade. They then cut it transversely, the transverse cuts being about a foot and a half apart; after which the different blocks thus formed are easily detached, one after another, from the mass. The process of cutting is facilitated by water being poured into the cuts, as the men proceed with them, the object of which is simply to ease the work, by preventing the spade from sticking firmly in the clay, when forcibly driven into it. The water is supplied by boys, who earn each about half the wages of a man. The blocks, when detached, are put into railway trucks, in which they are dragged, by means of an inclined plane, worked by horse power, out of the pits. They are then despatched in the same trucks to the port of Wareham, three miles distant, by railway—the trucks descending the line, which has a regular declination towards the harbour, by their own weight. On reaching the port, they are shipped in barges to Poole, where again they are shipped in larger vessels for Liverpool. When the clay is good and the vein deep, the cheapest process of working is by mining it. A perpendicular shaft is driven until the clay is reached, when the vein is worked in what are called "lanes." In Cornwall they would be termed levels. It is by the weight, and not the bulk, that the miners are paid—receiving so much a ton for what they raise. Their work being of a more dangerous description, their earnings are generally higher than those of the men engaged in the pits.

The nature of the arrangement between them is such that, beyond seeing that the work is not wholly neglected, the employers exercise little or no control over the men employed. They lay down some general rules, which must be observed by all, such as that no liquor shall be taken to the works, for the infraction of which they invariably discharge the transgressor. But the men may choose their own hours of working, provided they supply their employers with sufficient produce to meet the demand upon them. I have known work in the mines suspended at two o'clock. The wages are all paid weekly, the accounts being kept with the different parties at work. According to the quantity of work done, the sum earned is handed over to the head of the party, who divides it with his comrades in proportion to the amount of work done by each. As each works for all, and all for each, they keep a sharp look-out upon each other when actually at work. The proportion which each is to receive is, therefore, entirely regulated by the time for which he has been at work during the week. If he has been absent for a day, half a day, or two days, a deduction *pro tanto* is made from his share of the common earnings. I was very courteously permitted by the Messrs. Pike to inspect their books, and found that, whilst the miners generally earned from a pound to a guinea a week, the pitmen averaged sometimes from 3s. to 3s. 6d., and at others from 2s. 6d. to 3s. per day. The average earnings of the latter were from 2s. 6d. to 2s. 9d. a day. It is obvious how so large a demand for a particular species of labour at so high a price must affect the general rate of wages in the district.

To the stone-works at Swanage I shall have occasion hereafter to refer. These, together with Lord Eldon's improvements, have also a favourable effect upon wages in the neighbourhood of Wareham. The latter have not benefited the district as much as they might have done, inasmuch as they are being partly effected by imported labour. They have, nevertheless, afforded considerable employment to the resident population in the neighbourhood of Encombe, the only drawback to which is, that it has been, to some extent, casual instead of continuous. The works are in the hands of contractors, who, of course, look less to the employment of the labour of the district than to procuring the labour most adapted to their purposes.

The bargemen employed in carrying the clay from Wareham to Poole get 1s. a ton for the quantity carried. They have not steady employment, but their wages, when they earn them, are good, and exhibit a comparatively high average throughout the year.

It is by the demand for labour to which these different occupations give rise, that the value of agricultural labour is favourably affected in the neighbourhood of Wareham. But, even here, the wages of the farm labourer are, after all, as already said, only comparatively high. Except to carters, who receive 9s., the *maximum* paid is only 8s. a week. With this some of them, but not all, have a free house. In most cases they have their fuel in addition. This consists of turf, which they themselves cut, but which is carted to their houses by the farmers, who claim the ashes as sufficient compensation for their trouble, which is very little, seeing that the heath whence the turf is cut is generally hard by the labourer's hut. I regret to say that this is the most favourable report which I have to make as regards the wages and condition of the day-labourer on the farm in Dorset. Standing on this, then, as the highest point in the scene, the reader will have to contemplate a dreary level of misery and privation around him.

In inquiring into the condition of the labourer in the neighbour-hood of Wareham, I first directed my attention to the district ly-ing immediately south of the town, known as the Isle of Purbeck. This district varies much in its surface and general character, some of it being high and fertile, and other portions low, heathy, and ir-reclaimable. Close to the town, and between it and the arm of the sea into which the Frome discharges itself, a portion of the low-lying lands has been reclaimed from the waste, and now extends in one dreary and monotonous level of damp meadow land. The greater pro-portion of its surface is but little elevated above high water mark, and during the night it is generally overspread with noxious malaria, which commences to rise from it with the setting of almost every sun. Yet in this ungenial spot are several cottages, containing in all nearly 100 human beings. I examined several of them, and will describe a few, taking their inmates as I found them, bargemen, claypit men, and farm labourers together.

The first that I visited was a cottage occupied by a family of the name of Galton. The family consists of six persons—the father and mother, a son, and two daughters, and a grandchild, the illegitimate offspring of one of the daughters. When I entered, the only persons at home were the mother and the younger daughter. The mother in-formed me that her husband had steady work from Farmer Boyt, at 8s. a week, with the cottage free, and turf carried in. On the whole, the wages might be taken as amounting to about 9s. 6d. a week. They kept a pig, which they intended to kill at Christmas, and to which they looked as the only animal food which they were likely to have for the season. An open ditch, which served as a sluggish drain for the meadow, after touching one of the back corners of the house, which was a thatched mud hut, turned at a right angle, and extended along the back of it, right under the wall. The character of this ditch was indicated by the vegetation which thickly incrusted its stagnant contents. A little in front was another ditch, filthy in the extreme, though not quite so bad as the other. In front of the house was an ash-heap, where it would remain until the farmer chose to carry it away. The pigstye was behind, leaning against the wall of the fuel-house, which formed part of the building. So low was the hovel situated, that whenever it rained heavily it was completely inundated. Some time ago, after a heavy thunder-storm, the intrusive waters took possession of the whole floor, invaded the cupboard of the dresser, and rose, in an inner room, "half way up the legs of the bed." It was a long time afterwards ere the house got dry—indeed, it was not thoroughly so ere it was again flooded. It was about three years since the family had entered the house. They had all had ague shortly after doing so. The youngest daughter, the one then at home, had never been rid of it. Her sunken cheek, languid motions, and jaundiced complexion, all but too well attested the presence of the disease. The smells, I was further told, were sometimes very bad, but they were thankful that they were neither so numerous nor so offensive as those to which they had been accustomed at Newton, some miles off, where they formerly lived. There they had occupied a house from which the ague was never absent. Such was the domicile which they got rent-free, instead of an extra shilling in the shape of money-wages. But had they had two extra shillings, the poor creatures knew not where to get a better house, for there was none vacant in the district.

My next visit was to a hut but a few yards removed from that just described. It was one of a row consisting of four, being all thatched, and the crumbling walls constructed of mud and brick. In front of the door was a small close porch entered from the side. From this porch I stepped into the hut, in doing which I had to descend a step. The situation was as low and damp as that of the other cottage, nor was the house improved in this respect by the step down which had to be taken to gain the floor. There were but two rooms, one below and one above, which, as usual, served as the sleeping apartment. The lower room was dingy in the extreme, its dimensions scarcely exceeding 12 feet by 10. The floor was composed of small, rough, and irregular flags, and so close were the two floors together, that I had barely room to stand erect, without my hat, between the beams supporting the upper one. The tenant's name was Stockley, a common name in these parts.

He was 6 feet 2 inches in height, and had never stood erect in his own house. There was not a corner of it in which he could do so. All the wood-work was blackened with smoke, and clammy with moisture. The wall was bulging in on all sides, and seemed scarcely capable of supporting the crazy roof. The family consisted of seven—viz., the father and mother, and five children, all boys. The eldest boy was 16 years of age, and worked with Farmer Boyt, at 3s. a week. The second son was earning 4s. a week at the clay-pits. Both of them could read a little, but the second only could write—that is to say, he could write his own name. They all slept in the apartment upstairs. It contained two bedsteads, in addition to which a bed was made on the floor. One corner of the sleeping-room had to be avoided, on account of the floor having given way; it hung partly down into the lower room, so that the weight of a child almost would have brought it down altogether. About the middle of the floor the rents were so large, that I could see almost the whole of the sleeping-room through them. But the most extraordinary feature connected with this house was the provision made by the inmates for baling the water out, when the hut happened to be flooded by it. For this purpose, three of the flags were kept movable. I desired them to be lifted, and on their being so, discovered under each a large hole scooped out in the clay, each hole capable of containing about a gallon. When the water began to rise on the floor, which was not unfrequently the case, to a height which threatened to extinguish the fire, these flags were raised and the intrusive flood was drained into the holes in question. From these it was easily baled out by means of a tin dish. But for this device, the floor would be frequently several inches under water. When the water subsided the flags were replaced, not to be removed again until the next heavy rain should be followed by a tide within the dwelling. One of the three holes, which was under the only table in the house, was deeper than the others, and had always more or less water in it. But for this, the floor would never be dry. It was very damp when I saw it, but Mrs. Stockley called it dry. For this wretched den no less than £3 a year are paid as rent to Mr. Denis Brown, of Wareham. There is much, however, which might be done to it to render it more comfortable than it is. As it now stands, the whole fabric is scarcely worth one year's rent paid for it. I inquired why the family stayed in such a hole, and was informed that they had no alternative but to do so, as it was the only house they could get "convenient to their work." The ague was seldom out of it. Both father and mother had it on first taking the house, and not a year passed without some of the children being for a time stricken down by it. The youngest was just recovering from a severe attack of the small-pox. The mother was still annually attacked by premonitory symptoms of ague, but she was now accustomed to the disease, and stifled it at once by the use of active remedies. The other three houses of the row were somewhat larger and drier than this; but they, too, were damp, dark, filthy, and unwholesome. The whole row was not much more than fifty feet long—it contained in all eight rooms, and accommodated twenty-three people. They all slept in the roof of their respective domiciles, so that if the whole roof were thrown into one elongated chamber, and the occupants of the four houses lay side by side across the floor, each would have a strip of little more than two feet wide; in other words, they could scarcely so lie without touching each other. Distributed as they were, each sleeping room averaged about six occupants.

I found most of the denizens of this marshy and unwholesome plain in receipt of very good wages. But few of them were farm labourers, the majority being either bargemen or clay-pit workers. Stockley wrought in the pits, and his earnings averaged about 14s. a week. Two of his sons, as already shown, earned between them 7s., so that the united earnings of the family amounted to a guinea a week. Others, both bargemen and claymen, were in receipt of equally high earnings, and yet they did not appear to be a whit more comfortable than the Galton family, whose whole support was the 8s. a week earned on the farm. Mrs. Stockley complained that she and her family seldom tasted meat, and so did Mrs. Galton. The Stockleys paid rent, it is true, whilst the Galtons did not. But after deducting their rent, the earnings of the Stockleys were more than double those of the Galtons, whilst there was but one child more in the family. If the seven Stockleys were miserable on a pound a week, what must the six Galtons have been on 8s.? I confess it puzzled me at first to ascertain how it was that the one could not make 2s. go farther than the other made 1s. go. I requested Mrs. Stockley to inform me how the weekly earnings were spent. She soon disposed of the 7s. earned by the boys, by saying that they consumed all they got, and frequently more than they got. They worked hard, and fared, at least, as the men did. There was then the cost of their clothes and their shoes, of which they had but a scanty stock, it was true, but still more than would have fallen to their lot had they been earning nothing for themselves. But supposing the boys to be self-subsisting and no more, there were still the father's earnings, 14s., for the maintenance of the remaining five of the family. Taking the rent out of this, it would leave about 12s. 9d. as the fund for the support of five. But still for the support of the six Galtons there were but 8s. a week, and yet the Galtons did not seem to be more wretched than their neighbours. The secret by and by came out. The Galtons had 8s. a week steadily throughout the year, whilst the greater incomings of the Stockleys were casual and fitful. Stockley's employment was tolerably constant, but Galton's was steady and uninterrupted. The consequence was, that Mrs. Galton could, from week to week, take the exact measure of her means, and manage accordingly. Not so with Mrs. Stockley. The earnings of one week were no necessary indication of what those of the next week might be. In both cases the earnings of each week went as they came. But in the one case each week brought with it the same measure of comforts as the preceding one; whereas in the other, the comparative abundance of one week might be followed by the privation of the next.

"The working people can't stand an uncertainty," said a friend to me, who drew my attention to this point as intimately connected with the general condition of the labourer. Except in the case of purely agricultural labour, casual employment is generally accompanied by high wages. A man thus casually employed may average more per week throughout the year than the man having steady work, at low wages. But it is generally found that the former is frequently worse off than the latter. Nothing can better illustrate this than the case of the bargemen who ply their craft between Wareham and Poole. When engaged, they receive very good remuneration for their work. The barges do not belong to them, but they work them at so much per ton of goods actually carried. Their employment is not very constant, but they make good wages when they are engaged. Yet there is no set of men in the district more miserably off as a class than these very men. The Messrs. Pike have recently employed thirteen of them in manning a few barges connected with their clay works. Since the beginning of the year these thirteen have earned amongst them no less than £700. One of them, who was in a better situation than the rest, and whose earnings were frequently considerably over £1 per week, was some time ago detained by illness from his work. He had not been laid up a week ere he sent a begging letter to his employers. And so with most of them. If they are out of work for a few days, they wend their way to the union for relief. Their superior earnings avail them not, coming fitfully as they do—even though they come with sufficient frequency to give them a comparatively high average throughout the year.

None are more convinced than the poor themselves of the evils consequent upon uncertain employment and irregular wages. They are aware of their want of self-control, and some of them, more prudent than the rest, take measures to prevent their defect in this respect from being injurious to their families. Some of them who drink beer at their work, prefer buying it in small quantities, as they require it, to the cheaper course of laying in a large quantity at a time. Their reason for so doing is, that if they adopted the latter course, what they laid in would all be consumed at once.

The point to which I next bent my course was the village of Corfe Castle, once a parliamentary borough, returning two members to Parliament. It lies about four miles to the south of Wareham, immediately beyond the clay pits, and on the borders of the agricultural district stretching between them and the sea. On my way thither I passed through the village of Stoborough, about half a mile from Wareham. To do justice to the filthy aggregate of human dwellings passing under that name, is scarcely possible. There are hardly half a dozen houses in it fit to be inhabited, and yet almost every hovel swarms with more than its proper complement of inmates. Here, too, you have the farm labourer, the bargeman, and the clayman together. Here, too, you have different scales of wages giving rise to but slight differences in condition. The street, on either side, is one line of dung and ash-heaps. The cottages, which seem to be centuries old, have a dangerous and tumble-down look about them; and, indeed, most of them would by this time have been among the things that were, but for the stout brick buttresses which have recently been built against the walls for their support. There is a sink, with a light iron grating over it, before most of the doors, from which odours ascend, in hot or moist weather, of no very desirable kind. Notwithstanding this, there is much stagnant surface-water generally in the street. At the upper end of the village the houses seem actually rotten with age. Before one is a filthy duck-pond full of slime and garbage. A little way further up is a horsepond, in which turnips are sometimes washed before being given to the cattle. When I was passing, a boy was paddling in the water in search of the turnip-tops, which he was to take home to be cooked and eaten.

About two miles beyond Stoborough my attention was attracted by a cottage which stood a little off the road to the right. On examining it, I found it inhabited by a family of the name of Keats. It had recently been a stable, from which, by means of a little patching, it had been converted into a house. The walls were of mud, here and there strengthened, where they had been giving way, by patches of brickwork. The family consisted of six persons. There were two rooms on the same floor, there being no room above. The rooms were so low that here again I was puzzled to stand erect. The ceiling of the common room was a perfect wreck. It had formerly consisted of a layer of coarse plaster, spread over reeds, by way of laths, which were attached to the slender beams which stretched from wall to wall. The plaster was in places gone, and so were the reeds, so that at different points the whole anatomy of the ceiling was exposed. The whole too, instead of stretching straight across, hung downwards, like so much loose canvas suspended over head. Off from this room was the bedroom. It was about 12 feet long by 8 wide, yet it contained three beds, and accommodated six people. One of them was a girl of twenty-one, another a boy of sixteen. For this house a rent of £1 1s. is paid. It is on the property of Mr. W. Bankes, which is at present under the management of Mr. George Bankes, M.P. for Dorset.

Leaving this, I proceeded direct to Corfe. The old castle completely overlooks the town from its isolated, and once commanding, position. The grim old pile is rich in historic associations. During the "Great Rebellion" it was heroically defended for some time by Lady Bankes against the hosts of Cromwell. The name of Bankes is yet associated with many objects in its neighbourhood; prominent amongst them is an old almshouse, which is at the entrance of the town, and at the very base of the castle. It is no longer an almshouse, being now filled with a colony of poor, wretched, and squalid-looking tenants. The house, which occupies two sides of a court, is of some size, and it contains from seventy to a hundred individuals. I believe that rent is paid for every room occupied in the house. There is a stable-yard in front of the court which it faces. It is also, as I was told, under the management of Mr. Bankes. A short time before I got there, a large heap of dung had been deposited close to the gate leading into the open court. It was still in a state of reeking fermentation, and the smell to which it gave rise was offensive in the last degree. When I entered the court I found the whole population assembled, and bordering on mutiny. The dung heap in question was the grievance which had excited their ire. They were quite sure that it would bring the cholera amongst them, if anything would ever bring it; whilst some of them assailed me as if I had put it there, although I was perfectly ignorant as to who was the delinquent. I vainly endeavoured to obtain information in the town as to how this charity had become transformed into private property.

Corfe is a small place, but the great proportion of the houses which it contains are of a very miserable description. This is particularly the case in the lanes and outskirts of the town. I visited several of the worst description. One of the first of these was inhabited by a family of the name of Grant. There were twelve of them in the house. They had a good deal of room below, but only two sleeping-rooms above. In these were four beds; and it was with no little satisfaction that Mrs. Grant told me that they did not "sleep thicker than three in a bed." The family was then suffering considerably, owing to the husband and father being out of employment.

The next which I inspected was occupied by a family of the name of Brett. It had four rooms, two below and two above. It was very low, and the upper rooms were wholly in the roof. One of the lower rooms would, as regards size, have afforded tolerable accommodation to a small family. The other was a mere closet, the floor of which was almost wholly covered by the bed which occupied it. A child lay sick in the miserable and mouldy chamber. I ascended to the upper chambers. They had been plastered and whitewashed many years ago, but were then wholly out of repair. The roof rose on either side from the very floor, so that the only perpendicular walls were at the two ends, if walls can be called so which have not known the perpendicular for years. Had the two rooms been thrown into one, they would not have afforded available room more than 16 feet long and 10 wide. In the centre of the room I could stand erect, but nowhere else. Indeed, they virtually formed but one room, the thin deal partition between them not rising to the roof, and the door through it being too small to fill the doorway. In several places whole yards of the lath and plaster seemed to be hanging to the rafters only by hairs. At the farthest end of the inner room I touched the plaster thus situated with my stick. Down instantly came a large quantity of black dust, which formed a tolerably sized heap upon the floor. I touched it in another place with a similar result, the rotten thatch and clay falling, in this instance, on one of the beds. I was told that when the wind blew very hard and shook the house they could sometimes pick up "near a barrow full" of this debris in the room. When it was wet, too, for any length of time, the rain percolated through the rotten thatch and yawning plaster. In these two rooms, or rather in this one room, were four beds, which were occupied by twelve people. The whole number inhabiting this wretched tenement was fourteen. There were two families in the house—two sisters, with their husbands and children. These made thirteen; the fourteenth being the brother of the two sisters, a man tolerably advanced in life. One of the sisters occupied, with her husband, the small room below. The other, with her husband and six children, together with the five children of her sister and her brother—that is to say, the uncle of all the children—occupied the upper room, or rooms, if they could be called so. Several of the children were grown up, and one, who was then in the house, was a girl of seventeen. In winter, notwithstanding the number occupying it, the upper room was often bitterly cold, and no wonder, for one of the end walls seemed to have parted company with the roof, and leant outwards considerably. In summer, again, it was perfectly stifling, the small windows not sufficing to ventilate the room. Had the walls been perpendicular on all sides, they thought that they might get on, but the space being contracted, from being entirely in the roof, they were sometimes nearly choked "with our own breaths," as they said. The rent paid for this hovel was 1s. a week. I asked them why they did not seek for a better house, but was told that they could not get one for love or money. The two sisters had been bred in the house themselves. They were also married there on the same day, and for want of cottage room in the neighbourhood the two married couples had to settle themselves in the mother's house. There they have since remained, and have between them reared up in the same place no less than twenty-two children. "Yes," said one of them, with considerable emotion, "I have brought up eleven, and so has my sister, and ne'er a fire-place have we had but that one," pointing to the huge but cheerless hearth. They could scarcely speak with patience of the den inhabited by them, to which they applied the most uncomplimentary epithets. I inquired if they would be willing to pay more rent for better accommodation. "I would live on a dry crust to be able to do it," said the one. "That we would, and gladly," echoed the other. I then ascertained that a promise had lately been made them that the house should be pulled down and a new one erected in its place, which they were to have. But it appeared that this project had been abandoned, and that they were then promised that the house would be repaired next spring. It seemed, however, that the agent had just informed them that it could yet stand for two or three years as it was; which was very problematical, to say the least of it. But for a cowhouse, in the shape of a "lean-to," one of the end walls would have been down long ago. The inmates complained bitterly of the unsteadiness of their work.

This house is, like many others near it, the property of the Rev. Mr. Bond, rector of the neighbouring parish of Steeple. Of the reverend gentleman I heard none express themselves but in terms of the highest respect. Testimony to his humanity and kindheartedness was universally and ungrudgingly given. Surely he cannot know the state in which some of his tenants live.

I visited another house of his—the last, proceeding southwards, of the town. It was a long low building, situated by the roadside, on a slight declivity, and had formerly been a public-house, under the biblical designation of "Noah's Ark." The upper end was the fuel house, the lower, which was about two-thirds of the whole, having been the "public." The whole was now let to a man of the name of Gover, who had divided the lower part into two tenements, one of which he occupied himself, having sublet the other to a family of the name of Hood. This family possessed only a narrow strip of the habitable part of the house, in the end adjoining the fuel house. From being higher than the rest, the floor of the fuel house had always been considerably elevated above that of the cottage. It is through the fuel house that the Hoods have access to the strip which has been partitioned off for them. They would have to descend from the fuel house into it, were it not that a passage way has been cut through the elevated flag floor of the fuel house—which passage way is brought down to the level of the floor of the family room. About two-thirds of the elevated floor of the fuel house still remains as it was, forming a kind of platform in the end of it farthest from the habitable room. That room is but 14 feet long by 7 wide. There is no room whatever up stairs. This room has a kind of ceiling about six feet high, but the fuel house is covered in simply by the rafters and thatch. The family, if I recollect aright, consisted of nine, the husband and wife and six children, and the wife's mother. So contracted was the area of their only room, that when they were all assembled each had a little more than a square yard for his or her share. At one corner of the room was a deep recess, partly constructed out of what had formerly been a large fire-place, and divided from the room by a tattered curtain. This recess was completely filled by two large beds, in which slept the father and mother and five of the children. A close, unwholesome smell proceeded from this place, which was also swarming with vermin. On inquiring where the grandmother and the other child slept, I was directed to the fuel house. I searched for the sleeping place of the aged woman, and was horrified on discovering it. At one corner of the fuel house, and on the elevated part of the floor, two rough walls were built of stone, which, with the two walls of the house, formed the sides of the apartment. The two walls built inside were not more than five feet high. Over them was put a hurdle, and over that again a piece of canvas to keep the dust out, for the rotten thatch kept dropping from above. In one of the walls of the fuel house a hole was perforated, about eight inches high and five wide, which formed a window to the chamber. It had no glass, a few splinters of wood being nailed across by way of a casement. There was a small window-shutter, which swung upon a hinge inside, which covered up about two-thirds of the hole. The remaining third was kept open night and day for ventilation, and of course gave free admission to the cold and the elements. The dimensions of this crib were six feet long, five feet wide, and five feet high. The bed, which lay across it, occupied fully two-thirds of its space. Such was the dormitory of a woman on the eve of completing her 76th year. Her eldest grandchild, a girl of about 11, slept with her. I asked the poor woman if she was not sometimes very cold. "I be freezing often," was her answer. "I have lived very long to die in such a place," she continued. One may any day see at the London Docks packing-cases quite as large. Indeed, its position was like that of a large packing-case standing in the corner of a room. A friend, who was with me, likened it to a mouse-trap. For this house, with its appurtenances, two pounds a-year are paid, by way of rent, to Gover, Mr. Bond's lessee. The inmates stayed in the house because they could not do better. If they left it, they had no place to go to, although they were willing to make every possible exertion to pay even a higher rent for better accommodation, if it could be procured. It was with difficulty they could meet their present rent, for the father had but uncertain employment, and had then been out of work for four consecutive days. Their food, for weeks past, had been bread and "sweets"—garden vegetables, chiefly turnips and parsnips, going by the latter name.

Wherever I went, I found the uncertainty of work and the want of cottage accommodation the two great subjects of complaint. I was told by some of the more respectable people in Corfe that if there were twenty new cottages built in the town they would be readily occupied. So great is the want of room, that many of the labourers themselves would go to the expense of building if the opportunity of so doing were given them. To some extent this has been done, and the mode in which they have taken advantage of it shows that not only is more room wanted, but that their idea of physical comfort rises considerably above the character of the accommodation now at their command. On a heath between Corfe and Wareham, belonging to Mr. Bankes, small plots of ground, averaging two acres each, have been leased on three lives to some of the labourers. For these they pay at the rate of 5s. 6d. per acre. On each plot a house is raised at the labourer's own expense. I was curious to see these houses, and proceeded to examine them. I found them substantially built of mud, a compound of sand and clay, each being two stories high, so that the upper rooms were not wholly in the roof. There are generally four rooms to a house, the floors of the lower rooms being, in some cases, boarded, a great improvement upon the clay, the brick, or the flag. One at least of these rooms, too, is so comfortable that it can be used if necessary as a bedroom, so that the family can have the advantage of three bedrooms, which is the least that each cottage should contain. The rooms are lofty, likewise, as compared with those of the huts described. Such is the house which, together with two acres of land, a man may have for 11s. a year. True, there is the interest on the outlay for the house to be considered. Giving his own labour, during his spare time, to building the shell, the woodwork and other requirements will cost the labourer from £30 to £40. Allowing 5 per cent. for the greater sum, he will have his house and land for about £2 10s. a year, a less sum than many pay for the merest dens, without any land at all. One of the chief advantages of putting the labourer in this position is the degree of self-respect with which it invests him. Occupying what is virtually his own house, he is a comparatively independent man, and becomes a better citizen from feeling that he has some little stake at least in the preservation of order. I inspected one of the leases. It was carefully preserved in a voluminous covering of brown paper. On reading it, I found no provision for the renewal of the term. I was told that the understanding was, that renewals would be given, but it appeared that that was forgotten in drawing up the lease. They hold, therefore, but on three lives. In the case alluded to, the youngest life named did not then exceed nine years. The house may, therefore, be enjoyed for the next 50 years. At the same time, it cannot be forgotten that the term might possibly fall in in two or three. In some cases, more than one house has been built on the ground, which, of course, makes the rent lighter. By this means, an unproductive waste will eventually be reduced to cultivation, which will be a decided gain to the proprietor. Indeed, from the very first, he is a gainer, inasmuch as land which has been hitherto unproductive yields him 5s. 6d. per acre. Close by, a similar course has been pursued to some extent, on a heath belonging to Lord Eldon. Most of those inhabiting the cottages in question are clay pit workers. But it may be asked, why, if such a step is both profitable and humane, it is not more generally followed by other proprietors, and more largely pursued by those just named? The great drawback is that so often already alluded to—the fear of burdening the parish and the estates with rates.

But if cottages are so much in demand, it may be asked why, if the landlords will not build them, others, who are neither labourers nor landlords, do not do so? There could not be a more profitable investment of capital when the rents are regularly paid, and many would so invest if it were in their power to do so. But cottages cannot be built in the air, although their foundations are sometimes laid in water. Those who would willingly invest their money in building them cannot get the land on which to build them. All the land about Wareham is so strictly settled as scarcely to admit of this. If one of the most respectable inhabitants of Wareham wanted to build himself a house, it is questionable if he could get the land. Not that the landlords would in all cases refuse it, but that in many cases they cannot part with it. A rather ludicrous instance of this occurred a short time ago. A firm in Wareham had negotiated with one of the neighbouring proprietors for a lease of a certain piece of land for some works, which were to be carried on upon it; but when the agreement came to be carried out, the proprietor found that he had so strictly tied up the land that he could not give the lease.

This scarcity of cottages is a complicated evil. It sometimes drives families to the workhouse who would otherwise not be there, and, at others, serves to keep them perpetually on the parish, after distress has once thrown them upon it. In the Wareham workhouse, for instance, was a woman with her six children, her husband being at the time at work, and in the receipt of wages, but staying with his mother, because he could not procure a cottage for himself and family. The woman herself evidently felt her situation very much. She and the whole family would leave the workhouse if a cottage could be procured. Again, take the case of a man whose family is thrown into distress from a temporary suspension of his employment. On applying for relief, he is told by the guardians that they can do nothing for him unless he comes into the house. To this he has many objections, one of which is, that he has his cottage and his furniture—poor and scanty though it be, it is his own; and if he goes into the house his little establishment will be broken up, without the least chance of his recovering it when he comes out again. But the guardians are inflexible, and he must either starve or comply with the requirements of the law. At last he enters the house, and his little establishment is broken up. Some time afterwards he hears of employment, and leaves. But his cottage is now occupied by others, or it has in the meantime altogether disappeared. He cannot find another in which to shelter his family, and has to return to the workhouse. He is thus converted into what he never meant to become—a pauper; and being so, he makes up his mind to make the most of his pauperism. The chances are that he never makes another effort to retrieve himself, but remains with his family a permanent charge upon the rates. This is not an imaginary sketch of the pauper's progress, but one drawn to me as true in but too many instances, by one who had for years been the relieving officer of a district not far from Wareham.

In the town of Wareham itself are some of the worst tenements in this part of Dorset. There was one place the filthy state of which particularly struck me. It is called Hobb's-lane, and sometimes misnamed New-street. About its lower end there is, on one side of it, a cluster of six or seven houses, one of which is used as a Ranter meeting-house. In one of these lived a Mrs. Bess, with a couple of children, her husband working in the clay pits. She had two rooms, the lower of which was twelve feet long, seven wide, and about five high. The upper room contained but one bed, which very nearly filled it. For this house she paid 1s. a week. Next door to her lived Mrs. Lockyer, with her husband and seven children. The lower room, in this case, was but eight feet square and five high. The upper room was a little larger, as it extended over the space occupied by the staircase. Here the whole family slept in three beds, which left sufficient vacant room on the floor for a small box, and no more. Some time ago several of her children had the small-pox in succession. As she and her husband had had it before, they took the diseased child into their own bed, to save the others if possible from infection. When telling me her story the poor woman was in a stooping posture, although standing in the loftiest part of the room. Her husband was a bargeman, but his wages were most unsteady. They, too, paid 1s. a week as rent. Through the next house the back yard, which was common to all the houses, was drained. In this yard stood the house of Mrs. Lockyer's sister. It was no larger than the other, but she had only one child. About the beginning of the year, the authorities had the yard cleaned up from apprehensions of the cholera. The number of people to whom it was common was twenty-eight. Until that time it had not a single privy. There was a large hole in the centre, into which everything was cast. The overflowings of this hole passed by an open drain through one of the houses into the street. The house was that next Mrs. Lockyer's. The hole is now filled up, but the drain is still there, carrying off the filth of the yard. Within the house it is now covered with a board, which is lifted every time that the inmates wish to clean out the drain. The filth which it discharges is carried along the centre of the narrow lane, by the fronts of the other houses. This property belongs to Mr. Calcraft, but it seems that he has no immediate power over it, the houses being in the hands of lessees for lives, who draw the rents.

I was courteously accompanied over the Wareham workhouse by some of the guardians. In one of the sick rooms I found several paralytic patients, of all ages. One was in bed, and another, who was dressed, was sitting on the bed next him. This latter was a strong lusty young fellow, who in his countenance bore no signs of disease. The paralysis under which he laboured had, according to his own account, been superinduced by his wearing "damp shoes." I ascertained from the younger paralytic that he was from the village of Bere, about seven miles to the north of Wareham. He had come from Bere but a few days ago, and the wages which were being then paid in its neighbourhood did not exceed 7s. a week. Those who were not exactly ablebodied were getting but 5s. and 6s. Nor was house-room or fuel included in this. Whether they received 7s., 6s., or 5s., they paid rent for their houses, and had to buy their fuel, which cost them 3s. a load for cutting, and 9s. for carting. I lost no time in making my way to Bere, to ascertain if things were really as bad as represented. For five miles the road runs through an almost unbroken heath—for the other two, it is flanked by cultivated fields. The village is the property of Mr. Drax, M.P. for Wareham. I found no exaggeration in the statement made to me at the workhouse. The wages had not been misrepresented, nor had the workmen any perquisites, or "privileges," as they are more generally called. Their accommodation in the village was of the most wretched description. It is almost impossible to convey an adequate idea of some of the huts in this village. In one, known as the Will House, I found a widow and four children. It was a kind of parish house, and had, as she said, been for a long time a refuge for widows and orphans. The lower room, with its clammy clay floor, was not much more than ten feet square. The bedroom above was gained not by a staircase, but by a ladder, which let you through a hole in the floor. She paid no rent; but had been told that some repairs were to be effected, when it was expected that she would pay. She had an allowance from the parish. The next house, although not much larger, was more comfortable. It was inhabited by a married couple, who had paid no rent, but had themselves kept the house in repair; that is to say, they had kept it from tumbling about their ears. The next hut was occupied by an invalid couple and their four children. The eldest child was a girl of eighteen, the next a boy of fifteen. This house had a brick floor and was kept tolerably clean, although the poor creature who kept it so was in the last stages of consumption. Her increasing debility she attributed to palpitation of the heart. She showed me the bedroom up stairs; the climbing of the ladder by which it was reached so exhausted her that she nearly sunk upon the floor on gaining the top. There were three beds in the room, for seven slept in it, the seventh being an orphan child. "Had the child any claim upon you," I asked, "that you should keep it?" "O no," she said "but poor dear little heart, it had no friends, and I didn't like to see it go into the union." So true is it that the poor support the poor. It was all the more remarkable in this case, inasmuch as they themselves were chiefly supported by parish allowance, which amounted to 2s. and four loaves a week. The eldest girl earned something, though a mere pittance, by making buttons, and the boy sometimes made a shilling or two. The woman's husband seemed also in a consumption. He had been "off work" for nearly two years, and his eye was bright and his cheek flushed. He put out his tongue to show me the fever he was in. Its whole surface was white and furred. He lamented that, although there were about 1,500 people in the parish, there was not a single resident gentleman in it "to say a word for the poor."

I next visited a hovel which stood by itself on the opposite side of the road. I could scarcely make out how it stood at all, so broken and dilapidated did it appear on all sides. The floor was of earth, and the ceiling, which was of plaster and reed, was nearly all gone. Half the chimney-piece had fallen down. There was scarcely any furniture in the house. Here, also, the upper room was gained by a ladder. It contained two beds, the family consisting of six people. The only person at the time in the house was a girl of about 16. I asked her her name, whereupon she told me that her father's name was Purchase and her mother's Stansfield. I afterwards learnt that the father had run away from his wife and lived with this woman, by whom he had a family of four, of whom this girl was the eldest. The mother and two daughters slept in one bed, and the father and two sons in the other.

These are certainly specimens of some of the worst houses in and about Bere, but there are many others nearly as bad. For some of them a rent as high as £3 5s. is paid by labourers receiving 7s. a week.

Not far from Bere is another small place, called Kingston, the property of Mrs. Mitchell. Many of the houses are of the lowest description, and scarcely any provision has been made for draining.

In another direction is a place called Tingleton. The property on which it stands is in the occupation of Mr. Porcher. Here the condition of the labourer is in striking contrast with his state in the places already alluded to. His cottage is clean and comfortable, and he has, in most cases, about half an acre of ground attached to it, and all at a very moderate rent. The labourers who are badly off in the neighbourhood are constantly contrasting their condition with that of those at Tingleton.

I then proceeded to Winfrith, about twenty miles to the southwest of Wareham. Here the labourers are as badly housed as in Corfe or Bere. The wages in this district have recently been reduced from 8s. to 7s. In some cases, an attempt was made to reduce them to 6s., in the case even of able-bodied men. The reduction created quite an excitement in the district, and the labourers in a body waited upon Mr. Weld, the proprietor, who, however, told them that he could not interfere with the farmers. The consequence was, that, shortly afterwards, the horizon was lighted, in several places, with fires. Three incendiary fires have occurred at Winfrith, another, I believe, at Pimperne, on Lord Portman's property, and still another at a place called Compton, a little further to the north. A reward of £100 has been offered for the apprehension and conviction of the Winfrith incendiaries. Two of the farmers who have suffered are members of a Labourers' Friend Society, which had a meeting at Wareham about three weeks ago, at which prizes were distributed to the labourers. Two of these, viz., coats with brass buttons, have never been called for by those to whom they were awarded. They are still lying unclaimed at the hotel. On asking some labourers why this was so, they said that they were no longer to be gammoned by such professions. Others went so far as to justify the fires, as the only voice in which the labourer could speak with any chance of being heard. The prevalent feeling amongst them was very bad, and many were sorely annoyed that it was not the farmers, but the insurance offices, that suffered by the fires. A suggestive circumstance in connection with these fires is the almost complete silence of the local press respecting them.

On shifting the scene of inquiry to Blandford, I removed into the heart of a purely agricultural district. Notwithstanding this, I expected to find wages comparatively high in the immediate vicinity of the town—there being causes in operation to keep them up, as I thought, although not the same as those existing at Wareham. Around Blandford is to be found a numerous resident proprietary, the chief of whom are Lords Portman, Portarlington, and Rivers, Sir John Smith, Sir Edward Baker, Mr. Seymer, M.P., Mr. Farquharson, and Mr. Drax. The presence of these gives employment to numbers of the peasantry, and higher wages are paid by some of them than by the farmers. But still the wages of the district are not kept up—7s. a week being the ordinary rate for day-labourers. Carters and others, in somewhat confidential employments, have 8s. and 9s. Blandford is very much overcrowded, particularly in one or two of its lanes. This is chiefly attributable to the labourers having been driven from the surrounding parishes into the town. They have been driven in from the property of Mr. Farquharson and Lord Portman, but particularly from Milton Abbey, the property of Lord Portarlington. Lord Portman has enabled some of his labourers to emigrate. They can drive no more into Blandford, because every nook and crevice in the town is full. But the steadiness of the pressure is evinced by the fact, that whenever a house or a room becomes vacant the applicants are generally far more numerous than can be accommodated. This is not only the case in Blandford, but also in most of the surrounding villages.

It is by considering his circumstances in these villages that the condition of the labourer in this district can be best appreciated. In most of them, he is reduced to a point so low, that it is impossible to imagine him going beyond it compatibly with mere animal existence. Between Blandford and Wimborne is the village of Sturminster Marshall, which exhibits the very acme of physical wretchedness and intellectual and moral privation. Around it the average rate of wages can certainly not exceed 7s. a week. In the opposite direction, and about two or three miles from Blandford, are the two villages of Durweston and Stourpain—the former the property of Lord Portman, and the latter that of Lord Rivers. Both in appearance and actual comfort there is a striking difference between them. In Durweston the houses are in the main much better than those in the neighbouring village, whilst they are also less crowded with inmates. But there are two reasons for this. The first is, that some of Lord Portman's labourers have emigrated, others have gone to the contiguous parishes, and by both processes the estate has been relieved. The other is, that the village of Durweston is the residence of the celebrated "S. G. O.," who, by his exposures of the condition of the labourer, has made himself so obnoxious to Dorsetshire squires. It is to be regretted that his neighbourhood to Stourpain—for his residence is scarcely a mile from it—has not had the effect of improving it also. Although the property of Lord Rivers, his lordship has at present little, if any, control over it—most, if not all, of it being leased on lives, and some of it in the hands of those whose only source of income is the rents extorted from the miserable beings who inhabit it.

The first house which I visited here was a low wretched tenement, built of bricks, which were fast crumbling to decay. It was inhabited by a family of eight, bearing the name of Haywood. Some time ago they mustered twelve, and only two months since ten. Death had, about the latter period, taken two from their number. They had two rooms, the lower one being about 12 feet square, with scarcely any furniture, and a cold, damp, and broken earthen floor. The upper room, which was in the roof, was in a state of almost perfect dilapidation. It contained three beds, once occupied by twelve people, but now left to the eight who remain. When it rains, the beds have to be removed from place to place to avoid the water, which comes dripping through the roof. When the two died they had fever in the house. Several of the children were ill, but it proved fatal only to these. Six of them were at one time crammed into one bed, to avoid infection. Of the two who died, one was a young man, the other a child. "The buryings were five days apart." In each case the body lay in the sleeping room of the family until it was removed. The rent paid for this hovel is 1s. a week to one of Lord Rivers's lessees. There is no garden attached to it, and the same may be said of most of the houses near it. There is but one privy, and that is common to a whole cluster of houses. The eldest of the Haywood family now at home is a girl of twenty-one. The father is a labourer, in the receipt of 7s. a week. Their diet is bread and potatoes. They scarcely taste meat once a month, and then they will have but about half a pound amongst them. They have an allotment ground of 40 luggs, on which they raise their potatoes, and for which they pay 8s. 4d. a year. But for this, they say, they would be starving.

The next house also contained a family of eight. Their name was Allan. They had but two small rooms—the bed-room being off the common room. It contained but two beds. The father, mother, and three children slept in one bed—the children being put at the foot; the other three, all girls, occupied the other bed. The eldest girl was sixteen, the eldest boy at home eight. The family had occupied the house for sixteen years. The mother had never been well since she entered it. No wonder, for the house was cold to a degree. There was a kind of cellar below, which had formerly been occupied, but which was now nailed up. There was no ceiling below, and the wind came up through the floor. The window was almost half gone. It had originally consisted of twenty-four small panes, ten of which were broken—both glass and casement. It had been in that condition for more than five years, and was covered with brown paper or stuffed with rags. In the bed-room there was no casement at all. The hole which served as a window was nightly covered by a piece of bagging "to keep out the wet and the cold." The rent charged is £3 per annum. For the last year they have only paid 6s. They could not pay more, and did not like to say anything about repairs, as they were in arrear. But it was quite as bad as now, when the rent was regularly paid. Allan himself was a labourer at 7s. a week. There was a talk of lowering the wages to 6s. They were allowed no fuel, and had no "privileges." The parents got but little help from the family. "Mine do run upon daughters," said the woman, "and they get us little or nothing." In addition to this, her husband's work was not steady. It would be difficult enough, she said, to get on, even if it were so, but with "broken work" they would starve, but for an allowance of bread which she had from the parish.

The next house which I inspected was occupied by a family of the name of Read, consisting of husband and wife and two children. The rent charged was £3 10s. They had paid £1 15s. a few months ago. The man's earnings were only 6s. a week. He was not quite able-bodied. When I entered he was at dinner, seated in a dark corner, over a meal of potatoes and cabbage. The floor was of brick, and was kept clean. Above were two very small bedrooms, cleaner than most chambers of the kind that I had seen. There were great fissures in the wall, however, through which the wind could freely enter, but that it was prevented from so doing by broad patches of London newspapers pasted against the plaster, and thus put to a purpose similar to that assigned to Imperial Cæsar. The woman busied herself in making buttons. She has got as low as 3d. a gross for them. Working busily, she could make a gross in a week. The house was held of "Farmer Cole," one of Lord Rivers's lessees.

The next house, which was of about the same dimensions, was occupied by two old women who were supported by the parish. There were three children living with them, one of whom was deaf and dumb. Their allowance was 2s. a week and two loaves each. Out of this they had to pay 9d. a week for their barn to Farmer Cole, and had also to find their own fuel. Their diet was bread, with occasionally a little butter. They never tasted meat.

I visited several other houses, but they were all of the same class, and all equally bad. One occupied by a family of the name of Upwood, was particularly so. Its clay floor was full of holes, which formed receptacles for moisture during wet weather. The family numbered seven, and they all slept in the roof. Two of them slept in a bed which rested on a kind of elevated stage, near the angle of the roof, which was gained by a ladder. The eldest daughter, a tidy and interesting-looking girl, was seated at the window making buttons. These buttons are made with cotton thread sewn upon a small steel ring. She was getting 10d. a gross, but it would take her a week to earn it. She had to find the cotton too out of the 10d., which would reduce her earnings to 8½d. a week. She had been at work all that day since nine o'clock, from which hour till four o'clock, when she gave up work because it got dark, she had earned about a penny! No wonder that she was anxious to go out to service.

Adjoining this was Emily Bull's house, whose husband was a farm labourer at 7s. a week, without fuel. They had seven children, and the nine slept in three beds in one room.

I could multiply such instances, if necessary; but it is not so. Enough has already been said to convey some idea of the physical condition of the labourer in the district around Blandford. There are some of them tolerably housed, but seven-eighths of them are most deplorably accommodated. The illustrations already given, too, may serve as a type of the state of things in the vicinity of Shaftesbury. Drawing a circle around that place, with a radius of about five miles, the state of the labourer in the portion of it falling within the county of Dorset is so bad that it could scarcely be conceived worse. It is common to find eight occupying not only the same house, but the same bed-room. In one instance in which I found this the case, Samuel, the eldest of the family, was 22; Elizabeth, the next, was 20; and George, the next, was 18. The two lads were rather equivocal characters, which only made the arrangement all the more objectionable. Perhaps the spot in which the labourer is worst off in this neighbourhood is the village of Stour Provost, about four miles from Shaftesbury, and the property of King's College, Cambridge. In the immediate neighbourhood of Lord Westminster's residence wages may be a little higher; but their average around Shaftesbury is 7s. a week. Everywhere the labourer dreads a still further reduction to 6s. Thus the wretchedness of his actual circumstances is enhanced by his having still more gloomy prospects to contemplate.

Generally speaking the Dorsetshire labourer experiences but little competition from migrating Irish labour. There are sufficient hands in the county to perform even the extra work of harvest time, without importing labour for the purpose. Now it may be taken as an axiom, that where this is the case there are more hands than are required during at least three-fourths of the year. This is the case with Dorset, and goes far to account for the low state of the labourer within it. In Lincolnshire and in other parts of England, and in the Lowlands of Scotland, it is otherwise. There the number of hands suffices for the greater part of the year, but not for the harvest, when labour has to be imported. This will, to some extent, account for the superior condition of the labourer in these parts.

There has been considerable emigration from Dorsetshire, chiefly promoted by the larger proprietors. Multitudes more would go, were they not deterred from leaving the country by their profound ignorance of everything connected with the places whither they would be sent.

From what has preceded, it will have been seen that the staple dietary of the Dorsetshire labourer is made up of potatoes, bread, cabbage, and turnips, and that even of them he and his family have not always a sufficiency. I shall have occasion again to refer more particularly to the dietary of different union workhouses in different parts of the counties which I have visited; but, in contrast to the diet of the independent labourer in Dorset, permit me here to present you with the present dietary of the Blandford Union:—

"BLANDFORD UNION DIETARY FOR ABLE-BODIED PERSONS ABOVE NINE YEARS OF AGE.—NOV. 22, 1849.

	Break-fast.		Dinner.						Supper.	
	Bread.	Gruel.	Suet Pudding.	Bread.	Cheese.	Cooked Meat.	Vegetables.	Beef Soup.	Bread.	Cheese.
	oz.	pints	oz.	oz.	oz.	oz.	oz.	pints	oz.	oz.
Sunday										
Men	6	1½	16	...	...	...	...	...	6	1½
Women ..	5	1½	14	...	...	...	...	...	5	1½
Monday										
Men	6	1½	...	7	1½	...	...	...	6	1½
Women ..	5	1½	...	6	1½	...	...	...	5	1½
Tuesday										
Men	6	1½	...	...	...	5	16	...	6	1½
Women ..	5	1½	...	...	...	4	16	...	5	1½
Wednesday										
Men	6	1½	...	7	1½	...	...	...	6	1½
Women ..	5	1½	...	6	1½	...	...	...	5	1½
Thursday										
Men	6	1½	...	...	...	5	16	...	6	1½
Women ..	5	1½	...	...	...	4	16	...	5	1½
Friday										
Men	6	1½	...	7	1½	...	...	...	6	1½
Women ..	5	1½	...	6	1½	...	...	...	5	1½
Saturday										
Men	6	1½	...	4	...	...	...	1½	6	1½
Women ..	5	1½	...	3	...	...	...	1½	5	1½

"Old people of sixty years of age and upwards may be allowed 1 oz. of tea, 7 oz. of butter, and 8 oz. of sugar per week, in lieu of gruel for breakfast, if deemed expedient to make this change.

"Children under nine years of age to be dieted at discretion.

"Above nine years of age to be allowed the same quantities as women.

"Sick to be dieted as directed by the medical officer.

"Approved of by the Poor-law Commissioners,
February 9, 1837."

One hears a good deal in Dorset of the "privileges" of the labourer. These are generally extended only to the regularly employed labourers on the farms. The great bulk of the ordinary day labourers have them not. And, after all, even to those who have them they are worth but little. When a labourer gets a free house, he is compelled to put up with any hole that is offered him. When he gets his wheat at a shilling less than the market price, in nine cases out of ten he only gets "tailings," at their real market value. Sometimes he has his fuel, at others not; and his perquisites for his pig, if he has one, are meagre in the extreme. On the whole, he would be a gainer if all his privileges were compounded for 1s. a week.

Such is the condition in which I found the labourer in Dorset, viewing it, as I did, from three different centres of observation, illustrative of his condition throughout the county. If, as regards the condition of the labourer, Dorset does not merit the unenviable pre-eminence assigned to it by some, it must, at least, share that pre-eminence with Devon, Somerset, and Wilts.

LABOUR AND THE POOR.

THE RURAL DISTRICTS.

[FROM OUR SPECIAL CORRESPONDENT.]

INTELLECTUAL AND MORAL CONDITION OF THE LABOURER IN THE SOUTHERN AND WESTERN COUNTIES.

LETTER XIII.

Before proceeding to state the results of my observations, as regards the moral condition of the labouring poor in the counties which I have visited, it may be well to allude to their intellectual state in the counties of Somerset, Cornwall, Devon, and Dorset.

In dealing with this branch of the subject in reference to the counties of Bucks, Berks, Oxford, and Wilts, I took occasion to treat it in connection with two classes of persons—the adult labourers and the rising generation of labourers. I shall here follow the same plan; first considering the question in its bearing upon the adult labourer.

I regret to say that in the counties now more immediately in question, I found the same degree of ignorance and stolidity prevailing as in those previously considered. Cornwall may, to some extent, be regarded as an exception; both the mining and fishing populations of that county, but particularly the former, generally displaying a degree of intelligence very superior to that possessed or exhibited by the agricultural labourers around them. This is almost exclusively attributable to the peculiar character of their occupations—for the educational facilities which have been hitherto at their command have not been superior to those possessed by their brethren who labour in the fields. Their pursuits are such as to require constant watchfulness, and frequently to call into exercise the reasoning powers. This is especially the case with the miner, who has sometimes to make very nice calculations, which he does in his own rude way, but with wonderful exactness. It is generally upon themselves, and upon their knowledge of their respective crafts, that both fishermen and miners depend for the success of their enterprises and the amount of their gains. This stimulates them to industry, and quickens into activity their mental energies. But the position of the field labourer is little beyond that of a machine, which, in point of capacity, he also too closely resembles. His daily task is assigned him, and he performs it, but the work is the work merely of his hands, and is scarcely ever directed by his mind. There is, consequently, generally speaking, the greatest possible difference in this respect between him and the two classes of men alluded to. They are quick, shrewd, and calculating, whereas he is slow, stolid, and mechanical. The miners and fishermen, too, are generally lively and cheerful, whilst the farm labourers, as a class, are moody, sullen, and morose.

But there is a great difference between mere intelligence, and education in the ordinary sense of the term. The intelligence possessed by the miners and fishermen is the result merely of the education afforded by the peculiar nature of their occupations. As may be supposed, therefore, their range of intellectual activity does not much transcend the sphere of their labours. The mind which has been quickened into action, in any direction, is, however, more susceptible of improvement than that which has been permitted to lie wholly dormant. So it is with them. They are far more teachable than the rural labourers, although they have not been more taught. They are quicker in apprehension and more retentive of what is communicated to them than is the peasant; but, generally speaking, they are found deplorably ignorant as regards all subjects which lie beyond the line of their daily avocations. On conversing with them, one cannot but regret that so much intellectual power as they possess and exhibit should be left to direct itself into but one channel. A very large proportion of them cannot read, and I venture to say that the great bulk of them cannot write. Many of those who read do so with the greatest difficulty, whilst numbers who write can scarcely aspire to any higher achievement, in this respect, than the scrawling of their own names.

Taking the adult class of agricultural labourers, it is almost impossible to exaggerate the ignorance in which they live and move and have their being. As they work in the fields, the external world has some hold upon them through the medium of their senses; but to all the higher exercises of intellect they are perfect strangers. You cannot address one of them without being at once painfully struck with the intellectual darkness which enshrouds him. There is in general neither speculation in his eyes nor intelligence in his countenance. The whole expression is more that of an animal than of a man. He is wanting, too, in the erect and independent bearing of a man. When you accost him, if he is not insolent—which he seldom is—he is timid and shrinking, his whole manner showing that he feels himself at a distance from you greater than should separate any two classes of men. He is often doubtful when you address, and suspicious when you question him; he is seemingly oppressed with the interview whilst it lasts, and obviously relieved when it is over. These are the traits which I can affirm them to possess as a class, after having come in contact with many hundreds of farm-labourers. They belong to a generation for whose intellectual culture little or nothing was done. As a class, they have no amusements beyond the indulgence of sense. In nine cases out of ten, recreation is associated in their minds with nothing higher than sensuality. I have frequently asked clergymen and others, if they often find the adult peasant reading for his own or others' amusement? The invariable answer is, that such a sight is seldom or never witnessed. In the first place, the great bulk of them cannot read. In the next, a large proportion of those who can, do so with too much difficulty to admit of the exercise being an amusement to them. Again, few of those who can read with comparative ease have the taste for doing so. It is but justice to them to say, that many of those who cannot read have bitterly regretted, in my hearing, their inability to do so. I shall never forget the tone in which an old woman in Cornwall intimated to me what a comfort it would now be to her, could she only read her Bible in her lonely hours.

Take the ordinary day labourer on the farm, and viewing him from what point you will, what manner of man do you find him? You are first struck with the anomaly presented by the outward man. In his very dress he seems not to belong to the century in which he lives. The smock-frock was never the garb of active labour, and it certainly but ill beseems the labourer of these bustling and competing times. It would be no more in the way in the mine or the factory than it is in the field. Field-work requires a great deal of stooping, and perfect freedom of the limbs. The frock is neither adapted for the one, nor allows of the other. His gait, too, is awkward. The contrast between him and men engaged in other laborious occupations is sufficiently great to force itself upon the most passive observer. He seems to belong to an inferior grade of beings, when compared with the factory operative, the worker in the mines, the fisherman, the artisan, or the stable boy. They are dressed, more or less, in keeping with their work and with the times, and are quick and intelligent in their movements, whereas he is attired in the robe of centuries gone by, and is awkward, cumbrous, and mechanical in his actions. The state of his mind has been already adverted to. Education has advanced him but little beyond the position which he occupied in the days of William the Norman. The farm labourer has scarcely participated at all in the improvement of his brethren. As he was generations gone by, so he is now—a physical scandal, a moral enigma, an intellectual cataleptic.

Let it not be said that this picture is too strongly drawn. The subject is one which does not admit of exaggeration. Did space permit, or could any good purpose be served by it, I could adduce instances almost innumerable of the profound ignorance in which this class of British subjects is steeped. There is scarcely a field in the agricultural districts which does not exhibit a living illustration of it. Search any county throughout the south and west, and the examples start up around you in hundreds. I have found it so in all those which I have traversed—from Salisbury to the Land's-end—from Portland-bill to Oxford—in the vale of the Torridge, and in the vale of Aylesbury—by the Thames, the Severn, the Frome, the Stour, the Exe, the Camel, and the Plym. Where all is bad, it is sometimes difficult to point out the worst. So it is here. Cornwall may again be separated from the rest, for, even as regards the agricultural labourer, it forms an exception to the other three counties of the group. In that county, the labourer is quickened a little into intellectual life, by coming frequently in contact with those whose intelligence is superior to his own. But, even here, education, in its ordinary acceptation, has done as little for the peasantry as in Dorset, Devon, or Somerset. It is, perhaps, in the last-mentioned county that their intellectual gloom is the most rayless and hopeless.

But this has more to do with the past than with the present or the future. The existing generation has grown beyond us, and, as to it, we cannot now rectify the error, even if we would. The question of greatest interest to us, because the only one having a practical bearing, is, what is being done for the education of their offspring and successors?

In inquiring into the nature and extent of the educational machinery at work in the counties in question, I found that, as regards reliable and authentic information, I had to encounter the same difficulties as formerly. No one seemed to know anything of what was going on in this respect, beyond his own district, and few could furnish me with any very specific detail connected even with their own districts. This parish had one kind of school, that another—this one again had both—and that neither the one nor the other. On this, as on other subjects, people are often apt to be deceived by sounds, and are prevented only by careful inquiry from frequently running off with the most erroneous impressions. Thus, I was informed at Blandford that not only was there an excellent National school there, at which the children in the union were taught, but that all the surrounding parishes were provided with schools. "Have they all National schools?" I inquired. "No, not exactly that," said my informant. "They have all day schools, I presume?" I added. "Well," said he, "I am afraid I must say that some of them have only Sunday-schools." And so it is with many parishes in other parts of the county, which, we are told, are pro-vided with schools. Even in a secular point of view, the Sunday-school is better than no school at all. A few of the children who attend them are taught to read—but only a few, for the attendance is irregular, and the interval of a week which elapses between every two brief lessons affords the child sufficient time for forgetting the little that may have been learnt. Unfortunately, even when there are day-schools in the parish, it is only the Sunday-school that the labourer's child can at-tend. Labour in the fields, for 1s., 1s. 6d., or 2s. a week, absorbs all his time during the six days of work; and it is only on the seventh that his mind has any chance of receiving the slightest culture. When the child lives wholly with the farmer who employs him, it is only during a fraction of the year that even the Sunday-school is attended. He is kept steadily at work every day in the week, particularly dur-ing the season when the cattle are housed. It is thus that multitudes of the rising generation are rapidly growing up, and passing with-out improvement the improvable age. So far as they are concerned, their inheritance will embrace the ignorance as well as the servitude of their fathers. Reading is, of course, the only element of secular edu-cation taught at the Sunday-schools. You can almost always tell when the education of a child has been confined to these schools. He can sometimes read well, but knows nothing of either writing or arith-metic. In some parishes, where there are no day-schools, there is but one Sunday-school; in others there are several Sunday-schools; their circumstances in this respect depending upon the extent and zeal of the different sects which may inhabit them.

One cannot fail to be struck, on examining into this matter, with the newness of the machinery which he finds at work around him. In almost every other parish which you visit you are told by the clergyman that until he established one there was no day-school whatever in the parish. Nor is this the case only where the incumbency has been of long duration. I have been informed of it in numerous instances in which it has only taken place within the last three or four years. Even the very school-houses have, in most cases, a look of yesterday about them. In many of the rural towns particularly—and generally under the shadow of the church—you will find neat, small, and trim Elizabethan-looking buildings, the mortar of which seems yet scarcely dry. Here and there, again, you discover, but generally about the outskirts of the town, equally substantial but less showy erections, appertaining to the British and Foreign School Society. In numerous instances you find both.

I have already had occasion to state how far behind the educational exigencies of the times are many of the teachers of the National Schools. I was sorry to find the same deficiency existing, though not to the same extent, in connection with many of the rival institutions. The best that can be said of some of the National Schools is, that they are enlarged and improved dame schools. The British and Foreign Schools are more generally divided into departments, the women being usually found presiding only over the girls' department. Sometimes they have a third—an infant department—attached to them, where children of both sexes are taught (generally by a woman) up to a certain age, when they are drafted off into the boys' or girls' department, as the case may be. The following may serve as a specimen of some of the teachers even in these schools, in which one generally looks for efficiency in the work of education. The circumstance happened in Cornwall, in a parish in which there was no school but the British and Foreign School, which was attended by many children belonging to the Church. I was accompanied to the school by one who took a great interest in promoting the educational system to which it pertained. On entering the boys' department, I found about 120 of them assembled, most of whom were being noisily instructed in geography. At some distance before them was a large map of England, by means of which the teacher was testing their knowledge of localities. Finding the system pursued to be that of permitting all the boys to answer at once, I listened attentively, in order to test their proficiency, to some of the boys in the back rows, and found that all they did was to make an unmeaning noise every time a question was asked, leaving those who could to answer correctly and distinctly. In the noise of nearly a hundred voices this delinquency was undetected by the master. He shortly afterwards showed me several maps drawn by some of the boys. One of these was a large map of Scotland, which was the conjoint work of two of them. He evidently took great pleasure in showing it as something which reflected credit alike on master and pupils. On its being unrolled, the first thing my eye lighted upon was an immense arm of the sea, which, commencing at the head of the Dornoch Frith, stretched in a north-westerly direction nearly up to Cape Wrath, almost cutting the county of Sutherland into two nearly equal parts. It was painted so excessively blue that it was impossible to overlook it. I directed the master's attention to the county, and asked if he perceived nothing wrong about it. He said he did not; whereupon I pointed out the blunder to him, telling him that, independently of geographical teaching, my topographical knowledge of the locality enabled me to detect the error, as I had more than once ridden, high and dry, in her Majesty's mail, over the ground which the map had submerged with an arm of the sea several miles wide. He looked confused and annoyed, but said, at last, with great *naïveté*, "I'm sure it was so in the copy."

But, notwithstanding the undoubted improvements which have recently been effected in them, the Parochial Union Schools still constitute the most generally defective feature in our educational system. There are few of the unions now which have not in the workhouses the semblance at least of an efficient school. If you enter during school hours, you find all the children in the house attending, under the superintendence of a master or mistress—more generally the latter when the school is a mixed one, or of both when it is divided, as is sometimes the case, into separate departments for boys and girls. The children are all in the paupers' uniform, but are neat and clean in their appearance. The educational appliances with which the school is provided vary in the different unions. There is still a large proportion of them without the means of teaching geography; and many of those now provided with maps have been so so recently that the children have not as yet derived any benefit from them. That which is mainly defective in these schools is the system pursued. It is one of mere education without proper training. When I enter one of these schools, the first thing that is done is to place the copybooks of the children before me, after which I am asked if I would like them to cipher or read to me. But it is chiefly with the general training of the children that I busy myself, and it is this that I find so universally defective. They are taught reading, writing, a few rules in arithmetic, and some-

times a smattering of geography; but these things are generally taught
them in a way which opens up the mind a little, without, in the least
degree, improving the heart. The teachers are too often those who,
having failed in other pursuits, take to this occupation as a last resort.
Nor, indeed, is this to be wondered at, seeing that whilst the position is in itself a not very agreeable one, the remuneration is so low
as to tempt none but the most needy to accept it. The teachers must
reside with the children in the house. Sometimes they have separate
apartments for themselves; in other cases, they occupy the same dormitory as their pupils. In the Liskeard Union, I found the boys and
their teacher all in one room. It was large, and contained many beds.
Those of the boys stood side by side, in actual contact with each other.
That of the teacher occupied a corner screened off from the rest of the
room by a curtain. There was accommodation for forty-six boys, and
there he was put to keep watch over them, and to see that they slept according to the laws of the workhouse. Such a situation can be pleasant
neither for master nor pupils. Every one can enter into the feelings of
the master. The pupils chiefly regard him in the light of their constant
overseer by night and by day. To fill up the measure of their dislike
to him, he is called upon to be the instrument of their bodily pain
as well as the instructor of their minds; for when they transgress the
ordinary rules, not of the school-room, but of the workhouse, on him
generally devolves the task of administering the lash to them. Is it any
wonder that few who are really efficient men can be found to occupy
such a position? The guardians have frequently complained to me of
the difficulty they experience in supplying the place of a teacher when
a vacancy occurs. The difficulty is easily accounted for. The great majority of the teachers only take the post as a prelude to something else.
Their hearts are therefore seldom in their work, and their demeanour
towards the children is often harsh, and almost invariably cold. I have
found the poor creatures, when a kind word, accompanied by a kind
look, was said to them, start and look up as if they doubted the evidence of their senses. From these schools they are turned adrift upon
the world, with a slight smattering of the elements of education, but
without the slightest moral preparation for the rough life that is before them. It is this, with the results which have followed, that has
shaken the confidence of many good and thoughtful persons in these
schools altogether. It is this also which partly induces the guardians in
some of the unions to have the children sent to the national schools,
instead of having them educated in the house. The necessity of over

hauling the whole system of the union schools is now very generally canvassed in the country.

But in connection with this, as with other subjects, the truth, however startling or disagreeable, should be told. The farmers are now, in many instances, an impediment in the way of education. The church and upper classes are, more or less, favourable to it; but in the farmers, the employers of labour, is frequently found the great obstacle to its efficient promotion. I do not make this assertion hastily or without proof, for I find abundant evidence of it wherever I go.

To do justice to the farmers, a large proportion of them are insensible to the benefits of education. In many cases you cannot distinguish the children of the farmer, by their dress, demeanour, or intellectual culture, from those of the labourer; and this, too, not only in the case of "smock farmers," as the lowest class of them are termed, but also in that of some tolerably well off in the world. There are others who give their own children the benefit of the best education that they can afford, but who would deny the same boon to the child of the labourer. It is but a few days since I met one of this class. He did not like the present order of things at all. There was too great a tendency in society now-a-days to heave up that which was below to the top. Labourers were anxious to become masters, and so on. To educate the labourer was only to enhance this evil. The child should succeed his father at his toil. His own son was then at the University, and was studying for the church.

Such are, in too many instances, the men who, by becoming guardians of unions, are entrusted with the education of the poor. Some of them speak out openly, and express their disinclination to having them educated. They are obliged to comply with the letter of the law, but they care not for a master or mistress being qualified for the work of instruction. These are strong assertions, but they are borne out by facts, and every one acquainted with the views and conduct of the guardians of many of the purely rural unions—for it is of them only that I now speak—can attest their accuracy. The character of the teachers will generally bespeak that of the guardians. If they can distinguish between a good and a bad teacher, and do not remove a bad one—or if they cannot distinguish between them— they are not fit to be guardians. The cases are startlingly numerous in which they either cannot, or will not, make the distinction. I was informed by a gentleman, on whom every reliance can be placed, that when, some time ago, he entered the school-room of the St. Austle workhouse, he found the master setting a copy to a boy—"A blind man's wife need no painting." It was not even *needs*. In another school, the master, after showing me their copies, and making the boys read a little in my hearing, offered, as a test of their arithmetical proficiency, to "put them through a sum in sub*trac*tion." In another case, it was discovered that none of the children could write at all. An inquiry was instituted into this by the party whose duty it was to do so, and he discovered that the reason was that the schoolmistress herself could not write. He remonstrated with the guardians for having such a teacher, but they insisted upon it that she was good enough. Of what use was it to teach the children to write? It only made them bad servants, and they did not want them to write. The schoolmistress was afterwards removed by a higher power, but these same guardians re-elected her to her post. Whilst the party who moved in the matter had several letters from the guardians, insisting upon the sufficiency of her qualifications, he had also several letters from her to which was appended *her mark*. On another occasion, the same person, whilst examining a school, asked a girl what a quadruped was, the word occurring in her reading lesson. She could not answer. He then asked the schoolmistress if she did not teach them the meaning of such words. She replied that she did, and that they all knew it, but that "they were so stupid." He then desired her to point out one who could tell him the meaning of the word. She went round the whole school, but not one was found who could do so. It then occurred to him to ask her if she knew it herself. She coloured, stammered, and at last admitted that she "did not exactly know." He next asked her if she knew what a biped was. That she certainly did not know; but on being told that she herself was one, thought it was something awful, and afterwards complained to the guardians that her interrogator had called her names. I was informed of another case, in which a master was appointed who could neither read nor write. On being asked how he could undertake to teach, he said that he made the boys that could read teach those who could not, and that he listened to those who could read, and could easily tell when they went wrong. It would be unfair to infer that all the schools in question are thus miserably provided with teachers, but the system must be throughout a radically defective one which can admit of such cases even as exceptional.

The truth is, that there is much in our present system of educa-tion in the rural districts that is mere sham. We have a varied and tolerably extensive machinery apparently in efficient operation, but it is only when its working is closely inspected that it is found in too many cases to be anything but efficient. A great deal might be effected with the present educational apparatus, were it earnestly and honestly employed. But it is not so; and many a patriot and philanthropist is prevented from moving in the matter from a belief that the ground is now very generally occupied. It is, more or less, occupied, but not cultivated. It is only here and there that you find efficient schools, particularly in connection with the National Society.

In the parochial union schools geography is now much more generally taught than formerly—the guardians having at length discovered the stimulus which a little knowledge of geography gives to emigration. At first they could discover no use whatever in maps. "Maps!" said they, when it was first proposed to introduce them; "you'll be bringing in the dancing-master next." In illustration of the value of geography as regards emigration, the following was related to me. A gentleman, in want of a boy to accompany him to New Zealand, applied at a union school in which geography had not been taught. "Who'll go to New Zealand?" was asked of the whole school, but not one volunteered. The application was next made at a school where geography was taught. "Who'll go to New Zealand?" was again asked, and almost every boy in the school sprung forward, exclaiming, "I'll go!"—"I'll go!" On examining them, it was found that many not only knew its position, and other circumstances connected with it, but could also state accurately the different routes by which it could be reached. No sooner was the anecdote known abroad than the guardians of the surrounding unions immediately ordered maps for their respective schools.

Notwithstanding all that has recently been done for the cause of education, the proportion of children growing up utterly uneducated is very great. In almost every family such is the case with some. I make a practice of accosting almost every boy I meet, and inquiring into his education. I thus accosted one some time ago near Chewton Mendip, in Somerset, who was in his twelfth year, and had, according to his own account, been for some time at school, which, however, he had attended very irregularly. I asked him what he was learning, and he said it was the *a b-abs and the i b-ibs*. I then asked him if he knew the Queen's name, to which he replied in the negative. I frequently ask this question of boys, and find that in fully half the cases in which I do so, of boys from ten to fourteen, they cannot tell the Queen's name, nor have they ever heard of her Majesty. I put some questions in geography to a boy, who told me he had been learning it for two years. "What is the shape of the earth?" I asked. "Round, like an orange," he answered. "What is a promontory?" I next inquired. "Master always skips about the promontories," he replied. "What is an island, then?" I demanded. "Master skips that, too, sir," said he. "Well, what is a river?" This he answered correctly; but on further questioning him in connection with the very elements of the study, the reply in three cases out of four was that his master "skipped" the subject. Nor was this the child of an agricultural labourer. He was the son of a tradesman, living in a Cornish town, and attending school regularly. Let it be borne in mind that not only are numbers of the rising generation growing up defectively educated, but that a larger proportion of them are doing so without any education at all. Even in Cornwall, where, comparatively speaking, so much is done for education, by the different sects, this is the case to a very great extent. In treating of the Cornish mines, I have already had occasion to allude to the number of children engaged about them who could not read, and the still greater number who could not write. In a few years therefore, notwithstanding all the efforts which are being veritably or ostensibly made, a large proportion of those who are now children will be launched into manhood with all the stolidity and ignorance of their fathers.

Our social system is full of anomalies, but there is none greater, perhaps, than that presented by the parochial union school, such as it is. The child of the independent labourer is sent to toil at the age when he should be sent to school. It is only at irregular intervals that he enters a day school, and it is not always that he can attend a Sunday school. He never enters any school provided for him by law. But the child of the pauper finds a legal provision for the sustenance of his body and the culture of his mind. His day is not spent in toil, but is divided between his education and his amusement. When he leaves the school-room—which he attends, in summer for six, and in winter for five hours a day—it is to go to the playground, which he frequently finds provided for him with many of the appliances of childish sports. How different in their fates—the child of the independent man, and the child of the pauper! But where is the remedy for this anomaly? The evil is, not that the pauper is too well off, but that the child of independence should not be abreast, at least as regards his opportunities, with the offspring of poverty.

Having thus glanced generally at the educational system at work in the four counties in question, I now proceed to state the results of my observations as regards the morals of the labouring classes in all the counties which I have hitherto visited. In doing so, I regret to say, that the sketch which I am about to draw will be by no means of a favourable or encouraging description.

There are two things which strike every observer as exercising a most pernicious influence upon the habits and morals of the poor— the straitened character of their house accommodation, and the lowness of their wages. When I speak of low wages, I include casual work even at high wages—since, independently of the consideration that the average throughout the year may be low, those receiving them are frequently exposed to greater privations than are those steadily employed at low wages. But it does not follow that the ordinary day labourer in the fields is highly paid when only casually employed. If the rate of wages is but 7s. a week, and he is employed but for one day in the week, he gets but his fourteen pence a day like the man steadily employed. To low wages, therefore, a great proportion of the agricultural labourers have to add the terrible disadvantage of unsteady employment at the lowest rates. Taking the rate in Dorset as 8s. throughout the year, including the higher rates of harvest, there are many who will not average 5s. a week, taking the whole year round. In considering, therefore, the effect of low wages upon the condition and conduct of the poor, it is not enough that we take into account the nominal rate per week throughout a district, as there may be hundreds in it who are not realizing that rate for two consecutive weeks at a time.

The facts which I have from time to time stated, as illustrating the overcrowded condition of a very large proportion of the cottages, are so eloquent of themselves, that it is scarcely necessary for me to add anything as to the pernicious influence which such a state of things must have upon the morals of the poor. When families of from six to twelve individuals, of both sexes and of all ages, are huddled together night after night in two, three, or four beds, all in one room, what are we to expect as the result but a very general and a fearfully precocious immorality? I have met now and then with families crowded in their straitened dwellings who were, nevertheless, pious, lovers of truth, honest in their dealings, and exemplary in their conduct. But such green spots are rarely met with in the wide moral waste; and one marvels at their appearance at all. With the great bulk of the peasantry there is a laxity of morals which is as easily accounted for as it is painful to contemplate. The moral sense of many of them revolts at the circumstances in which they are placed; but the most startling feature connected with the whole matter is, the utter indifference which multitudes, who complain loudly enough of their physical privations, evince as regards the immoralities to which their condition gives rise. In thousands of breasts the distinction between right and wrong is but faintly traced, if it is not altogether obliterated. Perhaps, in all this they are more to be pitied than blamed, for the mode of life to which they are condemned would sap the morality of any class of people.

There are two classes amongst them who suffer from the manner in which the peasantry are herded together in their miserable dwellings. There are, in the first place, those who, from peculiar circumstances, may have reached maturity with some delicacy of feeling and purity of mind preserved to them, of which they are gradually robbed through the pernicious influences to which they are exposed. It is possible that some of these may successfully stem the torrent of immorality which would bear them down, and come pure and undefiled out of its filthy waters at last. But these are few indeed. It is possible, too, that some of them, having fallen away, may yet reclaim themselves, the virtues of early life triumphing at last over engrafted vice. But such instances are also of rare occurrence. There is, in the next place, that other class, and by far the more numerous one, the members of which advance from infancy to puberty aliens to shame and strangers to the common decencies of life. Of these, what can reasonably be expected, but that the vices which are sown broad-cast in them during their youth will grow with their growth and strengthen with their strength?

Let us consider, for a moment, the progress of a family amongst them. A man and woman intermarry, and take a cottage. In eight cases out of ten it is a cottage with but two rooms. For a time, so far as room at least is concerned, this answers their purpose; but they take it, not because it is at the time sufficiently spacious for them, but because they could not procure a more roomy dwelling, even did they desire it. In this they pass with tolerable comfort, considering their notions of what comfort is, the first period of married life. But, by-and-by they have children, and the family increases until, in the course of a few years, they number perhaps from eight to ten individuals. But all this time there has been no increase to their household accommodation. As at first, so to the very last, there is but the one sleeping-room. As the family increases additional beds are crammed into this apartment, until at last it is so filled with them that there is scarcely room left to move between them. As already mentioned, I have known instances in which they had to crawl over each other, to get to their beds. So long as the children are very young, the only evil connected with this is the physical one arising from crowding so many people together into what is generally a dingy, frequently a damp, and invariably an ill-ventilated apartment. But years steal on, and the family continues thus bedded together. Some of its members may yet be in their infancy, but others of both sexes have crossed the line of puberty. But there they are, still together in the same room—the father and mother, the sons and the daughters—young men, young women, and children. Cousins, too, of both sexes are often thrown together into the same room, and not unfrequently into the same bed. I have also known of cases in which uncles slept in the same room with their grown-up nieces, and newly-married couples occupied the same chamber with those long married, and with others marriageable but unmarried. A case also came to my notice, already alluded to in connection with another branch of the subject, in which two sisters, who were married on the same day, occupied adjoining rooms in the same hut, with nothing but a thin board partition, which did not reach the ceiling, between the two rooms, and a door in the partition which only partly filled up the door-way. For years back, in these same two rooms, have slept twelve people, of both sexes and all ages. Sometimes, when there is but one room, a praiseworthy effort is made for the conservation of decency. But the hanging up of a piece of tattered cloth between the beds, which is generally all that is done in this respect, and even that but seldom, is but a poor set-off to the fact that a family which, in common decency, should, as regards sleeping accommodations, be separated at least into three divisions, occupy, night after night, but one and the same chamber. This is a frightful position for them to be in when an infectious or epidemic disease enters their abode. But this, important though it be, is the least important consideration connected with their circumstances. That which is most so, is the effect produced by them upon their habits and morals. In the illicit intercourse to which such a position frequently gives rise, it is not always that the tie of blood is respected. Certain it is that when the relationship is even but one degree removed from that of brother and sister, that tie is frequently overlooked. And when the circumstances do not lead to such horrible consequences, the mind, particularly of the female, is wholly divested of that sense of delicacy and shame which, so long as they are preserved, are the chief safeguards of her chastity. She therefore falls an early and an easy prey to the temptations which beset her beyond the immediate circle of her family. People in the other spheres of life are but little aware of the extent to which this precocious demoralization of the female amongst the lower orders in the country has proceeded. But how could it be otherwise? The philanthropist may exert himself in their behalf, the moralist may inculcate even the worldly advantages of a better course of life, and the minister of religion may warn them of the eternal penalties which they are incurring; but there is an instructor constantly at work more potent than them all, an instructor in mischief, of which they must get rid ere they make any real progress in their laudable efforts—and that is, *the single bed chamber, in the two-roomed cottage.*

So well aware are parties resident in the country of all this, that in many families you will now see none but town-bred servants. True, this may partly be accounted for by the utter ignorance in which young women in the country are generally brought up of everything connected with the economy of a household. But this is not the only reason that is given you when you inquire into the cause of it. With many their prevalent demoralization weighs far more than the other consideration with those who reject the proffered services of the rustics. Yet how many in our towns, acting upon a contrary belief, look to the country as the only quarter where they can obtain honest and virtuous menials. This, I was told, had been done to a great extent in Bath, and I shall never forget the description given to me of the results by one of the resident clergymen of the city.

Perhaps, the most striking instance of the demoralization of a whole community, from overcrowding and other unpropitious circumstances, is that furnished by Sutton Courtney, in Berkshire, formerly alluded to in connection with the subject of education in that county. I was not then aware of the notoriety which this village had already attained. When England was first divided into unions, that of Abingdon was about the first to be marked off. The people of Abingdon were willing that the commissioners should draw any line they pleased, provided they only excluded Sutton Courtney from the union. Its character was then so bad that the people of the neighbouring parishes recoiled from the idea of being comprehended within the same division with it. The commissioners having acquainted themselves with the grounds on which this request was made, complied with it, and Sutton Courtney was erected into a union of itself, on the understanding, however, that whenever it amended its character it should merge into the Abingdon union. It is now part and parcel of that union, from which it is to be inferred that its character has somewhat improved. It was therefore in its amended state that I found it. Judging from its present condition, it must formerly have been inconceivably bad, or the people of Abingdon have been satisfied with very slight tokens of amendment. Despite the exertions of the zealous and independent vicar, the Rev. Mr. Gregson, whose efforts have not been without some success, the place is to this day a focus of intemperance and debauchery of every kind. Chastity is a thing little known in the village, and not at all respected. The want of it is regarded as no stain on a woman's character, nor does it mar her prospects in the slightest degree. Herself a prostitute, and the companion of thieves and prostitutes, she is just as likely to marry and get settled—as people in her class of life are generally settled—as is the honest and virtuous woman in localities possessing a higher standard of morality. I found more than one family of children going by different names. The mother was unmarried, and the different names indicated the paternity of the different children. Again, a whole family has been known to go by different names at different times. Thus, if the mother were living with a man of the name of Smith, the children took his name, but if she changed her paramour and lived with one named Tomkins the family would go by the new name. Children have thus been known to give to parties inquiring one name to-day and a different one to-morrow. It is distressing to witness the early age at which they commence a life of active immorality. Young girls may be seen at the public-houses sodden with gin or drunk with beer. There is, of course, no line drawn by them for the regulation of their conduct after this. Indeed, they are proficients in licentiousness ere they reach this point. The violence of their tempers, too, leads them into perpetual brawls and fights. I was told by one woman that when she had occasion to send any of them into the fields, she always sent a boy and a girl, because they would not quarrel; whereas if she sent two boys or two girls, they were sure to disagree and fight. The vicar has at length induced some of them to attend church; but when he first took possession of his charge, he used to find the men, surrounded by nearly all the women and children of the village, playing quoits before the church door on Sunday morning.

Perhaps the worst feature connected with the immorality prevailing amongst these classes is the apparent absence of all shame on the part of those guilty or that of their friends. It really seems in many places to be taken as a matter of course that a young woman will be found with child before she is married. Many are married as soon as they become pregnant. When marriage does not take place the child is generally consigned to the care of the mother of the girl, whilst she herself, when she can, goes out in the capacity of wet nurse. The grandmother will speak as coolly of the whole affair as did both mother and daughter in the case alluded to in a former letter from Cornwall, terming it a "misfortune," but the misfortune being more the necessity of maintaining the child than the stain on the woman's reputation. Indeed, I have reason to believe that in an immense number of cases young people come to a distinct understanding with each other to cohabit illicitly, until the woman becomes pregnant, the man promising to "make an honest woman of her" as soon as that takes place. This they find more convenient than marrying at once, inasmuch as the girl may be at service for herself, and the man elsewhere employed all the time. They meet occasionally, and are thus relieved at least of the responsibilities and the duties of housekeeping, living better on their separate earnings than they could do in a house of their own.

This practice of cohabitation before marriage is almost universal. It is not only a characteristic of low rural life, it is also so with the miners and the fishermen. Even in the fishing village of Mousehole, the people of which are in general so orderly, it is the case. And this, too, notwithstanding the extent to which temperance has prevailed amongst them. Total abstinence has not effected much in this respect for society. The miners and pitmen, too, are much more under the influence of constant religious teachings than is the rural labourer. And yet they are no better than he is, so far as the practice alluded to is concerned. When a young fisherman passes 18 he generally gets a man's wages. Immediately thereupon he gets a new suit of clothes and a watch, after which he fancies himself sufficiently set up in the world to commence a courtship, which generally leads to an early marriage by the course mentioned. In some parts of Cornwall the immorality of the females at work about the mines is notorious and proverbial.

It is on the Sunday evening that most mischief is done in this respect. No one can enter or leave a rural town at that time without being convinced of this. It is the time when servants, both male and female, are most generally permitted to go out, and it is therefore that for which they arrange most of their assignations. They have a slang of their own, in which their arrangements are pretty unreservedly made in the presence of those who, they think, have not the key to it. This, after some time, I became acquainted with, and I have frequently overheard them planning their assignations, which, in nine cases out of ten, were arranged for the first Sunday evening. The extent to which very young persons of both sexes participate in these arrangements is really shocking.

Nothing can be more fatal to the young girl, after the training which she has received at home, than the work to which she is so early consigned in the fields. She there often meets with associates, even of her own sex, who speedily qualify her for any criminalities in which she may be afterwards tempted to participate.

To every one all this must appear very horrible, whilst to some its relation will seem indelicate. But the only question worth considering is, whether or not it be true. If true, is it not better that it should be openly exposed, than that, existing, it should be suppressed for fear of offending the questionably delicate? It is unfortunately but too true; and being so, it is high time that the attention of society should be earnestly directed to the essentially demoralized state of the substratum at its base.

I was anxious to ascertain the effect, if any, produced by the late bastardy law in the different localities which I visited. But on this subject I found it extremely difficult to obtain any information of an authentic character. So far as the workhouses were concerned, the registers of births within them sufficed to apprise me of the true state of things. But on the subject generally, as affecting the parishes constituting the unions, I could only procure expressions of opinion, and these were sometimes singularly contradictory. The general impression, however, seemed to be that the law had had but little effect one way or the other. But to show how difficult it is to get correct information on this subject, I was told by some of the guardians in the workhouse at Wareham that they were inclined to believe that bastardy had decreased, not only out of doors, but even in the house; whereas, on inspecting the books, I found that quite the contrary was the case as regards the workhouse. I found that the number of illegitimate births which had taken place in the workhouse, since 1838 inclusive, was 53, giving an average of about 4½ per year. But for each of the last two years the number has been seven, or about 60 per cent. above the average of the last eleven years. This, however, is not to be taken as an indication of a similar increase outside, inasmuch as the greater difficulties than formerly which are now in the way of affiliation drive women into the house who would not otherwise, perhaps, have entered it.

In small parishes, where the clergyman is frequently brought into personal contact with the labourers, and where, from other causes, he exercises a direct influence over them, they may be found pretty regular in their attendance at church; but, generally speaking, their attendance is neither large nor constant, most of them moping about on the Sunday smoking and drinking, and some of them spending nearly the whole day in bed.

Another circumstance which powerfully affects the morals of the poor, is the lowness of their wages, and the physical privations to which they are thereby subjected. If a labourer has abundance of room for his family in his cottage, he will crowd them all into a single chamber, and let the other rooms if he can. The evils incident to his position are thus of a complicated character. In the great majority of cases he has not sufficient house accommodation, whilst in those in which he has, the lowness and uncertainty of his wages, and his consequent scanty command of the necessaries of life, induce him, when he can, to throw away the advantages of it. Thoroughly to elevate him, the work of improvement must be simultaneously pursued from different points.

A large proprietor being asked, when the conversation had turned upon the state of wages, how the poor could live upon the pittances per week which they earned so precariously, turned round, and said somewhat sternly, "they steal." This is true to a frightful extent throughout the counties in question. Petty theft, on his own and his family's part, may be regarded as part and parcel of a labourer's means. This is truly an alarming position in which to find so large a class of the community; but it is, nevertheless, their veritable position; and that it is generally known to be such throughout the country districts, is evident from the universal testimony to the fact borne by those who care for conversing upon the subject. Ask any one how families can live on 7s., 8s., or 9s. a week, and the answer almost invariably is, "They can't do so *honestly.*" The inference is irresistible that they live dishonestly; and so the great bulk of them do. This is more particularly the case as regards the article of fuel. In general I find them open, unreserved, and communicative on almost all other subjects; but the moment I touch upon the subject of fuel, their whole demeanour, in most cases, undergoes a change, and their awkward and incoherent statements are often in perfect contrast with their former readiness and consistency in reply. You can see at once that, whilst they tell you something, there is much that they are keeping back. In some places, furze is raised for fuel, and they are not so ill off in this respect; in others they burn turf, which they sometimes get for the cutting, although at others they have to buy it. When they have to buy their turf, or when there is neither furze nor turf, and they must look for their fuel to coal or wood, the greatest privations are suffered as the consequence of their very scanty supply. When they buy their wood, they buy it in faggots, a faggot being frequently little better than a bundle of green twigs. Even this they are not always able to purchase; when, unless they are permitted to take wood, which is very rarely indeed the case, they have to look to theft alone for their supply of fuel. In many parts of Cornwall, Devon, and Dorset, and in some parts of Wilts, they are comparatively well supplied by the furze and turf, but in the other portions of these counties—throughout the greater part of Somerset, and, I may say, the whole of Bucks, Berks, and Oxford—where they have nothing but wood or coal to burn, one universal system of pilfering prevails in respect to fuel. Both as regards themselves and others, this is a perilous alternative to which the poor are driven by the sad necessities of their position. Without expending any of their means in the purchase of fuel, they manage, in most cases, but to eke out a mere existence, generally on an almost exclusively vegetable diet. To buy as much coal, wood, or turf as would serve them, not only for culinary purposes, but also to warm, during the cheerless months of winter, their damp, cold, and desolate homes, would, in very many instances, make greater inroads than they could bear into their means of procuring mere edibles. The consequence is, that such fuel as they cannot buy or get in charity they are driven to steal. The evil of this is manifest, for it is generally through the instrumentality of the children that the wants of the household are thus supplied. Petty theft is thus the first positive vice with which they are brought in contact, and in the practice of which they are almost daily instructed. What is the consequence? The child who becomes an adept in stealing wood, is soon qualified for robbing a hen-roost. From that again to stealing a sheep there is but another step; and, in the words of a clergyman with whom I was conversing on this subject, "when a man goes out to steal a sheep he is ready for anything." Is it any wonder, seeing how many children are thus perniciously instructed, that so large a proportion of those who figure in the statistics of crime are juvenile delinquents? The course which this mischievous education takes with the child was well illustrated by an incident which happened as I was walking over his glebe in company with the vicar of Southleigh. On turning a sharp corner we met a boy on the road dragging home a piece of timber. On seeing us he immediately dropped it, assuming, at the same time, that half-frightened, half-ashamed look, which those who are not thoroughly callous assume on being detected in the very act of committing an offence. "Where did you get that piece of timber?" asked the vicar. "I found it on the road," said the boy, who was but eight years old. This was a falsehood, for he had taken it out of the neighbouring copse. The vicar sent for the mother of the child. Her plea was that she sent him for wood, but did not enjoin him to steal it. She well knew, however, that he could not get it without stealing it, and he well knew that he was not expected to come home empty-handed. What an education is this for a child! It may be said that it is but a trivial offence to take a piece of wood. But the evil is, teaching the child deliberately to do that which he knows and feels to be wrong. He does it *animo furandi*, and thus it is that the line between right and wrong is so early erased from his mind.

One of the objects of the coal clubs, established in some places, is to check this monstrous evil.

Let me say, in summing up the whole, that a pervading moral apathy is the general characteristic of the peasantry, when positive crime is absent—an apathy which leads, in too many cases, to an utter indifference to the distinction between right and wrong.

In connection with this subject, it is extremely discouraging to find how little good is effected by the education received in the workhouse. It is painful to find how few of the children who are turned out from some of the workhouses come to any good. This shows two things: first, how difficult it is to eradicate the pernicious influences of an essentially vicious domestic education; and secondly, how little proper training accompanies the mere act of teaching in the workhouse. In many instances have cases been pointed out to me of boys entering the gaol soon after leaving the house, and of girls returning pregnant to it a year or two after they had left it.

To many who have not been prepared for such revelations the foregoing may appear to be one sweeping calumny against the agricultural labourer. But it is not hastily that I have prepared this indictment, and to prove it I can call confidently into court the landed proprietor, the farmer, the guardian of the poor, the governor of the workhouse, the minister of the parish, and the magistrate of the county.

The Morning Chronicle, Saturday, December 1, 1849.

To THE EDITOR OF THE MORNING CHRONICLE.

SIR—Will you have the kindness to apply the enclosed Post-office order for 5*l.* to the relief of the consumptive couple at Bere, mentioned in your Correspondent's 12th letter, in *The Morning Chronicle* of Wednesday, Nov. 28, as being out of work, with four children and a little orphan whom they had in their true Christian charity adopted?

Faithfully yours,

Nov. 29, 1849.   G. H.

The REDUCTION of the TEA DUTIES.

To THE EDITOR OF THE MORNING CHRONICLE.

SIR—As "every little helps" in a good cause, I trust I may not be thought to infringe on the invaluable statements in *The Morning Chronicle* relative to "Labour and the Poor," if I mention one simple fact as to the price of tea in the rural districts. The aged poor in this village, in the west of England, use every effort to have a little tea; which is, in fact, to them the most grateful beverage, as well as their principal support, in connection with that *sopped bread* which is well known to west-country people as *"tea-kettle broth."* Now, sir, the general habit of the poor old folks in the villages is to go to the village shops for *one pen'orth* of tea—or what is called tea. For their penny, thus applied, they get *one quarter of an ounce!*—that is, these poor people are obliged to give 4d. per ounce, or 5s. 4d. per lb., for an article no better certainly than what their richer neighbours can buy at 4s. This fact I know, of my own knowledge; and surely it supports, in no trifling degree, your able advocacy, for the sake of the poor, of a reduction of the tea duties.—Wishing you all success in the "social and holy cause" in which you have embarked, I am, sir, your faithful servant,

A COUNTRY CLERGYMAN.

The Morning Chronicle, Monday, December 3, 1849.

To the EDITOR of the MORNING CHRONICLE.

Sir—I enclose you a bank note, No. 3,204, 13th October, of which you would oblige me by giving 2*l.* to the poor woman at Bere, in Dorsetshire, who so charitably took care of the orphan child; 2*l.* to the old man with the maimed knee, vainly struggling to obtain a livelihood as hot eel seller, for want of a little capital; and the other sovereign to any deserving needlewoman.—Requesting an acknowledgment,

I am, sir, your obedient servant,

Friday, Nov. 30, 1849.　　　　　　　　　　　　　　S. E. C.

The Morning Chronicle, Wednesday, January 23, 1850.

LABOUR AND THE POOR.

—◆—

THE RURAL DISTRICTS.

[FROM OUR SPECIAL CORRESPONDENT.]

THE STONE QUARRIES OF SWANAGE.

LETTER XXVIII.*

Before proceeding to describe the condition of the agricultural labourer in the counties forming the south-eastern angle of the kingdom, it may not be amiss that I should present the reader with a brief account of the quarries and quarriers of Swanage. Such a task may appear to be somewhat episodical in a series of communications having more especial reference to the state and circumstances of the agricultural labourers, with whom the parties in question cannot properly be classed. But if they cannot be strictly so classed, it requires no very great latitude of construction to bring their occupation within the category of labour in the rural districts. It is only thus that, like the miner and the fisherman, they can be brought within the range of the present inquiry; whilst their singular position, peculiar habits, and antiquated fashion of transacting business, render them more interesting as a study than even the laborious excavator in the mine, or the hardy adventurer who braves all weathers in pursuit of the mackerel, the herring, and the pilchard.

A little to the east of St. Alban's Head the coast of Dorset trends suddenly in a northerly direction. From the north side of the entrance to Poole Harbour it makes again to the eastward, stretching towards the Isle of Wight in a waving line, that terminates with the long point of sand on the extremity of which, commanding the entrance to the Solent, stands the historic fortalice of Hurst Castle. The town of Swanage, which is in the bight of Swanage Bay, is situated about midway between St. Alban's Head and Poole Harbour, having thus an easterly look-out, with the Isle of Wight visible in the distance, when

---

* Letter XXVIII. is reproduced here (out of publication sequence) to complete the Dorset letters.

the day is at all clear. The district of high land which rises abruptly behind the town, and stretches back for some miles in the direction of Corfe Castle and Kingston, is also known by the name of Swanage. This district comprises the stone quarries in question.

On approaching Swanage from the direction of Studland, the whole district behind it, sloping rapidly up from the sea, presents to the stranger the appearance of one huge rabbit-warren. It has a varied aspect, from the surface being in some places tolerably well cultivated, and in others still covered with down. But what strikes one most is the number of holes with which it appears to be perforated, and the quantity of rubbish which has been thrown up in the immediate vicinity of each. These are to be seen, in all directions, scattered not only over the face of the downs, but also amongst the fields which have been enclosed and cultivated. They impart to the district the singular appearance alluded to; and the stranger, ignorant of its real character, might, on approaching, fancy it a spot in which game of all kinds had enjoyed a succession of jubilees, ever since the establishment of the New Forest itself.

But these are far from being the tokens of the abandonment of the land either to game or vermin. They are the signs of busy industry, the results of the toil of generations of honest and hard-working men. The chief value of the district is not in its surface, but in that which is beneath. The holes which so thickly stud the hill side are the means by which the quarriers get at its hidden treasures. The small mounds beside the holes consist partly of the produce of their labours, and partly of the debris which they necessarily accumulate in the conduct of their operations.

The district in question is part and parcel of the Isle of Purbeck, so long celebrated for its marble and its different varieties of stone. The most southerly of the chalk ridges, which dips into the sea at the Needles, emerges from it again at the point known as Old Harry, immediately to the north of Swanage—this point, indeed, forming the northern boundary of the bay. From this point it proceeds inland towards Corfe Castle, stretching towards Dorchester and the borders of Devon, near which some of its spurs again dip into the sea. The strip of land lying between this chalk ridge and the Channel, and including Swanage, the greater part of the Isle of Purbeck, and the whole of the Isle of Portland, is rich in sandstone, and here and there in that peculiar species of marble which has entered so largely into the ornamental part of our ecclesiastical architecture. About Swanage and the Isle of Portland, the sandstone comes near the surface, and is easily quarried. Proceeding northward from the coast, it soon dips under the chalk—where, of course, it cannot be worked.

Swanage has long been celebrated for its quarries and its quarriers. Almost from time immemorial has stone been extracted from the hills which sweep around the bay, until now the whole country, for miles back, is so perforated and undermined as to resemble one huge catacomb. From the earliest period, too, the quarriers have existed as an organized body—bound together, not only by the tie naturally created amongst those engaged in common pursuits, but also by a number of ancient and revered articles, which they have invariably treated as a charter of incorporation. Indeed, for centuries they were known in their corporate capacity as the Company of Marblers. They still retain the articles, to which even to this day they pay especial reverence, and they still keep up to some extent the organization of former times. That to which they now cling, however, is more the form than the substance of bygone privileges—the skeleton of their organization being still perfect, although the flesh and muscle have long since dropped away from it. But much as the general objects of the original association have been departed from, there are still some points in respect to which they are to this day rigidly enforced.

Originally, the body of stone quarriers constituted a species of copartnery—each member being interested in the profits, and liable, *pro rata*, to make good the losses of the body. When such was the case, wardens were annually elected, under the articles, whose business it was to exercise a general supervision over the interests of the body, to dispose of the produce of its labour, and divide the proceeds amongst its members. The wardens thus chosen by the quarriers were invariably members of their own body; and during their tenure of office they were relieved from all duties, except such as pertained to the post which they were called upon to fill. Some of these are still performed by the wardens—for, to the extent of electing these ancient officers, at least, the old organization is still kept up. They are not, however, so numerous now as formerly, for the simple reason that their duties are more limited. The number now elected does not exceed two, who, with the secretary (whose position is permanent), constitute the entire official staff of the body. The quarriers have still common interests to watch over and promote; and in the furtherance of these they still act in their united capacity. But the general partnership of past times no longer exists—each, so far as his labour is concerned, being at liberty to promote his own individual interests, whilst it is competent for as many as please to unite in groups for the same object.

One of the main objects of the original association was to secure a monopoly of the quarrying trade of the district. To effect this it was made one of the articles that none but such as were made free of the company should be permitted to enter its works, or to have any share whatever in the business which it pursued. As it scarcely ever happened that any were made free of the company but the children of its existing members, it followed that strangers were effectually excluded, and that the business of stone quarrying, in that neighbourhood at least, remained a complete monopoly in the hands of a certain number of families. If antiquity be an essential element of true nobility, there are families at this moment in Swanage, with unbroken genealogies, extending back far beyond those of half the nobles in the realm. One can understand both the institution and the jealous maintenance of such a provision, so long as the whole body constituted one company with common interests and liabilities. But now that the partnership is effectually broken up, and the business is pursued individually, and not as a corporate concern, it may be easier to account for, than to justify, their continued adhesion to the rule for the exclusion of strangers from the quarries. They themselves have free warren of the wide field of competition around them, of which many of them, impatient of labour in the quarries, take advantage, and obtain employment in the metropolis, or wherever else Government works may be in progress—for it is generally to these that they flock. Should they tire of this, or should occupation elsewhere fail them, the quarries at Swanage are open to them on their return—for "once a quarrier always a quarrier" is the rule. It is this that renders so invidious their jealous exclusion of the stranger from their own peculiar field. They avail themselves of the right to compete with him on his ground, but will not suffer him to meet them on theirs. They have, of course, no legal right to exclude him. Any man who chooses may, if he can get a lease from the lord of the soil, take a quarry at Swanage, and work it. But there are a thousand ways in which they could annoy him and put him at a disadvantage; and to remain, under such circumstances, for any length of time amongst them, a man would require to be possessed of some means, and of an uncommon stock of fortitude. They are particularly jealous of the Portland men, who, on the other hand, are equally jealous of them. If a master-quarrier employs any stranger in his quarry, he is liable to a fine of £5—the mode of exacting which will be afterwards alluded to. In some cases there might be a mitigation of the penalty, but the fine would, in all instances, be inflexibly enforced if the interloper could be traced back to Portland. Indeed, the rule is, never to remit, and seldom to mitigate, the fine— a knowledge of which, on the part of the quarriers generally, renders the necessity for its imposition a matter of rare occurrence. An amusing instance of the extent to which the jealousy in question is carried, and particularly as regards strangers of their own order elsewhere, was related to me by a Swanage man who had attempted to smuggle himself into the quarries in Portland. When they find a stranger at work in the latter place they generally permit him to work for a week, at the end of which time they presume that he has earned enough to carry him out of the island. They then, when circumstances will admit of it, present a very ugly alternative to him—namely, to walk a plank, partly projecting over a cliff, or to quit Portland, never to return to it. My informant told me that, for the first week, he was treated with every possible consideration; indeed, he could not conceive of greater kindness than that which he experienced, particularly from the man who worked next to him—"Yet that was the very man who laid the plank for me when the week was out," said he; giving me to understand that the alternative alluded to was then quietly, but seriously, offered to him. As a sensible man, he preferred quitting the island to walking over a cliff into the sea. "And would you serve a Portland man in the same way?" I asked him. "Well, I am not sure that we would," said he; "but we would lead him such a dog's life of it, that he would soon be glad enough to be off." The system of exclusion is, perhaps, not now so rigidly adhered to in Portland as in Swanage—the Government works which have recently been carried on at the former place having tended, more or less, to break it down, from the large and constant influx of strangers which they have occasioned.

A quarrier cannot be made free of the company until he is twenty-one. He may be apprenticed at any age at which he may be found capable of working; but at whatever time that may be, his probation does not cease until he comes of age. It is to his father that he is generally apprenticed, or, if the latter is dead, to his nearest male relative, being a quarrier. It is not necessary, however, that the master should be at all related to the apprentice. It is to the father, however, that in the great majority of cases he is apprenticed, the business regularly descending from father to son. Indeed, the veriest infants, when males, are generally treated by their parents as the raw material for future quarriers. The father is entitled to the whole profits of his son's labour during the entire period of his apprenticeship. Should the father die during the term, the apprentice does not necessarily become his own master. In that case, the mother's interests are provided for—she being conditionally entitled to the profits of his work until he attains the age at which he can be admitted a freeman. The condition on which this right is secured to her is a very simple one, and one easily performed, being neither more nor less than the payment of a shilling into the funds of the company on the day of her marriage. This condition, which is within the reach of every couple, is almost universally complied with. The ceremony of admission takes place but once a year. The grand gala-day of the quarriers is Shrove Tuesday. On that day they meet at Corfe Castle for the admission of new members and the general management of their affairs, so far as they are still regulated in common. The apprentices who have completed their term, and are otherwise unexceptionable, are then admitted, and on payment of 6s. 8d. are enrolled freemen of the company, being thenceforth entitled for life to all the privileges which that honour confers upon them. On this occasion, the quarriers manage to combine festivity and amusement with business. I have already alluded to the condition on which the mother, in case of the father's death, is entitled to her son's earnings whilst he remains an apprentice. The last couple married during the year have to provide a foot-ball, which is regarded as tantamount to the shilling paid by others—the woman who provides the foot-ball being entitled to all the privileges of those paying the shilling. As soon as the young men who are found qualified have been admitted and enrolled members of the company, they are sent out to amuse themselves with a game at foot-ball, in which they very heartily engage. The articles of the company, some of which are supposed to date back as far as the reign of Richard II., are then read by the secretary to the seniors, who remain in conclave behind, the newly-made members not being admitted to so great a privilege until the following year. If there are any matters of general interest to be talked over they are then discussed, after which the elders adjourn to join the young men at their game. The festive board is not a feature overlooked amongst the ceremonies of the day, which generally, however, to the credit of those concerned, closes without riot or disorder. Such is the principal ceremony enacted at these annual meetings—a ceremony which has now reference more to the commemoration of past privileges than the maintenance of present ones.

The secretary is a man of no little authority with them. The influence which the present incumbent of that office wields is more of a personal than an official character. His name is Webber. He is at present chief clerk and book-keeper in the office of the Messrs. Pike, formerly alluded to as the principal clay merchants in the neighbourhood of Wareham. His original occupation was that of a stone-mason, which he still occasionally pursues, during his leisure hours, by way of recreation. His labours on such occasions generally take a funereal turn—the carving of gravestones being his forte as regards the chisel. Having received some education in his youth, he has turned it to the best advantage; not only thereby improving his own position, but acquiring an almost unbounded influence over the body to whom he originally pertained. He is not only their chief official, but also their friend and counsellor. "Mr. Webber," they will tell you, "is an understandin' man. He knows more about us than we do ourselves. He keeps us all right. Whenever we get into difficulty we always go to he." To the qualities of the intelligent observer and shrewd man of business, Mr. Webber superadds some touch of the poetic fire, as the file of the *Poole Herald* can testify.

The quarriers are now divided amongst themselves into two classes—the master-quarriers, and the ordinary quarriers, who give their labour for hire. This classification goes evidently no further back than the termination of their original arrangement, by which all the quarriers were upon an equal footing. The difference between a master and an ordinary quarrier is purely accidental—the two classes not existing as distinct orders amongst them. A master-quarrier is he who takes and works a quarry; and there is nothing to prevent an ordinary workman from taking a quarry if he pleases, and if the lord is willing to give him a lease. Many of the quarries are taken and worked by a single quarrier, all the aid which he receives in his operations being in the shape of hired labour. In other cases, several join together in a kind of partnership, working a quarry between them—being sometimes employed alone, and at others having hired labour in aid of their own. When one or more intend to take a quarry, the first thing to be done is to obtain a lease from the lord. This is generally granted without much difficulty, the lessees selecting their own ground, unless some good reasons exist for confining them in their choice. By the terms of the lease the landlord becomes, as it were, a partner in the adventure; his rent depending, as to amount, upon the quantity of stone yielded by the quarry. At

Swanage the stone produced is generally of two kinds—the solid block and the flat paving stone. The lord's dues are regulated by the number of superficial feet excavated in the one case, and generally by the number of cubic feet excavated in the other. They amount to a shilling for every hundred superficial feet of paving, and the same for every hundred cubic feet of solid stone. The lord has thus an interest not only in the goodness of the quarry, but also in the industry of the quarriers. One of the conditions of the lease, therefore, is, that the quarry shall be worked—a condition sometimes only complied with as regards its letter, when it is not the interest of the lessee or lessees either to work it constantly, or to give up the lease. It is seldom that anything in the shape of a written document passes between the parties, the leases having been verbal ones from time immemorial. And when a lease is once granted, the lessees cannot be dispossessed so long as they comply with the condition already alluded to. As to the scene of operations, too, they are only limited as regards the shaft; but, having sunk the shaft at the point selected when the lease is granted, they are at liberty to work under ground in any direction they please, and as far as they please, provided they do not transgress the bounds of the landlord's property, nor come within a hundred feet of another quarry which is being then actually worked. If they go beyond the bounds within which it is competent for the landlord to license them to work, and trespass upon another man's land, the party thus aggrieved has his remedy, as in ordinary cases. If they go within the forbidden distance of another quarry, the parties whose rights are thus invaded look not for their remedy to the law of England, either common, statute, or ecclesiastical, but to the code peculiar to the locality, and which may be designated as Swanage law.

For, amongst the other peculiarities of this singular district, it must be borne in mind that its people have their own code of laws, and their own mode of giving them effect. It is possible, no doubt, theoretically, that an English writ might issue into a Swanage quarry; but English law has, generally speaking, very little to do with the practical administration of Swanage justice. When a party is suspected of trespassing in the manner alluded to upon the rights of his neighbours, a meeting of the whole body is called, by whom the accusation is heard, and if a *prima facie* case is made out, a deputation is appointed to descend into the quarry and examine into the real state of the case. This deputation is not a mere committee of investigation, whose simple

duty it is to inquire and report—for it is contingently armed with ad-
ministrative powers, which it is enjoined to put in force, should such
a course be necessary, to do justice between the parties. Thus combin-
ing ministerial with judicial functions, the deputation descends into
the quarry, provided with compasses and other appliances necessary
for ascertaining the truth. If there is no ground for the accusation,
the charge is dismissed, and the matter goes no further, unless the
accusation be repeated; but if there is ground for it, and a trespass
has actually been committed, a fine is imposed upon the delinquent
party, according to the extent of his transgression. If the trespass is
one which is likely to be persevered in, it is the business of the deputation to take such steps as to render it impossible that it should be
so. To effect this, it is armed with very summary powers, which it
invariably exercises, whenever a necessity arises for putting them in
force. The mode of proceeding in such case is to destroy the portion
of the quarry in which the offence is otherwise likely to be continued. This is done by breaking down the roof, or otherwise destroying
the "lane" or level from which the stone is being excavated. When
this process is not likely to answer the purpose, or when its execution
might be attended with considerable risk or trouble, the end is more
speedily effected by walling up the lane with mason work, and thus
preventing the delinquent from having further ingress into it. It is
seldom that the offence is repeated after this, at least in the same direction; for the culprit is not certain that, should he again be caught
trespassing in the same quarter, he himself might not be walled bodily in as a warning to others. So tenacious are the quarriers of the
privileges which remain to them, that I am not sure that public opinion in Swanage would not sanction such a mode of procedure with
one who should prove himself incorrigible in their infraction. One
reason for enforcing the rule in question is that, if they approached
nearer each other, they might mutually endanger the stability of their
works, as will be seen when their mode of working is described. One
would think that their interest being thus mutual in the observance
of the rule, they would all be anxious to observe it. And so they are,
unless strongly tempted to infringe it. Thus, a vein of stone which is
being worked may be found to be both improving, and getting more
and more easy to work, when the prescribed limits are reached—and
then the temptation to transgress them is sometimes too strong to be
resisted. When the rule is being violated, the trespassers sometimes
work at night, so as not to be overheard. An amusing story is told of

two parties who were lately thus trespassing upon each other. They generally worked within the forbidden limits at night, until at length one of them drove his crowbar through the thin partition which separated them. The surprise of both may be imagined at seeing each other's light gleaming through the aperture which thus unexpectedly revealed them to each other. Mutual recrimination would have been worse than useless, so for a time the matter was prudently hushed up between them; but at length it leaked out, to the great scandal of the whole body.

For all purposes of action as a body, their organization is essentially democratic. They settle nothing by delegates—all matters of common interest being canvassed and determined in their primary assemblies. It is only when the time for action comes that they delegate their powers. Whenever a question arises which it is necessary for them to settle, the two stewards or wardens of the body go round to all the quarries—not exactly with the fiery cross—but with a notification to all the members of the body to attend a general meeting thereof at a time and place then mentioned. Nor is this a notification to be disregarded with impunity, the attendance being compulsory. The absentee, unless detained by sickness or other unavoidable cause, is liable, for non-attendance, to a fine of 3s. 4d.; and this being more than the average value of a whole day's work, it is seldom that any who can attend are absent for the sake of gaining half-a-day, which is the time usually occupied by such meetings. The place of meeting is generally the neighbourhood of some well-known quarry in as central a position as possible. At the mouth of most quarries there is a capstan used in drawing the stone out of the mine. The meeting is constituted under the presidency of the session warden, whereupon the business of the day is immediately entered upon. The assembly is usually addressed from the capstan, which is mounted by the different orators in succession. Sometimes the utmost order is preserved; at others, the assembly is somewhat disposed to be disorderly. "At times, sir," said one of them to me, "they do be all talking at once, except the warden, who keeps all the time calling 'silence!'" The matter, whatever it may be, being fully laid before the meeting, the next thing to be done is to come to some resolution respecting it. That being attained, the last business of the meeting is to devise the means of carrying its resolution into action. When the case is one of trespass, the mode of procedure is generally such as has been already described. When the body is called together to adjudicate upon the case of an interloper, the master-quarrier charged with having employed him is regularly put upon his trial. Should he be found guilty, he is condemned, as already intimated, to pay a fine of £5. Should he afterwards refuse to pay the fine, another meeting is convened, at which the whole matter is re-heard—when, if the former judgment is affirmed, the power of levying the fine, per force, if necessary, is delegated to a certain number of the body. These, after having given him sufficient time to reconsider his determination, proceed, if they find him still contumacious, to his quarry—and, without further warrant than the behest of the tribunal which appointed them, seize all the stone they can lay their hands upon, to the value of the fine imposed. A more lawless proceeding can scarcely be imagined—rendering, as it does, every man engaged in it liable to a civil action at least, if not to be criminally indicted, for the part he takes in it. Yet it is generally regarded in Swanage as one of the ordinary channels through which justice takes its course. Again, the body may be called together to consider respecting some real or fancied invasion of their privileges, or some nuisance which may have been instituted to their injury. The question then to be determined is, whether they will resist the innovation or abate the nuisance? If the case is one which admits only of passive resistance, the result is a simple resolution to resist; but if it is one calling for active measures, the means for taking them are immediately provided. It is but a short time ago since a case of this kind occurred. The grievance assumed the double aspect of the invasion of a right, and a positive nuisance. The offending object was neither more nor less than a weigh-bridge, which had recently been established upon a road over which the quarriers had long enjoyed the right of conveying as heavy loads as they pleased. They looked with the greatest suspicion upon the appearance amongst them of this appliance of civilized life, and immediately summoned a meeting to canvass its nature and consider its tendencies. The one they soon determined to be at least suspicious, and the other to be indisputably bad; so they resolved, by one and the same act, both to vindicate their right and abate the nuisance. The course determined upon was the very energetic one of demolishing the weigh-bridge, to effect which an executive commission was extemporized on the spot. This commission, armed with sledge hammers, was proceeding in the most orderly manner to the execution of its duty, when it was met by the *merchants* of Swanage—a set of men who will be afterwards alluded to—who did all in their power to divert it from its purpose. But all their entreaties were of no avail, until they at length pledged themselves that the offending object should be removed. On this the commission desisted, and the weigh-bridge was afterwards removed. The quarriers thus carried their point, and to this day they convey their loads over the road in question without being subjected to the annoyance of having them weighed, and of virtually paying a double toll—one for passing through the gate, in the neighbourhood of which the obnoxious machine was placed, and the other for the purpose of weighing. This may suffice to show how primitive is the state of development which society has as yet reached in Swanage.

When a quarry is taken, whether by one or more lessees, it of course requires several hands to work it. The number generally engaged in and about a quarry varies from six to twelve. When the adventurers themselves are in sufficient force to work it, no hard labour is called for. But it is seldom that you see a quarry where all those at work are master quarriers. It is not uncommon that you find two or three of them working a quarry in partnership, having five or six hired men about them to aid them in the work. The father is frequently found thus in partnership with his grown-up sons. In other cases a man, if his family is pretty numerous, may work his quarry with the aid of his sons alone, who may yet be all in their apprenticeship. The first practical operation is the sinking of the shaft, which is the only portion of the work requiring a little money capital on the part of the adventurer. The expenditure of this capital is, generally speaking, the best guarantee that the lord has that the quarry will be properly worked. The shaft is not sunk perpendicularly, as in most other mines, it being generally constructed at an angle of about 45°. It presents the appearance of a large hole in the form of a parallelogram, nearly perpendicular at one end, but slanting down at the other, at about the angle named. It is by the slant that access is had to the quarry, and the stone extracted is elevated to the surface. Along one side of this slant, or inclined plane, rude steps are constructed for the ascent and descent of the men. The rest of it is paved with flags, up which a truck is dragged with the stone which is being brought to the surface. Sometimes the motive power is a capstan—at others it is a horse. When the latter, the horse is, in some instances, joint property, and does duty at more than one quarry. The depth of the shaft is regulated by that of the vein under the surface. There are three veins of stone lying parallel to, and at pretty regular distances from, each other. To reach the first vein, the shaft, according to circumstances, must be sunk for from 40 to 70 feet. It is at the bottom of the shaft, when the vein is reached, and right under the perpendicular end of the shaft, that is to be found the real entrance to the quarry. It looks precisely like what it is—being neither more nor less than the entrance to an artificial cave. A horizontal passage is first driven from the foot of the inclined plane into the vein, from which "lanes" are struck off in different directions, in which lanes the quarry is worked. Generally, to get at the vein, a superincumbent stratum of solid but worthless stone has to be penetrated. Under this, and separated from it by only a very thin layer of clay, lies the first vein, in working which, the stone above forms a safe and substantial roof for the different lanes. They do not trust to it entirely, however, for as the lanes are widened, the roof is propped up by the rubbish which is accumulated. Thus, if a lane is originally constructed about eight feet wide, it is never permitted to exceed that width, for, to the extent to which the solid mass is excavated on the one side of it, the roof is propped up by the rubbish on the other. In some places the vein is six feet in depth, in which case it is all worked, when the men have sufficient room to stand at their labour. In others, however, it does not exceed three feet in thickness, when no more of the mass above or below is removed than is absolutely necessary to enable the men to work it. Thus, while some lanes are six feet high, others are not more than four, and the smaller the space, of course, the more laborious the occupation. Whenever they choose they can sink to the second or third veins. Many have gone to the second, but few to the third. Such as have done so have their shafts from 100 to 150 feet deep. The stone is excavated with comparative ease, lying as it does in horizontal layers, in contact with each other, and having numerous perpendicular fractures, which enable the men to detach it in blocks of different sizes from the mass. If the layers are thin, the produce is paving instead of block stone. Most quarries produce both, whilst in some the layers are occasionally found so thin that a species of slate stone is extracted from them. The stone is brought to the surface in the rough, where it is dressed and made ready for market by workmen who seldom descend into the quarry at all. This is frequently also the work to which apprentices are first put. The highest grade of work is that under ground. The work below is, of course, all conducted by candlelight; which, as may be supposed, does not add to the purity of the atmosphere in the lanes. Sometimes the quarriers complain very much of the "damps," particularly during the summer season. When the lanes are run very far back—and they are sometimes so run for hundreds of feet—it becomes advisable, as well for the additional working facilities which it will afford, as from sanitary considerations, to construct an additional shaft. Sometimes, for the sake of proper ventilation, a lane will be run through to an old quarry, which may be close at hand. At others, the owners of two contiguous quarries will agree to run a lane from one to the other for the same purpose.

When the stone is dressed and ready for market, it is conveyed in waggons to the harbour. The farmers who lease the surface under which the quarries are worked, claim the right of carriage between them and the beach. This claim is acquiesced in, but the result is that the quarriers pay a much higher freight than they would otherwise do. If in any case the farmer should decline the carriage, the quarrier can then look where he pleases for his means of transport.

All the means and appliances of labour about the quarries are of the rudest description. Main force is the element principally relied upon, but little aid being derived from machinery. Long as the district about Swanage has been quarried, and immense as has been the quantity of stone shipped from it, it does not, even to this day, possess a pier or jetty of any description. The vessels which receive the stone lie at anchor in the bay. The stone is dragged from the shore by very tall horses, in carts with very high wheels, as far into the sea as such an apparatus can venture with safety. From the carts it is consigned to the vessels, by means of barges, which are constantly plying to and fro. Could there be a ruder contrivance than this? Yet it is in perfect keeping with everything around.

But the most extraordinary characteristic of this singular social development still remains to be described. The world has long been divided on the subject of the standard of value, and the question of the currency is one that has baffled the most profound statesmen and the most astute economists. In Swanage these questions have received a very easy solution. The virtual standard of value is the article chiefly produced in the district—stone. But as silver is to the only standard of value, gold, in the national currency—so is bread to stone, the recognized and accepted standard in the currency of Swanage. This may be very new to the reader, but it is very ancient in this remote nook of Dorset. Stone is virtually in Swanage the standard of value, and the currency is composed of stone and bread. There is scarcely any coin in circulation in the district. All payments which are not made in actual money those so made being very few—or in goods, are made either in stone or in bread. The workmen in the quarries are paid in stone, and it is for stone that they receive in exchange such articles as they consume. It is quite true that there is a money value put on everything, but stone is almost the universal substitute for money. Thus when a master quarrier takes a quarry, and hires workmen to assist him in his operations, a money value is put upon their labour, and they are engaged at so much per day, or so much per week. But when the time of payment comes, no money passes between the master and his workmen, but a portion of the stone produced, equal in value (taking its current value for the week) to the sum at which the workmen were in each case hired, is set apart for them. Thus, if a man was hired at the rate of 3s. a day, instead of getting 18s. at the end of the week, he would get 18s. worth of stone. The stone so apportioned to him would in that case constitute his sole means for commanding the necessaries of life for himself and family. Sometimes, instead of the stone, the quarrier gives his workmen orders upon the merchant with whom he has credit. But still it is the stone that does it all, for it is upon the credit of the stone that the orders are executed. The course of dealing between the master quarrier and the merchant will serve to explain the whole system.

It is necessary to premise that the word *merchant* has, in Swanage, a peculiar local signification. There are here two classes of merchants in the ordinary acceptation of the term. There is, in the first place, the class of independent dealers who sell their goods for ready money, when they can get it, or for bread, which they afterwards convert into money, but who never deal in transactions having the transfer of stone for their basis. There is, in the next place, the class to whom the term *merchant* is exclusively applied, who keep a general assortment of goods, which they exchange for stone. Each merchant has a bakehouse attached to his establishment, the bread baked at which is one of the chief articles which he exchanges for the stone. His shop is thus, in one sense, a bank of issue; for he manufactures in it that which forms half the currency of the district—and its entire currency, in the way of small change. Every quarrier must have his merchant, as every man of business elsewhere has his banker. To establish a credit with a merchant, the quarrier must deposit stone with him, and the extent of the credit is regulated by the quantity of stone deposited. The merchant has what he calls his *banker*, which is neither more nor less than the spot of ground on which the stone left with him is deposited. The banker is like the vault, and the stone like the bullion deposited in it.

The quarrier may make his deposits in the banker when he pleases and to what extent he pleases, until the merchant, for reasons of his own, refuses to receive any more. An account is kept by both parties of the quantity deposited, as well as of the goods taken by the quarrier, or on his order, from the shop. When he wants to know how he stands he takes an account, and the balance, in the shape of stone, which remains to his credit in the banker, indicates the extent of his worldly means. When the stone is deposited a money value is set upon it, according to the current price of the day, that price being now about 21s. 6d. per hundred superficial feet of paving stone. The goods are also sold at a money value, so that the accounts between the parties are, as elsewhere, kept in money. When the quarrier pays his men in stone, they must have their merchant, as he has, to turn it to account. When he pays them by order on his merchant, he of course takes all the stone and deposits it, to his own account, in his merchant's banker. The merchants dispose of it as they best can, Southampton being one of their best and most accessible markets.

So far the system savours considerably of transactions based on credit. But there are, as it were, ready money transactions, in which stone figures as currency. A pair of boots, for instance, is sometimes paid for at once in stone. At some of the public-houses they take stone in deposit; at others, if a man wants a pint of beer, he must wheel a barrowful of stone to the house to pay for it. But in the great majority of transactions of the ready money kind, bread is the currency in vogue. Although the merchants keep a pretty varied stock, it is generally in the shape of different articles of food, bread being the principal. If a quarrier therefore, wants a coat, a pair of shoes, or anything else for himself or family which his merchant has not got, he has to go to one of the independent dealers who can supply him. But they not dealing in stone, and he having no credit with them, he is obliged to procure from his merchant that which they will take in exchange for what he wants. This is generally—in fact almost invariably—bread. He, therefore, draws for so much bread upon his merchant, which he carries to his clothier or his shoemaker, and gives in exchange for what he procures. It is in transactions like these that the system works with peculiar hardship to him. The result of the whole system is to make almost every necessary of life 15 to 20 per cent. dearer in Swanage than elsewhere in the neighbourhood. Thus the loaf which can be got for 5d. in Poole, is valued at 6½d. in Swanage. But it is only so valued to the quarrier when he takes it from his merchant. When he exchanges it for anything else, at the independent dealer's, he can only get 5½d. for it, or 5½d.'s worth. He thus loses a penny on every loaf which he turns to the purposes of currency. A quarrier in whose house I was seated, conversing on the subject, sent, during the interview, for some ale. His wife took with her a 6½d. loaf, and brought back 5½d.'s worth of beer. The stranger, ignorant of the purpose to which bread is thus applied, would be utterly at a loss to account for the quantity which he would see carried about in all directions. If a woman wants a piece of ribbon she must take a loaf with her to the shop. The dealers afterwards convert the bread into money at the price at which they receive it—those who ultimately consume it thus getting it at a penny a loaf less than the value at which it was originally issued from the merchant's establishment, and all at the cost of the poor quarrier. But this is not the only disadvantage under which he labours, for whilst his stone is taken from him at the lowest—and the bread and other articles which he receives from his merchant are given to him at the highest—possible rate, such commodities as he afterwards purchases from the dealers, by means of his bread, are highly overcharged; whilst that in which he pays for them is reduced at the counter fully 16 per cent. in value. Thus although the wages of a quarrier may nominally be 3s. a day, they are virtually reduced to 2s. by the series of peculations to which he is subjected. But even of the master quarriers, few can be said to average 3s. nominally a day. The average nominal wages of the working men, as contradistinguished from the masters, are from 2s. 3d. to 2s. 9d. a day. This, in reality, is but from 1s. 6d. to 1s. 10d. a day. They are also subjected to another great inconvenience by the length of time which sometimes elapses ere the merchants will balance their accounts with them. Some are careful to have a balance struck every year, but there are cases in which years elapse without any settlement of accounts. This leads some of them astray as to their real standing, whilst it begets reckless habits in the more thoughtless of them. These latter, so long as they have credit at their merchants, care little how they stand, so long as the day of reckoning is postponed. Others again, meaning to stand well, find themselves at last unexpectedly in debt, when they thought they had a balance in their merchant's hands.

There is little money in circulation in the town and district; house rents are exacted in money, and so are the lord's dues. To enable the quarriers to meet these demands, and also the rates which are levied upon them, the merchants, instead of goods, allow a certain sum of money to be drawn each week by their depositors. It is seldom that this sum exceeds 2s. 6d. per week to each depositor. This enables them to meet the demands in question, and also occasionally to buy a little fresh meat, which they do not often enjoy, and for which they have invariably to pay money.

They bitterly complain of the inconvenience and losses to which they are subjected from the almost total absence of money from their ordinary every-day transactions; and they are most anxious that some merchants would come amongst them, who, taking their stone at even a lower valuation than now, would pay them money instead of giving them goods for it. In this respect matters do not seem to be improving with them, the more advanced in life amongst them saying that there is less money in circulation now than formerly. But their universal desire is, at any reasonable sacrifice, to commute their present earnings into money. If a money system were established amongst them, instead of the present system of limited barter, not only would the price of the necessaries of life fall, and their physical comforts be thus increased, but the habits of some of them would be greatly improved.

Taking their condition throughout the year, they are, on the whole, considerably better off than the agricultural labourers throughout the country. Their houses are, generally speaking, vastly superior as regards accommodation, and consequently as regards cleanliness and healthiness, to those of the labourer in the fields. There is an abundance of the best material for constructing them at hand, and they are in many cases provided with four or five rooms. With the exception of Hop-about-lane, the houses in which are of a very inferior description, the dwellings of the quarriers in Swanage may be characterized as spacious, clean, and comfortable. Their furniture and bedding are also abundant and clean. They generally pay from £4 to £4 10s. in the shape of rent, in addition to which they pay rates amounting to nearly £1 more. Their diet, too, is also, in the main, better than that of the farm-labourer. They seldom eat fresh meat, but they consume more bacon than he does. But even of this they have a very insufficient supply, considering the laborious character of their occupation.

They are generally very ignorant, and in the majority of cases almost entirely illiterate. If any of them attend school, they are sent too early to work to derive much benefit from it. The boys, at about nine years of age, become useful about the quarry, and they are sent below as soon as they become strong and skilful enough for underground work. The bulk of the quarriers adhere to the Church, the rest being chiefly divided amongst the Methodists and Independents. On the whole, they are considered an orderly and well-regulated set of men.

But few, perhaps, of those who read this account were aware, before perusing it, that so rude and primitive a state of society is to be met with within a few hours' ride of the metropolis.

The Morning Chronicle, Monday, January 28, 1850.

THE SWANAGE STONE QUARRIES.

———◆———

To THE EDITOR of THE MORNING CHRONICLE.

SIR—I have read with great interest your communication of to-day, being No. XXVIII. in the series of letters upon "Labour and the Poor," and containing an account of the stone quarries of Swanage. I trouble you with this note, feeling it to be a duty to aid you by whatever can be contributed to render more complete your admirable reports, which are so well calculated to diffuse correct information on the state of our population, and thus to enable all better to understand, what very few now can appreciate—the real meaning of the words "Labour" and "Poor."

The details are so accurate and the facts so well related, that I cannot forbear requesting that, if the papers should appear in future in any other form, the error you have made in the description of the stone may be rectified. The stones of Swanage and Portland are lime stones, and not sand stones. Moreover, the articles of barter or currency, as you call them, are not always bread; but butter in red pans—or crocks, as they are called—and bacon in the side, form frequent media of exchange; articles of food generally, though bread and butter most frequently, being the currency.

There is another fact in connection with the position of the merchants, which, in estimating their power and position, is by no means unimportant.

The bankers are the only place of deposit on the beach for errot stone, and from this circumstance the owners exercise complete control over the trade; because, the freehold of the beach vesting in them, they keep to themselves the whole access to the water; and instances have occurred in which parties possessing every other means of establishing a trade have been ruined by the exercise of this power.

The "truck" system has so injurious an influence upon all this population, that I rejoice to find public attention thus awakened and directed towards a place where for so many years it has had uninterrupted sway.

There is a considerable manufacture of straw, in bonnets and hats, carried on by the female population; but this is all dealt with in the same manner as the stone.

Some years back the late Mr. Morton Pitt, who owned a large district in this neighbourhood, commenced extensive operations in building and road-making, with the view of converting the town of Swanage into a watering-place. The public, however, very feebly supported it, and although the late lamented Sir W. Follett resorted to this place in his last illness, but very few of his rank or position are aware of the great beauty of the surrounding scenery and the delightful retirement it affords.

The difficulty of access from the metropolis has prevented its becoming a place of much resort; but as there is now railway communication to Wareham, it is to be hoped that the public may have an opportunity of informing itself, and that thus this interesting locality being brought under the influence of public opinion, the result of more extended acquaintance with the district will be, that the condition of the inhabitants will be improved by their having a fair opportunity to receive and economize the well-earned reward of their toils.

Within the memory of many now living, all the streets of the metropolis were paved with the stone of Swanage only. It became gradually displaced by that of Yorkshire, which (being a laminated sandstone, quarried in open air, and hence more uniform in thickness and larger in size) has now altogether superseded it.

So that, while in former times the supply of London was a very important part of the trade of the town of Swanage very few freights are at this time sent in that direction; and of paving, not 20 vessels in a year reach London.

I am, sir, yours respectfully,

London, Jan. 23.   T. P.

LABOUR AND THE POOR.

—◆—

THE RURAL DISTRICTS.

[FROM OUR SPECIAL CORRESPONDENT.]

NORFOLK, SUFFOLK, AND ESSEX.

LETTER XIV.

Before proceeding, as I propose to do, separately and in detail with the counties which are named at the head of this letter, I shall briefly state the extent and population of that portion of the eastern district of England comprised in the counties of Norfolk, Suffolk, and Essex. These three counties together contained in 1831 a population of 1,003,868 souls. In 1841 the number had increased to 1,072,716, being about one-fourteenth of the entire population of England and Wales. Assuming that the population has increased in the same ratio during the eight years since 1841 as in the years previous to that date, the present population of the three counties would be about 1,130,716. Between the years 1831 and 1841 the increase had been at the rate of 6.8 per cent., while the increase for the whole of England and Wales had been 13 per cent. Consequently, the increase in this portion of the eastern district is 6.2 per cent. below the average per centage of increase in England and Wales. The three counties contain within their boundaries 3,190,060 acres, or a superficies equal to about one-twelfth of the whole of England and Wales. From this it is evident that, since the population of these three counties—being equal to only one-fourteenth of the entire people—is spread over one-twelfth of the surface of England and Wales, the pressure of population is below the average of the whole country. The number of inhabitants to 100 statute acres is, for Essex, 35.2—for Suffolk, 32.5—for Norfolk, 31.9. There are 16 counties which have a lower number of inhabitants to 100 acres than Norfolk—19 have less than Suffolk—and 24 less than Essex.

Having thus dealt in a very general manner with the whole of the group of counties, I shall now proceed to touch very briefly upon the leading physical and social features of the county of Suffolk; and I shall afterwards enter fully into the more immediate subject of my inquiry—viz., the condition of the labouring classes of the county.

The county of Suffolk is in length from north to south about seventy miles, and its breadth from east to west is about fifty-two miles. On the east it has the Ocean for its boundary; the rivers Yare, Waveney, and Little Ouse divide it on the north from Norfolk; the river Lark divides it from Cambridge on the west, and the Stour separates it on the south from the county of Essex. It contains 1,515 square statute miles, or 969,600 acres. The greater portion of the county is of diluvial formation. In the north-western parts it is chalky—while Norfolk crag and London clay are to be met with in various other parts. The soil is not generally what might be called rich; a great portion of it is of a light and poor character. It has been calculated that there are within the county 40,000 acres of rich loam, 80,000 of marl, 150,000 of sand upon a subsoil of crag (and occasionally of a rich character), and about 100,000 acres of poor sand and chalk. 250,000 acres are considered to be under tillage, 500,000 in pasture, and 229,200 wooded or unproductive. The tillage of Suffolk bears rather a high character, and the farmers generally are not deficient in practical or scientific skill. The chief products of the county are—cement, stone, lime, marl, bricks, salt, corn, horses (for which it is famous), cattle, butter, cheese, and malt. There are also considerable manufactures carried on at Ipswich. The sea coast is low, and is considered dangerous on account of the sand-banks and shoals which abound in its neighbourhood. There is scarcely a town of any size in the interior that cannot avail itself of the facilities afforded by the various rivers for inland navigation. There are about 52 miles of railway completed within the county, which connect the principal towns in its central and western districts.

In 1831 the population of Suffolk was 296,317; in 1841 it had increased to 315,073. Assuming that the increase of population for the eight years since 1841 has been in the same ratio as during the ten years previous to that period, it will be found that Suffolk has increased since 1841 at the rate of 5.4 per cent.—which, upon the census of 1841, would be equivalent to 16,000, and would make the present population amount to 331,073.

The number of persons returned as agricultural labourers in the census of 1841 were—males, above 20 years of age, 31,237; under 20, 4,935; females, above 20, 566; under 20, 132; making a total of male and female agricultural labourers, of all ages, of 36,870. Of farmers and graziers there were 5,380, from which it would appear that the average number of labourers employed by each farmer or grazier was not quite 7, but only 6.7. The number of domestic servants, male and female, was 17,174, or rather more than 5 per cent. of the whole population; and of this number 7,081 were under 20 years of age. The amount of real property assessed to the property and income tax is £1,717,825—being 1.07 per cent. above the average of the same amount of population throughout England and Wales. The number of independent persons in the county was 7,499, or 15.1 per cent. below the average. About 30,000 of the population are employed in trade, commerce, and manufactures; among whom may be reckoned 1,343 in connection with fisheries, or otherwise engaged in shipping, 879 employed in silkworks, 169 in the woollen and worsted trade, 322 in weaving, 75 spinners, 412 engaged in the malt trade, and 131 in ironworks. The number of inhabited houses in 1841 was 64,041, being at the rate of 4.9 persons to each house—the average number of persons to each house in England, exclusive of Wales, being 5.5. There is, therefore, it would appear, a larger amount of house accommodation in Suffolk than the average of the whole of England. The number of individual depositors in savings banks has increased from 9,332 in 1840, to 13,038 in 1847. The amount of deposits in the former year was £280,913; and in the latter, £375,145. In the years 1840, 1841, and 1842, the average amount of each depositor was, during each year, £30—and for the remaining five years, it was £29 in each year. In 1847, the average amount of each depositor was £2 more than the average of England and Wales; in each of the years, 1840-1-2-4-6, it was £1 more; and in 1843 and '45, the amount was equal to the average.

Foremost and most important, among the labouring classes of Suffolk, stand its agricultural labourers, amounting, as we have seen, to not less than 36,870 persons, of both sexes and all ages. But this number represents only those who are actually employed in agricultural work. The subject of the present investigation is, "Labour and the Poor"—and although 36,870 may be the number of those whose industry is devoted to the purposes of agriculture, yet the inquiry must be extended to those who, unable from youth or other circumstances to labour in the fields, are still dependent upon agriculture for their support. A calculation has been made by Mr. Porter, in his "Progress of the Nation," founded upon the census of 1841, the result of which is, that there were then in the United Kingdom 3,343,974 persons engaged in agriculture, including occupiers, farmers, graziers, and labourers—and that there were dependent upon them 13,604,915, or about four times the number of those actually employed. The number of agricultural labourers in the county of Suffolk was in 1841, as has already been stated, 36,870. Assuming the same ratio to exist in the case of the labourers alone as with respect to the occupiers, farmers, graziers, and labourers collectively, it would follow that the number of persons dependent upon agricultural labour is four times as great as the number of those who are actually employed as labourers. Adopting this proportion, therefore, as the basis of our calculation, we shall have in the county of Suffolk 147,480 persons of all ages dependent upon agricultural labour for their support. To this number, however, must be added the increase which has taken place in the population since 1841, at the rate of 5.4 per cent.; and we shall then have a total of 156,012 persons—or very nearly one-half of the whole population of Suffolk—who are either actually engaged in, or dependent upon, agricultural labour for their subsistence.

Upon comparing the number of agricultural labourers with the quantity of land upon which they are employed—including only pasture and arable—the proportion will be about 4.9 to every 100 acres. Upon making the same calculation with respect to six other agricultural counties—viz., Lincolnshire, Norfolk, Essex, Sussex, Dorsetshire, and Wilts—I find the proportion of labourers to 100 acres is as follows:—Lincolnshire, 3; Norfolk, 4.1; Essex and Sussex, 4.8; Dorset, 2.7; Wilts, 7.7. The amount of agricultural labour employed in Suffolk, in proportion to the cultivated soil, is therefore greater than in any of the counties above enumerated, with the exception of Wilts. The annual value of the agricultural produce of Suffolk may be taken to be—

250,000 acres of arable land, at 7*l.* per acre .. £1,750,000
500,000 acres pasture, at 6*l.* per acre 3,000,000

Total £4,750,000

Being at the rate of nearly £130 to each labourer employed. The sum which may be considered as paid for wages to the persons so employed—as near as I have been enabled to judge from the information I have received as to the rates of wages and the amount of employment given during the year, in various parts of the county, would be as follows:

The total number of male labourers above 20 years of age is 31,237, of whom there were—

One-fourth, or 7,809, at 12s. per week,
  for 52 weeks £243,250
One-fourth, or 7,809, at 9s. per week,
  for 52 weeks 182,728
The remainder, amounting to 15,619, at
  an average of 7s. 6d. per week, for 40
  weeks 234,270
Total male labourers above 20 years of
  age .... ———— £660,248
566 female labourers, above 20, at 5s. per week, for
  40 weeks 5,660
4,935 males, under 20, at 3s. 6d. per week, for 40
  weeks 34,545
132 females, under 20, at 2s. 6d. per week, for 40
  weeks 660
                                        ————————
              Total £701,113

During the harvest month the labourers, however, receive double
wages; and the amount so paid—taking the above calculation as the
basis—would be £60,311, which, added to the sum paid in regular
wages, makes a total of £761,424 paid in wages for agricultural labour
in Suffolk, being equal to about £21 per annum to each labourer.

Having thus referred to the general statistics of labour, I proceed
to what may be regarded as the more immediate object of my inquiry,
viz., the condition of the labourer himself. In so doing I shall first
deal with what I consider to be of the most paramount importance
with respect to the well-being and comfort of the poor—I mean their
physical condition.

In travelling through the county of Suffolk, perhaps the first thing
which would strike the attention of the traveller would be the fact
that he would scarcely see a single cottage untenanted. Upon making
inquiries into this subject, I have uniformly been told that, notwithstanding the increase which has taken place in the population, there
has been comparatively little or no increase in the amount of cottage
accommodation for the people. Many of the cottages, especially those
in the immediate neighbourhood of the larger towns, are greatly overcrowded with persons who work in the town, and who wish to live
near their work. In too many cases, the occupiers of the cottages, re-
gardless of the want of decency and comfort which must follow from
such a practice, are in the habit of taking in these persons as lodgers,
in order to obtain assistance in paying their rents, which in the great
majority of instances are enormously high, compared with the accommodation provided. Where the owners of the soil reside among their

tenantry, or where the estates are left to the management of persons who take an interest in the welfare of the people, it will be found that the cottages and tenants are the most comfortable. In many portions of the eastern districts of the county this is peculiarly the case. I might mention numerous instances of this which have come under my own notice. The cottages upon the estate of the Earl of Stradbroke, near Halesworth, have both a comfortable and an ornamental appearance. They are generally built of brick, with tile roofs; few, if any of them, have less than four rooms, and they have also suitable out-offices, and are well supplied with cupboards and pantries. They are generally only one story in height, the bed rooms being on the same floor as the parlours and kitchens. The cottages also upon the estates of Sir Edward Kerrison, near Stradbroke, are remarkable for their neat and comfortable appearance. They generally contain four or five rooms, and in all cases they have pieces of ground either attached to them or at a small distance, varying from an eighth to a quarter of an acre in extent. There are probably few gentlemen in the county who have successfully devoted so much time and attention to the improvement of the cottages upon their estates as the Rev. Mr. Benyon, at Culford, who resides about five miles from Bury. Nothing can exceed the neat and pleasing appearance of these dwellings. They are built with blue flint stones, which are dug in the neighbourhood, and they are faced with bricks. The roofs are slated—the colour of the slates and of the blue flints being agreeably relieved by the facings of brick. Each cottage has four rooms—some, which have been more recently erected, contain five. On the ground-floor there is a "keeping-room," used as a pantry, or larder; a back-kitchen, fitted with a copper, stone sink, and other conveniences; a small room which is used as a cellar; a sitting-room in the front of the house, about 14ft. by 12ft., and 7ft. in height; and two bed-rooms up stairs. At a short distance from each set of cottages (they are generally built in pairs, and in some cases there are three standing together) there is a wooden erection with a tile roof, enclosing a place for fuel, a privy for each cottage, and an oven. In some instances the oven and coal cellar are under the same roof with the cottage, and the privy stands a short distance from the cottage. Mr. Benyon informed me that his tenants were always regular and punctual in the payment of their rents, and he believed that a great improvement had taken place in their moral condition since their dwellings had been improved. The cost of the double cottages averaged about £170, or £85 each. Attached to each of them is a quarter of an acre of land.

The cottages at Buxhall are also deserving of the highest commendation. The Rev. Mr. Hill, late rector of the parish, has devoted a great deal of time and attention to the best mode of constructing labourers' dwellings. A few years since he received the gold medal of the Agricultural Society for the best essay upon the subject. His excellent and amiable wife accompanied me to several of the cottages; and it must be a source of gratification to them to see that their praiseworthy efforts for the improvement of the condition of their tenants have been crowned with so complete and signal success. The cottages are built of clay, made up in the form of large bricks and dried in the sun; they have thatched roofs—it being very generally supposed that the thatch, when well done, is warmer in winter and cooler in summer than slate or tile roofs. The cottages are built in pairs, and have each two rooms on the ground floor, one of which is used as a pantry, and two rooms above. The kitchen, or down-stairs room, has a brick floor, and is provided with an oven and a small cupboard. The whole of the rooms are well lighted. There is no ceiling to the lower room; the rafters and timbers are stained to imitate dark oak, and they afford a very pleasing contrast to the whitewashed walls. The cottages are well drained, and have a good supply of water. The chimneys are built in an octagonal shape, with small white bricks, of a somewhat ornamental style, and they give to the houses a pleasing picturesque appearance. The cost of the pair of cottages just described was somewhat under £120. One of the rules enforced by Mr. Hill upon letting his cottages is—"no pigs, no poultry, no lodgers." He stated to me that he had adopted this rule in order to allay or remove the jealousy which is very generally found to exist on the part of the farmers towards any of their workpeople who are in the habit of keeping either the one or the other of these. They have an opinion—whether well founded or not I cannot say—that keeping pigs and poultry does not tend to improve the honesty of their labourers; and they fear that occasionally some portion of their grain might find its way into the corn-binns of the cottagers. The rule against taking lodgers has been framed with the view of preventing the overcrowding of cottages. With respect to the payment of the rents by the tenants, Mrs. Hill informed me that they were always punctual to the day. "Last Michaelmas-day," she said, "twenty-eight of the tenants dined with us, and every one of them brought his three guineas for the year's rent to the very halfpenny."

In addition to these individual cases, which might be multiplied to a considerable extent, a decided improvement has also taken place in the neighbourhood of some of the larger towns. And for the most part the better class of cottages are clean and neat in their appearance. In some of the newer-built ones, the boards of the upper rooms and the stairs leading to them are almost milk-white. You feel as if it would be no great hardship if you were compelled to take your meals off them—they are so perfectly clean. The walls, both externally and internally, are generally kept well whitewashed. The different articles of furniture are also remarkably clean; the chimney-pieces are frequently ornamented with a pair of bright brass candlesticks; sometimes a small shelf contains a few articles of crockery—a fancy beer mug generally occupying a rather prominent position among its companions. On the ground-floor you may find some four or six strong, and perhaps not very modern, wooden chairs—a chest of drawers—a table or two, one of which supports a tea-board, with a youthful Moses or a grey-headed David for the centre-piece; and in a great many instances you will not fail to hear the drowsy ticking of a Dutch clock in the corner, and to see a magpie chattering in his wicker prison, with a cat sleeping comfortably on a clean and unassuming rug. You will almost invariably notice in cottages of this description the signs of a genuine, though untutored taste for the "fine arts," manifesting itself in a few antiquated and gaudy-coloured pictures, which hang around the room. Many are the saints of high renown, such as St. Ignatius, St. Augustine, St. Ambrose, and others, who keep watch and ward over these homely hearths. It does not appear that these humble pictures are held in estimation in consequence of any peculiar reverence which the people entertain towards the sainted originals—for in many cases they do not know whom they are intended to represent. The price of them, including frame and glass, is generally one penny, and it is no doubt in consequence of their cheapness that they are so generally patronized. There are not a few of the cottages which have cheap likenesses of the Queen and Prince Albert—and by the side of these I saw, in several instances, what purported to be likenesses of the Prince of Wales and the Princess Royal. The cottage libraries, unfortunately, are generally of very minute proportions. This, however, is easily accounted for by the fact that so few of the inmates are able to read. The sleeping apartments of the tenants in the better class of cottages are also, in the great majority of cases, remarkably cleanly and neat in their appearance.

Having now glanced at the condition of the better class of the dwellings of the poor, I shall proceed to draw aside the veil which conceals from the superficial observer the wretched condition in which vast numbers of the peasantry of Suffolk are to be found in their miserable homesteads. I have now lying before me the description of upwards of eighty cottages in different parts of the county, which I have visited since my arrival. I shall give the reader a few of them, arranging them in classes according to the number of apartments in each. The first class to which I shall refer is that consisting of cottages with only one room, but which, in the great majority of cases—by means either of a wooden partition, or by hanging up some old quilt, or even articles of apparel sewn together, over a line stretched across the room—is made to serve the purpose of a dwelling and sleeping room. The number of these one-roomed cottages is, comparatively speaking, small in proportion to those of other classes.

The first cottage of this class which I visited was in the neighbourhood of Stradbroke, and was occupied by a widow and her three daughters. The entrance was so low that you had to stoop in order to gain admittance. The building lay back at some distance from the road, and in the rear of another row of cottages, which I shall presently have occasion to refer to. It was lighted by means of a small window, about two feet square. The thatch—and, indeed, the whole building—was fast going to decay. A wooden partition divided what might be called the sitting-room from the bed-room. The furniture of the place was of the most wretched character, consisting of two or three old chairs, a small table, a stool or two, and a few articles of crockery ware. Upon a sort of bench lay six loaves of bread, which the family had just received from the parish. "My mother," said a girl of about 18, to whom I addressed myself upon entering, "is a widow; she is out at wheat-dropping"—an operation which consists in dropping the seed wheat into small holes made for its reception in the ground by means of a "dibble," or "dibbler," in cases where it is not sown in the more usual manner, either by broad-cast or in drills. "She can earn sixpence a day when she's at work at it, but she can't always get it to do; and sometimes when she can she can't go, because of leaving that poor creature alone"—pointing at the same time to a miserable idiotic-looking young woman, who was engaged in making lace-edging upon a pillow in her lap. I was struck with the peculiarly delicate manner in which she referred to the poor creature, and I asked her reason for speaking of her in such terms. "Because, sir, she do go wrong in her head, and if she was left at home by herself there's no knowing the mischief she wouldn't do. She broke this, and that, and that," pointing to several articles of crockery and a square or two of glass in the wretched window, "the other day, when mother was out, and I wasn't at home to take care of her. When the poor thing's able to work she makes sometimes a penny, sometimes three-ha'pence a day, but when her fits comes on she can't work at all. My mother gets 1s. 6d. a week and six loaves from the parish. We haven't got any garden. We pay 1s. a week rent. My other sister is eight years old; she can't do anything either, for she's afflicted too." Adjoining this cottage was another, occupied by a newly-married couple, which was constructed upon the same plan. There was little or no furniture in the room; the wife was apparently in a deep consumption; her voice was almost gone, and it was with difficulty that I could understand what she said. Upon a few rags, spread upon two old chairs, in a recess between the window and the chimney, lay a weakly, sickly-looking infant, ten weeks old. "My husband," she said, "is out of work, and has been since harvest. I haven't been well since my confinement, and am so ill now that I can hardly get about. We have been married two years. When I was first married my husband earned 8s. a week. Through his being out of work we have got behind in the rent, but I hope we shall soon be able to fetch it up. We haven't got no garden, and we pays eighteen-pence a week, when we can pay it." The place was remarkably clean, notwithstanding the abject poverty of the tenants.

Another cottage which I visited—which may probably be considered an exceptional case, inasmuch as no rent was paid, but which I mention in order to show into what miserable hovels some of the poor people are glad to creep for shelter—was near Barrow. The building had once formed, to all appearance, a double cottage. The thatch of one portion of it was lying upon the ground, mingled with the timbers which once supported it—a portion only of the clay walls of one of the cottages remained standing. The thatch which had already fallen had left exposed to the wind and rain the portion of the adjoining cottage, between the thatch and gaping flooring, which formed the partial covering of the lower room. This room, which was a tolerably good sized apartment, was roughly and unevenly paved with bricks, the great majority of which were broken and cracked. Gleams of sunlight found their way through the broken thatch and crevices of the floor overhead, while the light from a small window, in which was scarcely an unbroken square of glass, lent its miserable aid in showing the dreary wretchedness of the place. The furniture consisted of one old chair, a three-legged stool, a smaller stool; and nearly in the centre of the place, lay, upon its side, one of those antique tables, with its labyrinth of legs, in which the genius of our ancient cabinetmakers was wont to indulge itself. Upon the broken flap which lay uppermost, stood a broken basin and teapot. A few sticks of wood burning with a flickering blaze revealed the spot where once a fire-place stood, and in an old iron pot suspended over them the few potatoes were boiling which were to serve for the scanty meal of the day. Upon a line, which was stretched across one part of the room, immediately in front of the door, hung a tattered quilt, to conceal from view, or to shelter from the cold draught, a wretched stump of a bedstead, where, upon an old straw mattress and covered with a few rags, slept together at night the husband, the wife, and the three children who tenanted this desolate abode. "It's a cold place, indeed, sir," said the wretched woman, in a touching tone of sadness and despair. "My husband has had no work since harvest; the farmers turned off as many as they could then, when they'd got the harvest in. I don't pay any rent for the place; Mr. Bailey lets me live in it for nothing, to take care of the sticks. If it was not for this I don't know what we should do, nor where we should put our heads." I asked her if she was not afraid of the place falling down, and her answer was that she expected it would every day.

The next class of cottages to which I shall call the attention of the reader consists of those having a room on the ground floor, and a bed-room above; and in cottages of this character the greater proportion of the labouring population reside. Mr. Twisleton, in his report upon the sanitary condition of the labouring population of Norfolk and Suffolk, thus speaks of these cottages, and his description entirely agrees with all that I have witnessed myself. He says, "Although they may be sufficiently commodious for a man and wife and very young children, they are manifestly uncomfortable, and the having only one bedroom is even indecent for a man and wife and large growing family; but I have seen many instances where a man and his wife and six children of different sexes have slept together in one room, on three, and sometimes only two beds. The annoyance of thus herding together must be almost insufferable, and several mothers of families among the labourers have spoken to me with great propriety and feeling against the practice, saying, 'that it is not respectable or decent, and that it is hardly bearable;' 'that such a thing is not right for a Christian body in a Christian land;' and they have used other expressions of a similar import. In order to diminish the evil, they have recourse to various expedients, such as putting curtains to the beds, or dividing the room into two parts, by pinning old counterpanes together, and sometimes by cutting up, and sewing together, old gowns, and stretching them across the room; all of which schemes are attended with the inconvenience, that in a crowded apartment, where pure air is a scarce luxury, they have a tendency to check still more its healthful circulation. The having only one room below is almost equally inconvenient, and where it is necessary to wash linen, to cook, to bake, and to perform all the ordinary household work in the same room, with children running and playing about, it is difficult for even the most tidy person to prevent her house from being, to use a favourite phrase of the district, in a constant 'muddle.' However, it not unfrequently happens that two or three of such cottages have a bake-house and wash-house in common, which, of course, lessens, to a certain extent, the discomfort of having only one day room."

The first of the cottages of this character which I visited was at Wortham, a place just bordering upon the boundary of Norfolk and Suffolk. The exterior of the building presented a most wretched and dilapidated aspect. There were a few miserable articles of furniture in the lower room, consisting of two or three chairs and an old table. In the upper room was an old stump bedstead, upon which the husband and wife slept, and in two corners of the room lay a heap of indescribable looking rags, which marked the spot where seven children, the eldest of whom was fourteen, were in the habit of sleeping. There was no fire in the lower room, and the woman was suffering extremely, and expecting every hour to be confined with her twelfth child; she had seven living, and had buried four. Her husband was out of work. There was no garden or ground, and the rent for the hovel was £4 per annum. At a place called Coombs, near Stowmarket, there were a great number of wretched hovels of this description. I may, perhaps, state, in passing, that there are few places which bear a worse character, either in respect to cottage accommodation or the character of the inhabitants, than Coombs. Within the last three years no less than seventeen persons have been transported from it for various crimes, principally that of incendiarism. The population, I believe, does not exceed a thousand. Here is an account of one of the cottages. The lower room was so low, that when I had taken off my hat I could scarcely stand upright. The brick floor was several inches below the surface of the ground on the outside, and in damp or wet weather the inmates are constantly obliged to sweep the water away, as it either oozes up through the brick floor, or, entering by the doorway, creeps sluggishly towards the hearth, which is the lowest part of the room. Throughout the whole of the place the effects of the dampness and moisture were everywhere visible; the lower part of the walls of the cottage were stained with damp to the height of upwards of two feet. Although the weather was dry, the bricks were wet and damp; and the woman, suffering from asthma and shivering with cold, sat with her feet upon a log of wood before a small fire, which had not sufficient heat to dispel the dampness from the chimney jambs. There was a little bit of garden, "but it is not enough to pay for the labour," said the poor man. "I sold the potatoes off it last year, but they didn't fetch the price of the seed." He had been out of work for some time. His wife earned 1s. 6d. a week by washing. They had no relief from the parish. "They won't give us anything," said he, "except we goes into the house, and as long as I can arne a sixpence anyhows, they sharn't part me from my wife." "No, that they sharn't," chimed in the woman, "I'd work the flesh off my bones afore I'd be parted and locked up like a felon; and I've never done nothing to desarve it, but have worked hard all my life, and this is what it's come to now!" "If I could only arne eight shillings a week," said the man, "aye, or even seven, all the year round, I wouldn't thank King George to be my uncle. But there's a many worse off than we are in this place. There's a poor man over the way that's got nine children, and hasn't got nothing to do either. Thank God we haven't got none. If we wur to go to the house, we should have to leave all our few things here, exposed like a desolate wilderness. They're not worth much—what would they fetch at auction? Why, not 5s., but then we don't want to lose 'em, they does very well for us." The rent of this place was £3 10s. per annum. The poor people had got in arrears with their rent, "but the landlady," said the man, "is a good'un and don't press us."

Another case, of which I was informed by the Rev. Mr. Baddeley, the rector of Halesworth, was one in which misery and wretchedness of every kind appeared to culminate. The rev. gentleman stated that he was called upon to visit a poor woman, who was suffering severely from a cancer. Beside her, on a heap of rags on the floor, lay her unmarried daughter, eighteen years of age, moaning in the pangs of labour. Upon his next visit the mother had expired, the daughter had become a mother, and, huddled together in the upper room, lay the corpse, the living mother and her child, seven other children, and the husband, who had been for some time out of work.

I could enumerate cases to a still greater extent which would show the disgraceful condition of many of these double-roomed cottages in the rural districts. There are many of a similar character to be found at Rattlesdeen, at Metford, at Ranshold, at Sutton, Selland, Gipping, Dalham, Woodbridge, and many other places which I have visited; enough has, however, been stated to show their general character.

But it is not only in the rural districts that these wretched dwellings are to be found. Clustered together in many of the larger towns in the agricultural districts similar abodes are to be met with. At Stowmarket, at the back of the Fox Inn, is to be found a close, confined, and badly-paved court, called "Cabbage-square." In company with the Rev. Mr. Freeman, of Stowmarket, I visited the place. Three sides of the court were occupied by twelve houses, there being four on each side; the fourth side was a dead wall, which formed the back of the premises of the Fox Inn. There were no gardens to the houses, back or front—no water, and one common privy to the whole of them. The interior of some of the houses which I visited presented an appearance of wretchedness and misery quite in keeping with the dreariness of their external appearance. The entrance to the court was through a narrow and dirty passage, in which there was scarcely room for a couple of people to walk abreast. Mr. Freeman informed me that the place had been recently greatly improved, under the orders of the Sanitary Board, and that previously to that time it was almost impossible to approach it in consequence of the heaps of filth and ordure with which it abounded. The rent of each house was 1s. 7d. per week. In the town of Bury, which bears a high and deservedly good character for its general cleanliness, similar haunts are to be found. Mr. Brown, the able and intelligent superintendent of police in the Bury district, accompanied me to a place called Hong's-lane, than which a more miserable-looking place could not be conceived. It consists of a row of red brick houses, 26 in number, which, though they have been only erected four years, are already in the most ruinous condition. The front walls of the houses are in many places cracked from top to bottom. There is scarcely a window in the whole row which has not some of its glass broken; some of the windows are stopped up with rags of all colours and shades, others have pieces of paper pasted over them. In front of the houses is a dead wall, extending the whole length of the buildings to the height of the upper windows, totally excluding the current of fresh air. The place is approached at each end by a low and narrow archway, through which, while stooping, you have to pick your way amid the filth and garbage with which it abounds. It is the resort of prostitutes, poachers, thieves, and others of the worst character. At the back of the row, and extending the whole length, was a wall equal in height to the top of the windows of the lower room. The distance between the back of the cottages and the wall was about three feet, and this space was used as a general receptacle for filth and refuse matter. At each end of this filthy tube, for I can designate it by no other name, was a privy, the two being used in common by the whole of the inhabitants. The first den which I visited was in the possession of a labouring carpenter. From some injuries which he had received he had not been enabled to do any work for the last fortnight. He was a widower, and there were six children at home. The eldest boy, twelve years old, appeared, as he walked, more like a moving heap of rags and tatters than anything bearing the semblance of a human being. How his rags were kept on was a mystery which I believe none could solve, and if they had been taken off, it would have been impossible for the owner to have put them on again. They were never taken off; in fact he slept in the rags, as did his other brothers and sisters, for in the upper room there were no beds, no sheets, no blankets, no counterpanes. Three heaps of shreds, more filthy, if possible, than those upon the backs of the wretched children, and more loathsome from the vermin which they harboured, showed the spots where each group of this miserable family sought in sleep the short-lived bliss of unconsciousness of misery. The fetid smell of the room was overpowering.

Three doors removed from this was another place, which we visited. Its external and internal appearance were even worse than the one just described. Of the twelve small panes of glass in the upper window, five were broken, and in the lower one, about as many. Upon my entering the room in company with the superintendent of police, a woman, miserably clad in an old gown, with apparently no other article of clothing upon her, and with a young child three months old in her arms, addressing my companion, said, "You are not come for Tom again, are you? 'Cause if you have, he isn't here—that's all I can say." Having satisfied her upon that point, and explained to her the object of our visit, we learned from her that her husband was at work on the railway near Diss; that he sent her 8s. a week, that she had seven children, the youngest being three months old. "I can't get no meat," she said, "only once a week; to-day we had a herring and potatoes for dinner. Sometimes I buys a sheep's head and pluck, and that lasts me nearly all the week." We requested permission to see the room upstairs, but she objected to it, telling us that "it wasn't fit for no Christian to see." Judging from the condition of the room in which we then were, it must have been miserable indeed. The only articles of furniture were two very old chairs and a small table; on the shelf over the fireplace, a broken basin; on the window sill, a stone bottle and a few dirty cloths.

I shall only detain the reader by a description of one of the cottages next in point of superiority, many of which are greatly superior to those that it has been my painful duty to describe. They consist of three apartments, and in some cases, by means of a small out-house attached to the dwelling, they are made to comprise four. Vast numbers, however, of them are miserably built. We will take one of this class situated at Barrow-green, a place distant about five miles from Bury. There is a group consisting of about thirty cottages, situated at the lower end of the green or common. Along this side of the common runs a large ditch, over which you pass to arrive at the group. One row of six cottages faces the common, in front of which is a piece of ground, divided, by means of a number of shattered fences, into as many pieces, of about four yards long and three wide, as there are cottages. These plots of ground, dignified by the name of gardens, are, in point of fact, little more than enclosures for the reception of the filth and refuse of each cottage. At the back of the buildings is a privy, which, like many others in this part of the country, is common to a number of cottages. Having taken off my hat, which in visiting a large number of these cottages is a mark of homage which you are physically compelled to pay if you would wish to obtain an entrance, I found myself inside one of a class of cottages called three-roomed ones. It was Saturday, and the woman, with her little girl of nine years of age, was busily engaged in washing and cleaning the dwelling, their damp and humble abode. Against the back wall of this cottage a small outhouse had been erected, which was just large enough to contain a bed, and was lighted by a small window, which looked out on the fields. Immediately underneath it—the outer wall of the outhouse forming, in fact, one of its sides—was a ditch of about two feet in depth. "I can't have that window open," said the poor woman, "in summer, because if I did I should be *pisoned*, it do stink so. The place is always damp with it, and I'm never without the *rheumatis*." She hereupon showed me a portion of her arm, the sinews of which were shrunk, and when attacked with cold or rheumatics she was unable to make any use of it. Her son was a pedlar, and the upper room—or rather loft, for, like most of the upper rooms of these cottages, it was immediately under the thatch—was used as a store-room for his wares and trinkets. She had lived in the place thirty years, had had three different landlords, none of whom had expended a farthing upon the premises. "It is almost impossible to keep the place clean. Look here," she said, pointing to the different places from which the plaster and rubbish were constantly falling, "as fast as I sweep it up it comes down again." Her husband was in constant work, but could not, she said, "afford to buy a pig, even if they had a place to keep it in. They used to grow a little *sauce* (potatoes), upon the common, but they won't let us now. Sometimes we can manage a goose, when we can't a pig, because that'll run on the common; but they're a goin' to enclose it, and then we shan't be able even to do that. They don't encourage poor families as they ought to do here, but it is not much matter to me. I don't think I shall be here long. My eldest daughter is at Port Phillip, and I take on very much about it; she was married very early, against my will, and was not *yoked* very pleasantly either. I have many a hearty cry when I think of how I have brought my family up." I left the poor woman in tears. There was a tale of real woe, I doubt not, to be gathered, but the poor woman was so affected that I declined to pursue the subject further.

The next subject immediately in connection with the dwellings of the labourer is that of rent. It is impossible to arrive at anything like a fair average of the rent paid for the cottages, as it varies so much, not only in different districts of the county, but, in some cases, actually within the same parish. At Buxhall, the cottages built by the Rev. Mr. Hill let for £3 3s., while close by him, and in the same parish, there are others, not containing a greater amount of accommodation, which let for £6 and even £7 per annum. At Woodbridge there are a number of wretched one-roomed cottages, the property of the Rev. Mr. Taylor, a dissenting minister, the rent of which is 1s. 4d. per week, while in many other places cottages of a similar character can be had for 9d. and 1s. Upon the estate of Sir E. Kerrison a comfortable four-roomed cottage, with a rood of land, lets for £3 10s.; while there are several cottages close by his estate which, without any garden, let for £4. As a general rule, it may, perhaps, be stated that in the neighbourhood of towns the rent of the cottages is higher than in places further removed from them; and it will also be generally found that the cottages built by gentlemen of property upon their own estates let for a considerably less sum than those built by private speculators. One great cause of the enormously high rents which are paid by the poor people is, that in a great many cases the cottages are built by persons of very small capital. A tradesman in a country town, as soon as he is able to scrape together a little money, forthwith begins to look about for a piece of land upon which he can build one or more cottages; but through his not having fully counted the cost, he finds that before the building is completed his small capital has run out, and he is compelled to borrow money at a high rate of interest upon the mortgage of the cottages—and thus, having interest to pay upon the borrowed money, as well as to obtain a return for his own investment, he is forced to obtain the largest amount of rent he can from the unfortunate tenants. The number of cottages which are either in this situation, or which have fallen into the hands of those who had advanced money upon them, is very great.

Generally speaking, there appear to be no universally recognized conditions upon which the tenant holds the cottage. In some, but comparatively few, cases the repairs are done at the expense of the landlords. In the majority of cases the tenant bears the cost of repair, or puts up with the want of it. Upon the estates of Sir E. Kerrison and other gentlemen the landlord charges himself with the repairs. Upon the Culford estate, the property of the Rev. E. Benyon, very strict rules are adopted with respect to the tenantry. The following is a copy of the regulations to be observed by the tenants on his estate:—

"REGULATIONS TO BE OBSERVED BY THE COTTAGE TENANTRY, AND THOSE RENTING GARDEN ALLOTMENTS, ON THE CULFORD ESTATE:—

"1. Each occupier is to keep his cottage, with the buildings belonging to the same, clean and in good order.

"2. Any injury committed to the walls, doors, oven, or windows, or upon other fixtures, as locks, grates, cupboards, shelves, &c., to be made good by the tenant; reasonable use and wear thereof being allowed.

"3. All fixtures that are actually the property of the tenant, are, on his leaving the cottage, to be offered to the Rev. E. R. Benyon, at a fair valuation, and should he decline the purchase, they must be removed before the tenant's quitting the premises, and without injury to the walls, or any part of the buildings.

"4. No person, in addition to the immediate family of the tenant, is permitted to reside in any cottage, without a written authority from the steward of the estate.

"5. No gleaning corn is allowed to be threshed in any cottage.

"6. The gardens are to be cultivated with the spade, and on no account to be ploughed.

"7. No occupier is to underlet his garden, or any part of it.

"8. All fences, gates, posts, rails, &c., are to be kept in repair, and the hedges neatly trimmed, by the tenant.

"9. No horse, pony, or donkey is to be kept without a written authority, as aforesaid.

"10. Should the Rev. E. R. Benyon, or his steward, notice any tenant neglecting to conform to these regulations, they will be compelled to remove him from possession of his cottage and garden, by notice, according to the covenant in the agreement under which he holds possession.

"As the principal object desired by the Rev. E. R. Benyon is the welfare and comfort of his tenantry, it is hoped they will see the advantage that must arise from conducting themselves respectfully and orderly, and keeping their cottages and gardens as directed; a proper attention to which will alone secure to them their respective occupations."

The observance of these regulations is enforced by a written agreement signed by each tenant. If the tenant refuses to leave when called upon to do so, the landlord has the power, under the Small Tenements Act, of forcibly removing him, upon application to the County Court. I was informed, however, by his steward, that it was very rarely that this power was called into requisition, the tenants, generally speaking, being very careful to fulfil the terms of the agreement.

One of the great evils of which, perhaps more than anything else, the poor people complain of, is that of their being compelled to pay the parish-rates in addition to the sum they pay for the rent of their cottages. Speaking to a poor woman, who resided in a cottage of her own near Woolpit, and whose husband was in almost constant work, she said:—"One of the most cruellest things as I know is to make the poor dear people pay the rates. I'm better off than some of 'em because I don't have no rent to pay, but there's a *hape* of people that can't afford to pay it nohows. There's my poor daughter has to pay 2s. 9d. or 2s. 3d. every time they call for a rate, and I'm sure they're often obliged to go without wittles to pay it. It's a cruel thing—it makes the poor dear people run in debt for things they ought to pay for, and puts things in their minds that they never thought or dreamt on, and I hope and pray that some good gentleman will take the matter up, and write to the Government and let 'em know how the poor labourer is put upon. Everything comes from them—if they warn't to work what could the rich folks do? They'd starve, and yet they makes him pay the rates. Oh, it is a cruel thing, indeed it is. The poor dear labourer has to go a *throshing,* tearing his poor inside out, and can't get nothing when he's out but his bit of bread and a drop of water from the ditch, without even a crum' o' pork, and then when he comes home, why all that's for him is to go to the pail for a *soop* o' water, or have perhaps a little *wake* tea, or boiled water with a crum' o' sugar in it—perhaps not that."

The wages of the labourer vary rather considerably in different portions of Suffolk. Previously to the harvest the maximum paid to field labourers was 9s. a week. In many other parts, principally in the western division, the wages were not more than 8s. Since the harvest, however, there has been a very general reduction of 1s. per week, and in the neighbourhood of Clare and Cavendish the farmers had very generally come to a resolution to reduce the wages to 6s. for married men, with a proportionate reduction in the wages of the women and unmarried men. But although 8s. or 9s. per week is the nominal amount of wages paid to the labourers, it is in fact somewhat more than that. During "hay time" and harvest an increased rate of wages is paid. During the hay-making season the labourers get in some cases double wages, in others about 50 per cent. more; that is to say, a labourer who may have previously been receiving 8s., will then make 12s. per week. In addition to the money increase, they also have what they call "fours," which consists in having bread and cheese and beer at four o'clock. During the harvest month, too, the men generally get double wages, or in cases where it is done by piece-work, a number of men join together and take so many acres, which they undertake to reap at a certain price. In such cases the men will earn upon an average from £3 to £5 during the month. A custom prevails in many parts of the county of giving the men three bushels of malt at the close of the harvest. During the harvest, in addition to their wages, the men are allowed what is called "a taking supper," which is a supper given to the men at the time of making the agreement; the "half-way supper," when the work is about half completed; and the final supper, called the "harvest home," when the grain is carted and stacked.

The appropriation among the labourers generally of their earnings is usually, that the amount earned in harvest pays the rent—the hay-making wages go for clothes—and the produce of the gleaning pays the shoemaker. In too many cases, unfortunately, this mode of distribution cannot be adhered to. The majority of the labourers have nothing to do during the winter, and where they can, they are compelled to run in debt for the necessaries of life, and the extra money earned in harvest too frequently goes to pay off "the old score." A few extra weeks of wet weather, or sickness in the family, is quite sufficient to destroy all their nicely-adjusted financial schemes. If you ask the labourer how he manages to pay his rent, live, and clothe himself upon his wages, the usual answer given to you will be something of this sort, "Why, zur, I don't know how we manages; if you wur a labouring man yourself you would know, I *dur* say." There can be no doubt as to the truth contained in the latter portion of the answer, but as to any information you can get upon the subject it is almost out of the question. It is, in fact, a mystery to themselves, and it is no wonder that they are unable to explain it to you.

But the wages as given above include only those paid to married men; a custom very generally prevails of giving the unmarried considerably less than the married men. Few of the unmarried men get more than 6s., the majority but 5s. per week; but, so far as the value of the labour obtained by the farmer is concerned, there can be no doubt that they are able to get a much larger amount of work from the young unmarried men than from the married and older ones. And in this point of view it is manifestly unjust to make a difference in the wages of the two classes. Besides the injustice of the proceeding, the policy is of the most doubtful character; by giving a young man of 20 years of age and upwards a lower rate of wages than they would give to one who was probably his junior, but who could call himself a married man, they almost compel them in self-defence to marry early, and, in the great majority of cases, additional burdens are, in consequence, thrown upon the parishes. Accustomed up to the period of his marriage to live under the roof of his parents, allowing them a portion of his earnings for his food and lodging, and when thrown out of work having his parents to fall back upon—which in a great many instances is the case—he knows nothing of the extreme privations which others less favourably situated than himself have to endure. He is married however; he is entered upon the farmer's list as a married man, and forthwith his wages are raised from 5s. or 6s. to 8s., or perhaps

9s. His wife may or may not possess those peculiar qualities which are indispensably necessary to the labourer who desires to make both ends meet. For the first five or six years of their married life they are subject to the greatest privations. The expenses of a family of four or five children have come upon them, and the earnings of the husband, even if in constant work, are insufficient for their support. The children are too young to earn anything wherewith to assist the general stock; the wife is unable to earn anything, because the family is too young to be left. Sickness perhaps comes upon them; the husband is unable to work; and finally the union receives the whole of them; and the farmer who grudgingly paid him his paltry pittance of five or six shillings a week as an unmarried labourer, has to reap the fruits of his injudicious economy, by supporting the labourer, with his family, in a state of idleness. Many instances of this have come under my own knowledge.

The wages paid to boys under 16 seldom exceed 3s. per week, and the women seldom earn more than 5s. I have not met with any case in which a higher rate than that has been paid, and for one who is paid so much there are hundreds who receive less.

The diet of the labourer may be summed up in two words—bread and potatoes. Meat is comparatively unknown to them. "I can assure you solemnly," said a labourer to me, who was in pretty constant work, "I don't get a bit of mate from one month's end to another." "Last Sunday," said a poor woman whose cottage I visited, "we had a bit of pork that I gave 9d. for; it was the first bit that we'd had for many a long week. What we didn't eat for dinner on Sunday my husband took with him when he went to work on Monday." "Lor, bless you," said another, "we shouldn't know ourselves if we got meat." "My son," said the poor woman whose residence I have described at Barrow, "sometimes buys a pig to sell again, and then we has his head." A poor woman residing in Hare-court, Bury, whose husband earned 8s. a week at a maltster's at Fornham, and who was necessarily absent all the week in consequence of the distance from his home at which he was compelled to work, gave me the following as their weekly expenditure:—

```
Rent ..................... 1s.  6d.
One stone of flour ......... 1   8
Baking .................. 0   3
A piece of pork on Sundays ... 0   9
Potatoes ................. 0   1½
¼ oz. tea ................. 0   1½
¼ lb. sugar .............. 0   1½
¼ lb. butter ............. 0   3
                        _____
       Total .......... 4   9½
```

leaving 3s. 3½d. for the support of her husband during the week, out of which he had to pay 1s. a week for his own lodging. They had no family, had lived twenty-seven years in the same house, and owed only one week's rent. "We never gets pork, except on Sundays, and then my husband is at home. I don't think about none all the week, and it is no use a thinking about it, if you can't get it," said the sharp little woman, resuming her work at making flour sacks, at which she informed me she could "arne," if she got up before daylight, and worked all day, the remunerating sum of 6d. When she was mending sacks "she only got a halfpenny a piece," and they took her almost as long to mend as a new one did to make. She "couldn't mend more than four dozen in a week."

Having thus dealt with the condition of the labourer, with regard to his dwelling, his wages, and his diet, I propose in my next to give the reader the result of my inquiries with respect to the numerous incendiary fires which have recently taken place in the county, with some account of the wages and condition of the labourers in those localities where the fires have occurred.

LABOUR AND THE POOR.

——◆——

THE RURAL DISTRICTS.

[FROM OUR SPECIAL CORRESPONDENT.]

NORFOLK, SUFFOLK, AND ESSEX.

Letter XV.

I propose in the present letter to enter somewhat more in detail into the condition of the agricultural labourer as regards his work and his wages, and to point out a few of the evils in connection with these subjects which tend to produce that feeling of sullen discontent which is so generally prevalent among them—particularly in those portions of this district where of late so many incendiary fires have taken place.

I shall first deal with the question of wages. In my previous letter I stated that the wages of the labourer averaged from 7s. to 9s. per week. Nothing, however, could be more erroneous than to suppose that the actual amount paid to the labourer is equal to that sum, or, on the other hand, that it is his good fortune to receive such a sum during the entire year. The system of hiring the labourer by the week is one which is comparatively rarely adopted in Suffolk; when, therefore, we are told that the wages of the labourer are 8s. per week, it is, so far as the great body of agricultural labourers are concerned, a perfect delusion. Labourers are paid by the day, not by the week—and only for the number of days during which they are actually at work. If, in consequence of wet or unfavourable weather, they are unable to work, the wages for such days are deducted from what, by courtesy, are called their weekly wages. If a day's sickness or domestic affliction keeps the labourer at home, the same principle is acted upon. In fact, upon the day which was set apart for the General Thanksgiving, the wages of great numbers of the labourers were stopped, on the plea that no work was then done by them. I am happy, however, to state that the instances of such hardship, and of such total disregard to the comforts of the poor, which came under my own notice, were comparatively rare. Those of the farmers who acted in so ungenerous a manner towards the labourers were principally confined to a small district in the western division of the county, to which I shall presently have occasion more particularly to refer.

The full wages of 8s., or even 9s. per week, are little enough to keep body and soul together; but when from that sum are deducted the wages of every day, or of every portion of a day, upon which the labourer is unable to work, the manner in which he exists becomes a mystery indeed. "There's some weeks," said a poor fellow to me, "that we only get 4s.—sometimes less than that—and in very wet weather we gets nothing at all." "How, then," said I, "do you manage to subsist, and pay 1s. 6d. a week for that cottage of yours?" "We can't do it on our wages, you may be sure," he said; "the truth is, master, that we're often driven to do a many things those times that we wouldn't do if we could help it. It is very hard for us to starve, and we sometimes pull some turnips, or p'raps potatoes out of some of the fields, unbeknown to the farmers." Is it to be wondered, if the poor man is thus tempted to commit these acts of depredation in order to preserve his miserable existence?

It has been very generally stated to me by the farmers, when I have spoken to them upon the subject, that the labourers are now much better off than they ever were, and they generally put their proposition in these words:—That 8s. a week wages, with wheat at 42s., is much better than wages at 9s., with wheat at 56s. Taking the two extreme points thus selected by the farmers, there could be no doubt as to the perfect truth of the proposition. But how stands the fact? The minimum of wages is not 8s. (or at the rate, rather, of 8s.) per week. In the great majority of cases, they are not higher than 7s.; and within the last fortnight, and since writing my last letter, there has been an extensive reduction to 6s. per week. Speaking to a labourer, whose wages had been gradually reduced from 1s. 4d. a day *before,* to 1s. 2d. *after* harvest—and now finally to 1s. per day—I asked him if he did not think that he was better off with low than with high wages, supposing that wheat was at a proportionately high price? He replied—"We can get more bread for the money, and that's some consequence to poor men like we, but they don't lower the rent to us when they lower the wages. When I was getting 9s. a week I had to pay eighteenpence a week for rent, and I must pay the same now when I am only getting 6s. a week; and then I don't know how long I may be able to get 6s. The farmers have nearly got in all their seed, and then we may go about our business. And then if I ain't got no money to buy the bread, why what's the consequence if it's cheap or dear?" Viewed in this light (and many of the labourers are shrewd enough to look at the question in this way), the condition of the labourer must be bad enough. As a general rule there can be no doubt whatever, that when the price of corn is low the condition of the labourer is vastly improved, as compared with what it is when the price is high. In order to ascertain, if possible, the relation between the price of wheat and the condition of the labourer, as shown by the amount of pauperism, I have extracted from a number of returns on the subject the average number of persons receiving in-door relief, and the average amount expended in out-door relief, in the county of Suffolk, during each of the three years ending the 29th of September, and also the average price of wheat at each of the same periods. The following is the result of my inquiries:—

	1847.	1848.	1849.
Average number of in-door paupers	3,199	2,932	2,935
Average amount of out-door relief	£2,802	2,315	2,219
Average price of wheat for quarter ending Sept. 29	67s 1d	51s 3d	45s 9d

Mr. French, who is vice-chairman of the board of guardians of the Hartismere union, stated to me that he had paid considerable attention to the subject, and he had come to the conclusion that the labourer was generally much better off when the price of corn was low than when it was high—and, as a consequence, that in all well-managed unions the amount of poor-rates and the number of paupers were then considerably reduced. A most intelligent master of a union workhouse on the borders of Norfolk and Suffolk also made the following statement to me, as the result of considerable experience:— "During the high price of flour I have invariably found more paupers come into the house, and altogether a larger proportion of destitution in the union." He also states that at one time, when corn was high, he had, out of 396 persons in the workhouse, 114 who were able-bodied labourers.

If this be the case, the question arises, how is it that at present, throughout nearly the whole of the county, there is such general and wide spread distress, and so much of complaint and dissatisfaction among the labourers? This conducts me at once to the second subject with which I propose to deal—viz., the employment of labour by the farmers. I have taken considerable pains to ascertain, in the course of my inquiry, whether there existed generally throughout the county an excess of labourers—whether there were more hands than could be profitably employed by the farmers upon the cultivation of their land; and I have uniformly been told, by persons conversant with the subject, that, so far from there being a redundance of labour, there was not enough to cultivate the land properly. Most unfortunately, however, for the comforts of the labourer, there is a very large proportion of the farmers of Suffolk who have gone on making additions to the size of their farms, without increasing in the same proportion the amount of capital with which to cultivate them. The difficulty and embarrassment in which they are consequently placed, prevent them from employing the number of hands which they would otherwise require on their farms, or from sufficiently remunerating those whom they do employ. I have met with many farmers who sympathize deeply with the depressed condition of the labourer, and who would be willing to give increased employment if it were in their power so to do. The consequence is, that at the present moment there is a considerable number who are out of employ; those who are employed are receiving extraordinarily low wages, and they generally expect that, as soon as the seed wheat shall be all sown, and the weather shall become in the least unfavourable, the opportunity will be taken of discharging many more of them. The favourable state of the weather for the last few weeks has, indeed, enabled the farmers to employ a good number of men in the fields. Had the weather not proved so propitious, the numbers out of employ would have been very largely increased. I have endeavoured to ascertain, from the various unions of the county, the increase in the number of able-bodied paupers, in the hope that it would afford some guide in forming a conclusion as to the number of persons actually unemployed. The returns, however, for various reasons, do not afford the full amount of information on the subject which was to be desired. The average number of able-bodied paupers receiving in-door relief in the county of Suffolk was, for the thirteen weeks ending September 29, 1848, 119; and for the same period of the present year the number was 174. The number of able-bodied paupers actually receiving in-door relief, in the week ending September 29, 1848, was 101; and for the week ending September 29 of the present year, the number was 166.

Of course it will be understood that these numbers only refer to the able-bodied paupers receiving in-door relief. They do not show the extent of pauperism in the county, for no account is taken of the insane, the sick, the infirm, or the children, who may be receiving in-door relief; nor do they apply to the number of able-bodied labourers who may be receiving out-door relief in consequence of the sickness of their families, or other exceptional causes. Although the principle of the Poor-law is to give no relief to the able-bodied, except in the workhouse, still there are many cases in which the boards of guardians relax a little the stringency of the rules. An instance of this kind came under my notice a short time since. A labourer applied to the board for relief; he was asked of course the usual questions as to the state of health of his family—he had six children. There was an evident desire on the part of the guardians to afford some slight relief, which they knew would be only of a temporary character, rather than be burdened with the expense of maintaining the whole family for an indefinite period in the workhouse. They accordingly strove hard to make out a "case." The applicant stated that his family were all well, and that he only wanted a little assistance to help him in the meantime, as he hoped to get something to do in the ensuing week. The guardians pressed the poor man still more closely. "Is not your wife poorly?" "No," replied the honest applicant. "Are you quite well yourself?" "Yes, I'm pretty well myself." "Is there none of your children ill?" "No." "Not one?" "No." "None of them got the ringworm, or anything the matter with their heads?" "No" was still the answer of the applicant, evidently not perceiving the design of the board. "Have any of them," at last suggested a member of the board, "had the ringworm lately?" "Why, yes," said the poor man, "a little time ago Billy caught it some-where." The applicant was ordered to withdraw—the consciences of the board were sufficiently elastic—one of his children had had the ringworm—it was a case of illness—and the man was ordered out-door relief. The following week the man was in work again. Repeated instances of this kind take place among the guardians, and they are generally considered rather liberal towards the poor. The number of able-bodied paupers receiving in-door relief, does not, therefore, af-ford complete information as to the number of labourers who may be unemployed, although, by comparing one period with another, some idea may be formed as to the amount of employment. There are, how-ever, many labourers who, when unemployed, refuse to apply for re-lief, as they are aware that, if able-bodied, the workhouse would be the only relief offered them—and sooner than subject themselves to such restraints as would be there imposed upon them, they endeav-our by some means, fair or foul, to support themselves until they are enabled to get employment. We have, therefore, no means of ascertaining with accuracy the number of persons who are at present out of employ; but there can be no doubt whatever, from the statements I have heard in various parts of the county, that the number is considerably greater than it has been for some years past, and that the coming winter is expected to be one of great hardship for the poor.

Another of the causes of complaint which I have frequently heard among the labourers, is the hardship of having to walk some ten or dozen miles in the course of the day, in going to and from their work. The necessity for this has arisen from the practice which exists in the neighbourhood of some of the larger towns—upon the part of some of the close parishes, or of the owners of extensive estates— of endeavouring to evade the operation of the law of settlement, by pulling down the cottages, or turning out the tenants just before the expiration of the term which would make them irremovable. Upon several properties in the neighbourhood of Bury, for instance, I have been informed of cases where, upon the slightest possible pretext, a whole family has been driven off the estate. The poor people thus driven away are unable to obtain accommodation in the villages in the immediate neighbourhood, the owners of property there not wishing to run the risk of having any burden thrown upon their parish—and they accordingly seek shelter in some of the wretched back streets and lanes of the larger towns. In several instances I was told by the labourers themselves that they had to walk one, two, three, or four miles to work on the very estate from which, as tenants, they had but a short time since been removed. I was informed of the case of one family which had been driven off an estate situated a few miles from Bury, under circumstances of the greatest hardship—though, it must be added, that there are few gentlemen who have devoted more time and attention to the improvement of the cottages and the condition of their tenantry than the owner of the estate in question. The plea for the removal of this family was, that the mother had been seen to pick up a few small potatoes which had been left upon the surface of the field, after the bulk of the crop had been removed. After having been turned out of the house, the whole family took up their abode within the porch of the church for two days, determined that they would not be driven out of the parish, although they might be evicted from their dwelling. From the church, however, they were finally removed as vagrants, and, travelling on to Bury, they obtained lodgings in the wretched place to which I referred in my former letter, viz., Hogg's-lane.

Several other instances like this came to my knowledge as having occurred in the neighbourhood of Bury. In the various other parts of the county through which I have travelled I have made it my business to inquire into the existence of such a practice, and I feel bound to state that the result of my inquiries was such as to lead me to the opinion that it is not carried on to so great an extent as I was led to suppose, except in some comparatively few cases, where close parishes exist in the immediate neighbourhood of large towns. I found upon inquiry that in a great number of cases where cottages had been pulled down, others had been erected in their stead of a more commodious character, and in some cases nearer to the farms. Taking the whole county, I do not believe that the number of cottages pulled down has exceeded the number of new ones that have been built. The insufficiency of cottage accommodation remains, however, still as great.

Another complaint on the part of the labourers is founded on the unfeeling manner in which they consider that they are almost invariably treated by their employers. They feel, to use their own words, that "they are treated like slaves." It is seldom, they say, that the farmer will condescend to speak to them, except in terms of reproach or abuse. There is no display of anything like kindly feeling towards them, nor any desire shown to improve their condition. But, amidst the general ill-feeling which subsists, it is gratifying to witness, in some instances, the display of kindlier sentiments between the parties. On the day before that set apart as Thanksgiving-day, I was in company with two farmers who occupied, one upwards of 500, the other about 700 acres. Having heard a rumour among the labourers, of the intention of many of the farmers not to pay the men the wages for that day, I was anxious to ascertain from the farmers themselves if there was any foundation for such a report. I accordingly addressed myself to the one who occupied the larger farm, and asked him if he intended to pay his men their wages if they did not work? "Pay 'em! no—certainly not," said he; "they're not agoin' to work, and why should I pay 'em for adoin' nothing? I've told my foreman not to give 'em anything." Shortly afterwards I addressed myself to the other farmer—an aged, grey-haired man, whose warm and benevolent-looking countenance strongly contrasted with that of the former. His answer to my inquiry was—"Why, to be sure I do; I wouldn't think of stopping the wages of the poor fellows on such a day. Lor' bless me, I'd rather give 'em something extra if I could afford it, than stop anything." Upon further inquiry I learned that the latter was paying his men 1s. 4d. per day—

the former had on the Saturday night previously reduced the wages to 1s. per day. It would be idle to ask whose labourers were most likely to be the best contented, and which of the two farmers received the greater amount of labour from the men in return for the wages paid.

Unfortunately it is the fact, be the cause what it may, that there does exist throughout the county—but to a considerably greater extent where low wages are paid—a very large amount of ill-feeling on the part of the labourers; and considering, as they most unhappily do, that they are ill-used and underpaid, it cannot be a matter of great surprise, if among them there should be found numerous instances in which they have blindly and wantonly endeavoured to wreak their bad feelings upon those whom they consider to be the causes of their grievances.

Within the last two months the crime of incendiarism has been fearfully on the increase in some portions of the western division of Suffolk, and in those portions of the counties of Essex and Cambridgeshire which lie contiguous to it. Incendiary fires are not, unfortunately, of rare occurrence in Suffolk. There have been times during which the people have, as is almost the case at present, been nightly alarmed by the sight of blazing ricks and farms in various parts. I find, upon inquiry, that during each of those periods the wages, as compared with the price of wheat, were remarkably low. The years 1816 and 1817 were the first in which incendiarism prevailed to any extent. The price of wheat in 1816 was 85s. 9d.; in 1817, 89s. 1d. The wages in the former year were 10s.—in the latter, 11s. per week. In 1825 incendiary fires again became numerous: the price of wheat was 68s. 7d., the wages 8s. 6d. In 1843 and 1844 the evil again broke out: wheat in 1843 was 54s. per quarter, wages 8s.; in 1844 the price of wheat was 51s. 3d., and wages in some parts were as low as 7s. per week. In the years 1843-4 there were not less than 89 incendiary fires in the county of Suffolk, the vast majority of which were in those portions of the county where the wages were the lowest. The average price of wheat for the quarter ending 29th September, 1849, was 45s. 9d.; the rate of wages in those portions of the county where the fires have recently occurred being 7s., but now reduced to 6s. per week. It is not my intention to enter into any inquiry as to what may or may not be considered a fair rate of wages to be paid to the agricultural labourer. Any person who may be disposed to enter into the inquiry as to the proportion which the wages bear to the price of corn may easily do so by ascertaining the quantity of corn, which the wages would purchase at the different periods.

Adopting, for a moment, the standard advocated by the farmers, of 8s. per week when corn is at 42s., the quantity of corn which could be purchased by wages of 8s. per week would be about 6 pecks; but with the present wages, in some parts, of only 6s. per week, but little more than 5 pecks could be obtained. The reader may easily calculate for himself the value of the wages, upon the standard of the farmers themselves, for the different years in which fires have been of the most frequent occurrence.

Since August last there have been no fewer than seventeen incendiary fires in a portion of the county of about fifteen or twenty miles in length, from north to south, and about twelve or fifteen in breadth. This district forms the southern part of the western division of the county, adjoining the district about Soham, in Cambridgeshire, on the west, and the district of Saffron Walden, in Essex, on the south. In these portions of Essex and Cambridgeshire the fires have been almost as numerous as in the county of Suffolk, and no doubt they have their origin in the same cause. The value of property thus destroyed has been, I am informed, not less than £14,000. Indeed, to such an extent has the system prevailed, that certain districts of Suffolk, Cambridge, and Essex have been placed under "ban" by the fire offices, several of them having refused to insure farm property there.

I have endeavoured as far as possible to ascertain the causes of these incendiary fires, and I have been unable to arrive at any other conclusion than that they originate in the distress and discontent of the labouring classes. Individual cases have occurred in which the fires, to all outward appearance, are not traceable to this source. Several fires have happened in cases where a comparatively high rate of wages was paid, where the labourers were generally contented, and where every possible exertion was made on the part of the employer to furnish them with work and to improve their condition. A gentleman who occupies a prominent position in one of the parishes where several fires have occurred, informed me that in 1844 he had paid considerable attention to the subject, that he had been present at many of the fires, and that the conclusion which he then came to was, that they were almost universally attributable to the low rate of wages; and that he had no doubt whatever but that the same cause applied to the fires of the present year. Indeed, the prevailing opinion among all thinking persons appears to be that they are owing to the very general depression and discontent of the people in those parts where the fires occur.

It does not appear that there are anything like secret societies among the peasantry, where the fires are planned or concocted. There is, however, a very general opinion among the police and others, that there is scarcely a fire which occurs the perpetrator of which is not pretty generally known in the neighbouring village. At Dalham, Gazeley, and several other small villages in the Risbridge union, there is evidently a great desire on the part of the people to screen the offenders. The people of Dalham uniformly refuse, I was informed, to render any assistance in putting out the fires, and upon one occasion they actually cut the hose of the engine, and fired upon the firemen who were working it.

Many persons are of opinion that the fires are, in the majority of cases, the work of one man only; and they support their opinion by the following fact. A short time since a man was transported from Dalham for the crime of poaching. His son, who resided in the parish, and carried on the trade of a basket-maker, was frequently heard to state that he would be the ruin of the parish. Numerous fires took place shortly afterwards, and there is no doubt that many of them were the work of this individual. The plan which he used to adopt upon such occasions was to place a small bundle of shavings, sticks, and other matters, well besmeared with pitch and other combustible materials, made up in such a manner as that ignition should not take place until he was enabled to get to some distance from the spot. In several cases these bundles had been discovered unignited; and upon examining them they were found to contain chips of osier—which circumstance, he being a basket-maker, naturally led to the inference that the bundles had been placed there by him. On one occasion, a portion of a handkerchief with some of these chips, which was traced to his possession, was found upon the premises after a fire; but, although the man has been tried upon several occasions, the authorities have not been able to procure a conviction. The man has now left the district, and the fires have been somewhat less in that immediate neighbourhood. The labourers themselves who are employed, even at miserable wages, are almost by common consent acquitted of being wilful parties to these acts of incendiarism.

The prevailing opinion on the subject appears to be, that the fires are not generally referable to one common origin, but that, in a great majority of cases, they are traceable to a spirit of wicked and wanton mischief on the part of boys—and perhaps even of vagrants—excited and brought into action by a spirit of imitation, and that, the fires having once broken out, a ready means of gratifying revenge is placed before their view, while the cheapness and ease with which lucifer matches may be procured offer facilities for giving effect to the feelings of hatred or hostility excited towards particular individuals.

There appears to be no reason whatever for supposing that the administration of the poor-law has anything to do with producing these fires. Indeed in several of the unions in which fires have occurred, the law has been carried out by the guardians with a total absence of anything like harshness or cruelty, and the provisions of the law are even frequently strained with the benevolent view of affording the fullest possible relief. Generally speaking, there is not, in these districts, so strong a feeling of dislike to the poor-law among the labourers as may be found in some of the unions where no cases of incendiarism have occurred.

I have heard an opinion expressed that a great number of incendiary fires were traceable to boys. After the age of 16 the boys become paupers in their own right. The parents begin to think that it is time that the boys should earn something for themselves; the boys also think that they ought to assume the habits of men, and they wish to become independent of their parents; they accordingly endeavour to get work, but they are boys in the eye of the farmer, and they have not the requisite qualification for high wages; they are unmarried; they are not able to earn more than from 2s. 6d. to 3s. 6d. a week. They soon get tired of working for so small a sum; they spend a short time in the workhouse; becoming dissatisfied there, they meet with other boys of the same age who are similarly situated, they talk over their grievances, and become sullen and discontented with everybody and everything; they leave the house literally with their hands against every man, and avail themselves of the first opportunity of indulging their feelings upon the property of those who may or may not have done them some real or imaginary wrong.

There are many fires which are considered as the work of the incendiary, but which might perhaps be ascribed to other causes, such as accident or negligence. A few days since a large fire occurred a few miles from Bury, which for some time was considered to be the act of an incendiary, but it came out some time afterwards that two little boys had been playing with some lucifers in the neighbourhood of the farm, and by accident had set fire to one of the stacks.

Referring to individual cases of incendiarism, it is curious to observe how, in the great majority of cases, the fires occur in districts
where either a low rate of wages is paid, or where the labourers deem
themselves improperly treated. Speaking to many of the labourers
upon the subject, they have not unfrequently made use of expressions towards those whose property had been destroyed, such as—
"Oh, sarve him right;" "He was a grinder;" "He was a strict, hard-
fisted fellow;" "He was very hard upon his men," and other terms of a
similar character. On the other hand, some of the fires have happened
in cases where the farmers bore the highest possible character. In one
case a farmer of about 500 acres received the prize at the Stow Agricultural Society for employing the largest amount of labour in proportion
to his occupation. Another farmer possessed the general reputation of
farming higher, and employing more hands, than other persons in the
district. A short time since an extensive fire occurred near Kirtlinge,
which destroyed the whole of the property. A portion of the premises
had been burned down last year; they had but just been rebuilt, and
the workmen had not left more than a few days, when a fire again
broke out, and burned the whole of the newly-erected premises, together with that portion of the old which escaped upon the previous
occasion. The farmer bore an excellent character. Two fires recently
occurred in Fornham, in both of which cases the farmers bore a high
character, and were in the habit of paying a better rate of wages than
most of the farmers in the neighbourhood.

But while, on the one hand some farmers who bear a good character among the labourers have suffered, there are many instances in
which they have been spared, although fires have been constantly taking place around them. A large farmer, residing five or six miles from
Bury, and farming upwards of 1,000 acres, was a singular instance of
this. "He is a good man—a good fellow," said a labourer to whom I
was speaking; "he is one of the best men we have round here, and he
hasn't had so much as a hay-rick, or barley-stack, set on fire. Aye! a
better man never trod shoe leather than he. The poor men all like him;
he isn't ashamed to speak to 'em when he sees 'em, and he's always glad
to help a poor fellow when he's in want." Neither in 1843 nor in 1844,
when so many fires occurred, was there a single fire upon his farm—
nor have there been any during the present outbreak. Upon many of
the estates that are well managed, and where there is a resident proprietor, comparatively few cases of incendiarism have occurred. On
the estate of a gentleman near Lavenham it was found necessary to

remove one of the tenants, in consequence of some bad conduct upon his part, and on the following day a barn upon the estate was fired—there being no moral doubt that the evicted tenant was the guilty party. The case could not, however, be brought sufficiently home to him to procure a conviction. No other instance of incendiarism has occurred upon the estate, although it is situated in the very heart of the district in which so many fires have taken place.

But although there are cases in which the farmers who bear a high character have suffered, and likewise cases in which they have escaped, there are also many in which farmers who are very generally disliked by the labourers, who give very low wages and afford but insufficient employment, have escaped injury. You may frequently hear the poor people speak in terms of almost unmeasured abuse of some of the farmers; and, in looking over the list of fires, you expect to find some of their farms included. Such, however, in a great many instances, is not the case. Any theory which may be set up on the subject is, therefore, liable to be immediately overthrown by some case or cases which may be cited, and which it is impossible to reconcile with any preconceived opinions. Difficult as it may be to explain many individual cases, we have, however, the broad facts before us, that in the northern and eastern parts of the county fires are comparatively unknown, and that the rate of wages is higher there than in the other portions of the county; and that in the southern and western parts of the county, where fires are constantly taking place, the rate of wages is, generally speaking, lower. In the former case, wages average from 8s. to 9s. per week; in the latter, from 6s. to 7s. per week. How far low wages may tend to produce this state of things is a question upon which the reader will form his own opinion.

Before leaving the labourers of Suffolk, I will shortly refer to the state of education among them. Upon this question blue books are silent, and any attempt to arrive at a conclusion would be certain to result in failure. One mode that is generally adopted of arriving at information upon this point is by taking the number of persons who in any particular district may have signed the marriage register with their mark, not being able to write their names. Adopting this standard, it appears that the number of men so signing the register in the county of Suffolk, in the year 1847, was not less than 1,083—being 42 per cent. above the average of all England and Wales upon the like number of marriages. There is no doubt that this is an enormous per centage, and it must also be remembered that this applies to the whole county, including persons of every class and condition who were married during that year. It is but fair to suppose that among persons in better condition than the agricultural labourers, there would be but few probably who would be unable to write their names. Among the tradesmen there would be also a far greater proportion to be found, able to write their names, than among the labourers. How many of the agricultural labourers of Suffolk were able to sign their names would be a curious point upon which to obtain information, and one which would be necessary if we wished to arrive at the state of education among that numerous body. Unfortunately the information is not forthcoming; but we are fully justified in assuming that among the labourers, as a body, there is to be found a far greater per centage of persons who cannot write their names than would appear from taking the average of the whole county. Of course the evidence adduced by the marriage registers applies only to the state of education among the adults—the people of the last generation. What is the case as regards the rising generation? Here, again, we are left to grope our way almost entirely in the dark. We search in vain through the enormous pile of blue books for information upon this all-important subject. We have accurate accounts of crime and pauperism, exports and imports—nay, even of the number of herrings cured, dried, salted, and otherwise disposed of; but, with the exception of the case of pauper children, we have no educational statistics upon which we can rely. After some considerable trouble I have been enabled, however, to obtain "The Result of the General Inquiry made by the National Society into the state and progress of the schools for the education of the poor in the principles of the Established Church, during the years 1846-7, throughout England and Wales." This Return does not include schools connected with dissenters, nor Church of England preparatory schools, nor grammar schools. The preface to this voluminous document states that, although every care had been taken to insure accuracy in the details, still there was no doubt that many inaccuracies were to be found. From these returns I have collected that there are in Suffolk 699 schools, having 32,667 scholars under their charge—being a proportion of 1 in 9 to the entire population of the county. By the minutes of Council on Education, for the last year, I find that the number of pauper children receiving education in the schools connected with the workhouses is 1,043. The number of scholars in connection with the Wesleyans is, I believe, about 4,000. As to the numbers in the schools connected with other bodies of dissenters, I have no means of obtaining information. Probably there may be about the same number as in connection with the Wesleyans. The number of children in connection with the Roman Catholics is, I believe, very small—probably not exceeding 100. I have no means of ascertaining the numbers attending the various private schools throughout the county. The total number of children in connection with the schools of the National Society throughout England and Wales is computed at 1 in 11½ of the entire population; in the county of Suffolk the proportion appears to be 1 in 9. It would appear from this, that the state of education among the children is rather in advance as compared with the whole of England and Wales. The education of the children of the agricultural labourers is, however, remarkably deficient; and in this respect the pauper children are placed in a much more favourable position. There is a school in connection with each of the workhouses, where the children are taught the rudiments of education, and in several of the schools which I visited considerable proficiency was exhibited in some branches of instruction. At the pauper school at Stowmarket many of the boys write excellently, and are good bookkeepers. At the Blything Union, many of the children have made considerable progress in the art of navigation, and have obtained employment in the navy; and some of them have obtained marks of merit for their good conduct. As an instance of the want of education among the pauper children in some parts of the county, and of the benefits likely to result from the establishment of pauper schools, I may mention the case of a school which I visited at Wortham, in connexion with the Hartismere Union. During the examination of the children, a number of questions were asked and answers given—among others the following:—

"Why was Lazarus seen afar off in Abraham's bosom?

"Because he was Abraham's father.

"What is a publican?

"A Pharisee.

"What was Matthew?

"A fisherman.

"What did the Jews expect the Messiah to be?

"A false prophet.

"What is faith?

"The substance of anything seen.

"How many Houses of Parliament are there?

"Three—two.

"What is the upper one called?

"The house of dukes.

"What is the lower one called?

"The house of gentlemen.

"Who puts on the taxes?

"The Queen.

"Suppose you were to send a person to the House of Commons, who would he represent?

"Gentlemen.

"If you were to send one, who would you send?

"You, sir (to the chaplain).

"What would you send me there for?

"To collect money."

It must, however, in justice, be stated, that considering the short time during which they had been receiving instruction, they had made considerable progress in many other branches; many of the boys and girls read well, and some of the girls wrote an exceedingly good hand. The late master of the workhouse, I was informed, had been in the almost constant habit of neglecting his duties, and the guardians were finally compelled to remove him. During the short period in which the present able master, Mr. Dunlop, has been engaged, a marked improvement has taken place in the children.

It is pleasing to notice the great exertions which are in many cases made on the part of landed proprietors to afford the means of education to the children of their tenants. There is scarcely a large estate upon which one or more schools have not been erected—the salaries of the masters, and other expenses attending them, being defrayed by the proprietors themselves. Among schools of this class may be mentioned those of Mr. Shaw, of Kersgrave Hall, near Woodbridge; of Sir Edward Kerrison, of Stradbroke; of Mr. Benyon, of Culford; and of Mr. Kerrison, of Broome Hall, who has also established an industrial school in connection with one in which the usual routine of education is taught. Great credit is also due to the great body of the clergy throughout the county for the manner in which they have exerted themselves to provide the means of education for the children of the poor. In many of the parishes are to be found small schools, which are supported entirely from funds derived from the miserable stipends of the country curates. There is still, however, a great want of school accommodation throughout the entire county. There are four parishes in the immediate neighbourhood of Ship-meadows, a district lying between Bungay and Beccles, in which there is not a single school, with the exception of a small Sunday-school, conducted entirely by the wife of one of the curates—the parties residing in the parishes not being able to raise a sufficient sum either to establish the schools or to allow them to obtain any assistance from the Government grants. There are other parishes in which, unfortunately, there is no school accommodation whatever—and in many the schools are of the most wretched character.

The Morning Chronicle, Monday, December 10, 1849.

THE MORNING CHRONICLE

ON

"LABOUR AND THE POOR."

The demands constantly made to obtain the early Numbers of THE MORNING CHRONICLE containing the Letters on "LABOUR AND THE POOR," in the Metropolitan, Agricultural, and Manufacturing Districts, have induced the conductors of that Journal to direct the Republication of those Letters in

SUPPLEMENTS

(containing Twenty-four Columns each), to be given twice a-week, commencing on Friday, the 21st of December.

The sole object of these Supplements being to enable the Public to obtain the complete Series, they will be discontinued as soon as the Letters which shall have been published previous to the 21st of December have been republished, as parties desirous to possess the Letters that will be published after that date will have it in their power to do so, by ordering, from the 21st instant, copies of the regular daily publication of THE MORNING CHRONICLE, in which the Series will be continued.

The Supplements will be supplied GRATIS with THE MORNING CHRONICLE of the days on which they appear; and all persons desirous of Completing their Sets are requested to forward their orders to the Publisher of THE MORNING CHRONICLE, 332, Strand; or to their respective News-agents.

LABOUR AND THE POOR.

—◆—

THE RURAL DISTRICTS.

[FROM OUR SPECIAL CORRESPONDENT.]

NORFOLK, SUFFOLK, AND ESSEX.

Letter XVI.

Following out the plan which I had prescribed to myself, I now proceed to give the results of my inquiries into the condition of the labouring classes of the county of Norfolk.

This county is one of considerable extent: there are but three counties—viz., York, Lincoln, and Devon—which are of greater dimensions than Norfolk. Its area comprises 2,024 square miles, or rather more than 1,290,300 statute acres. On its northern and eastern side it is bounded by the German Ocean. The Wash separates a portion of the western part of the county from Lincolnshire, and the Ouse divides the remaining portion on the same side from Cambridge, while the Waveney and the Little Ouse divide it on the south from Suffolk. Its greatest length from north to south is about seventy miles, and its breadth from east to west about forty-two miles. The small rivers which run through the county, such as the Wensum, Yare, Waveney, Bure, Ant, and Thirne, afford great facilities for inland navigation. There are about 170 miles of railway constructed, which connect together all the most important towns. Two lines of communication are opened with London—one by the Eastern Union system, and the other by the Eastern Counties; and by means of the Norfolk railways the whole of the manufacturing districts are brought into connection with the county.

The population of Norfolk in 1841 was 412,664—of whom there were, above twenty years of age, 94,982 males, and 95,967 females; while of those under twenty, there were 104,119 males, and 117,596 females. 384,594 of the persons so enumerated were born within the county, and 28,070 elsewhere. Between the years 1831 and 1841, the rate of increase in the population appears to have been checked in a most remarkable manner. In 1811, the population was 291,999, being an increase of 18 per cent. as compared with the previous ten years; in 1821 the number was 344,368, an increase of 13 per cent. over the previous decennial period; in 1831, 390,054, or an increase of 13½ per cent.; while in 1841, the rate of increase was found to be only 5¾ per cent., the population having only increased during the ten years to 412,664. The number of inhabitants to 100 statute acres in Norfolk, according to the census of 1841, was 31.9, being a proportion of not less than 25.8 per cent. below the average of England and Wales; there being fifteen other English counties with a less number to 100 acres—one county, viz., Sussex, having the same number—the remainder having in each case more than Norfolk.

The estimated rental of the county is £1,957,822, the assessed rental £1,928,422, and the amount assessed to the property and income tax £1,972,558. The number of persons returned as "independent" in 1841 was 10,358, being a proportion of 10.4 per cent. below the average of England and Wales upon the same amount of population. The actual annual value of the real property assessed to the income and property tax in 1843 was £2,327,371, being a proportion of 4.55 per cent. of real property above the average for the like population throughout England and Wales. In 1831 there were only 6,168 depositors in the savings banks of Norfolk, the amount of whose deposits was £198,554; in 1846 the number of depositors had increased to 19,250, and the amount of their deposits to £562,373. The mean amount of each depositor in 1841 was £31, and in 1846 £29.

Having thus briefly alluded to a few of the more prominent features in connection with the county of Norfolk, I am anxious, before proceeding to describe the condition of the labouring classes, to call the attention of the reader to the state of the ancient city of Norwich. There were, in 1841, in the city, 14,023 inhabited houses and 812 uninhabited. The population was 62,344; of this number there were males under 20 years of age, 12,766; females, 13,807; above 20 years of age—males, 15,403; females, 20,268. Of the total number, 56,847 were born in the county, and 5,497 elsewhere.

In former times Norwich was particularly famous for its extensive manufactures of crapes and woollen goods. I was informed by Mr. Yarrington, who had been formerly extensively engaged as a manufacturer, that in 1791 there were not less than 100,000 hands employed in immediate connection with the establishments at Norwich. Great numbers of these persons were employed in the surrounding parishes, and many even in the county of Suffolk. At that time one firm alone exported annually 40,000 pieces to Germany, Spain, and Portugal; and upwards of 70,000 pieces of the coarser kind of goods were also required for the Russian trade. Since that period, however, the trade of Norwich has sadly fallen off. As you pass through the great majority of its narrow, gloomy, ill-paved, and irregularly-built streets, traces of ruin and decay everywhere present themselves to view; and there is no doubt that ere long, despite the exertions of a few capitalists, and even the recent infusion of new blood among them from London and elsewhere, the city of Norwich will lose its importance as a manufacturing place, and become the centre and capital of an extensive agricultural district.

Various reasons have been assigned by the manufacturers for the great falling off in the trade. The complete isolation of the city from the other seats of manufacture, and its distance from any large port, is considered to have had some effect in bringing about its present state. The high price which the inhabitants have to pay for coals, as compared with other manufacturing districts where coal abounds, has also placed them in a disadvantageous position. For a long time the manufacturers of Norwich held out against the introduction of steam power into their factories, and it is only within the last few years that it has been introduced to any extent. Their powerful rivals in the North did not fail to take advantage of this omission on the part of the manufacturers of Norwich; and in a short time the Paisley people were enabled to take the lead of them in nearly the whole of the markets. Another cause of the decline, which has been frequently stated to me, is to be found in the fact that the trade of Norwich is in the hands of so few persons. There are not more than a dozen manufacturers, and the majority of these are inert and apathetic. There is nothing in them of that "go-a-headism" which is to be found in the other large manufacturing towns in the country. Knowing full well that there is always an abundant supply of labour in the market, they delay till the latest moment giving out the work, and until they "can safely feel their way," as they call it—that is, till they know that some particular kind of fabric will "take." The evil arising from the adoption of this course falls with tenfold force upon the unfortunate workpeople. Day after day, and week after week, they are compelled to drag attendance at the different factories for the purpose of obtaining a supply of work. The manufacturer declines to give out the "shoot;" there is nothing like constant employment for the people; they are driven to the parish for relief, and the

enormous poor-rate of the city—at present not less than £40,000—
is the burden imposed upon it owing to the want of energy on the
part of the manufacturers. Another evil arising from this system is
one which may be said to be felt more by themselves, although it ultimately falls upon the workpeople; that is, the comparative want of
originality of design. There are one or two enterprising manufacturers among them, who at considerable expense produce new designs
in shawls and dresses, some of them of a very beautiful character. So
soon, however, as these articles make their appearance, the design is
copied by others, and worked upon an inferior article—the market is
glutted, prices fall—and the public, having purchased inferior articles,
cease for the future to patronize the Norwich manufactures. Among
some of the manufacturers there is a very strong feeling on the subject,
and they entertain great hopes that the establishment of the schools
of design will eventually be the means of remedying the evil.

The chief articles of manufacture in Norwich are woollen, silk,
and cotton goods, crapes, paramattas, stuffs, camlets, &c.—the materials used being principally worsted and silk. Being anxious to see
for myself the mode of employment at the principal factories, and the
condition of the workpeople, I called upon the owners of the several
mills, stated to them the object of my visit, and, in almost all cases,
every facility was afforded me for obtaining the information which I
sought.

The first mill which I shall notice will be that of Messrs. Grout,
Martin, and Co., who, in addition to their factory at Norwich, have
a very large one at Yarmouth, and another also at Ditchlingham. The
number of hands usually employed by the firm is—at Norwich, 600;
at Yarmouth, 800; and at Ditchlingham, 350; being a total of 1,750.
The number employed at the time of my visit was considerably below
the average. The first department into which I was shown was an extensive fire-proof store-room, in which were enormous bales of silk
of different sorts, from Italy, India, and China. The first operation in
connection with this manufactory consisted in sorting and dividing
the various qualities of the silk—a process in which great care and
discrimination are required. The silk, having been thus prepared, undergoes the next process—winding; an operation which is carried on
in two large rooms, well lighted and ventilated, of 75 feet in length
and 40 in breadth. There were engaged in this department about 80
persons, chiefly females, whose average earnings by piece-work were
from 4s. to 6s. per week. From the winding-room I was conducted to

the "throwing-rooms." There were two rooms in which this process was carried on, in each of which about forty persons were employed, many of whom were young girls, not exceeding eleven years of age. The lowest amount earned during the last week was 2s. 6d., and the highest 7s. 6d. The next stage consisted in winding the silk from the larger to the smaller bobbins, for the convenience of the "warpers." About eighty persons were employed in this operation, whose average earnings were about 6s. per week. The silk having been wound upon bobbins, or "horns," of the proper size, was then handed over to the warpers. The "warping," which in most factories is done by hand, is here performed in the most ingenious manner by steam-power. In this room there are about fifty of these small warping machines, each attended to by one person; and a small dial-plate attached to the frame, the hands of which are moved by gearing wheels, registers the number of yards made by each machine. In this room the average earnings were from 7s. to 8s. per week. The warp having been prepared, the next and final process of manufacture is the weaving. Leaving the warping-room, we proceed therefore to the weaving-room, where sixty power-looms are in almost constant employment. There was generally one person to each of these looms, but some of the most experienced and active hands undertook the management of two of them. There were a few learners also at some of them. The number of persons here employed was about sixty; and the highest amount earned during the week by the weavers was 8s. Some of the less skilful hands did not earn more than 4s. 6d. or 5s. The whole of the weaving in connection with this establishment is done on the premises, no portion of it being given out to the hand-loom weavers to work upon in their own homes. Every part of the establishment was remarkably clean, and the condition and appearance of those employed were calculated to remove a great many of the unfavourable impressions which some persons might be led to form of the injurious effects of factory employment.

From the crape and gauze manufactory of Messrs. Grout and Co., I proceeded to that of Messrs. Willett, Neville, and Co., of Pottergate-street, who are extensive manufacturers of all kinds of fancy materials, such as Irish poplins, gros de Naples, waistcoatings, bandannas, barege and woollen shawls, "Lindianas," and various other fabrics of a similar nature. There are several jacquard looms at work on the premises. The various processes of preparing the materials differ but little in detail from those pursued in the mill of Messrs. Grout and Co. The use of the jacquard loom constitutes the greatest point of dif-

ference between the two establishments. The rate of wages paid to
the weavers at the jacquard looms is about 12s. per week, but they are
not employed on an average more than seven months in the year. The
weavers of bandannas, mousselin de laines, and other fabrics, earn
about 8s. per week, but there are very few of them who are in constant employment. There were about 200 hands employed—below
the usual number; this being considered the worst part of the year,
the autumn goods having been done with, and the sale of the spring
goods not having commenced. In the case of Messrs. Willett and Co.,
who have a considerable number of power-looms, the work done at
this period of the year is almost exclusively spring goods, which are
manufactured for stock. There were connected with the manufactory,
or at work upon it, about 540 persons.

The next factory which I visited was that of Mr. Middleton, of
Calvert-street, the principal articles manufactured being paramattas,
bareges, and poplins. There were 100 power-looms on the premises,
all of which were at work. The total number of persons employed,
both on the premises and at their own homes, was about 420. When
in full work they have employed as many as 800 hands. In order that
I might fully satisfy myself on the subject of the wages paid to the
workpeople, Mr. Middleton, in the most courteous manner, allowed
me to look over his pay-book, from which I made the following selec-
tions, at random, of the amounts paid to individuals during various
periods:—

PAID TO MEN.

No. 1. June 16 to Oct. 27 . . . . £8 13 8
No. 2. July 7 to Nov. 24 . . . . 18 6 7
No. 3. Oct. 3 to Nov. 23 . . . . 1 17 10½
No. 4. Oct. 30 to Nov. 21 . . . . . . 2 1 9
No. 5. Oct. 27 to Nov. 24 . . . . . . 1 4 3½
No. 6. Nov. 3 to Nov. 24 . . . . 1 15 9

PAID TO WOMEN.

No. 7. Nov. 6 to Nov. 23 . . . . 1 5 8

In all these cases the parties employed did the work at their own
homes, and they have to pay for winding, beaming, candles, and other
expenses. The amount to be deducted for these items, I was informed,
was about 20 per cent. Making these deductions, we shall have, therefore, as the average earnings per week of

No. 1 . . . . 19 weeks, at . . . . 7s. per week.
No. 2 23   „   . . . . 13s.   „

[This person, I was told, is the best weaver in the city, and can always command employment of the best kind.]

```
No. 3 .... 7 weeks, at ....   4s. 6d. per week.
No. 4 .... 3      „      ....  11  8      „
No. 5 .... 4      „      ....   4  9      „
No. 6 .... 3      „      ....  10  8      „
No. 7 .... 3      „      ....   6  8      „
```

The earnings of some of the persons employed on the power-looms were as follows:—

```
No. 1 ... From March 25 to Oct. 22 ... £12 15 0½
No. 2 ...   „   April 27 to Sept. 28 ...  10 10 4½
No. 3 ...   „   April 14 to Oct. 30  ...  12  7 1½
```

One penny per week is the whole amount of deduction to be made from the earnings of this class of weavers. That sum is charged for gas, for lighting the factory. The average earnings per week for these three persons would therefore be:—

```
No. 1 .... 30 weeks, at ....  5s. 2d. per week.
No. 2 .... 23      „     ....  8  10      „
No. 3 .... 29      „     ....  8   6      „
```

At the manufactory of Messrs. Clabbon and Co. the principal articles manufactured are figured silks, for dresses, and "fill-over" and other shawls. The firm expect to be able to employ a large number of hands shortly upon fabrics of this kind. Mr. Clabbon informed me that he had but thirteen power-looms, only one of which was at work, and that he would be glad to get rid of them all, as he found that the power-looms did not suit the weavers' work, and that their introduction into Norwich had done great injury to the trade. They had a number of jacquard looms which had been lying idle for several years, but which he expected to set in full work very shortly; indeed, so great a demand was there for this kind of loom, that they could scarcely be purchased at any price, although a few months since they would not realize the price of old iron. The numbers then employed by the firm did not exceed 200, though when in full work they usually employed 500 hands. The average earnings of the weavers were about the same as those in the mills already referred to. Within the last few years increased employment has been given to the workpeople by the introduction of manufactures of different kinds from those previously carried on—among which may be mentioned cotton spinning, silk and satin weaving, mohair yarn spinning, and the manufacture of Leicester goods.

A large factory has recently been erected by Mr. Jay, in King-street, for spinning mohair and Alpaca yarn. The number of persons employed in, or connected with, this factory was about 250. The wool employed is of a peculiar character, and is now imported in large quantities from Constantinople. As in the case of the silk, the first process which the wool undergoes is that of sorting, according to its different degrees of fineness and coarseness. The persons employed in this portion of the work earn from 18s. to 23s. per week. The wool having been sorted, it is then sent to the combers, who work chiefly at their own homes, and who earn, when employed, from 15s. to 20s. per week. A great deal, however, depends upon the ability of the workman. The wool, when combed, is handed over to the spinners and twisters, about 100 of whom, chiefly girls, are employed in three large rooms of the factory. The rate of earnings (they are all paid by piece work) ranges from 2s. to 4s. 6d. per week. The young beginners and learners seldom get more than 2s. per week; and many of them are, I was told, "dear at that price." From the "winders and twisters," the yarn proceeds to its final stage, that of "reeling," and when completed it is made up into hanks, in which state it is exported. The persons employed as "reelers and hankers" earn from 6s. to 7s. per week. A very small proportion of this yarn is consumed in the home manufactures, the principal portion of it being exported to France. The recent convulsion in that country greatly injured the trade. So great a demand, however, is there at present for this kind of material, that Mr. Jay informed me he could employ double the number of hands if he could obtain additional "sorters;" that being considered the most particular branch of the manufacture. In France the article is used very considerably in the velvet manufactures, and for covers for sofas and ottomans, chairs, and other articles of furniture. Some portions of the finest kind are made up into ladies' bonnets, and used also in the manufacture of dresses, many of which are sold for poplins. About this time last year the earnings of the spinners did not average more than 2s. per week, owing to the great falling off in the demand for this article of manufacture.

The circumstances which led to the establishment of a cotton-spinning factory in Norwich were as follows: a few years since vast numbers of the weavers were out of employment, and in the almost constant receipt of out-door relief. Mr. Geary, one of the then guardians, suggested that some employment should be found for the able-bodied within the workhouse. The guardians, however, refused to expend any money in the purchase of machinery for the employment of the people, but after a considerable time they allowed Mr. Geary to set up some machinery at his own expense—the guardians stipulating that, as a return for this privilege, they should have the whole amount earned by the parties. Mr. Geary, however, closed with the offer, and at the end of twelve months, having expended upwards of £500, and kept a number of persons constantly at work, he asked the board to take the management into their own hands. This they refused to do, and Mr. Geary finally resolved upon carrying on the experiment at his own establishment. The machines were accordingly removed from the workhouse, and with them all the persons who had been employed upon them. From that time the trade has been steadily and constantly increasing. Having seen the thing fully established, Mr. Geary gave up that branch of the manufacture to his nephew, Mr. Sultzer, who now carries on the business. In this factory there are employed about 50 men and boys in making, polishing, and finishing the reels upon which the cotton is sold. The men earn from 12s. to 14s. per week, the boys from 8s. to 9s. About 200 girls and women are employed as winders and reelers, the best hands earning from 7s. to 8s. per week, the inferior hands from 4s. 6d. to 5s. 6d. From 50 to 100 girls of all ages are employed in the different processes of sorting, cutting, gumming on the tickets, and other multifarious duties, with wages ranging from 2s. to 6s. per week. The number of reels manufactured weekly is about 150,000. In addition to the cotton spinning which is carried on in Mr. Sultzer's factory, about sixty or seventy persons are employed in weaving silk and satin. This branch of manufacture is carried on exclusively in Norwich by Mr. Sultzer, who was the first to introduce it. It was considered for a long time that the Norwich weavers, having been so long accustomed to other kinds of work, would not succeed in the manufacture of silk. The enterprise of Mr. Sultzer has, however, completely decided that question in favour of the weavers of Norwich—having already wove some satins which have been considered fully equal to the best made in Spitalfields. The earnings of the weavers in this case, as in all others where they are paid by the piece, depend greatly upon the ability and skill of the individual. While at Mr. Sultzer's mill, a weaver brought home a piece of satin upon which he had been occupied four weeks and two days. The amount which he received for his work was £2 16s., being at the rate of 14s. per week. Deducting the expenses of winding, candles, and other things, his wages would average about 11s. or 12s. The total number of hands employed was between 500 and 600.

There is no manufacturer in Norwich who exerts himself more laudably for the promotion of the comforts of his workpeople than Mr. Sultzer. He has recently built several comfortable cottages in the neighbourhood of the factory for the accommodation of the persons employed by him, and he is now erecting warm baths for the use not only of his own workpeople but for the public generally. In the whole of Norwich there is no such thing as a public bath, and it is intended to give a warm bath and a clean towel to every person for one penny. Mr. Jay means also to form a bath for his workpeople. In both cases it is intended to keep up a constant supply of warm water from the engine connected with the factory. No person known to be of a bad or immoral character is allowed to continue at work at Mr. Sultzer's factory, and provident habits are encouraged, as far as they can be among the workpeople, by the formation of coal clubs and provident societies. Upon the payment of a small sum per week to the coal club, a quantity of coals is sent in at cost price to the subscribers at the cheapest time of the year. The object sought to be gained by the provident society or club is that of inducing the workpeople who can spare it to deposit a portion of their earnings with their employer, who invests it in separate accounts, and in the names of the individual depositors, in the savings bank. Mr. Sultzer informed me that he had known great benefit to be derived from this system, as the workpeople were enabled to lay by a few shillings, without the risk of its being discovered by their more improvident relatives, who would be certain to obtain it from them when they felt they wanted any little assistance.

At Mr. Geary's factory about 520 persons, of both sexes and all ages, were employed at the time of my visit. The articles manufactured here are—netted shawls, braces, webbing for shoes, belts, and a variety of miscellaneous articles of that character. Connected with the brace department there were 109 girls, mostly very young, employed in preparing the brace ends, sewing on the buckle, and making the button-hole. There were 49 of them who were "seamers," 34 "buttonhole workers," who were at work on the premises, and 26 who worked at their own homes. I inquired of the children—for the great majority of them appeared to be from ten to twelve years old—how much they could earn in the week? One said she could make four gross in a week, which was 3s.; two others could make the same quantity; one made three gross and a half, which was 2s. 7½d.; two others made three gross, equal to 2s. 3d.; while several of the newer hands could not make more than two gross, and some not so many as that. Mr. Geary informed me that he was anxious to avoid employing the children when too young, but he was constantly pressed by their parents to take the children and give them work. Many of them had been brought to him to employ when they were scarcely fit to be left without a nurse. I was surprised to see, among the little children, some girls who were considerably older, and some even young women; and upon inquiring as to the cause of their being so employed, they informed me that they liked the work much better than anything else, although they could not perhaps earn so much at it as they could at other work; still it was regular, and for that reason they preferred it. All the work in this department was of course done by hand with the common needle. The whole of the children appeared to be perfectly contented, and to all appearance were in excellent health and spirits. In another portion of the building are to be found upwards of one hundred boys, who are employed in making shoes and slippers. The usual mode adopted in the city is to teach the boy the business in four years, upon payment of £5 as premium—the boy receiving a shilling a week for the first year, two for the second, three for the third, and four for the last year. The plan pursued by Mr. Geary is to take the boys, without any premium, for four years, teach them their business, and pay them for whatever amount of work they may perform. The boys are regularly indentured, and undertake to remain four years; Mr. Geary undertaking, on his part, to teach them the trade, and to find them employment during that period. At the expiration of the term they are at full liberty to stay with their employer, or to seek employment elsewhere. The boys are all kept in constant work, and during the first year many of them earn from 3s. to 4s. per week, while the best and oldest hands earn from 12s. to 14s. In the rooms in which the netting belts and webbing were wove there were 50 power-looms, and about 60 persons employed, whose average earnings were from 5s. to 6s. each per week. There is an evening school for adults in connection with this factory, which is under the management and care of Mr. Geary. There is also a tolerably large school in connection with the factory of Mr. Sultzer.

In addition to the factories already referred to, and which I have personally visited, there are various others. There is a large establishment conducted by Messrs. Toler and Co., who are principally shawl,

paramatta, and fancy dress weavers. This firm manufactures more of
the kind of shawls called "fill-overs," many of which fetch a very high
price, than any other manufacturer in the city. The number of hands
employed by them in all branches, including hand and power-loom
weavers, is probably from three to four hundred. About three hundred
persons are employed at the Lakenham factory, conducted by R. W.
Blake, Esq., in spinning mohair, in the same manner as at Mr. Jay's
factory. At the Yarn Company's works, at St. Edmund's, there are
about 400 persons employed in spinning yarn for the weavers, to
manufacture into Orleans cloth, paramattas, challis, and various other
fabrics. Messrs. Bolingbroke and Co. also manufacture considerable
quantities of woollen and fancy goods of various descriptions. They
have a number of hand-looms on the premises, for weaving paramattas and other fabrics, which are almost constantly at work. The whole
of their fabrics are manufactured by hand, it being the only firm in
the town which does not use steam power. I was not able to learn the
exact number of hands employed, but was informed that the numbers
ranged from 200 to 300. A large factory has recently been built, called
the St. James's Power-Loom Factory, which was built by a company
of shareholders, and the various manufacturers occupy portions of the
building, paying rent to the proprietors for the use of the looms and
the power.

The whole of the factories which I visited were remarkably clean,
the floors of nearly all of them being cleansed once in every week.
There was an air of comfort and cleanliness about the whole of them,
that contrasted strangely with the wretched habitations of some of
the handloom weavers whom I subsequently visited. There are none
of the mills which work more than ten hours, and in none of them is
the relay system adopted.

Before proceeding to give an account of the condition of the
working-classes of Norwich, it will be as well perhaps if I endeavour
to give the reader some faint idea of what may be termed the sanitary
condition of the city itself. Norwich is built upon the river Wensum,
which, at a short distance from the city, forms a junction with the
Yare, by means of which a direct communication is afforded with
the sea, at Yarmouth. The site is composed of a light soil upon a
substratum of chalk, gravel, and sand, and being for the most part
built upon rising ground, the city possesses a considerable amount of
natural drainage. Its extent is about a mile and a half in length from
north to south, and about a mile and a quarter in breadth from east

to west. The city was formerly surrounded by walls, great portions of which still remain, though in a very ruinous condition. In some of the best localities a considerable portion of the ground is laid out in small gardens attached to the houses, but in the parts occupied by the working classes the houses are densely built. The streets in those parts are built without the slightest pretension to anything like regularity or plan, and it is next to impossible for a person not born in the place to find his way about without the assistance of a guide. Indeed, many of the inhabitants of the city are themselves perfectly bewildered in the endless labyrinths of streets and lanes which beset the adventurer on every hand. The great majority of the streets are so narrow that there is not room for vehicles to pass each other, and the greatest possible annoyance is constantly felt by persons who may be desirous of making anything like progress in these narrow and tortuous districts. Many of the streets, even in the better portions of the city, are wretchedly paved, and persons who, like myself, may have been employed for hours together in walking over what by courtesy is called the pavement, may probably be enabled to form some faint notion as to the penance endured by some of our ancestors. In addition to their being badly paved, the streets are also miserably lighted. In fact, the place appears to have been constructed with the view of affording as much inconvenience as possible to the unfortunate pedestrian, who, by duty or inclination, may be led to perambulate its thoroughfares.

As regards those portions of the city and the suburbs where the working classes chiefly reside, the poverty, wretchedness, and vice of the inhabitants, added to the decaying state of the houses, bear witness to the comparatively prostrate state of the manufactures of the town. The houses inhabited by the working classes are generally in the most dilapidated condition. Within the boundaries of the city you must search for the working classes in narrow lanes, courts, and yards, the entrance to which from the adjoining thoroughfares is through low and narrow openings or archways. Here will be found rows of wretched cottages, built in most cases back to back, ventilation being almost entirely excluded. Where the cottages face each other, in many cases they are not more than three feet apart. Down the centre of these places an open kennel or drain—perhaps not even that—carries off the refuse water, either into the adjoining streets, or into some receptacle, where it is allowed to soak away into the surrounding soil. Great numbers of the houses, both within and without the city, are situated in yards and alleys below the level of the adjoining streets. These places are appropriately named "holes," such as "Dyble's Hole," and others. Many of these "holes" are to be found in the lower parts of the city, abutting on the river, where the ground is constantly damp and moist; while heaps of filth and rubbish, open binns or privies, decaying vegetable and other matters, are constantly contaminating, by their offensive malaria, the unwholesome atmosphere in which the wretched inmates live. During the recent visit of the cholera the authorities aroused themselves to a sense of their dangerous position, and everything was done which wisdom could dictate. Many of the places which for years before had never known cleanliness received a coat of whitewash for the first time; gutters and drains were laid down along the surface, large quantities of lime were distributed in all parts of the city, the receptacles of filth were emptied and cleansed, and many of the chief nuisances were removed. These well-timed exertions were so far successful that not more than forty persons died of cholera; but of this number nearly the whole were inhabitants of the worst parts of the city, such as may be found in the neighbourhood of Lower Westwick-street, St. Swithin's; King-street, St. Julian's; and Cowgate-street, St. James's. I was informed that there are not more than 3,000 houses out of the whole number in the city that are supplied with water, the remainder having to obtain their supplies either from the river, into which all the filth of the city flows, or from cocks belonging to the water company, where the water is laid on for a few hours each day. Many of the houses are over-crowded to an enormous extent, and in several instances I have seen two or three families living together in houses barely sufficient for one family. There are no public baths or washhouses, nor any public parks or places set apart for recreation.

It is not easy to ascertain with anything like precision the number of persons employed as weavers in Norwich. In the year 1838 an inquiry was instituted by the Government into the condition of the hand-loom weavers of Norwich; and upon that occasion it was found that 5,075 was the total number, employed and unemployed. Since that period, however, considerable changes have taken place in the trade of the city, and the number of hand-loom weavers has considerably diminished. According to the census of 1841, there were in Norwich 2,344 weavers, 121 persons engaged in cotton manufactures, 106 persons returned as factory workers; shawl makers, 62; silk manufacture (all branches), 1,277; woollen and cloth manufacturers,

394; worsted and yarn, 253; gauze and stuff weavers and spinners, 83; making a total of about 4,650 persons employed in the silk and woollen manufactures of the city. The more recent introduction of the power-loom, since 1841, has, however, again affected the distribution of the various workers. The inquiries which I have been led to make upon the subject of the number of persons employed in connection with the manufactures of Norwich, have led me to the conclusion that the present number of hand-loom weavers is about 2,500; weavers employed in the power-looms, 750; making a total number of weavers of about 3,250. The numbers employed in the yarn, mohair, and worsted manufactures do not exceed 1,000 of both sexes and all ages; about 1,200 persons, chiefly children, are employed as winders; and the number of warpers, pickers, sewers, dyers, packers, hot-pressers, havel makers and drawers, slaie and shuttle makers, &c., may be set down at about 500—making together a total of 5,950 persons employed in the different branches of manufacture connected with the city. Deducting from this number the 1,200 winders, who are for the most part children, we shall have 4,750 persons, of whom it will not be too much to suppose that two-thirds, or 3,100, are married people with three children. There would then be a portion of the population of Norwich, amounting to 14,050 persons, who were either engaged in or dependent upon manufactures for their subsistence.

I was anxious to ascertain as correctly as possible the earnings of the weavers, both at their own homes and in the factories, and for this purpose I visited numbers of the hand-loom weavers at their own homes, and obtained from their own mouths statements of the amount of their earnings and their mode of life. In my next I shall give the reader the information which I have thus collected upon the subject.

LABOUR AND THE POOR.

———◆———

THE RURAL DISTRICTS.

[FROM OUR SPECIAL CORRESPONDENT.]

NORFOLK, SUFFOLK, AND ESSEX.

Letter XVII.

Having received from some of the Norwich manufacturers statements of the earnings of their workpeople, I resolved to visit one or
more of the weavers employed in each department of manufacture,
for the purpose of obtaining their statements on this point, and of informing myself generally as to their social and moral condition. I was
told that the employers would be certain to give me only the earnings
of the best workmen, and that the other side would be equally certain
to give me the lowest amount of their earnings. I found, however, in
a great many cases, that the information afforded me by the weavers
was perfectly correct, as I had subsequent opportunities of verifying
it by reference to the books of some of the manufacturers by whom
they were employed.

The condition of the hand-loom weavers of Norwich, like their
brethren of Spitalfields, has for many years been of the most distressing character. Low wages and uncertain employment have reduced
this class of operatives to the lowest possible state of wretchedness
and misery. During the last twenty years the rate of wages has been
gradually but constantly diminishing. In the year 1844 the distress of
the Norwich hand-loom weavers appeared to have reached its climax.
In the month of February of that year, an address was issued by the
Hand-loom Weavers' Union to the inhabitants of the city of Norwich
and its vicinity, in which the wages they then obtained for their work
were compared with the amount received in 1829. According to that
statement, a hand-loom weaver received for weaving a piece seventy
yards long, or eleven dozen nine skeins of yarn, 6s. 4½d.—being at
the rate of 6½d. per dozen. If the fabric were checked with two shut-
tles, 1d. per dozen more was paid. None but the most expert and able
workman could weave, upon an average, more than one piece in the

week, and after deducting the expense of winding, candles, and other things, the amount of his earnings for the week would not exceed 5s. 3d.—being about 9½d. for weaving sufficient material for a lady's fancy dress. Several conferences took place between the workpeople and the manufacturers on the subject of an increase in their wages, and a scale of prices was ultimately agreed upon in 1846, which has since been pretty generally adhered to. What those prices were the reader will be enabled to judge from the statements made to me by the manufacturers, which I have already given, and from those of the workpeople, which I shall now proceed to detail.

The first person that I visited was a weaver residing in White Lion-court, St. Paul's, who was employed in weaving barège—a fabric of a light gauzy nature, used for ladies' dresses. The court in which he resided was approached from the main street by a low and narrow archway. There were twelve houses in it, of two rooms each—there were no back premises to any of them; but in the front were small patches of ground of about eight or ten feet in length, by about the same in breadth. A row of eight houses occupied one side of the court; the other was occupied by a stable and slaughter-house. At the bottom, or lower end of the court, were four houses, of the same description as the others, in the corner one of which dwelt the weaver above referred to. Immediately facing the entrance to the house, and joining the little fence, was the privy, used by the whole of the inhabitants of the court; by the side of it was an open bin, into which all the refuse matter was thrown, and into the bottom of which the soil from the adjoining privy drained. Some rain had fallen on the night previous to my visit, and the contents of this open cesspool, oozing through the walls, were streaming sluggishly down the path to the house. A part of this filthy fluid was absorbed by the ground, but some parts of it not unfrequently found their way into the house, the floor of which, as if to invite its entrance, was nearly a foot lower than the ground outside. As usual, the loom was in the upper room, which was used as a work-room, bed-room, and in winter, to save a second fire, as a sitting-room. A diminutive little woman—all Norwich weavers are so—was busily engaged at the loom, and during the intervals of putting the fresh bobbins on the shuttle, I obtained the following information from her:—"I do the best kind of barège work. If I commence work at light, and keep on till eleven at night, without being called off to do anything else, I can weave eleven dozen in a week, and I should get 11s. 11d. for that—that is 13d. a dozen. I pay a girl, who does the winding, 2s. a week and her dinner; then 'beaming-on,' candles, and other expenses would be about 10d.—so that would leave me 9s. 1d. for my week's work. I am rather a privileged person, and if there is any work to be got, I usually have the preference, but I am often obliged to 'play.' Before I had the last two canes I 'played' a week, and I played a month right out at Whitsuntide: that was because I couldn't get any work. I suppose for the last twelve months I have played four at least. I am married, and have four children; they are all at school. My husband sometimes works at the other loom. When I do not have this girl to wind for me I can get it done for a penny a dozen."

A person unacquainted with the process of winding could scarcely form an idea of the quantity of manual labour thus performed for a penny. The "dozen" referred to is a dozen skeins, each containing 560 yards, or 6,720 in the dozen; and this quantity has to be transferred from the hank or skeins to small bobbins for the shuttle, by means of a small wheel, turned by the hand of the winder. A great loss of time constantly takes place in consequence of the threads of silk breaking, and of the constant change of the bobbins required when full. At the winding it is physically impossible to earn more than from 2s. to 3s. per week. Of course the great proportion of this kind of work is done by young children or old persons; but that is not always the case. The person employed as winder in the above instance was a young woman of eighteen years of age, and she received 2s. a week and her dinner; but in addition to winding she was expected to assist in the household duties, in taking care of the children, and other matters, while the woman was at work.

The next person I visited was a fancy barège weaver, residing in Light Horseman-yard, Pockthorpe. This place, like the former, was approached by a narrow covered passage, leading out of Pockthorpe into a square court with eight houses—some of two and others of three rooms. The waste water and filth from these houses were conveyed along the surface by means of drain tiles, which had recently been laid down; but previously there had been no drains whatever, the whole of the refuse water either finding its way along the passage which it had worn for itself, or soaking into the ground. The place was disgustingly filthy, and the greatest care was required in stepping to avoid the filth, which abounded in the place. There, as in White Lion-court, the privy was common to the whole of the inhabitants, and in order to avoid repetition of a disgusting fact, I will state at once that in no one of the numerous courts and alleys which I visited was there to be found a house possessing an exclusive right to a convenience of this kind. The house in which the fancy barège maker resided consisted of three rooms, one above another. It was an old and ruined place; the stairs (which lay open to the court) were fast decaying; and the flooring of the rooms creaked as you walked over them. The lowest room of the three was occupied by the eldest daughter of the weaver, 24 years of age, who was married. The second room was used as a day room for the family and a bed room at night for the husband and wife and two youngest children, one of whom was six months old. The upper room was occupied by the loom, and was used as a sleeping room by the remainder of the family, eight in number. The part nearest to the window was occupied by the loom; at the opposite side of the room were two stump bedsteads side by side, and almost touching each other. Across the frames of these a few cords were stretched, and a coarse kind of sack filled with straw lay upon each. Upon neither of the beds was there any blanket. "There is but one in the house," said the poor man, "and that we have down stairs." One of the beds had an old coverlid, the other a dirty sheet and coverlid. In one corner of the room lay, rolled up, what was called, "the third bed"—a bag of straw without any bedclothes whatever. "My eldest son is nineteen," said the weaver, in answer to my questions. "My eldest daughter, eighteen years old, and the six other children sleep together in this room. My wife and me sleep down stairs with two of the children; there is an old feather bed there, but it's a very old one—it was given me when I was married, twenty-five years ago. I have never been able to buy any since I have been married. Since last Christmas I have earned—take one week with another—p'rhaps 8s. I can earn, some weeks, if the children do the winding, p'rhaps 14s. a week. I have nothing in pawn; indeed, I've got nothing that they'll take in. I have not drunk a drop of beer since the 28th of last February. I am a teetotaller. Lor, sir, the work is so irregular; all this week I sharn't earn sixpence. They keep me dragging up to the warehouse day after day, and they always say, 'There's no shoot to-day, come to-morrow;' and so it goes on. It would take us 7s. or 8s. a week for bread, if we could have all we could eat; but it's never less than 6s., and when we can't pay for it we're obliged to go on tick for it at the 'fogging shops;' that's where they sell heads and plucks, and all them sort of things. I don't think we have to pay any more for bread in consequence of credit; some other things we do, I dare say; and I often think the flour is very short weight. I have to pay 1s. 9d. a week for rent." The whole appearance of this family and of their house and furniture was of the most wretched and deplorable character. The eldest boy was out of work—the daughter worked at the factory, and gave a portion of what she earned to her parents for her wretched food and lodging.

The next case was that of a paramatta weaver, who resided in Dible's-hole, a place situated close to the city walls, in the parish of St. Paul. The access to this Dible's-hole was by means of a narrow passage, flanked on one side by the ruins of the old city wall and upon the other by some wretched-looking houses. Upon descending four or five steps on the left hand, I found four cottages, with a small piece of ground in the front of each, of a few feet in extent, with here and there a sickly looking dahlia, or a consumptive looking chrysanthemum, struggling against premature decay. Proceeding as directed, I entered one of these cottages. I found there a sallow looking individual, 36 years of age, with a family of five children. Having informed him of the object of my visit, he gave the following account of himself and his earnings:—"I have only two rooms in this piggery—a place not fit to live in. My eldest child is eleven years old, my youngest was born yesterday. My wife is confined upstairs, in the room where the loom is. Three of my children, myself, my wife, and the young *babby* sleep together; the other two children sleep in a small crib by the side of us. I have been obliged to keep the loom at work although my wife is lying there. The noise of the loom has made her very poorly. I pay 17s. 6d. a quarter rent for the place. I am a paramatta weaver, and as the house I live in belongs to my master, I am pretty well employed, more so than the generality of the weavers. I generally work from six in the morning till ten at night in the summer, and in the winter from half-past six till nine o'clock, and when at work I can earn 10s. a week; but then the candles cost me 7½d., and when my wife is not able to do it, I have to pay, for winding the bobbins, 1¼d. a dozen. My average work is about eighteen or twenty dozen in a week. I generally lose two or three days in getting the work, and as much in putting it on the loom. I have been married twelve years, and have had eight children. My wife has got but this one gown. [An old ragged washed-out gown was here produced by an old woman, who attended to act as nurse during the confinement.] She has none but that one to put on, when she gets up. Three of my children go to school, and I pay 6d. a week for them. I am determined to bring up my children as well as I can—I would rather stint myself of food, to give them a little education. It is a mystery to me how ever we get through it. I have been in this wretched way for years, till I am quite sick of it. I went a day or two since to Mr. ——, and his wife gave me some soup on account of my wife being so poorly, and I took a bit of the meat out of it, and, so help me God, that is the first bit of meat I have tasted for months. My children never see a bit of meat, except what they may see at the butchers' shops, as they go to school. Mrs. —— was kind enough to lend me a bag of linen for my wife, or I don't know what ever we should have done. There are a many of the weavers worse off than myself, because when there is any work to be got I always get the preference. I have always been suffering ever since I was married, and I am never without some trouble; some of my children are always ill, and when some are born others of them are dying. I have only five out of the eight we have had. I have got nothing at the pawn shop, and before I would go to the pawn shop I would lay down and be trampled on. What little I have got I mean to keep as long as I can. For the last five or six years I have not been out of my house except to go to work. I cannot go to church if I would, for I've got no clothes fit to go in. After paying for the candles, the winding of the bobbins, and the 'beaming-on,' I don't think I make more than 8s. a week. Very often when I go out of doors the fresh air seems to be too much for me, and I often stagger and roll about as if I was drunk." The account of this man's earnings was fully corroborated by a reference to the pay-book of the person by whom he was employed. The furniture and everything about the house was more cleanly and comfortable than might have been expected under the circumstances in which the family were placed.

The next person upon whom I called was a widow employed in weaving gauze—a material which, when dyed, is used as crape for mourning. The house in which she resided was in St. Martin's-lane, in a situation far preferable to many of the others which I had previously visited, and it contained two rooms. In the window of the lower room were a few onions, a few reels of cotton, sweetmeats for children, and other small wares of a similar character. The upper room was occupied by the loom and by the two beds in which herself and family, consisting of three children, slept. The room was miserably close and sickly, and everything bore the appearance of the greatest want and misery. The following is the account which she gave of her condition and employment:—"This is a piece of double super gauze. I get 4s. 6d. for weaving it; when finished it will be about 32½ yards long. It will take me a week and a half to finish it; sometimes I am a fortnight over a piece—I was a fortnight over each of my last two pieces. I have to play a good deal. I played a week when I got this last 'cane.' My children do the winding, or else I should have to pay for that out of what I get. When I first commenced weaving crape, I could earn 14s. a piece. It was a better material then than it is now, and you could do the work a good deal quicker. They have been gradually reducing the pay for it every year, till it is now only 4s. 6d. a piece, if double; the 'singles' are only paid 4s. a piece. The warp and shoot are both silk. I have been a widow eight months; my husband was a pipe-maker, and I was very comfortable when he was alive. He lay ill best part of a twelvemonth before he died, and I was greatly put to, to get on at all. I have five children, three at home; two are married. My eldest son is a pipe-maker at Greenwich; when my husband died, he started off, and took all the things away that he could. I have had one letter from him since he has been away, but he has never sent me any money, although he is in good work, I believe. I get 3s. a week from the parish—that is, a shilling for each child. I have tried to sell a few things in the shop below, but I can't get on; the people over the way have got all the connection. I bought half a gross of lucifers for a shilling, and I have only sold two of the boxes all this month, and I only got a halfpenny for them. I haven't sold a shilling's worth for more than a week. My constitution is very much broken, and when I do sit up and 'watch' (work by candle-light), I can't earn enough to pay for the candles, and I often think I shall have to give it up and go into the house. I pay 1s. 7d. a week for rent."

Of all the branches of weaving there appears to be none so wretchedly paid as that of the gauze and crape weavers. Three-halfpence per yard is the miserable amount paid to the weaver for this kind of work—its selling price being from 3s. to 4s. per yard. During the last four months, owing to the large number of deaths from cholera, the trade in this department has been more than usually brisk.

Several of the manufacturers are in the habit of employing persons at Wymondham in the manufacture of gauze and other articles, as they can get the work done even cheaper there than in Norwich. A few years since a large portion of the population of Wymondham were weavers. The failure of a large firm, however, in 1845, was the means of throwing vast masses of them out of employment. Many of them are in the most distressed condition, and are glad to take work at any price. The weavers of Norwich complain sadly of the disastrous effects of this competition for work, which they say the manufacturers are not slow to take advantage of when they wish to make any reductions in their wages.

A case of this kind came under my own knowledge. A weaver of Wymondham was employed to make a quantity of gauze, for which he was to receive 9s. The work had taken him a fortnight to complete, and in order to finish it within that period he had worked from fourteen to sixteen hours per day. It cost him a shilling for a return railway ticket from Wymondham, and he lost a day's time in bringing home the work; he paid 1s. 3d. for winding the bobbins, and used a pound and a half of "short eights" candles while at work. His account would, therefore, stand as follows:—

	s.	d.
Railway fare to take home the work ...	1	0
Winding the bobbins	1	3
1½ lb. of candles	0	7½
	2	10½

Deducting this from the 9s. paid for his work, the net earnings of the poor man for the fortnight would amount to the sum of 6s. 1½d.! I am not aware what was the amount of rent which he paid for his cottage.

Leaving the gauze weaving, I proceeded to inquire into the rate of wages paid for bandannas and silk handkerchiefs. A person who kept a beer-shop in Colnsey-street, used chiefly by the weavers, was employed in this branch of manufacture. Among others, the following answers were given to my inquiries:—"I was last employed in weaving silk handkerchiefs; they were made with cotton warp and silk shoot, and were 33 inches square. I had two dozen of them to make, and by working 14 hours in the day I was able to do 18 of them in a week. I finished the two dozen in ten days, and was paid 16s. for them. Out of that I had to pay 2s. for winding, for 'beaming-on' 4d., and the candles were about 7½d. I paid 1s. 3d. for twisting-in; if I had done the twisting-in myself I should not have been able to have got the job done as soon as I did. All that made 4s. 2½d., which left 11s. 9½d. for myself for my ten days' work. I had to play a long time before I could get that work, and I have just got a little job that will take me a week. It is a fortnight since I took my last work home." Nothing, perhaps, would show more strikingly the depressed state of the weavers of Norwich, as compared with former times, than the statements made by this weaver with respect to the amount of the business in connection with the beer-shop. The large room in which the weavers used to assemble to hold their convivial meetings was occupied by the loom. No meeting had been held in it for the last twelvemonths. The sale of spirits would not pay the license, and it had not been renewed for several years. The present consumption of the house is about half a barrel of beer per week, and that only of one sort. The house was formerly the chief place of resort for the weavers, and its former proprietor had managed to save a considerable sum out of it. "They have no money to spend now," said the landlord; "they can't get enough for bread hardly. They used to draw two or three barrels of porter a week, but the last I had all turned sour long before it could be drawed off."

I was informed that the work which was best paid in connection with the weaving trade was that called the "havel work," which consists in preparing the havel for the weaver. I accordingly visited several of the persons so employed, to ascertain what was the amount of their earnings. One of these workpeople was a woman living two or three doors from widow Smith, the gauze weaver, whose case I have already referred to. Her house was remarkable for the neatness and cleanliness of its interior. She had two children, and her husband worked as a carpenter. "He is a steady man," the wife said, "although he is my second husband, and he is in pretty constant employment. I get for drawing havels for nets, or barèges, 1s. 6d. per 1,800. I can do two of them in a day with my little boy helping me. That of course is 3s. a day—when you get it. I pay a girl sixpence a day out of that, to give me the 'ends.' But, Lor' bless you, sir, we play more than half of our time. Since Christmas I haven't played so much as I did before, because we are always busier after than before Christmas. When I have got no work I am obliged to keep my end-drawer, and pay her just the same as though I was in work. If I wasn't to keep her I shouldn't p'r'aps know where to find her when I wanted her. Take all the year round I suppose I can earn 7s. or 8s. a week, but then you must take the 3s. off that for the girl, and that only leaves 5s. for myself. When the work comes in I am obliged to work a good many hours—a long time after my husband and children have gone to bed. Ah! then there's extra candles and fire—you must reckon them. I can't tell you how much to set down for them, because I don't keep any account." It appears, therefore, that the net earnings of a person employed on the best kind of work are about 5s. a week all the year round, subject to a charge for extra fire and candles. As this statement was so much at variance with all that I had previously heard on the subject, I resolved to call upon some other person employed on the same work, in order to see whether it would be confirmed. I was accordingly directed to the residence of a person similarly employed. Her statement was as follows:—"I am 21 years old; my father and mother keep a little shop. When about 13 years old, I used to work at Messrs. ——'s factory, where I used to earn sometimes 3s., sometimes 4s. a week, according to the work. I used to live with my father and mother, and give them 2s. 6d. a week for my food and lodging. I was sometimes out of work, but not very often. My father and mother, brothers and sisters, all slept together; there was but one sleeping-room. I was sent away from the factory because a young man kept me out all night. Mr. —— heard of it, and he discharged me, because he makes it a rule not to employ any persons of bad character in his factory. I was seventeen when this happened. I couldn't get any work. I had no money to give my father and mother. I was obliged to have clothes, and I took to learning the havel work. While I was learning, I used to 'go out;' what else could I do? There's many a one obliged to do the same. Why, what's a poor girl to do when she's out of work, and got no money? I have been off and on the street for the last four years. When there's no work, I am obliged to do it. I live at home now with my father and mother. They must know that I go out. How can they think I get clothes, and money for them, if I didn't get it in that way? Don't I earn a good deal at the havel work? Yes, when I am in work I can earn 10s. or 12s. a week, but then there's half my time I'm doing nothing except the streets. Take all the year round I am sure I don't earn more than 5s. a week. I wouldn't go in the streets if I wasn't compelled to do it, and then we are obliged to dress nice if we 'go out,' and all I can earn at the havel work goes for clothes."

I next directed my inquiries to the shawl weavers, and found one of this class of persons residing in Bull-close, a place formerly set apart for bull-fights: it was a comparatively open space, and much better ventilated than the majority of the residences of the weavers. This person was employed in weaving fancy shawls. With respect to his earnings, he said, "In the course of last year—and I have just been making the calculation from my books—my earnings appear to have been about £30; my expenses were, I reckon, about £5 10s.—the extra rent which I have to pay for an additional room for the loom would be about £1 6s.—the cost of candles would be about 12s. during the whole year, as I have to burn three or four when I *watch;* that would leave my clear earnings about £22. I may say that I stand a much better chance than hundreds of weavers in the town, because when any new design comes out they don't want anybody to see it, and as I am well known to them, I have an opportunity of earning something when the others have not. Very often when I finish a shawl it may not be liked, or some alteration will have to be made in the pattern; and if it is not approved of, I have to take down all my *harness*. When I am what you may call 'going along,' I can earn clear, perhaps, 3s. in the day, but then I don't do that but very seldom. There is no end to the time that is lost in putting the things in harness and altering them. The manufacturer perhaps tells you to shoot it with some other colour, and that takes time to alter the loom. Then there is a great deal of time lost in taking the work home, or in getting other work or orders back. The masters appoint a certain time in the day to receive the work, and unless you can get it in by that time, the rest of the day will be lost. Sometimes it takes two or three weeks to put the loom in order, and you are not allowed anything for the loss of time. Sometimes, if you beg and pray of the master, when the pattern doesn't turn out well, they'll give you a couple of shillings perhaps, but that's only as a kind of charity; they won't allow that we ought to get anything for putting the loom in harness."

There is another kind of shawl, called the "fill-over" shawl, for the manufacture of which Norwich is highly famed. I was directed to a person employed upon this kind of work, residing in Silver-road, Pockthorpe, and who was considered one of the most able hands at the "fill-over" weaving, and was specially selected to make one of these shawls as a present to Jenny Lind, at the time of her late visit to Norwich. This person stated that it took him five weeks to prepare what is called the "tow" for the weaving of Jenny Lind's shawl. "The pattern," he said, "took well, and I was employed for three-quarters of a year in making other shawls of the same pattern. I could make about one of them in a week, and I was paid 24s. 10d. each for making them. Out of that, I had to pay the 'winder' 2s. 6d.; for 'shoppage,' or hire of loom, 2s. 6d.; a 'tire-drawer,' a boy to pull the tires while weaving, 7s.; for 'picking,' 6d.; and at night I had to have three candles going at a time, which would cost about 1s.; the whole expenses would, therefore, be 13s. 6d., which would leave me clear 11s. 4d. for my week's work. Miss Lind was very kind to me, and so she was to every one who made anything for her; she sent Miss —— round to all that she could find, and gave 'em all anything that they wanted. When she came to me I said I didn't want anything; I thought it would be imposing like upon her, but Miss —— said 'You must have something;' then my daughter said, 'Father, I think you want a good greatcoat;' so Miss —— sent a tailor to measure me for one, and she paid for it, and I hadn't had one for a many years before that. Miss Lind did a world of good for the poor weavers when she was here, and they all adore her for it." I visited several other "fill-over" weavers, and found that the amount of their earnings was about the same as that already stated. One of them stated that he was out of work five months out of the year—another had "played" three months out of the last four—and a third said that he was out of work half of his time. There appears to be every prospect of a large amount of employment in this branch of weaving for the next four months, as I was informed that the Norwich manufacturers "were determined to put an end to the reign of silk and velvet mantles, polkas, and visites, which had for several years been so injurious to the shawl trade."

Where there is such an enormous amount of unemployed labour, it will very naturally be expected that the poor-rates are proportionately high. The rate for Michaelmas, 1848, was 1s. 7d. in the pound; for the corresponding quarter of this year it is only 1s. 2d., the amount ordered for the quarter being £7,200; of this sum about ten per cent. would remain uncollected. Last year there were as many as 13,000 persons at one time on the relief lists of Norwich, being nearly one-fourth of the entire population of the city. When the weaver is out of employment, his only resource is the workhouse; but here he is met with the greatest difficulty. The authorities of Norwich have calculated that a weaver can exist fourteen days without work before he will require relief—or, in other words, that the price which he gets for his work when taken home will be sufficient to maintain himself and family for the following fourteen days—strangely forgetting that the work for which he may be paid has taken him perhaps a week or a fortnight to make. By far the most rational and correct conclusion to come to would be, that the amount which he receives for his work would be required to defray the expenses of maintenance incurred while the work was in hand, rather than that it should be available for future support. The board of guardians of Norwich do not, however, view the matter in this light. When the weaver applies for relief to the board, he is furnished with a certificate, of which the following is a copy, which he has to get filled up and signed by the party who last employed him:—

"TO THE RELIEF COMMITTEE OF THE CORPORATION OF
GUARDIANS.

"Norwich, ... 184......

"The bearer .... has not
worked for me since the .... day of .... when he received .... shillings and .... pence.

"This certificate is not to be used as a begging petition."

If upon the production of the certificate it is shown that the applicant has practically solved the mystery of a weaver's existence for
fourteen days without work, he is handed over to the superintendent
of the weaving rooms in connection with the workhouse, and forthwith, after existing fourteen days without work, he is set to weaving;
and if he has a wife and one child, he may earn at weaving 6d. in the
day, for which he will be paid at night, when his work is completed.
According to the number of his children will be the proportion which
he will be allowed to earn; if he weaves more than the given quantity,
he is not paid for it, and if he earns less he gets nothing. The workhouse at Norwich is totally inadequate for its purpose. It will only
accommodate 355 persons, and the guardians consequently contrive
to make the labour test, in connection with the fourteen days' non-
employment, a substitute for the workhouse test.

It is only very lately that the guardians would sanction the system
of giving employment to the weavers at all. The consequence was,
to use the words of my informant, "the place was literally eaten up
with paupers, who were constantly receiving out-door relief." But the
means of giving employment to the weavers, even upon the present
system, are miserably deficient. The great majority of them are receiving out-door relief, for there is no room for them in the workhouse,
and when once they get upon the lists they have no inducement whatever to obtain work, as it is always precarious and uncertain; and if
they should succeed in obtaining any, if only for a week, or some
other short time, they know that they will not be able to obtain relief
until they have again been fourteen days without work. One of the
guardians, speaking to me upon the subject, said, "that although it
was a saving to the rate-payers, still the benefit would be derived by
the poor themselves, from the extension of the system upon an improved principle; and the giving of increased accommodation in the
workhouse would be infinitely better, as it would have the effect of
diminishing the enormous amount of idleness and vice which was inseparable from the existing state of things in Norwich." Owing to the

smallness of the workhouse, it is impossible to carry out anything like an efficient system of classification among the paupers. The young, able-bodied, and the old men are found together in the same ward; and women of abandoned character are placed in the same ward as the virtuous and better class of females. In fact, the Norwich workhouse presents a vast number of those repulsive features which were so common to establishments of this kind previously to the passing of the New Poor-law. By one very numerous class of females it is invariably used as a lying-in hospital. Upon the occasion of my visit to the house, as the females were passing in to their dinner, the master pointed out several of them to me, who had been in three, four, five, and one even six times, for the purpose of being confined there. The influence which the association of such persons exercises upon the better class of females is almost incredible. Numerous attempts, I was informed, had been made to obtain increased workhouse accommodation, and the subject had been repeatedly brought under the notice of the guardians; but hitherto all these efforts have been unsuccessful, as it is invariably treated as a party or political question. I send a copy of the dietary table, from which it will be seen that at all events insufficient diet is not one of the grounds of complaint:—

	Breakfast.				Dinner.							Supper.				
	Bread.	Cheese.	Treacle.	Tea.	Meat.	Yeast Dumpling.	Potatoes.	Suet Pudding.	Bread.	Cheese.	Pea Soup or Milk Broth.	Bread.	Cheese.	Butter.	Tea.	Meat Broth.
	oz.	oz.	oz.	pint.	oz.	oz.	oz.	oz.	oz.	oz.	pints.	oz.	oz.	oz.	pint.	pints.
Sunday.																
Men	6	1	-	½	-	-	-	16	-	-	-	6	-	½	½	-
Women	6	1	-	½	-	-	-	14	-	-	-	6	-	½	½	-
Boys from 9 to 16 years of age	6	-	¾	½	-	-	-	14	-	-	-	6	¾	-	½	-
Girls from 9 to 16 years of age	6	-	¾	½	-	-	-	12	-	-	-	6	¾	-	½	-
Monday.																
Men	6	1	-	½	-	-	-	-	6	1	-	6	-	½	½	-
Women	6	1	-	½	-	-	-	-	6	1	-	6	-	½	½	-
Boys from 9 to 16 years of age	6	-	¾	½	-	-	-	-	6	¾	-	6	¾	-	½	-
Girls from 9 to 16 years of age	6	-	¾	½	-	-	-	-	6	¾	-	6	¾	-	½	-
Tuesday.																
Men	6	1	-	½	4	5½	12	-	-	-	-	6	-	-	-	2
Women	6	1	-	½	4	5½	12	-	-	-	-	6	-	-	-	2
Boys from 9 to 16 years of age	6	-	¾	½	3	5½	8	-	-	-	-	6	-	-	-	2
Girls from 9 to 16 years of age	6	-	¾	½	3	5½	8	-	-	-	-	6	-	-	-	2
Wednesday.																
Men	6	1	-	½	-	-	-	-	6	-	2	6	-	½	½	-
Women	6	1	-	½	-	-	-	-	6	-	2	6	-	½	½	-
Boys from 9 to 16 years of age	6	-	¾	½	-	-	-	-	6	-	2	6	¾	-	½	-
Girls from 9 to 16 years of age	6	-	¾	½	-	-	-	-	6	-	2	6	¾	-	½	-
Thursday.																
Men	6	1	-	½	4	5½	12	-	-	-	-	6	-	-	-	2
Women	6	1	-	½	4	5½	12	-	-	-	-	6	-	-	-	2
Boys from 9 to 16 years of age	6	-	¾	½	3	5½	8	-	-	-	-	6	-	-	-	2
Girls from 9 to 16 years of age	6	-	¾	½	3	5½	8	-	-	-	-	6	-	-	-	2
Friday.																
Men	6	1	-	½	-	11	-	-	-	-	-	6	-	½	½	-
Women	6	1	-	½	-	11	-	-	-	-	-	6	-	½	½	-
Boys from 9 to 16 years of age	6	-	¾	½	-	11	-	-	-	-	-	6	¾	-	½	-
Girls from 9 to 16 years of age	6	-	¾	½	-	11	-	-	-	-	-	6	¾	-	½	-
Saturday.																
Men	6	1	-	½	-	-	-	-	6	1	-	6	-	½	½	-
Women	6	1	-	½	-	-	-	-	6	1	-	6	-	½	½	-
Boys from 9 to 16 years of age	6	-	¾	½	-	-	-	-	6	¾	-	6	¾	-	½	-
Girls from 9 to 16 years of age	6	-	¾	½	-	-	-	-	6	¾	-	6	¾	-	½	-

It is pleasing, among the many unpleasant things connected with Norwich, to witness at least one institution which has already produced an incalculable amount of good—and that is the "Boys' Home." The object of this institution is to afford a home for the workhouse boys, entirely removed from the contaminating influences of such an establishment. A house has been taken and fitted up at a short distance from the workhouse, where the boys are fed and lodged, and to which they return at night from their various occupations in the city. Each boy gives a portion of his earnings for his food and lodging, and even with the small amount of support it has already obtained, the receipts from the boys are sufficient to cover nearly the whole of the expenses. The institution owes its origin to Mr. Bailey, the workhouse schoolmaster; and the account which he gave me of its rise and progress was as follows:—

"I was appointed schoolmaster in November, 1842. I found the children at that time in very great ignorance, there having been no schoolmaster previously. After I had been engaged about six months I asked the chairman of the school committee whether he would permit me to take the children out for a walk. He referred me to the school committee, who were rather fearful that I should lose some of them. I promised I would keep a vigilant eye upon them, and by promising to repeat their 'frolic' (as some of them called it) if they behaved properly and orderly in school—and, to the best of my recollection, I never forfeited my promise—I gained their confidence in a great measure, and began to think there was some hope of reforming them, and ultimately of their becoming good members of society. In order to test this, I selected a boy of about sixteen years of age, into whom I thought I had instilled a little morality. I asked him whether he would prefer being employed out of doors, or still continue an inmate of the house? I saw a smile and a doubt upon his countenance as he replied, 'I'm fearful you are laughing at me, sir.' I said, 'Henry (for that was his name), do you ever remember my doing such a thing as that?' He said, 'No, sir.' I took no further notice at the time to him about it, but called upon the chairman of the school committee, and submitted to him my plan, which was this: I proposed to find the boy lodgings with some respectable poor person, if the committee would allow me 1s. 6d. a week, to assist him to pay for linen and lodging. This, through the influence of the chairman, they granted. The result of the experiment has been, that the boy has never been an inmate of the workhouse since. I found, upon making my intentions known among my friends, that I could find more places for my boys than I could provide lodgings for. Upon my again applying to the same gentleman he immediately took the necessary steps to provide a home for them. The following are the results: Fifty boys have been admitted, of whom two only have returned for bad conduct. Some of these, I have ascertained, are earning from 10s. to 12s. a week, others are living as indoor servants, and, I am happy to say, retain their places with good characters. Some few have left Norwich."

I might add that the boys whom I saw were all looking remarkably well; their sleeping apartments were well ventilated, clean, and comfortable, and their diet was both good and substantial.

Many of the low lodging-houses of Norwich are of the most disgraceful character. I visited several of them—some during the day, others at night. One, which I visited during the day, was a public-house. The house itself was in the most wretched state of dilapidation; one of the windows and frame were entirely gone from the staircase, and as you ascended the rickety and crazy stairs some care was necessary to avoid falling through the large space which was thus left open in the walls. In one of the rooms, used as the sleeping room, were six beds, and a "shake-down" or two on the floor. The window of this room was broken in several places, and old pieces of paper, rags, and other materials were used to stop up the holes. The adjoining room to this was occupied by the landlady, who, I was informed, was gone to London for a few days, on particular business. Two other beds, besides that of the landlady, were in this room, and in one corner, on the floor, I observed what seemed to be another bed. Above these rooms was an extensive loft, extending the whole length of the building, the access to which was by means of an old ladder. Upon inquiring, I was told that no person ever slept there, for the end of it had fallen away, and the roof was in such a state as to leave it entirely exposed to the weather. As I could not exactly reconcile the fact of the ladder being there with the statement that it was never used, I ascended into the loft to see for myself. So far as the condition of the place was concerned, it was worse even than the description which I had heard had led me to suppose. Upon going to the further end of the wretched place, towards what I at first thought a heap of rags, I was surprised to see some movement among them, and upon approaching somewhat nearer, I found to my astonishment an old woman lying there. Upon announcing my discovery to the daughter of the landlady, she feigned to express considerable surprise, and after a short pause, she

recollected that "there was an old woman went up there the day before yesterday, but she thought she was gone." In the bed-room with
the six beds a young tailor was sitting at work, making a pair of boy's
trowsers, for which he was to get 3d. He had been in the habit of
sleeping in the room, off and on, for the last three or four years, and
he appeared perfectly astonished when I asked him whether there was
any separate apartment for the women. His reply was, "Lor, no; we
all sleeps together here; last night there were fifteen of us in all—three
married men with their wives, and the rest of 'em were single chaps
and any girls they liked to bring with 'em; for the landlady wasn't at
all partikler in that respect, though she tried to get another 3d. out
of 'em when such was the case. Sometimes, when there's a married
woman at all nice in that way sleeping here, she hangs some of her
clothes on a line across the bed-post; but we don't have much of that
here." The daughter of the landlady informed me that when one room
was full, her mother let out the beds in her room, and very often a part
of her own bed, and "was noways partikler who it was to, so long as
they paid." The back part of the premises was in the most filthy state.
There was no privy to the place: a large hole dug in the ground formed
the receptacle for the refuse and filth of the house; while nearly the
whole surface of the yard was covered with night-soil.

The other house of this description which I visited was also a
public-house. I visited it on Sunday evening, as I was informed that
there would be more "company" there then than on any other night.
Upon arriving there, I was shown into the sitting room of the tramps
and travellers. It was a small room, about ten feet square, in which was
a very large fire, and, seated in two rows upon each side of the room,
were 25 persons, male and female. The heat, smoke, and close smell
of the room were almost overpowering; and a gentleman who accompanied me was obliged to leave almost immediately. Upon inquiring
of them, I found there were among them persons from the following
places:—Liverpool, 2; Hereford, 2; Newcastle, 3; Derby, 2; Norwich,
1; London, 4; Manchester, 2; Salford, 1; a Dutch girl from Holland,
who sold brooms; 2 from Essex, 2 from Ireland, 1 from Scotland, and
1 from Cornwall. The total amount of money which they had was
1s. 7¼d. Of the number present twelve had none; one had a farthing;
three, a halfpenny; four, a penny; one, five farthings; two, three half-
pence; one, twopence; and one, twopence three farthings. Four out of
the company could read and write; five could read, but not write; the
remainder could neither read nor write. I then inquired how often any

of them had been in prison for any offences? "I was in once for a week for begging," said a young urchin of ten years old. "I was lagged for poaching, and got two months for it," said another. A boy of sixteen years old said, "I had six weeks of it on the wheel once, and another time I had a month without it." "I had seven years over the water," said a somewhat elderly man from Liverpool, "but I didn't leave old England, and arter three years I got my discharge." "I can't tell you how often I've been in," said a desperate-looking character who sat in the corner; "they've had me so often I begin to think they won't have me any more. Last time I was in London I got a month for a 'winder' job, for I am a deuced sight better off in *quod* than out of it." "You're quite right," said a thin and sickly-looking man who was sitting next to him; "a *pal* tramped along with me from Ipswich yesterday, and he said, says he 'Jim, what's the best thing to get a month for?' I recommended the *winders*, and he said he'd do it; and as he's not come here to-night I s'pose he's better off." "I have been," said another person, who from his peculiar deformity was called my lord, "in almost every gaol in England, and I could tell you some queer things about some of 'em." "Well, I've not been in anywheres yet," answered another, a broken down respectable-looking person, "but I don't know how soon I shall be there, if I don't get something to do soon; I can't go on for ever like this." "Nor I haven't either," said a young, stout, and determined-looking character, "but if I can't get something to-morrow, blow me if I don't do something to get in." "They had me up once for singing in the streets, and gave me seven days for it," was the answer of another, who, in answer to my question, said that he was a ballad-singer. "I sings 'em and sells 'em, but the cursed blues won't let a fellur get a honest living now-a-days. As soon as you jist tip a stave, up they comes bouncing, and says, 'You musn't make that noise there,' or calls the singing some other disrespectable name. Lor', in my earlier times, I've made lots of money. You knowed Greenacre, I s'pose?" "Well, what do you think I made out of his dyin' speech?" "Why, twelve bob. I came down from London with a lot of Mannings, but somehow they didn't go so well as I expected. I don't think the people have got so much money as they used to have." "I've never been either in a prison or a workhouse yet; and, please God, I never will," said a journeyman carpenter. "I've seen better times, and I hope and trust I shall see 'em again." None of the other persons had been in prison, but four of them had occasionally received parish relief.

I found upon further inquiry that ten of the persons present had not paid their lodging for the night, and had not the means of doing so—twelve of them had had nothing to eat since breakfast—one had had a piece of bread given her by a fellow tramp—five had had some bread and cheese for their dinner—one some bacon and bread—and two (a husband and wife) a herring and some potatoes. One of the women, who was married, was nursing a weak and starved-looking child, of about ten weeks old. The little creature, as it lay upon the mother's lap, frequently gasped and started convulsively; its breathing was short, and a distressing and gurgling noise appeared to come from its throat, as if on the point of death. During the time I remained in the room, I suffered considerably from the oppressive and heated atmosphere, and had several times to request the door to be left open. The sufferings of the child must have been intense, seeing that it had been in the confined room during the whole of the day. I asked the mother if the child was ill; she said it was very ill, and with apparent unconcern, "she didn't think it would live long, it wasn't a healthy child from its birth." I asked her how many children she had, her answer was "five as counts." Upon desiring to know why the others were not entitled to some consideration in the reckoning, she said "the first never counts for nothing—my husband acted on the old saying about here, 'No child, no wife,' and I had one afore I was married." There were three sleeping rooms in the house, containing together seventeen beds, most of them placed side by side so closely that there was not room to pass between them. They were much cleaner than those I had seen previously, but here, as at the other place, "they were no ways partikler" about the separation of the sexes—not the slightest attempt being made for that purpose.

The Morning Chronicle, Saturday, December 15, 1849.

The Correspondent of *The Morning Chronicle* who is roaming through the kingdom in order to spy out the nakedness of the land in the rural districts is now prosecuting his inquiries in Essex. Last week he was in Chelmsford, and inspected many of the houses, and inquired into the state of the poor in this neighbourhood: after which he left for Tendring hundred, to prosecute an investigation into the burial clubs, which the criminal annals of the country have rendered so notorious.—*Chelmsford Chronicle.*

LABOUR AND THE POOR.

—◆—

THE RURAL DISTRICTS.

[FROM OUR SPECIAL CORRESPONDENT.]

NORFOLK, SUFFOLK, AND ESSEX.
THE HERRING FISHERIES AND FISHERMEN OF YARMOUTH.

Letter XVIII.

Before proceeding to describe the state of agriculture and the condition of the agricultural labourer in Norfolk, I propose, in the present letter, to give some account of the fisheries and fishermen of Yarmouth. Although there are several places besides Yarmouth where fishing-boats are fitted out, both in Norfolk and Suffolk, still, as most of them find their way to that town with the produce of their fishing, it will be unnecessary to enter into any details respecting them. The same remark will also apply to the port of Lowestoft—the boats which belong to that port being all registered as belonging to Yarmouth.

The borough of Yarmouth itself stands upon a narrow neck of land at the extreme southern end of the county of Norfolk. On one side of the town is the sea, and upon the other the river Yare, which at this part forms the boundary between the counties of Norfolk and Suffolk. The quay is perhaps one of the finest in England, being upwards of a mile in length and of proportionate width, and colliers and other vessels are able to discharge their cargoes immediately upon it. Great quantities of agricultural produce are constantly brought down to Yarmouth from Norfolk and Suffolk for the purpose of being exported, coastwise, to various parts of the country. Not less than 100,000 quarters of corn were exported from the town during last year, and upwards of 200,000 tons of coals were brought into the port for the consumption of the neighbouring counties. Great quantities of the produce which was formerly sent by way of Yarmouth is now, however, carried by the railways, and the trade of the place has consequently fallen off during the last few years. The gross receipts for Customs duties at the port of Yarmouth were, in 1846, £52,457; and in 1847, £59,784. The amount received by the corporation for pier dues during the year ending the 3d of January, 1845, was £10,188, being upon an average of 6d. per ton on 269,289 tons of coals—2d. per ton on the register tonnage of 224,880 tons—and 1d. per quarter on 304,118 quarters of corn. The number of arrivals and sailings was 2,837.

Quay Side, Yarmouth

There are few towns in England which are more densely populated than Yarmouth in proportion to its extent. In the Eastern counties there is no town which approaches anything near to the same proportion. Ipswich, one of the chief towns of Suffolk, has an area of 7,020 acres, to a population of 25,384—being about 3.6 persons to an acre. Bury St. Edmund's, also in Suffolk, has 3,040 acres, to a population of 12,538—or 4.1 to the acre. Colchester and its liberties has 11,770 acres, with a population of 17,790—being no more than 1.5 to the acre. Harwich, a port of Essex, stands upon 2,060 acres, its population being 3,829, or about 1.3 to the acre. Norwich contains 5,920 acres, and a population of 62,344—being 10.5 to the acre. Yarmouth, however, contains 1,270 acres, and its population amounts to 27,750—being at the rate of not less than 21.7 persons to the acre, or more than double that of Norwich, six times that of Ipswich, five times that of Bury

St. Edmund's, and nearly fifteen times that of Colchester and Harwich. The extraordinary density of the population of Yarmouth may be accounted for by the peculiar style of building which is adopted. Along the whole line of the quay, and running at right angles to it, are a vast number of narrow streets, or "rows," as they are called—few, if any, of them exceeding six feet in width. These "rows" are numbered consecutively from 1 to 136; there is no foot path up any of them—they are paved with small round stones, and drained down the centre. Many of them are so narrow that an ordinary-sized vehicle would be unable to pass through them; hence the curious little carts or barrows which abound in the town, of about three feet in width, with the wheels placed under the body, in order to take up as little room as possible. The poor-rates are generally exceedingly heavy. In 1848 there were only twelve unions, in the whole of England and Wales, which were rated higher than Yarmouth, the rates being then 4s. 10½d. in the pound for the year. Since that period the rates have even increased to 1s. 7d. in the pound for the quarter—being at the rate of 6s. 4d. in the year. The last rate, which was made at Michaelmas, was only 1s. 2d. in the pound for the quarter. The annual value of the property rated to the poor is £34,315, and the number of paupers relieved during the year ending Lady-day, 1848, was 9,795.

The enormous extent and importance of the herring and cod fisheries of the east and north-east coast of Great Britain may be judged of by the following facts. The number of boats, decked and undecked, which are employed in the fisheries is 14,126. The fishermen and boys who man the boats amount to 59,859; coopers, employed in the manufacture of barrels for the salt and dried fish, 2,334; persons engaged in packing, repacking, cleaning and drying the fish, 28,254; labourers otherwise employed in carting the fish, bringing it ashore, and other matters, 7,074; fish curers, 1,572. 1,636 men, with a tonnage of 22,758 tons, are annually employed in carrying salt for the fisheries direct from Liverpool or other ports, and 2,325 men, with a tonnage of 31,926 tons, obtain employment in exporting the fish, when cured, to foreign ports. The number of men, therefore, employed in connection with the fisheries is—

Fishermen and boys	59,859
Coopers	2,334
Packers and cleaners	28,254
Labourers	7,074
Fish curers	1,572
Employed in carrying salt	1,636
Employed in the export trade ..	2,325
Total persons employed ...	103,054

The tonnage of the vessels employed is—

Boats employed in the fisheries .	90,273
Carrying salt	22,758
Exporting the fish	31,926
Total tonnage	144,957

The total value of the boats, nets, and lines, employed in these fisheries, is £908,586. The number of square yards of netting used in the herring fisheries is 68,014,243, and the number of yards of long and hand lines, and buoy ropes, is 23,151,729. The quantity of herrings cured during the nine months ending January, 1846, was 526,032 barrels, 140,632 barrels branded, 266,373 exported, and 117,606 assorted after the Dutch mode. The number of barrels which were taken, and promptly disposed of for immediate consumption, during the same period, was 295,664. In the cod and ling department, the total quantity taken was 491,650 hundred weights. Taking the value of the barrel of herrings at 20s., and the cod and ling at 10s. per hundred weight, it will be found that the value of the produce of the fisheries of the eastern and north-eastern coast of Great Britain is not less than £1,592,132.

The exact proportion contributed by Yarmouth towards this enormous amount I am not able to state. The returns which are published by the Board of Fisheries do not give the number or tonnage of the boats in connection with Yarmouth—that port being included with Dover, Portsmouth, and Gravesend, in the London station. Having been given to understand that a register of the fishing-boats belonging to the town was kept for public inspection at the Custom-house, I applied to one of the officials of that establishment for information as to their number and tonnage. I was, however, told that the required information would take some time to obtain, and he could not undertake to furnish me with it for less than a sovereign. I then inquired

A "Row," Yarmouth

if I could inspect the register myself for a few minutes, but was informed that "that document was locked up." Nothing but the golden key would unlock this treasure. Not feeling disposed to submit to an imposition of so gross a nature, I determined to endeavour to obtain the information, as near as possible, from some of the boat-owners themselves; and from them I learned that there were from 80 to 100 herring-boats then out, and that this number included those which were connected with Lowestoft, and that the average number of the men and boys employed in each boat was ten. The quantity of fish cured and sold at Yarmouth is considerably more than that brought in by these boats, as great numbers of both north and west country boats bring their fish there for sale.

The tonnage of the boats employed in fishing varies from 36 to 55 tons, and they are generally called "luggers." Most of them carry three long masts, two and sometimes three topmasts. A boat of 54 tons would cost about £550. The suit of sails would cost £78, and the nets £280. The warps and bowls for the nets would be £100, and 60 small barrels used to buoy the nets in the water, at 4s. each, would cost £12—in addition to which there would be seven warps of 120 fathoms in length, to which the nets are made fast. The greater part of the net is purchased at Bridport; but before it is used it has to undergo the process of tanning with bark. It will take about a hundred weight of "lint"—the material of which the nets are made—to make four nets. The women employed in mending the nets are called "beatsters," and each boat will afford employment in this kind of work to two women during the entire year. A great number of children and women are also constantly employed as "braiders," and in forming the meshes of the nets.

The herring fishery is by far the most important and extensive in connection with Yarmouth, and the fame of its "bloaters" is almost world-wide. The herring season usually commences about Michaelmas, and continues for about 12 or 14 weeks, the boats being almost all "made up" by the 8th or 10th of December. Great complaints are made by the owners of boats—the great majority of whom are also curers of fish—of the badness of the late season; not so much on account of the numbers of fish caught, as of the ruinously low prices at which they have been sold. Various reasons were given me as the cause of this depreciation. One of the principal causes was the prevalence of the cholera and "the ignorance of the doctors" in prohibiting fish. "It was ridiculous," said a large owner and curer to me, while he was expatiating on the healthful and beneficial qualities of the "bloater," "to suppose that erruns hurt people; it is quite the contrary, they does 'em good. I know several people who won't eat nothing but erruns when they're poorly, and they always gets well again." Whether the faculty were really correct or not in including fish in their prohibitory diet-table, will, I suppose, for some time, remain an open question between the respective parties; the effect, however, has been most injurious to Yarmouth. "I'll give any one £500, and be glad to do it," said my friend, the advocate of the healing virtues of the herring, "who'll pay me what I'm out of pocket this season."

Another cause of complaint among the Yarmouth owners is the formidable rivalry which they have to sustain against the west-country boats, which bring their fish into the port, and, by increasing the supply, tend to reduce the prices. During the last season more than a hundred of these boats entered Yarmouth for the purpose of disposing of their fish. In consequence of the different system which is adopted in the west-country boats, as compared with those of this town, the fish are generally sold at considerably lower prices than would suit the convenience or profit of the Yarmouth people. The men in the west-country boats engaged in the herring fishery have generally a share in the boat, and they usually divide among them whatever they get. Having only the expenses of the boat to defray, they can afford, and are always anxious, to part with their fish at any price. Their nets are generally mended and repaired by themselves; they have consequently none of the expenses for labour which the Yarmouth fisherman has to bear. The boats and nets too, being their own property, are generally taken greater care of by the crews than by those of the Yarmouth boats, who are engaged upon a totally different system, which I shall presently state.

The complaints of the Yarmouth people do not, however, stop here. In addition to the decreased consumption caused by the cholera, and the increased supply of their western rivals, they have to lament an almost total cessation of demand on the part of great numbers of French boats which used formerly to visit the town in order to purchase fish. A few years since twenty or thirty French boats used constantly to come into the port and purchase great quantities of herrings, which they were in the habit of taking back to France as the produce of their own fishing. They would perhaps catch a few herrings themselves, buy the rest at Yarmouth, and take them home and receive the bounty money from the French Government on the quantity which they were supposed to have caught. A French cutter is now constantly stationed in the harbour to prevent this species of smuggling from being carried on. The effect of this has been, I was informed, to reduce by £5 or £6 the price of the "last" of herrings.

I have already stated the cost of a boat, with its nets and lines, as required for the fishing trade. I shall now enter somewhat more in detail into the current expenses of the boat, and the quantity and value of the fish taken. The crew of a fishing boat consists of from ten to twelve persons, varying according to the size of the boat. They are of various grades—a master, a mate, one oarsman, one whaleman, one net ropeman, one net-stower, one yunker, and four capstan men, and sometimes a boy. The payment of the men is regulated by the quantity of fish which they catch. The master gets 16s. per last—a last consists of 13,200 herrings; the mate 10s., the oarsman and whaleman 9s., the net ropeman and net stower 6s. 6d., the yunker 4s. 6d., the capstan men from 4s. to 4s. 6d. each, and the boy about 3s., making a total of 82s. 6d. per last paid for wages to the crew. Some of the herrings were sold this season for £3 10s. and £4 5s. per last.

This, however, does not include the cost of their provisions. The boat's stores generally consist of 3 cwt. of bread, 10 nine-gallon casks of table-beer, half a firkin of butter, ½ cwt. of Dutch cheese, 1 cwt. of beef, 10 lbs. of coffee, and 4 stone of sugar. The consumption of beer among a crew of ten men and a boy is usually a nine-gallon cask per day. Each boat is also provided with 10 or 12 tons of salt for the herrings, in case the boat should not be able to make Yarmouth while the fish remain sweet. In addition to the wages and provisions for the crew, there is the wear and tear of the nets. "It costs me a hundred pounds a season for mending the nets of my boats," said the individual to whom I have before alluded; "there's Mr. Dogfish, he bites 'em to pieces, and soon wears 'em up. Then there's the string for mending. 'What does that cost?' Why, it would puzzle a Philadelphia lawyer to tell that. There's 45 or 46 cwt. of net, besides all the running in twine; and then there's the tanning of it before it can be used."

In addition to the expense of taking the fish, the owner has to pay a number of additional expenses before he can have them landed. Owing to the want of sufficient depth of water the fishing boats are unable to come nearer than about half a mile from the beach. The fish are consequently obliged to be brought to shore in ferry boats, rowed by a somewhat important body of men, called the beachmen (to whom I shall have occasion presently more particularly to allude), in baskets called "swills," each holding about 500 herrings. The charge made for conveying them to the beach is 10s. per last. They have then to be taken up the beach to the shore in small carts at a charge of 5s. per last, and 1s. extra for the trace horse to assist in drawing them up the loose sand. The owner of the boat has, therefore, to pay £4 2s. 6d. per last as wages to the boat's crew, and 16s. per last for the landing the fish—making together £4 18s. 6d. per last, in addition to the cost of provisions for the men, which is about £2 per last, and the wear and tear of the nets and boats. The whole of the expenses may be taken together at about £7 per last, and when the herrings are sold for less than this price, of course the greater the quantity the men take, the greater will be the loss to the owners. It must not, however, be supposed that it is the invariable rule at Yarmouth for the fishermen to sell their herrings for a less sum than they pay to catch them. The love of gain of the people, which is almost proverbial, forbids any such rash or unfounded conclusion. A passing cloud may have darkened for awhile their brightest expectations; but there are already some glimpses of returning prosperity. I had the curiosity to inquire the price of some herrings which were for sale, and was informed that it was £10 5s. per last; they were not, however, of first quality, being all "shotten." The curers have a great quantity of dried herrings on hand, which they expect to be able to dispose of at improved prices, and as many of them have been bought at very low rates, they may probably, upon making up the accounts, find that the improved value for the dried will counterbalance the depreciated prices of the fresh herrings.

Comparatively few of the persons actually employed in fishing are natives of the town. "The reason is," said a Yarmouth man to me, "it don't pay us to go out for such low prices; we can't do it for the money." By far the greater part of them are farm labourers, from various parts of the counties of Suffolk and Norfolk, principally from those portions of the county adjoining the sea coast. Immediately after the harvest they start off in search of employment to Yarmouth, and various other small ports on the coast of Norfolk; a great many of them are "Norwichers." They usually enter into an agreement with the owners to stay during the herring season. On making the agreement the men are required to state where they came from, the name and address of the person who last employed them, and the name of the last boat, if any, in which they may have sailed. These precautions are adopted, as I was informed, in order "That if any of the men are lost, or washed overboard, we may know where they came from, and can send their friends word as to where they're gone to." When mishaps of this kind take place, the children or widow of the lost man receive the full share of the earnings which would have been paid to the husband or father had he been alive.

Each one of the boat's company has his peculiar duties assigned to him. The master, of course, has the entire command. The duty of the mate is to assist the master. The oarsman attends to the oars, the whaleman to the nets. The net ropeman looks after the rope to which the nets are attached. The net stower attends to the stowing of the nets. The yunker is generally employed in skudding the nets, and occasionally goes to the capstan. The duties of four capstan men are indicated by the name they bear, and the duty of the boy is to curl the warps, and make himself otherwise generally useful; one important branch of his duties consisting in serving the beer to the men.

The mode in which the herring fishing is carried on by the crew is in this manner:—Each herring net is composed of a number of meshes, or holes, of about an inch square, and is 24 yards long, and 200 meshes deep. From the mode in which the herring swims in the water, it is obvious that they would not be able to enter the meshes if they were not more than an inch in depth. The mode adopted to overcome this difficulty is that of reducing the width of the meshes by reducing the width of the net; and, consequently, increasing their depth till they hang in the form of a diamond of about one-and-a-half inch in length by half an inch in breadth. This is effected by "setting the nets," which are 24 yards each in length, upon 16 yards of rope. The net—or "lint," as it is called—is then made fast to the warp by what are called the "season ropes." About eighty or ninety of these nets are attached together for the herring fishery, making together a quantity of nets of 700 fathoms, or four-fifths of a mile in length. The quantity of net run out in the mackerel fishery exceeds 2,000 fathoms, or very nearly two and a half miles. The herrings, when caught in the meshes, seldom live more than a few minutes; if caught round the gills they die almost immediately.

The quantity of fish caught will vary, of course, considerably, according to circumstances. One person informed me that a boat in which he was employed a few years since had brought in ten lasts of herrings in four hours; and in another case that he knew, 18 lasts were brought in during the same period. "But there's not been such a catch as that this year," said he. "Sometimes we're out for a whole fortnight, and don't get so many as we can eat; and sometimes we're obliged to beg a few of our neighbours for our own eating. Last year I fished the October month out, and only took 2,800 herrings. One of the best seasons I ever had in my life was about six years sin', when we catched 43 last, and got home to Yorkshire on the 28th of October. If it's a good season, no boat ought to make less than £450 or £500." When on board, the fishermen seldom or never take off their clothes when they go to sleep; they are all ready, "booted and drawered," to jump up on deck directly, to haul in the nets if they have a sufficient take. At the latter end of the season the men, I was told, are not so good as at the beginning; they get lazy, careless, and tired, and the "take" of the boats is generally very small in consequence.

The amount paid to the men, as before stated, depends entirely upon the quantity of fish taken, without reference to the prices at which it may be sold. The masters have come to a determination to make an alteration in the system for the future, and to pay the men only for the fish they take, in proportion to the price at which it is sold. To any attempt of this kind the fishermen are most decidedly and unanimously opposed. For several seasons the plan has been attempted to be carried out, but hitherto the masters have always failed. At the commencement of the present season a similar attempt was made to induce the men to go out upon those terms, but they one and all refused. The difference between the parties at one time threatened to assume a rather formidable character; the owners, however, gave way "for this time," with a mental reservation that next season there should be some alteration. The earnings of the men during the present season have been generally somewhat above the average. The quantity of herrings taken has ranged from twenty-five to forty lasts for each boat: the earnings of the men would therefore range from £6 to £9 for the lowest class or capstan men—from £8 to £13 for the "stowers and ropemen"—and from £11 to £18 for the "oarsmen and whalemen;" the mates receive from £12 to £20, and the masters from £20 to £32 for the three months. There may be some who have earned a less—some probably a larger—amount than that stated above. I have met with several labourers who have returned from the fishing, and in no case have I found that their earnings were under £5 for the season (about three months) independently of their provisions. The north-country boats which come into Yarmouth do not, generally speaking, make so much as the Yarmouth boats, as they almost invariably make for port on the Saturday, where they remain over the Sunday—few of them being willing to carry on their operations on that day.

At the conclusion of the herring season, the mackerel fishing commences. The usual period for commencing is about Christmas, and it generally lasts till April. Many of the Yarmouth boats go as far as Plymouth to look after the mackerel. When they take them they are usually sold at the nearest port, whence they are conveyed by railway or other conveyance to the London markets. In the case of the mackerel fisheries, the men are all paid by the share. The fish are usually sold at public auction; a portion of the produce of the sale is reserved for the nets, another portion for the boat, and, after deducting the cost of the victuals and other expenses, the remainder is divided among the men, in proportions agreed upon.

The sole and turbot fishing is carried on almost the whole of the year. The men employed in this department are paid by the week. The master gets 12s. a week, and a shilling in the pound on what the fish realize; the men get from 14s. to 16s. per week; and the boys from 2s. 6d. to 5s. The vessels employed in this kind of fishing are generally cutter-rigged craft. They visit Holland, the Humber, and the Silver Pit, for soles; and many of them carry large quantities of ice on board, in which the fish taken are kept if they are not able to make land soon.

The Yarmouth fishermen are generally considered to be very hard and close in their dealings. I have heard it frequently stated that "the Yarmouth people count the scales on their herrings," and that "if one of the men loses a scale off, he gets the sack from his master." The saying, "dog eat dog," is invariably applied to the dealings of a Yorkshireman and Yarmouth man with each other. "The Yorkshireman," they say, "bites hard, but the Yarmouth man bites harder." The fact of their close-fistedness in money matters may, perhaps, have something to do with the character which they generally bear for "pluck." "They are the pluckiest set of fellows," said one of them to me, "that's known anywheres; they're like terriers. Fight! Aye, they'll fight a millpost. They're the terror of the publicans; in Norwich they'd as soon see as many devils come in as Yarmouth folks." I was also informed that at St. Ives, when the people heard that a Yarmouth boat was in the harbour, they instantly closed the public-houses, apprehensive lest they should be favoured with a visit. "Wherever they go," said one of the publicans of Yarmouth to me, "they make everybody else in the house uncomfortable, and won't spend any money neither."

From the men engaged in fishing I shall now proceed to another branch of employment in connection with the herring trade of the town—that is, the curing of the herrings. There are two things of which the Yarmouth man is proud, perhaps justly so—his boats and his bloaters. "There are no ships in the world," said one of them to me, "that can come up at all to the Yarmouth build; they stand higher at Lloyd's than any others, they'll stow more, sail quicker, and stand the longest." In praise of his "bloaters" the Yarmouth man will often wax eloquent and even poetical. "The errun, sir," said my friend who was so strong an advocate for the restorative qualities of herrings, "is a cold water fish. The Yarmouth fish is a better sort of fish than's caught anywhere else; all depends upon the quality of 'em, and what they lay upon; and the season, too, is half the thing. Why, sir, the October erruns, caught on the Brown Bank—they are as different as different from any other speshus of fish. We like the short, thick, shiny, bright, pulky erruns. Them erruns you get in Midsummer time ain't got no roes; there's no doing nothing with 'em; you can only cure 'em as inferior sorts of bloaters. The errun is always better when the water's cold. Why, do all you can, you can't make a Yorkshire errun a Yarmouth one: they haven't got the taste nor yet the flavour of 'em. You know them there great Scotch erruns that's caught in the summer time. Well, they go out to the Mediterranean before us. Well, our erruns go after 'em, and soon knocks 'em out of the markets there. They supersedes the Scotch wheresomever they goes. Now, take a barrel of these Scotch erruns—I don't care how treated—and put a bloater by the side of 'em. Why, lor' there's as much difference between 'em as— what? Aye, as between a primrose and muck. Only put your nose to 'em you can smell 'em at once; they've a nasty rank smell; and then when you open 'em the bone is as coarse as coarse; but open one of our little pulky ones, and you'll find it as fine as silk. You won't see one Scotch errun out of a hundred but'll always be as black as a coal at the back bone; but the little bloater is as red as a cherry and as sweet as a rose." Such are a few of the transcendant qualities of this excellent fish, the Yarmouth herring, as stated by one of the corpulent and enthusiastic curers of Yarmouth. The reader will no doubt feel some anxiety, after so glowing a description, to hear something of the process of curing, and the mode by which the men of Yarmouth are enabled so successfully to distance their competitors in the herring trade.

We will accordingly accompany our friend to his large curing establishment, and, premising that the fish are all landed, and stowed in the sheds, we will hear in his own words the mode adopted in the curing of herrings. The first part of the building which we will visit will be a large room, the floor of which is sloping at each end, and paved with bricks. In the centre of the room, and at the foot of the slope, a drain is formed for carrying off any refuse matter that may flow into it. Upon these sloping floors the herrings are laid, preparatory to undergoing the first process. Our friend will now describe the process of salting:—

"You know, sir, there are two kinds of erruns that we make; one is the bloater, the other is the dried uns. The dried uns we send to the Mediterranean, to Venice, Leghorn, Tuscany, and other places, where there's many Catholics. The erruns we use for this are the ones that comes in late, when the boat is out a long time, and they are obliged to salt 'em aboard. When they come in here we lay 'em upon these here sloping floors and bury 'em in salt, and you'd be surprised if you were to see how they sweats. Lor' bless you, we can't do nothing with 'em till we've sweated all the blood out of 'em. Sometimes it takes ten days or a fortnight to get it all out. When they've sweated enough I keep nine old women and five men—we call 'em 'rivers'—who hang 'em on the 'spits,' about 20 on a spit. They open the gills with their fingers, and push the spit through 'em; then they're hung up to dry in the drying-houses." The spit is merely a stick of about a foot in length. The drying-houses are large spacious buildings of about 20 feet in height. In most cases the floor is three or four feet below the surface of the ground outside. The reason of their being sunk was in order to gain as much room as possible, the corporation of Yarmouth having forbidden the erection of drying-rooms above the height of twenty feet, as they would prevent the view of the sea from most of the houses. Some of these drying-houses have from seven to fourteen compartments, which are called "rooms." The house which I visited was a ten-roomed house. The rooms are formed by beams or "balks" laid across the house, at distances of about four feet from each other, and about eight feet from the ground. Resting upon these "balks," and reaching to the top of the building, are a number of racks about a foot apart, upon which the ends of the spits with the herrings upon them are supported. Each room will contain about fifteen tiers of herrings, one above the other. As the spits are placed very close to each other, each room will contain about a last, or 13,200 herrings. Upon the floor and beneath the herrings large oak logs are kept constantly burning, the air is excluded as much as possible, and the herrings are gradually smoked and dried. The dried herrings for exportation are generally smoked for ten days or a fortnight. When sufficiently dried they are taken down, packed in barrels, and in this state are exported.

But hitherto we have only witnessed the process of curing the dried herrings for exportation. The pride of the Yarmouth man—the bloater—is seldom or never exported; they are entirely for home consumption. "The bloaters take a very small time in preparing. They come in, for instance," said my friend, "in the morning; they're hung up over the fire a night; they're lightly salted for home at once; and in four or five hours they are packed and sent away; some of them hang all night, but less than that is enough for 'em." A number of men were engaged in packing the herrings in hampers for the London markets. Opening one of the hampers, "Them bloaters that they're packing," said the master, "some of 'em was in the water 24 hours ago; they are now off for London." He then took one of the herrings out of the basket to show me. "Look at it," said he; "it's as mellow as a pear; its eyes is as bright as a diamond; its gills is as fresh as fresh: why it's almost alive. We don't make 'em very salt, as they're not intended to keep long. The most time that they'll keep good is about ten days or a fortnight, but I never like 'em after three or four days; they lose their flavour after that, and gets crumbly, and falls to pieces when briled." Some of the herrings, when taken, are broken and damaged by the nets and the rough usage which they get in landing. Before the herrings are sent away to market, they have to be sorted. The broken ones are thrown aside as "plucks," and when sent to market in barrels they are marked with the letter P, and sold accordingly.

There are from two to three hundred persons, male and female, employed in curing the herrings. The women earn from 5s. to 7s. per week, the men from 12s. to 15s., according to the nature of their employment. About 100 coopers are also pretty constantly employed in making barrels for the exportation of the fish when dried and cured.

Having given some account of the fisheries, the fishermen, and the curers, I must not omit to notice one very important body of men in connection with Yarmouth, known as the "beachmen." The life of the beachman is one of constant excitement, toil, and danger. I have already stated that, owing to the want of sufficient depth of water, the fishing boats are not able to come near enough to the beach to land their fish. One of the duties of the beachmen is to bring the fish ashore in what are called "ferry boats;" and another very important part of their duty consists in affording assistance, in case of distress, to the numerous vessels which are constantly getting aground on the Cross Sands and at Scroby.

The beachmen are formed into companies of about twenty each, one of whom is called the captain, and they divide equally among them the proceeds of whatever they make. For bringing the herrings ashore the charge is 10s. per last; an account is kept of the quantity they bring ashore, and at the end of the season they are paid by their employers. They do not get paid as the work is done, but have to wait till the close of the season—and in some cases, like most people who are in the habit of giving credit, they have to divide a back debt. "I think," said one of these beachmen, "that there will be some trouble in getting our money this year from all of 'em, the fish has sold at such low prices, and some of the masters won't be able to pay us." In a good season the company will divide from £200 to £300 among them.

The herring season is considered by them to be their harvest. "The mackerel work is poor work," said one of them, "you may consider yourself well off if you can get 5s. or 6s. a week." Their charge for bringing the mackerel ashore is a shilling per hundred, and they are paid for their work at the end of each week.

When the herring and mackerel seasons are over, the beachmen are comparatively idle, their chief business then being to look after wrecks, and sometimes they earn an extra shilling in taking people out on the water for pleasure. One of the men with whom I entered into conversation stated that "after the season is over we have nothing to do but pleasuring; sometimes they make special constables of us at the time of the races. When we ain't employed at that, we go hovelling and knocking about to see what we can do. There ain't been many wrecks about lately. We have always one of our company on the look-out, and he gives the signal when there is anything. We've been out all today swiping after an anchor dropped by one of the fishing-boats, but we couldn't find it. It won't give us much when we get it. The Cross Sands, where there are the most wrecks, is about seven miles from here. Scroby is about two-and-a-half. There's thousands of folk as never tells the tale of that place; they don't want much to go to pieces when they once gets on there. When we go to a wreck, if the vessel is stranded, we get one-fifth for ourselves, and the owner gets four-fifths. When there's a wreck, the people of course always gives us the most valuable things first, as they are naturally anxious to save them. The preventives keep a very sharp look out after us, and so do the insurance people. You can hardly get a bit of rope even of the length of your finger here. Sometimes when we get a cask of liquor we broach it. We don't think there's any harm in that. The money that we get at the end of the herring season is all eat up before we get it. We are obliged to go in debt for what we want, for they won't let us draw anything on account; and then there's a great deal of 'sleight' (wear) upon the men's clothes. Here's a pair of shoes I've got on; I've only had 'em six weeks, and now they want soleing and heeling. Well, then there's the boot stockings (large worsted stockings, which reach above the knee); they cost 2s. 6d. a pair. They chafe a great deal with the sand and wet, and soon wears out. Then the trowsers, they're fustian, and cost about six or seven shillings a pair. The blue flannel slops, they costs about 7s. a piece, but they're very warm; and then there's the Guernsey frocks that goes over the slop, they're 7s. and 8s. each; and then there's the oily trowsers and oily frock that goes over 'em all to keep the wet out, they're 10s. or 11s. each; the sou'-wester would be about a crown. When we are bringing the fish ashore, the serf runs so high and so strong that it often washes the fish out of the boats, and we are almost always wet head over ears; we have sometimes three and four fresh suits on in a day; if we haven't got but one suit, of course we are obliged to keep on the wet one. I pay £5 a year rent for my house, and that's about the price paid by all the beachmen, though the rent is mostly paid by the week. We are obliged to live as near as we can to the shore, as we don't know when we may be wanted. I used to live in a house close by the shore, but they have pulled them all down lately, and they won't build any more small houses unless they touch the rates (are rateable). Some of us are obliged to keep watch about the beach all night, for if there was to be anything start up for us to do we couldn't collect all our men so quick as we ought, and unless we were all to be here when the boat pushed off, we shouldn't get any share of what the boat got. Unless we can touch the boat we don't have any share. Sometimes, when the men are not able to get in the boat, they'll run after it up to their waists in the water to touch it, and if they can do that they get their share. I once got £50 for just touching the boat in that way. If one of the company is hurt in the boat, he gets his full share, just the same; and if he is sick, or unable to work, he has a share allowed to him which lasts as long as he is sick, and when they 'turn up,' we 'shoots' a little among ourselves to bury him, or if there's a widow, we give it to her. If the man belonged to a club, we 'shoot' just the same, and raise enough, and over, to bury him. I have belonged to a club for 31 years, and have never had but two months' money from it. I pay 1s. 10d. a month—that is, 1s. 6d. for the box, and 4d. for beer. If any man is catched groggy at the club, or caught swearing, he is fined a shilling. There's another club for beachmen and seamen, where they pay 2s. 6d. a month, and if you are cast away or lose your clothes, fresh clothes are given, and you are sent home free of all expense. These are called the 'half-crown' clubs; the members of the club have a small medal, which is tied round their necks by a piece of ribbon; it is sewed up in a piece of cloth, and is always worn under the shirt, next to the skin. So if a man gets cast away in Cornwall, or anywhere, he has only got to show his medal to the club there, and they will send him home, and give him what he wants. Then there's the Muster-roll Club; every man who goes aboard a ship is obliged to pay to that a shilling a month—it is stopped out of his pay. It is in connection with the Merchant Seamen's Fund." "Ah, I subscribed to that club for a long time," said an old weather-beaten looking man, who belonged to the same company of beachmen; "and what do you think I got when I was cast away on Greenland, and was there for six weeks? Why, I got half-a-crown."

From all that I have seen of the beachmen of Yarmouth, they appear to be comparatively well off. They are all strong and hearty-looking men, inured to danger, and appear capable of undergoing almost any amount of hardship. There is no weather so rough or stormy that it will prevent the beachman pushing off to the assistance of a vessel in distress. That their impelling motive is gain there can be no doubt, and to obtain their end they will encounter dangers from which many of the most hardy and experienced mariners would shrink. It not unfrequently happens that after rowing in the roughest weather for several miles to a wreck, cheered with the bright vision of the large amount of salvage they will have to divide, they find to their great disappointment, that it is but a collier or corn-laden vessel, with little or none of the more valuable cargo which best repays the adventurous beachmen, as they are paid only according to the value, not the quantity, of their salvage.

As far as the beachmen are concerned, there is no doubt but that they manage, with one thing or another, to do pretty well all the year round. Those who are actually employed in the fishing boats return to their homes at the end of the season, with the amount of their earn-ings; but many of them soon contrive to run through them. When their funds are exhausted, they apply to the farmers for work, and if not able to obtain it, they become burdens upon the different parishes till the farm-work revives. After harvest they again betake themselves, like other amphibious creatures, to the sea, and again go through the same routine of fishing, farming, and pauperism.

========

LABOUR AND THE POOR.

—◆—

THE RURAL DISTRICTS.

[FROM OUR SPECIAL CORRESPONDENT.]

NORFOLK, SUFFOLK, AND ESSEX.

Letter XIX.

With the single exception of Lincolnshire, there is perhaps no county in England which has made such rapid strides in agriculture as Norfolk. The farmers are almost proverbial for the readiness with which they undertake improvements, and for their great desire to arrive at perfection in the machinery by which the cultivation of their land is carried on; and in nothing perhaps is this feeling more strongly exemplified than in the fineness of the "tilth," or surface of the soil, owing to the great number of ploughings bestowed upon the land, and to the complete pulverization of the clods by the various formidable-looking machines used for that purpose.

It is but a comparatively short time since the county of Norfolk might have been styled, with the utmost propriety, a county of warrens and sheep-walks. The farmers of those times, destitute of that ardent desire for improving their farms which now characterizes them, were content to follow in the track laid down by their ancestors; and so long as they were able to obtain, by a small amount of exertion, some eight or ten coombs of wheat or barley from the land which they might have under tillage, they appear to have been perfectly satisfied. To the untiring exertions and liberal policy of the late Earl of Leicester is mainly to be ascribed the present high position which Norfolk holds among the agricultural counties of England. Large quantities of fens have been reclaimed, and barren heaths have been cultivated; and where they formerly existed, the most luxuriant crops of wheat and barley are now obtained. In many of these districts as much as fourteen and sixteen coombs of wheat to the acre have been produced, and from sixteen to twenty of oats—a coomb being equal to four bushels.

Taking the average of the county, it has been calculated that the produce per acre is from six to eight coombs of wheat, and from ten to twelve of barley. With respect to the character of the soil of Norfolk, it is exceedingly varied. It has been said of it, that "All England may be carved out of Norfolk, for here are fens and heaths, light and deep, sandy and clay grounds, meadow lands and pastures, arable and wood lands." In the east and north-east parts of the county there is a great quantity of vegetable and alluvial soil, with rich loam interspersed with portions of sandy and gravelly soil. In the neighbourhood of Norwich the soil is gravelly; near Acle, clay abounds; and adjoining it a fine vegetable soil of great depth is to be met with. From thence to Yarmouth there is an extensive district of marshy land. Towards the north, also, there is an extensive tract of marshes, which, in winter, are almost always under water, and produce only a coarse kind of feed, or "rowen." In consequence of these marshes being the property of a great number of small proprietors no really efficient system of drainage has yet been attempted. In the neighbourhood of Holkham, the seat of the Earl of Leicester, the soil is, for the most part, a light kind of loam and gravel, upon a substratum of chalk and marl; between Wells and Holkham the soil is particularly fine. About Castleacre and Newton the soil is generally of a light gravelly nature, but there is a great deal of very good and productive land. Near Downham and Marshland there are immense quantities of fen and marshy land. In the neighbourhood of Downham, I was informed, some land had been sold, within the last five years, at £45 the acre, which, a few years since, was not worth more than £7 an acre. In that part of the county lying between Brandon and Thetford a great proportion of the land is merely sheep-walk, and some portions of it are let at as low a rate as 3s. 6d. per acre. About Taverham and Drayton the soil is light and sandy, and almost entirely upon a subsoil of chalk. It is computed that there are, of light sand, 140,800 acres; of good, 268,000 acres; of marshland clay, 38,400 acres; of various loams, 576,000 acres; of rich loam, 94,720 acres; and of peat, 52,480 acres, within the county. Of these various kinds of soil there are 50,000 acres of unimproved common heath, 60,000 acres of sheep-walk and warren, and 15,000 of wood and plantation. Assuming these numbers to be accurate, there would be not less than 1,045,760 acres under cultivation within the county of Norfolk; and of this quantity it will not be too much to assume that one-fifth, or 209,152 acres, are pasture, and the remaining four-fifths, amounting to 836,618, arable land. It is somewhat difficult to form an estimate of the value of the agricultural produce of this county. In some parts the crops are wonderfully large. I was told, at Fakenham, by a farmer, that he had never known the crops so fine and so heavy as they were this year in the Holkham district. Great quantities of the land had produced from 14 to 16 coombs to the acre. "The crops," said he, "are such that we can defy all price." Let us assume that £7 per acre represents, upon an average, the gross produce of an acre of arable land—and £6 that of an acre of pasture. There is no reason whatever to suppose that the produce of Norfolk is below the average; and in the absence of more accurate data on the subject, we must assume that the gross value of the produce of the arable land is not less than £5,856,326, and of the pasture land £1,254,912—making a total of £7,111,238 as the gross value of the produce of the land under cultivation in the county. The average amount paid for tithe, as calculated from a list of forty commutations, is—for arable land 6s. 6d., and for pasture 2s. 5¼d. per acre; which gives as the total amount paid upon arable land £271,906, and upon pasture £32,779, or a total upon arable and pasture of £304,684. The quantity of rape and linseed cake imported into the county in 1843, for the purpose of feeding and fattening cattle, was 26,366 tons. The total quantity of grain and flour exported from the various ports in the year 1843 was 536,766 quarters. Of the quantity of bullocks, sheep, and pigs fattened in the county, I have not been able to obtain any information upon which reliance could be placed; the quantity, however, must be enormous. The cattle market at Norwich is one of the largest in the country; but as the market is rented of the corporation, the parties having the management uniformly refuse to give any information as to the actual number of cattle or sheep sold there. Some idea of the immense quantity sold at the market may, however, be formed, from some returns which were published on the subject in 1837, from which it appears that the quantity sold at Norwich market, during the year 1836, was—of sheep, 214,480; pigs, 29,207; cows and calves, 4,032; beasts, 40,390; and horses, 1,882; and I have been informed that since that period the quantity has considerably increased. At Lynn market, in 1843, the numbers sold were—sheep, 53,665; pigs, 25,172; and bullocks, 16,368.

One of the main causes which have led to the great improvement in the cultivation of Norfolk has no doubt been the almost universal adoption of giving leases to the farmers. In order to reclaim the thousands of acres which formerly were mere barren heaths, a large

outlay of capital was necessarily required, and it was not to be supposed that farmers would invest their capital in undertakings of this
sort unless they were guaranteed such a permanent possession of the
land as would in all probability allow of a fair return upon their investments. In order to afford this necessary security the late Earl of Leicester adopted the system of granting leases of fourteen and twenty-
one years to all his tenants. Following his example, most of the other
large landed proprietors of the county adopted the same course, and
at present there are comparatively few farmers in Norfolk who do not
hold their farms upon leases. Mr. Burroughes, M.P., the member for
East Norfolk, and a proprietor of upwards of 8,000 acres, has within
the last few years given leases to every one of his tenants. Lord Wodehouse, who is also an extensive proprietor in the neighbourhood of
Wymondham, has also given notice to those tenants who have not
already obtained leases, that he is prepared to grant them upon the
most just and liberal terms. The beneficial effects of granting leases
are, perhaps, nowhere to be seen more strikingly than in the county
of Norfolk. The appearance of farms cultivated under lease, as compared with those belonging to yearly tenants, is such as cannot fail to
strike even the most superficial observer. The farms held under lease
may, in almost all cases, be distinguished by their high state of cultivation, the neatness and trimness of the hedges and fences, and the
good state of repair in which the houses and farm-buildings are universally kept. The question of leases is one also which bears intimately
upon the condition and well-being of the labourer. A person holding
a farm under a yearly tenancy will be careful not to expend more, either in improvements or in labour, than he considers will be repaid
by the value of the crop; his expenditure will be only proportionate to
the interest which he possesses in the land. On the other hand, the
farmer who feels that he has a security for a number of years in the
produce, will naturally exert himself to the utmost in the cultivation
and improvement of his farm; and in proportion as he does so, will he
be able to give an increased amount of employment to the labourer.
And from all the inquiries which I have made upon the subject—and
I have taken some considerable pains to inquire into the matter—I am
firmly convinced that a far greater proportion of labour is employed
upon farms held under lease than upon those held under uncertain
tenures; and not only is there in such cases an increased amount of
employment for the labourer, but he is also generally better paid, and
his condition is in every respect more comfortable. As to the periods

for which the leases are granted, considerable discussion has taken place among those immediately concerned in arriving at a satisfactory solution of the question, and various terms have been mentioned to me, each of which has been supported by a considerable show of argument. It appears, however, to be admitted upon all hands that leases under fourteen years would not secure to the tenant a fair return for the additional outlay which he would be supposed to make. Several farmers with whom I have spoken on the subject advocate very strongly the insertion of renewal clauses in the leases, which, in the case of a fourteen years' lease, would give to the tenant the option of renewal at the end of ten years, and in cases of leases of twenty-one, a renewal at the expiration of fourteen years. In the leases which have recently been granted by Mr. Burroughes, clauses are inserted, giving the tenant compensation for unexhausted improvements upon the expiration of the lease. This arrangement is one which has given very general satisfaction to the tenants, and if universally adopted, would tend to remove any apprehension as to the injury which the land might sustain, during the small unexpired term of a lease, in consequence of the tenant withholding from the farm its fair proportion of labour or improvements.

Great numbers of farms are, however, still let by the year; in some cases it being stipulated that twelve or eighteen months' notice shall be given by the landlord if he wishes to remove the tenant, and by the latter if he desires to give up his occupation. But when the landlord is the party desiring to remove the tenant, he is bound to pay to him the value of all unexhausted improvements. The interests of the labourer are also deeply affected, in addition to the extent to which the practice of giving leases may prevail, by the nature of the covenants as to the cropping of the land. Many of the compulsory clauses, which at present regulate the rotation of crops and the mode of cultivation, operate injuriously to the interests of both the tenant-farmer and the labourer. There is a very general feeling against the continuance of many of the old compulsory clauses. There are but few cases in which a tenant, holding under a long lease, can cause any injury to the land by the system of cropping which he may adopt, without inflicting upon himself even a greater amount of injury. One large farmer, who farmed upwards of 1,000 acres, gave me as his opinion—and assured me that it was one very generally shared throughout the country, both by landlords and tenants—that when once some general rule as to cropping was laid down, the less the farmer who was disposed to invest his capital was interfered with or fettered by arbitrary clauses, the better would it be for the landlord, the tenant, and, above all, for the labourer. "I know," said he, "a case where there are clauses which prevent the farmer from drilling his turnips and from mowing wheat; and another which prohibits him from 'shacking the stubble,' and even letting the sheep feed off the wheat stubbles before October. Why, when a man is hampered with such regulations as these, how can he cultivate the land, or employ as much labour as he might wish on his farm? The fairest and most proper covenants that I know of are just these—and I don't think anybody could object to 'em, because they're for the good of all parties:—I wouldn't allow of two white crops following each other. I wouldn't have any pasture broke up, and I'd let the farmer sell his hay, his straw, and even his green crops, so long as he laid out as much as he sold 'em for in artificial or other manure. Well, then, when there was any draining to be done, a part of the expense should be paid by the landlord, and not all by the tenant."

The clauses in the agreements which most injuriously affect the tenant-farmer, and through him indirectly affect the labourer, are those which reserve to the landlord the exclusive right of shooting game. Vast quantities of game are preserved in Norfolk, and a very general and wide-spread feeling of dissatisfaction exists upon the subject among all the tenant-farmers with whom I have spoken on the subject. The great difficulty appears to be as to what should be the amount of remuneration to the tenant for the loss that he sustains by the depredations of the game. The system at present adopted is that of making a certain reduction, agreed upon by both parties, from the rent. The farmers, however, complain that a fixed amount of reduction does not meet the case fully. The injury done by the game frequently exceeds very considerably the amount allowed as compensation. This evil is more particularly felt in the neighbourhood of large preserves, where the quantity of game has been allowed to increase to any very great extent. I have been informed of several cases in which the loss by game has been enormous. Upon one farm, twelve acres which were sown with barley did not yield more than forty coombs, while the average yield ought to be from 90 to 100 coombs. In consequence of this continued falling off in the crops, and the inability of the farmer to obtain anything like adequate compensation, the amount expended in labour had fallen off to one-half; and no labour of any kind, except what was absolutely necessary, or required by the covenants, was performed upon that part of the farm. "I should employ ever so many more men," said the farmer to me, "in draining and trimming the hedges; but it is no use, the birds eat up all the profit." There is one complaint which I have frequently heard made by the farmers in connection with game; that is, that the numbers are not kept down so much as they were formerly—that the destruction of the game is not "steady." The railways, they say, have increased the facilities for the friends of the squire to visit him, and the game is usually reserved for the periods at which the visitors and guests may arrive. Another reason why, they say, there is not so much shooting going on daily, is because the owners do not wish to make the birds shy by too frequently visiting them, as by so doing they would not be able so easily to supply the large quantities to the dealers in game who are in the habit of purchasing of them. This system of reserving the game for "battues" of this kind is, if not loudly, at least very generally, complained of by the great body of tenant farmers; and in too many cases it operates most prejudicially to the interest of the labourer.

So completely identified with the state of agriculture are the interests of the agricultural labourer, that it is impossible to fix upon any one of its various phases, or to consider any of the modes by which it is carried on, without being at once led to connect with it its effects upon the condition of the labourer. Not only is he interested in the tenure by which the land may be held, and the covenants by which his employer may be bound, but he is also interested to a great extent in the system of cropping which may prevail in the district in which he resides, and upon the farm on which he is employed. A few years since, the "six-course shift" was the one most generally adopted throughout Norfolk. Under this system, two white crops were generally taken in succession. These were followed by turnips, barley, and sometimes oats, and the course was invariably finished by a two years' layer. Under such a system, it is obvious that the whole of the land could only come under tillage once in every six years. For some parts of the county, the "five-course shift" prevailed. A number of varieties were introduced in connection with the five-course shift, into which it is obviously not my province to enter, but the object of the farmer in all such cases is to employ as small an amount of capital as possible, and to secure the largest return for the smallest possible outlay. The rotation of cropping which is now most generally adopted, especially in the western division of the county, is the four-course shift. In some portions of the county, in the neighbourhood of Cromer and in the hundreds of Tunstead and Happing, the six-course is still adhered to—while near Fellrigge, and in some portions of Flegg, the five-course is still adopted. In the fen district, and in marshland, wheat and beans are grown without any intervening crop, and such is the extraordinary fertility of these districts, that the same course has been continued for upwards of twenty years. There can be no doubt whatever that the adoption of the four-course shift, setting aside the fens and marshland, is the one which affords the greatest possible amount of employment to the labouring classes, inasmuch as the whole of the land comes under tillage once in four years, instead of once in five or six, as would be the case under the five and six-course shift. The old notion that it is necessary to allow the ground to remain for one year in the four, five, or six, as "dead fallow," is in most parts of Norfolk completely exploded, and it is generally found that no difficulty exists in keeping the ground clear by a judicious system of green cropping.

The comparative effects upon the labourer, of large and small farms, has for many years been a *vexatio questio*, which has been agitated with more or less violence in the whole of the eastern counties of England. It is a question of considerable importance, the satisfactory solution of which would be attended with a vast amount of good. The limits of a single letter would barely suffice to enter fully into a consideration of the various arguments, *pro* and *con*, which have been advanced upon either side. Feeling strongly that it was a question deeply affecting the interests of the labourer, I made it my business to make somewhat extensive inquiries as to the opinions entertained upon the subject by the farmers, and even by the labourers themselves. The man whose farm is too small for his capital is far more likely to afford increased employment to the labourer than the farmer whose holding is too large for his capital. I have been repeatedly told that the small farmers were constantly suffering from the want of capital, and unfortunately they appear to have many companions in this respect among the larger occupiers. The small farmer who may bestow his own labour upon his farm, may, and often does, struggle on against difficulties of an almost overwhelming nature; but the privations which his want of capital necessarily produce are shared only by himself and family, or, at least, are confined to a very limited number of labourers. Not so, however, with the large occupier, holding his 500 or 1,000 acres: a large proportion of the labour of a district must necessarily be dependent for employment on the farm, and when, through want of capital, the farmer is unable to afford the necessary employment, they have no other resource but crime or the workhouse. I apprehend there are very few farmers who, if they were candid enough, would not say—and several of them have told me frankly—that if their farms were half their present size, they would be able to employ nearly as many labourers as they now do upon their larger occupations. "The truth is," said one of the farmers of Norfolk, when speaking to me on the subject, "my capital is not more than enough for 400 acres, and I've got upwards of 800. What's the consequence? I am obliged to stint it, both in manure and in labour, and my case isn't a single one. I'll be bound to say there's many of us that would be glad to give up half their farms if it wasn't for the shame of the thing. They must do it, though, some of 'em, or else go to the wall altogether, depend upon it." The opinions of great numbers of the labourers, who can frequently form a pretty shrewd opinion upon such matters, are similar to that of the farmers just referred to, and, in speaking to many of them on the subject of their employment, they will frequently say, "Master can't afford to do it, d'pend upon it he can't; he has got too many irons in the fire," or "Master wants to have as much ground as the squire, but he arn't got the money to work it." I have frequently heard such exclamations as these from the labourers with reference to their employers. Want of capital, therefore, is an evil which applies equally to many of the large as to many of the small farmers, and any argument founded upon it with respect to the one, applies equally to the other.

In many parts of Norfolk and Suffolk the farms are exceedingly large, and in many cases the occupiers do not appear to be suffering from insufficiency of capital—consequently a fair amount of employment is given to the labourer. In Suffolk, Mr. Capon, to whom I have before alluded, farms upwards of 6,000 acres, and is famed for the large number of labourers which he employs. Upon the Culford estate, consisting of upwards of 11,000 acres, there are but eight tenants; and from all I can learn the labourers are well employed and comfortable. In Norfolk the farms, generally speaking, are also very large. Upon the estate of Lord Leicester, consisting of 40,000 acres, I believe there is no farm of less than 500 acres, while many of them are of 1,000 and 1,500, and even 2,500 acres. In order to bring into cultivation this extensive district, it was absolutely necessary that farmers possessed of both capital and skill should be induced to take the farms, and probably the only mode by which this district could have been brought into cultivation was under the large farm system.

Mr. Baker, who is the steward to the Earl of Leicester, informed me that in his opinion a larger proportion of labour was employed upon large than upon small occupations. He stated that upon a farm of 1,000 acres there would be 16 or 17 labourers employed—while upon the small farm almost the entire amount of the work would be performed by the occupier himself, assisted by members of his family. Mr. Kent, however, who is a most strenuous advocate for the advantages of small farms, stated that in the village of Stanton, in Suffolk, there are several small farmers whose united occupations amounted to about 130 acres, and that these small farms give employment to the occupiers, their sons, and about five labourers. Exclusive of the labourers the employment would be at the rate of about one man to every ten acres. According to this statement the number employed upon the 1,000-acre farms must be enormously below the proportion employed upon the small farms. In many parts of Norfolk there appears to be a growing desire, upon the part of some of the farmers, to increase the size of their occupations. In the neighbourhood of Wymondham and Attleborough, within the last ten or twelve years, all the small farms of 150 to 200 acres have been allowed to merge into one holding, and several of the farmers about there have their 1,000 acres, who formerly held but 400 or 500. An example of this kind might be mentioned in the case of Mr. Howse, who occupies at present four distinct farms, comprising together upwards of 1,000 acres. In order to prevent as much as possible any injury to the labourer, in consequence of non-employment, Lord Wodehouse stipulates with all his tenants that they shall employ a certain amount of labour on their farms. In point of fact, a farmer with 1,000 acres usually employs but very little more labour than is employed upon one of 500 acres, or even less. I was informed of two light-land farms—one of 400, the other of 550 acres—on which the average cost of labour per acre was, for the former, £1 8s., for the latter £1 15s.; while in the case of a large light-land farm of 1,650 acres, the cost of labour was only 14s. per acre; upon two others, of 1,400 acres each, it was only 12s.; and in the case of one of 2,400 acres, the average cost was 21s. The average weekly wages upon the two smaller farms were 10s., while upon the farm of 2,400 acres the weekly wages did not exceed 9s. If any dependence is to be placed upon the accuracy of official statistics, it would appear clear that the large farms do not employ a due proportion of labour. The number of agricultural labourers of both sexes, and all ages, in Norfolk, is 41,647; the quantity of land cultivated, including pasture and tillage, has been computed to be 1,045,760 acres, which would give a proportion of about 4.1 labourers to the 100 acres, or 41 to a thousand. The numbers employed upon a farm of 1,000 acres rarely exceed seventeen; taking twenty, however, as the number employed, it would appear that a large farm does not employ more than about one-half its due proportion of labour. The evil which would result from this non-employment of labour, upon the large farms, appears to be checked in some measure by the increased employment upon the small ones, especially in cases where the small farmers have a sufficiency of capital. There is, however, in many parts of the county, but little surplus labour to be met with. In the Tunstead and Hopping Hundred, there have not been for the last five years any able-bodied persons in the workhouse. When I visited it there was but one able-bodied pauper in the house. In the Wangford Union there is generally a larger amount of unemployed labourers than in most other unions. The master of the workhouse there informed me that he had had at one time as many as 396 paupers in the workhouse, of whom 114 were able-bodied. In the week ending Michaelmas, 1849, the number of able-bodied was 43, as compared with 42 in the corresponding period of the last year. The total number of able-bodied paupers in the different unions of Norfolk, in the week ending September 29 of the present year, was 142; the number being 116 at the same period of 1848. The average number of able-bodied receiving in-door relief for the 13 weeks ending the same period of the present year was 155, as compared with 127 in the corresponding period of 1848. There is, perhaps, no county in England in which machinery is more extensively employed in connection with agriculture than in Norfolk. The slightest improvement in any of the agricultural machines is certain to meet with a cordial reception among the Norfolk farmers. The first thing which would strike a visitor to any of the large model farms which are to be met with in Norfolk would be the extensive array of agricultural implements of all kinds, many of which, to a novice in such matters, would be alike formidable in appearance and mysterious in application. The reader will not expect me to give him an account of the various "clod crushers," "pulverizers," and "scarifiers," which are in high esteem among the farmers; it is sufficient for my purpose to state that machinery is very extensively employed, and that it is by its constant use that the farmers of Norfolk, many of whom are styled "farmer princes," have attained to their present deservedly elevated position.

Any description of the agriculture of Norfolk, as it affects the condition of the labouring classes, would obviously be incomplete which did not take cognizance of the continued and persevering attempts which have been made to extend the growth of flax in this county; and there is no person, perhaps, to whom the thanks of the community are more due for labours and exertions in this respect than to Mr. Warnes, of Trinningham. For the last eight or ten years he has constantly devoted both his time and his fortune in promoting and bringing to perfection the growth of this useful article. Everything that could be done by public meetings and by pamphlets on the subject, and by the formation of flax-growing associations, has been done by him to bring it prominently before the public, and he has now the satisfaction of witnessing the benefits to the moral and social condition of the people, which have been already caused by the partial growth of flax in the parish in which he resides. As I had heard in travelling through the county a great deal with respect to the growth of flax, and the great employment of labour afforded by it, on the farm of Mr. Warnes, I determined upon visiting it myself, and the results of my visit were such as fully to convince me that neither the benefits of the undertaking nor the exertion of Mr. Warnes had been overstated.

Trinningham, the parish in which Mr. Warnes resides, is a small parish in the North Erpingham hundred, comprising 510 acres. In 1841 its population consisted of 222 persons. It is situated upon the coast, at the extreme north-eastern part of the county, and the soil is, generally speaking, of an inferior character. A portion of the land in Mr. Warnes' occupation is upon the edge of the cliffs, in some cases 200 and in others 300 feet above the level of the sea, and within the last few years three or four acres have fallen into the sea. The condition of the inhabitants was a few years since most deplorable. Typhus fever was seldom absent from the wretched and overcrowded hovels of the poor; the want of decency among the people was almost universal; and the amount of pauperism far exceeded that of the adjoining parishes, owing to the almost entire absence of the means of employment. Since the introduction of flax, however, this state of things has passed away. The poor-rates are merely nominal; there are no paupers in the parish. A commodious school-room has been erected, where previously none had existed; and the cottage accommodation is ample, and of an excellent character. "Previously, little or no employment was provided for the weaker hands; now both old and young find an abundance. The money thus circulated amongst children augments their parents' wages, and thereby large as well as small families derive ample maintenance. The moral and physical state of the village will bear comparison with most. Not an instance of illegitimacy has occurred for many years, nor a conviction for theft. The children, educated at a school unsupported by Church or State, are trained to habits of industry through flax-dressing, and early find situations at service." Such is the account of the change which has taken place in this small village, as given in a letter written by Mr. Warnes, a copy of which was recently published in the public papers, and, so far as I was enabled to judge, the benefits have not been in the least exaggerated. Many of the cottages are newly built, and afford ample accommodation to the labourers. Those which have been recently erected are built of rubble and brick, and are mostly thatched; they contain from two to four rooms each. A porch is built in the front of the new cottages, which has the effect of remedying the great inconvenience so universally felt by the poor, of having the doors of their rooms open at once into the street or road. By the use of the two doors, the outer and inner one, the cold draughts of air are prevented from entering, and the rooms are kept cleaner and warmer with a less amount both of labour and fuel. I visited several of the little cottages, and was gratified to see the comfortable state in which most of the tenants were living. The furniture of the rooms was good, and remarkably clean; while on the shelf over the fireplace were to be seen a crowd of such little toys and ornaments as clearly indicate a state of comparative prosperity and contentment among the people. To each of the cottages a small piece of garden ground was attached, varying from an eighth to a quarter of an acre; and at a short distance from the house, and neatly thatched, was a small house, or sty, for the pig. In one of the houses dwelt a man and his wife and six children. The man was by trade a jobbing carpenter, and had for years borne an exceedingly bad character. Whenever he had it in his power he was almost always drunk; he disliked work, preferring to spend his time at public-houses and beer-shops, where he would collect a few pence by playing on a fiddle. Last winter, as usual, the man, with his family, became an inmate of the workhouse. After he had been there a short time, he obtained a little temporary work; he was discharged, and two of his children resumed their old employment, at flax-dressing. "When I had finished my job," said the poor man to me, "I went to the board for an order for re-admission into the house. When I was there I saw Mr. Warnes, and says he to me, 'Why don't you try to get some work?' I said, 'I had tried, but couldn't get none.' Then he said, 'Why don't you come and try to work at the flax along with your children?' and so I went, and after a week or two—I didn't get on very fast at first at the scutching—but I soon got into it, and after a few weeks we *yearned* altogether such a thing as a pound. I sold the fiddle, and we are now all quite comfortable. I have never known what it is to want a meal's victuals since I've been at work at the flax. My children have all got clothes, and we're not put to any of the shifts we used to be. When any of the young uns wanted clean clothes they were always obliged to go to bed and stop there without any on, till they were dried and ready for 'em to put on. It's not so now, for they've all got a change of clothes at least. When I'm not at work a doing of odd jobs in carpentering, there's always something for me to do in the scutching room." This is one instance among many in which the cultivation of flax has been made subservient to the wants of the people, and has removed a load of pauperism which formerly weighed heavily upon the parish. The contrast which the parish of Trinningham presents to many others by which it is surrounded is peculiarly striking in respect to the condition of the labourers. It is the usual custom, I was informed, in a great many of the adjoining parishes, for the farmers to send their teams in order to convey the labourers with their families to the union workhouse for the winter months, and as many as seventy persons have been seen thus to pass through Trinningham on their way to the union workhouse. There is now no able-bodied labourer, nor any portion of his family, in Trinningham, who may not obtain employment throughout the whole of the winter months in scutching and preparing the flax for market. One of the peculiar qualities connected with flax is, that it can be prepared at any time, as it is found that the fibre improves by being stacked after drying and kept for a considerable time. There is, therefore, no necessity for scutching it at any particular season, or within any limited time, and a means of employment is thus afforded for wet or other weather, when field operations are necessarily suspended. On the occasion of my visit, the weather was such as totally to preclude the possibility of carrying on any field labour. The snow had been upon the ground for several days previously—a thaw had set in, and with it a constant and heavy fall of rain; it was one of those days when the country presents one of its most dreary aspects. The men employed upon the farm were not, as in most other instances would have been the case, sent home for want of employment, but, on the contrary, were all busily engaged in the barn in "beetling" the flax, while upon another portion of the premises fourteen persons, some of whom were children, were employed in scutching it. At the blacksmith's shop close by were standing idly together three or four stout able-bodied men, belonging to a neighbouring farm, who had nothing to do that day on account of the wet; while several others, similarly circumstanced, were intently looking on at the proceedings of those engaged upon the flax. I asked several of them why they were not at work, and they informed me that they had been to the farm, but were told that there was nothing for them to do. I asked them if there was no threshing going on, and was told that there was not then, and that what threshing there was to be done would be done by the regular men. The land occupied by Mr. Warnes does not exceed seventy-five acres, and the number of persons employed upon it is never less than nine men and a boy, while sixteen others are employed in the various processes of preparing the flax for market. The amount paid in wages last winter to the persons employed in preparing the flax was £109 8s. So eager, indeed, are some of the people to get to work, that during last winter they were in the habit of coming at three o'clock in the morning to commence their labours, the work being all paid for by the quantity done.

In addition to the amount of employment which the cultivation of flax affords, it also possesses the additional recommendation of being highly remunerative to the grower. I cannot forbear, while upon the subject, although it may be considered somewhat beyond the natural scope of my inquiry, from referring to a few of the results which have been obtained by Mr. Warnes. He states that, through the cultivation of flax—in connexion with fattening cattle with native produce, box-feeding, and summer grazing—three bullocks and three sheep may be fattened where only one of each was kept before, and that the triple quantity of manure thus obtained produces a corresponding increase in the production of the soil. In fact, there is no instance in the whole of the county of Norfolk where so many cattle are fattened upon so small a holding as upon that at Trinningham. He has at present twenty-three bullocks, which are being fattened entirely upon the produce of his farm, made into a compound which entirely supersedes the use of foreign oil-cake. The bullocks are seldom kept in the boxes more than six months; and by the adoption of this plan he is enabled to secure a double return in the year. "The last 23 bullocks," said Mr. Warnes, "which I sold, cost me £8 15s. per head; the price at which they were sold was, on an average, £16 5s. They were fed entirely upon linseed and turnips; and I expect to clear as much by those that are now in the boxes. With respect to the flax, the fibre produce of 14 acres was sold last year for £238 16s. 6d.; the value of the seed, at 20 bushels to the acre, and at 6s. per bushel, was £84, and the value of the chaff, which forms a part of the food of the cattle, I estimate at £15—making the total value of the produce of the 14 acres of flax £337 16s. 6d. The sum expended in the preparation of the flax, as wages, was £109; and the rent, seed, and tillage, were £2 11s. per acre, or £35 14s. for the 14 acres, being a total expense of £144 14s., leaving a clear profit upon the 14 acres of £123 2s. 6d.—to say nothing of the value of the manure obtained from the cattle, and the increased fertility obtained thereby upon the other portions of the farm." As showing the enormous amount of additional employment which would be given by the extensive cultivation of flax, Mr. Warnes informed me that the firm of Messrs. Marshall and Co., of Leeds, consume in their manufactory 30 tons of flax in the week, or 1,500 tons per annum, to produce which would require 6,000 acres, and the employment of 2,000 adults or 6,000 children in its preparation. The wages of the adults at 10s. per week, or of the children at 3s. 4d. per week, would amount to £52,000, being at the rate of £8 13s. 4d. per acre, exclusive of the amount which would be expended for labour upon the culture of the plant. The quantity of flax imported in 1845 was 1,418,323 cwts., the value of which exceeded £5,000,000. Making every possible allowance for the very sanguine opinions which Mr. Warnes entertains of the benefits which would result from an extended growth of flax, it certainly does appear that a large field for additional labour would be opened by its cultivation. "From the most careful calculations," he says, "which I have been able to make upon the subject, founded on my own actual experience, I firmly believe that one acre sown with flax out of every hundred now under tillage, would produce at least 35,000 tons of linseed more than ever were imported of oil-cake in one year—afford employment for double the present redundant population—and then not supply half the demand for the fibre." Even though these calculations should prove inaccurate, still, if the growth of flax can produce elsewhere results similar to those which I have witnessed at Trinningham, there can be no doubt that the sooner it is cultivated to a greater extent, the sooner will the enormous amount of pauperism decrease, and comfort and contentment be more generally diffused among large masses of the labouring agricultural population.

One of the chief causes which appears to have prevented the extensive growth of flax by the farmers is the opinion very generally entertained that it is of an exhaustive character. Mr. Warnes informs me, however, that when grown in connection with the box feeding of cattle, so far from its being an exhaustive crop, it is entirely the reverse. Last year he had twelve acres of wheat, the greater part of which was sown upon land upon which flax had been grown in the previous year. He states that he never had such fine crops, and that they were superior to any others in the parish. In fact, upon several occasions he has obtained two crops in the year from the same land—one of flax, and one of turnips. The flax ripens earlier than the wheat; and he was last year enabled to pull it in sufficient time to sow the turnips upon the same ground; and many of the turnips which I there saw were of an enormous size, the whole crops being considerably above the average of many other farms which I have visited.

The rents of the farms in Norfolk vary very considerably in different parts of the county. In some parts the arable land is let at rents as high as 50s. per acre, and some of the pasture at upwards of £3. Taking the average of the whole county, the rent of the arable may be taken at 21s. per acre, and that of the marshes at about 30s. per acre. An immense increase has of late years taken place in the rental of the county on some of the marsh land. I was informed that the increase had been as much as from 60 to 80 per cent., and upon some of the good class of soils 30 per cent. According to the returns under the property-tax for 1815, the estimated rental of Norfolk was £1,102,352—the rent per acre 17s., and the estimated profits of occupiers £698,882. The amount assessed under the property-tax was £1,439,977; under the income and property-tax established in 1842 it amounts to £1,945,558, being an increase of £505,581. In the neighbourhood of Wymondham, the farms which form a portion of the property of Lord Wodehouse are let at sums varying from 20s. to 25s. Some of his best lands are let at from 30s. to 50s. per acre. In the parish of Selfield good heavy land, principally clay, is let at from 30s. to 35s. per acre. At Attleborough the rent is about 30s. per acre; the land belonging to Mr. Burroughes, M.P., I was informed, lets at from 30s. to 40s. per acre. Speaking to Mr. Baker, the steward of the Earl of Leicester, on the subject of the rents upon his lordship's estate, he said, "That is a very ticklish subject, but you may fairly set it down at 5s. an acre less than any other of the same kind in Norfolk. Upon some of the light-land farms the rents do not exceed 16s. per acre, in some cases 18s. and 20s.—few exceeding 25s. per acre." The amount of tithe varies very considerably. The rent-charge upon the average is as high, and in some cases higher, than it was some years since, and many of the farmers complain sadly of the bargains which they made under the Tithe Commutation Act. Upon several farms the tithe is as high as 10s. 6d. per acre on the arable land; in other cases, 9s., 9s. 6d., 8s., 7s. In two cases out of a list of nearly a hundred which I have seen, the amount is only 1s. 6d. and 1s. 9d. The tithe upon pasture land varies from 1s. 9d. to 3s., the great majority being between 2s. and 3s. the acre.

There is perhaps no subject to which greater attention has been paid by the farmers of Norfolk than to the improvement of their farm-buildings; and the man must be blind indeed who could travel through the county without being struck by their excellent appearance. But not only is it in their external appearance that these great changes have been effected, but in what is indeed far more important—their internal arrangements. In this, as in everything connected with the improvement of the agriculture of Norfolk, are to be found traces of the enterprising spirit and genius of the late Earl of Leicester. The great farm at Holkham is a model worthy to be followed by every agriculturist, and many of the large farmers upon the property have shown a laudable desire to follow the example set them by his lordship. The Holkham great barn and cattle buildings are constructed with a view of obtaining the greatest amount of convenience and accommodation, and also of avoiding the expenditure of unnecessary labour as much as possible. The cattle stalls are all well ventilated, and care is taken to avoid the effects of extreme cold. At Weasenham, upon a farm of Mr. Overman's, I was informed that the buildings were of the most superior character, and afforded an admirable illustration of the great amount of convenience which may be obtained by judicious arrangement upon a comparatively small farm. I cannot omit allusion to the farm-buildings of Sir J. Cullum, Bart., a short distance from Bury. The arrangement of the buildings, and their adaptation to the various purposes required of them, are probably not to be surpassed, if equalled, in the whole of the eastern districts which I have visited.

The improved cultivation of Norfolk has, of necessity, led to the inclosure of a great deal of common lands; and it is computed that there are at present 27,000 acres of uninclosed and waste land which would well repay the cost of inclosure and cultivation. Among these commons might be mentioned a large one at Cossey or Costissy, Fakenham, Messingham, Kipton, and numerous others. The inclosure of some of these lands would be attended not only with an increase of production and employment for the labourers, but would also tend vastly to their social and moral improvement. In the neighbourhood of these commons I have almost invariably found the greatest amount of want, wretchedness, and vice among the population. The cases of Barrow, in Suffolk, and Cossey, in Norfolk, afford abundant proofs of this. Speaking of the beneficial results which have attended the inclosure of one of these commons, Mr. Bacon, in his prize essay on the agriculture of Norfolk, refers to the case of a village which was noted, not many years since, for the comparative immorality and want of its inhabitants, and for its large heath and ling grounds, which were in common. The proprietors determined to effect some alteration if possible, and accordingly proceeded to bring part of the common into cultivation. The heath and ling were ploughed in as deeply as the plough would admit of, where they were suffered to decay; the ground was cropped and gradually brought into cultivation; and the result has been that a considerable portion of what was once a barren heath is now studded with farm-buildings and cottages, while the crops are such as to afford ample returns for the outlay of capital and skill. Excellent crops of wheat, barley, and rye were last year produced upon it, and the culture and quality of the turnip crops proved how much had been effected by the personal attention and exertions of the proprietors. The effect upon the village has been, as might have been anticipated, a great reduction of pauperism, and a comparative increase in the comforts of the people themselves. One of the chief evils attending the non-inclosure of these common lands is the great inducement afforded to the building of an inferior class of cottages for the poor people, who flock to such places for the sake of enjoying the rights of the common. The cottages consequently become overcrowded, and the greatest possible amount of wretchedness and vice is to be found in such places. A large quantity of common land has very recently been inclosed in the Hartismere Union, in the county of Suffolk. The interests of the poor are, however, carefully provided for, as a large portion of the inclosed land is set apart for allotments, and four or five acres are reserved as a place of recreation for them. But it is not only the common lands which are being brought under cultivation to a great extent, but large portions of land have been reclaimed, or are in course of reclamation, from the sea. A bill has very recently been obtained, authorizing the reclamation of 32,000 acres on a portion of the Norfolk estuary, between Lynn and Wisbeach, towards the expense of which the corporation of Lynn are to contribute £120,000.

The Morning Chronicle, Monday, December 24, 1849.

THE SUFFOLK LABOURERS.

———◆———

To the EDITOR of the MORNING CHRONICLE.

Sir—In justice to the cause of truth, I have to request your insertion of the following plain statement of facts connected with a case mentioned in your article upon the condition of the labourers of Suffolk. The case is that in which an ejected family are stated to have taken up their abode in the church porch, previous to their removal to Bury. This identifies it with what actually occurred in the parish of which I am the incumbent. The case of the poor man mentioned in your recent article was simply this:—On this property none but the idle and the good-for-nothing—and these are but very few—are without employment, even in the winter. One mode of employing the people is in planting; and at first the plantations are set with potatoes, and so made to repay somewhat of their original cost. The potatoes, thus lying exposed, had been very much plundered, though every cottager has, generally, ample garden room to supply his own wants; and the owner of the estate publicly declared that he would make an example of the first person detected. This person was the woman of whom your Correspondent speaks. She was not merely caught in the act of stealing a few potatoes, but nearly a bushel of potatoes was found hidden by her, after she had solemnly declared that what she had in her apron was all she had taken. Notice to quit was immediately sent to her husband; but he declared that he would not go, and defied his landlord to turn him out. I expostulated with him, advising him to go at once, and reminding him of others who had been removed for similar offences, and had been allowed after a year or two to return, on promise of good behaviour. All, however, was to no purpose. Nearly six months were allowed him to try and find a new home; but he took no steps whatever, reckoning, I believe, upon the forbearance of his landlord. If he had got the better of his landlord, pretty well all the discipline which has been such a blessing to this estate, both temporally and morally, would have been at an end. At least, having been once infringed, it would have been ten times more difficult to keep up than before. But the man was removed, and went to the church porch, agreeably to a notion prevalent, I hear, in some parts of Norfolk and Suffolk, that every parishioner has a right to shelter there. He remained there eight or nine days, and at last removed to Bury.

This is the simple truth, by inserting which you will much oblige your obedient servant,

W. PRIDDEN,

Rector of West Stow and Wordwell.

West Stow Rectory, Bury St. Edmund's, Dec. 18.

LABOUR AND THE POOR.

—◆—

THE RURAL DISTRICTS.

[FROM OUR SPECIAL CORRESPONDENT.]

NORFOLK, SUFFOLK, AND ESSEX.

EASTERN AGRICULTURAL DISTRICTS.

LETTER XX.

The total number of persons employed in agricultural labour in the county of Norfolk was, in 1841, 40,647. Of this number there were—males above 20 years of age, 34,006; under that age, 5,751; females above 20 years of age, 731; under, 159. The number of farmers and graziers in the county was at the same time 7,452. From these figures it would appear that the average number of labourers employed by each farmer or grazier was 5.4, the average number so employed in Suffolk being 6.7. As far as I have been enabled to judge from the information which I have obtained upon the subject, the amount of wages paid annually to the agricultural labourers of Norfolk would be about the following:—

> The total number of male labourers, above 20 years of age, according to the census of 1841, was 34,006:—

	£	£
Of whom one half, or 17,003, may be said to receive 10s. a week, for 52 weeks	442,052	
One-fourth, or 8,500, 7s. 6d. per week, for 52 weeks	144,092	
One-fourth, or 8,503, 8s. per week, for 40 weeks	136,048	
Total male labourers, above 20 years of age	———	722,192
5,751 males under 20, 5s. per week, for 40 weeks		57,520
731 females above 20, 5s. per week, for 40 weeks		7,280
159 females under 20, 2s. 6d. per week, for 40 weeks		760
Extra, hay and harvest wages		65,843
Making a total of		£853,595

Being rather more than an average of £21 per annum to each labourer employed, or about £81 expended for manual labour to each 100 acres under cultivation in the county.

The number of persons dependent upon agricultural labour, adopting the same proportion which I used for the county of Suffolk, would be 162,588, or rather more than one-third of the entire population.

The principal means of employment in Norfolk, independent of agriculture and weaving, are, domestic servants—males, 4,365; females, 18,074; total, 22,339. The number of persons returned as labourers, whose particular occupation is not specified, is, of both sexes, 5,652; of millers, there are 1,141; seamen, 1,597; dressmakers and milliners, 2,389; and of boot and shoemakers, 5,689. This latter occupation is one which, during the last few years, has increased to a considerable extent in the county—more particularly in Norwich, where there are several very large manufacturers, some of whom employ two or three hundred persons. The principal manufacturers of the city are Messrs. Winter, Ford, Keisch, Kemp, and Wright. The average earnings of the persons employed may be taken to be from 7s. to 12s. per week—the shoe-binders ranging from 3s. to 5s. per week.

At Taverham there is an extensive establishment for the manufacture of paper, where a large portion of the paper used for the *Times* newspaper is made, and where upwards of 100 persons, male and female, are constantly employed. About fifty women, employed in the various occupations of sorting and preparing the rags, earn upon an average 8s. per week; and the same number of men, engaged in the various processes of the manufacture, earn from 2s. to 3s. 6d. per day. Several boys are also employed, whose wages vary from 4s. 6d. to 7s. per week.

The wages of the agricultural labourers vary considerably in different parts of the county. In the northern part, 9s. to 10s. may be considered as the average rate, and the labourers are pretty well employed. Throughout the eastern parts of the county, the wages are lower, and the labourers, generally speaking, are neither so skilful nor so well employed. Being situated close to the sea, their labour is chiefly divided between agriculture and fishing. During the herring and mackerel seasons, great numbers of them go to sea, where they remain for two or three months, and then return to their agricultural employment.

Their return invariably causes a diminution of wages; the farmers are anxious to employ as many of them as possible, in order to keep them from becoming burdens on the parish; and, to enable them to do so, they are driven, in most cases, to reduce the rate of wages. The consequence is, that in these districts the rate of wages is much lower than in many of the other portions of the county. In the southern and western hundreds the rate of wages is from 8s. to 9s. per week. In many of the parishes, however, the wages are considerably lower, and I have met with many cases in which they have not exceeded 6s., and still more where only 7s. per week have been paid. At Great Melton, a short distance from Norwich, it was proposed among the farmers that a general reduction of wages to 7s. should take place. It was, however, finally agreed that the reduction should be to 8s. per week. That reduction has accordingly been generally made; but in several instances, I am told, the farmers are giving but 6s. in that parish. A labourer at Wymondham, who was employed upon the farm of one of the largest occupiers in that district, told me that his wages had been reduced from 8s. to 5s. 6d. per week. "Master," he said, "did that because I had two children at work on the farm; one of 'em arned 2s., t'other 2s. 6d. a week, and he told me they would make up the difference." Women and girls are usually employed in weeding, turnip hoeing and pulling, and stone picking. Their average earnings are from 6d. to 8d. per day. The children are usually employed in keeping pigs, or as "scarecrows," to keep the birds away from the seeds, and similar occupations; their wages vary from 3d. to 6d. per day.

The hours of labour in Norfolk, Suffolk, and Essex, vary according to the season and the mode of employment. A large proportion of the farm work is done by piece or task work, and the labourer in such cases regulates the duration of his labour as may best suit himself. When employed by the day, eight hours is about the regular time of employment. In some parts, the custom is, in the winter, for the labourer to go to work at seven in the morning, and to leave at half-past eleven for dinner; to return at half-past one, and continue till dark. During the summer, two or three hours is not unfrequently allowed for dinner. The reason assigned for allowing so long a period for dinner is, that the horses may be allowed a proper time for rest, and that both labourers and horses may be able to leave off work at the same time.

The food of the labourer and his family is principally bread, potatoes, and frequently, in Norfolk, the Norfolk dumpling, which consists simply of the dough of which the bread is made, the difference between bread and dumpling being merely that the one is boiled while the other is baked. In the neighbourhood of Fakenham I met with a family whose food was chiefly bread and turnips, and I was informed that that was a very general diet with the people about there. In none of the cottages that I have visited in either of the three counties have I ever seen such a thing as a piece of fresh butcher's meat. That it may be had occasionally there can be no doubt, but it is certainly at very rare and long intervals. When meat of any kind is purchased it is mostly bacon or salt pork, and the labourer invariably finds it more economical to purchase that kind of food than fresh meat—the high price which they have to pay for any little piece that they may want being quite sufficient to deter them from its purchase. While at Bury, I was informed by a butcher who carries on a somewhat extensive business, that the "shins" and "stickings" of beef which he was in the habit of selling in the town for 1½d. per pound, he could sell on Saturday to the poor for 5d., "bone and all," when it was cut up in pieces of about two or three pounds weight. About Swaffham, Yarmouth, and Lowestoft, red herrings and salt fish will be found occasionally to enter into the dietary table of the labourer. In one cottage which I visited, I found the woman busily employed in chopping up some pieces of fat pork, which she was about to mix up with some cold potatoes and flour for dumplings, by way of "a treat for the children, because it was Mary's birth-day." The prices which the poor people have to pay for their grocery, such as tea, sugar, and coffee, is enormous. When in Norwich, I obtained several samples of sugar at 3½d. and 4d., and 5d. per lb., and compared them, in several places which I visited, with the sugar for which the poor people had paid at the rate of 5d. and 6d. per lb., and according to the opinion of the poor people themselves, my sample at 3½d. was as good as their fivepenny, and my fourpenny better than their sixpenny, while my fivepenny was fit for the squire.

The cottage accommodation of the labourer is in many parts of Norfolk lamentably deficient. A few praiseworthy efforts have been made on the part of some of the landed proprietors to remedy the evil, but their exertions have by no means kept pace with the wants of the population. The cottages built by the Earl of Leicester, at Holkham, are among the most substantial and comfortable of any in the three counties through which I have travelled. There are about 90 cottages altogether at Holkham. One row of six cottages, each containing two rooms, is chiefly occupied by the widows of the labourers, and are let to them at a guinea per annum. There are about 20 three-roomed cottages, built together in groups of four cottages, the whole forming a crescent, which has a most pleasing and attractive appearance. The rent of these is three guineas a year each, and they are occupied by persons with small families, or by those who have none. The larger cottages contain four rooms, and a small back kitchen and pantry, the rent being four guineas. To each of the cottages there is a piece of garden ground attached, varying in extent from 15 to 20 perches. On the ground floor, the front rooms are 17 feet by 12 feet, and about 7 feet in height. The back kitchen is of the same height, and is about 13 feet by 9 feet. The pantry is about half the size of the kitchen. On the upper floor there are three bed-rooms. At a short distance from each cottage there is a washhouse, a dust-bin, a privy, and a pig-cot. The drainage is excellent, and the cottages are well supplied with water. The cost of building the cottages was, I understand, from £110 to £120 each. Not only is there a great amount of unwillingness on the part of the proprietors generally to build cottages for the labourers, but in too many instances there is an evident desire to destroy or pull down numbers of those that at present exist. In the neighbourhood of Norwich, the extent to which the destruction of cottage property has been carried on was, in the words of my informant, "fearful and disgraceful." In Drayton parish, fourteen cottages have been pulled down within the last few years, and none have been erected in their stead. In the Horsted Hundred, twenty-five of the cottages have been ordered to be destroyed. At Long Sutton, Pulham, Wackton, and various other parishes, the destruction has also been carried on to a great extent, though I was not able to learn the exact number which had been destroyed. I was informed of the case of a large landed proprietor in the vicinity of Norwich, some of whose property being required by the railway company, it was expressly stipulated in the sale that no cottages whatsoever should be built upon any portion of the ground. In point of fact, it is impossible to obtain a piece of ground, for building purposes, in any of the villages within eight or ten miles of Norwich. Many of the estates have been *entirely* cleared of tenantry. To such an extent has the system been carried on, that there are at present in Norwich not less than 500 agricultural labourers, who have to walk to their work distances varying from three to seven miles. Every expedient to prevent the labourer obtaining a settlement in the rural parishes is resorted to by the occupiers. In Wackton parish, one of the modes of removing the paupers was, to set a number of persons, principally weavers, who had some claim on the parish, and who, in all probability, had never had a spade in their hands before, to dig up a common in the middle of January, the snow at the time lying upon the ground several inches deep. The poor wretches were told that they must dig a certain portion of the common before they could obtain any relief. The first thing which they did was to dig in the snow what they called "the grave" of the magistrate who had given the order. So far as the experiment was concerned, it was perfectly successful, for after two or three days the greater proportion of the persons left their employment, and contrived to settle themselves, by one means or other, in the city of Norwich, or in some of the surrounding open parishes. The effect of this conduct, in addition to the injury inflicted upon the paupers, has been most materially to enhance the rates of the adjoining parishes. In Long Sutton, for instance, a number of small cottages have been built; they are crowded by the evicted of the other parishes and the rates are 6s. in the pound, while in the parish of St. Michael, which adjoins it, and where the cottages have been pulled down, the rates are only 2s. 6d. in the pound. This system is not, however, confined to Norwich; for it has been carried on to a great extent in the neighbourhood of Castle Acre, which is an open parish, the consequence being that whilst Castle Acre is overstocked with inhabitants, and the cottages there are densely crowded, there are not in the surrounding parishes anything like sufficient hands to cultivate the land. It is owing to this excess of labourers in one district, and the great want of them in the neighbouring parishes, that the custom has sprung up within the last few years of employing the people in what are termed "gangs," a system which, there can be no doubt whatever, is attended with a considerable amount of evil to the persons employed.

The principle upon which this "gang system" is carried on is the following. A farmer residing in or near Castle Acre may wish to have some particular piece of work done, the performance of which will require a considerable number of hands. In such a case he would apply to a gang-master at Castle Acre, who would contract to do the work, and to supply the labour. The gang-master would accordingly get together as many hands as might be necessary, and they would be sent in a gang to the place of work. In cases where the work can be done by women and children as well as men, the gang is composed of persons of both sexes and of all ages. During the time they are at work, they are superintended by an "overseer," whose duty it is to see that they

are steady to their work, and to prevent the use of any bad language
or the occurrence of any misconduct. The overseer generally accompanies the gang both to and from the place of work. This system,
although it works well for the employer, has in many cases a directly
contrary effect upon the workpeople. The farmer gets his work done
well, quickly, and cheaply; and the prospect of work to be obtained in
the gangs at Castle Acre has drawn together a vast number of labourers from the surrounding districts, till at length, to use the language
of one of the overseers of the gangs, published a few years since, the
parish has become "the coop of all the scrapings in the county; for
if a man or a woman do anything wrong, they come here, and they
think, by getting among them here, they are safe." The employer is
not only benefited by the system, but also the gang-master, inasmuch
as it has the effect of raising him in some degree to the position of
a master instead of a labourer, and as such affords him great local
power, and an indefinite kind of patronage. But the system operates
most injuriously upon the employed. In the first place, it is a mode
of getting them to do the largest possible amount of work for the
smallest amount of pay. The gang-master contracts for the work by
the piece, and the labourers are compelled to work as hard as though
they were working by piece-work for themselves; while, in point of
fact, they are only receiving day labourers' wages. It not unfrequently
happens, also, that after the gang has walked some four or five miles
to the place of work, wet or unfavourable weather may prevent them
from performing the task for which they were employed, and they
thus have to walk there and back without receiving any remuneration.
Many of the children are employed from a very early age in these
gangs, and are thereby debarred from the opportunities of receiving
instruction in the schools. The Rev. Mr. Hogge, rector of South Acre,
stated, in 1843, that the congregating together of such numbers as 70
or 80 in each of the gangs must naturally produce, from its very com-
position of good, bad, and indifferent, great immorality. He had been
a resident in the parish upwards of 40 years, and could affirm, from
his own personal knowledge, that the gang system had produced, and
was still producing, on the rising generation, morally, physically, and
intellectually, immense evils. The Rev. Mr. Gordon, of Cremworth,
also stated that the mischief which these gangs caused to society was
extensive, and very much to be deplored. The Rev. Mr. Bloom, vicar
of Castle Acre, was also of the same opinion. He stated that his aversion to the system as then constituted was decided and uncompromis-

ing. The appendix to the report of Mr. Dennison, who was appointed a special assistant commissioner to inquire into the employment of women and children engaged in agriculture, contains a mass of evidence on the subject, and as it entirely coincides with all that I have been enabled to learn, I shall here transcribe some portions of it. The first is from the evidence given by Mrs. Sculfer, a labouring woman of Castle Acre:—"Fuller (the name of the gangsman) works boys and girls together; I know that this now is the case, because the lads come up and call my girls. The lads who work with the girls are all ages. I know the gangs generally bear a very bad character, but I don't know myself that any ill-conduct goes on in the fields. It's my belief that it's the ruin of 'em. They never settle to anything after it. My eldest girl has a thorough dislike to it. She almost always goes crying to her work. She would almost rather do anything than it. The children here generally go out so early that there can't be any schooling. There are many go out at six. They can 'quick' and single turnips, and they like the small ones for that better than the large ones. ... Fuller takes the children in a waggon; *then they ought to stop all night;* but my husband won't allow it, for they sleep in barns or anywheres—that's what they said. There's pretty work for boys and girls! We wouldn't agree for ours to stop by no means—not if they lost their work. ... Fuller keeps a flour-shop, and forces all his gang to deal with him. When my husband worked with him I was obliged to deal with him. My girls don't board themselves, else they'd be obliged to deal with him. He says he would give those who would deal with him 1d. a day more." Two other witnesses, a mother and daughter, spoke very ill of the gangs, of the bad language used in them, and of what had taken place in the fields; and with reference to the gangsmen, they said that some of them were as big blackguards as were anywhere to be found. Another witness, a young woman aged nineteen, stated, "If we're idle, he (the overseer) would mob us, or send us home: he daresn't beat us." One of the overseers himself stated—"I don't think there's anything done amiss as they come from work: they are so tired, poor things, and glad to get home after walking ten or a dozen miles. I believe that, owing to the gang system, 70 out of 100 girls are very imprudent girls—prostitutes. They sit working along with the lads in the day time, and make appointments at night. But still, if you was to come in among them when they're at work, you wouldn't know but that they were all very prudent women and girls. ... I shouldn't like myself to take a wife out of the gang." Another man, a labourer, said,

"Ganging is what leads 'em into so many bad ways. That's what causes many girls to be out of nights when they ought to be at home. My girl (11 years old) went five miles yesterday to her work, turniping; she set off between seven and eight; she walked; had a piece of bread before she went: she did not stop work in the middle of the day; ate nothing till she left off; she came home between three and four o'clock. Their walks are worse than their work. She is sometimes so tired she can't eat no victuals when she comes home. The gangs are very bad schools for manners; they have ruined many a girl: it is a very bad system for girls. I'm forced to let my daughter go, else I'm very much against it. I earn nothing myself. She does not like it at all; she hears so much blackguard bad language, and she's never used to hearing that at home. The overseers can't always see or hear them, if they're ever so sharp—they're often a long way off. It's the ruin of a girl to be in such a place as that. Gathering stones has hurt my girl's back at times. Pulling turnips is the hardest work; they get such a hold of the ground with their roots, when the land's strong, it's as much as we can do sometimes to get 'em out, pull as hard as we can pull. It blisters their hands, so that they can hardly touch anything. My child's hands have been blistered by it." Another of the witnesses stated: "My children's hands are so blistered pulling the turnips, that I've been obliged to tie them up every night this winter." The wages of the gangsmen or overseers is about 12s. or 15s. a week. Children of seven years old usually earn 3d. per day, the elder ones 4d., and women about 9d. The report also states that there were at that time 23 farms, containing altogether 18,000 acres, and situated in the surrounding parishes, upon which these gangs from Castle Acre were employed. Many of the evils attending the gang system which were rife in 1843 are still in existence, and appear to be inseparable from it, and it has clearly had its origin in the destruction of the cottages of the labourers, or in suffering them to fall into decay. Till the landowners shall have retraced their steps, it will be vain to expect that the system can be put an end to; and so long as the circumstances of the parish remain as they are, the gang system, however well regulated, must always be accompanied with some degree of hardship and immorality, and be destructive to the comforts and happiness of those who are employed.

From such an utter want of regard to the comfort and well-being of their labourers on the part of too many of the farmers and landed proprietors of both Norfolk and Suffolk, it is pleasing to revert, if but for a moment, to the laudable exertions of such persons as Messrs.

Ransome and May, of Ipswich, in improving the social, moral, and physical condition of their workmen. The number of men employed in the extensive iron works of Messrs. Ransome and May ranges from 1,000 to 1,400. During the last few years, upwards of 150 cottages have been built by the firm for the accommodation of their workmen. They are situated at a short distance from the factory, and are built for the most part of red brick; each contains at least four rooms; a small piece of ground is attached, though, from being in the immediate vicinity of a large town like Ipswich, the quantity of ground is of course rather limited; the houses are well drained, and there is a good supply of water. There is also a mechanics' institution and a school in connection with the factory: to the former there is attached a considerable library, to which any of the workmen have access upon payment of a small weekly subscription, and they have also the privilege of taking the books to their own residence to read. This attention to the interests of the workmen has been, I am informed, attended with the best possible results, and there is a very general and marked improvement in their social and moral condition.

In a great many instances, in Norfolk, the greatest estrangement of feeling exists between the agricultural labourers and their employers. This is produced on the part of the labourer, not more by the total want of interest displayed in his well-being by the employer, than by the numerous acts of petty unkindness which they are too often called upon to endure. In visiting the dwellings of the poor, and inquiring into their condition, you are constantly compelled, in addition to their tale of misery, to hear the recital of some acts of harshness and oppression. Among numerous instances of this kind which I have now lying before me, I select a parish, of which Mr. —— is the sole proprietor. This gentleman is possessed of a considerable amount of property— the whole of three parishes, and considerable portions of two others, belonging to him. He has also large estates in Suffolk and in Ireland. The houses in these parishes are generally of the most wretched character; and were it not for the existence of an extensive establishment for the manufacture of paper in the neighbourhood, the condition of the labouring classes would be miserable indeed. The first tale of distress which I heard from the poor people was that of a widow occupying a small two-roomed cottage. Two of her sons were grown up young men; her daughter was also grown up; and they were all in the habit of sleeping in one and the same room. The husband of the widow had been shot by some poachers, having been mistaken by them for one of the squire's gamekeepers, and she was left with three children, the eldest of whom was, I believe, about ten years of age. By unremitting exertions, the poor woman had been enabled to bring up her family, without being any burden to the parish. The squire allowed her to live in the house rent free. At length, through old age and illness, she was compelled to leave her employment, and to apply to the parish for assistance. Two shillings per week were allowed her by the guardians; the squire refused to assist her; and now, when upwards of 70 years of age, he has called upon her, either to pay him rent for the wretched hovel in which she had previously dwelt rent-free, or leave the parish altogether. Another case which I was compelled to hear from the poor people was also that of a poor widow, residing in the same parish. Her husband had worked for seventeen years for the squire. Through some accident which he met with, he was laid up for some time, and finally died, and he was buried by what is called "a shake of the hat;" but his employer would not give one farthing towards the expenses. A large farmer, also residing in the immediate vicinity, for whom the deceased had worked three or four years, desirous of treading in the footsteps of his landlord, refused to assist in any way towards his burial. The curate of the parish gave up his fee, headed the subscription, and the poor man was buried. Some few months after, a friend of the poor widow got a memorial drawn up, which she intended to take round among the neighbours, to see if it was possible to raise some small sum with which to assist her friend. The curate headed the list with a contribution. The poor woman subscribed the same amount, and immediately started off to the hall, to obtain the squire's subscription. The kind-hearted woman was "abused" for her interference, and told to send the widow up herself. The widow accordingly went, but returned no richer. Arrived at home, "I hardly knowed what to do," said she; "I felt almost as if I was going mad; I burst out crying, and oh, sir, if I had only knowed what I was to get at the hall before I went, I would have gone without a bit of victuals for a fortnight, sooner than I'd a gone a near him." The squire's son was on a visit to the hall; and hearing of this distressing case, generously despatched one of the servants with a liberal sum for the poor widow. The high esteem in which the son is held by the poor people, speaks volumes for his liberality and generosity. "If we can only hit upon the young'un," said a poor old man to me, "there's no case of distress but he'll do something for."

As I before stated, the cottages in Taverham parish are in a miserable condition. The poor people can get no water, except what they obtain from the stream, into which all the refuse water of the paper-mill flows. There is a well, but it has been for some time out of repair: the iron work belonging to it is completely useless. The cost of putting it in repair would be about £2. The proprietors of the paper-mills offered £1, the poor people raised 10s., and the squire was applied to to assist with the remaining 10s. The application was refused, and to this day the decayed iron and frame work bear witness to the great amount of suffering and privation which in this, as in other parishes, is endured by the agricultural labourers, where their interests are neglected by those whose duty it is to assist in ameliorating their condition. One of the guardians of the parish, and an extensive farmer in the district, appears to be equally desirous of distinguishing himself by the harshness of his conduct towards the labourer. How far he has succeeded in his object, may be ascertained from the following facts, which came under my notice. A poor man, somewhat advanced in years, was employed upon the farm at 6s. a week; he was principally employed in "mucking" for wheat. A short time since he was sent by his master to the residence of a clergyman, a distance of ten miles, with a live pig. Upon his arrival at his destination he received some refreshment and a shilling for himself. On the following Saturday, when the poor man was paid his wages, instead of receiving 6s., as usual, he received but 5s.—the shilling that he had received from the clergyman being stopped from his wretched pittance of 6s. a week.

It would be scarcely possible to conceive anything more wretched than was the condition of this place a few years since. There was no school in the parish; the walls of the churchyard were broken down; a roadway existed through it; and some portions, I was told, were even occasionally planted with potatoes; two of the bells of the church had been sold to defray the current expenses of the church, for the squire would not subscribe anything towards it, nor allow a church-rate to be made. The living is worth £300, and the patronage is vested in the squire and the bishop alternately, the last appointment being with the squire. The rector is non-resident, the present curate receiving £80 per annum. He has only been appointed a short time, and has already effected a great amount of good by the establishment of schools for both adults and children within the parish. "But if it had not been for the gentlemen at the paper mills," said he, "I do not know what I should have done; and in cases of distress I have no one else to apply to."

The adjoining parish of Felthorpe presents a marked contrast with respect to the exertions made to improve the condition of the people. A system of allotments for the labourer is there carried out; there is a horticultural society for giving rewards to the cottagers, while employment is afforded to the poor people by a most liberal-minded lady, Mrs. Fellowes, who employs them in knitting stockings and other things, pays them a certain price for the knitting, and then distributes among the poor people the articles which they may have made; and by one and all of the poor her name is held in the highest esteem.

The system of granting allotments to the labourer has been attended with an incalculable amount of good in the counties of Norfolk, Suffolk, and Essex. The effect of giving the labourer a small piece of land upon which he can grow his own vegetables, and perhaps a coomb or two of wheat, has been to wean him from the ale-house, from the ill example of bad company, and to give him something akin to a feeling of independence, while it has taught him to feel that he has a small stake in the country. Generally speaking, the farmers are opposed to the system. There are, however, many exceptions to the contrary: they consider that the labourers will be apt to husband their strength for their own allotments, and that they will not be able to get a fair amount of work out of them. In many cases the farmers expressly prohibit the labourers from growing any wheat on the allotments. The reason given to me by a farmer for this prohibition was, that the labourer might frequently be able "to make free with my corn, and sell it along with his own to the miller; but if the miller knows that the men don't grow corn when they come to him to sell any, they'll know at once that they haven't come by it fairly." If suspicions of this kind were allowed to prevail generally, the obvious effect would be to prevent the labourer producing anything whatever upon his allotment. From all that I have seen of the labourers themselves, I think that suspicions of this kind are generally unfounded. In many cases the farmer, suffering himself to be actuated by his suspicions, also forbids the labourer from keeping either pigs or poultry, lest they should be kept at his expense. When once, however, the labourer is in possession of his allotment, and is able to procure a few things from it, his condition becomes at once improved, and the temptation to dishonesty is removed; and so far as experience goes, it entirely supports this view of the case. Mr. Cooper, a large farmer of Halesworth, in Suffolk, informed me that the farmers' club of that place had recently carried out the allotment system to a very great extent—£40 had been given away by the society during the present year in prizes to the labourers, for either the best cultivated allotments, or for the finest production. Since the introduction of the system, the minds of the labourers have been greatly improved, and throughout the whole hundred, consisting of 54 parishes, they have not had a single prosecution for felony during the last twelve months. In distributing the prizes to the labourers, Mr. Cooper, the chairman of the club, informed me that he told the labourers that since they had been placed in a position to know the value of property by its possession, they had learned to become honest. He congratulated them upon the result, and trusted that they would continue to act upon the same good principle. A unanimous expression of "we will," from all the labourers present, evinced at once their gratitude and their resolution to adopt the good advice thus given them. Mr. Johnson, who is the banker of the town of Halesworth, and also a magistrate, informed me that since the introduction of the allotment system, there had been a very general improvement in the condition of the people, and that at the last quarter-sessions there was not a single case of felony to be disposed of. In the county of Norfolk similar good effects have been produced by the allotments. The Rev. Mr. Gurden, of Cranworth, stated, that when he first came to reside in his parish, he was struck with the discreditable appearance of the poor land, which had been set out at the time of the enclosure for the benefit of the poor, while the labourers were perambulating the several parishes in search of employment. He called a meeting of the parish, and succeeded in hiring some of this land, which he divided into portions of half an acre each, and let them to the labourers. A strong prejudice existed among the farmers to the plan; but he felt it his duty to persevere, and guard, as well as he could, against some of the evils which he was told would be certain to result from the experiment. Each tenant was bound by his agreement to keep a pig for not less than six months in the year, and to apply the manure to the ground. Upon inquiry into the account of the income and expenditure of the half-acre, he found that the labourers had, in one or two cases, cleared £5 during the year, after payment of all expenses, and had fatted four pigs. No doubt, whatever, he adds, could exist of the general benefits arising from the allotment system, while the thankfulness of the poor who cultivate the allotments testifies to the good opinion entertained of them by the labourers. In

Essex, also, the system of allotments is very generally carried out, and some of the cottagers' gardens are admirably cultivated.

The produce of the allotments is in some cases wonderfully large. I have already referred to the case of £5 having been cleared off the half-acre in one year, and four pigs having been fatted. I have been informed of several cases where wheat had been grown at the rate of from 16 to 18 coombs per acre upon these allotments in the neighbourhood of Stradbroke, in Suffolk. The value of a small piece of land to the labourer may be estimated from the statement of a Mr. Sillett, a tradesman residing near Saxmundham, to the effect that upon two acres of land he had been enabled to support himself, his wife, and two children, and to make a clear profit besides of £25 15s. per acre. The account appeared to me incredible, and I took some trouble to inquire into the accuracy of the statement; and from all I could learn it was perfectly correct. Many of the labourers to whom I have spoken upon the subject have said that, without their allotments, they do not know whatever they should have done last winter when out of work. One of them stated that he had lived almost entirely during the winter months on the produce of his "bit of ground." "When I comes home," said he, "at night, my missus always has something ready for me out of the garden, and I fancy my *taturs* and cabbage, and everything, is ever so much sweeter and better off my own ground than if we'd got to buy 'em. I growed eight bushels of *taturs* last year, and they served us nearly all the winter. Then this here little bit I keeps for radishes, *inguns*, and them sort of things, and in the summer it's very nice to have a few of 'em with your tea—it relishes it, like. Then in the little bit of ground at home we grows a few flowers, and they look very pretty, you know. Sometimes my missus cuts a few, and puts 'em in a mug with some water to 'em, and then we can see 'em in the room without going into the garden, and then you know, sir, it does you good to look at 'em, and know that you growed 'em yourself." I have met with several instances in which the labourers have given expression to their feelings in almost the same words. Many of them have informed me that they have been enabled to pay the rent of their cottages out of their allotments.

But even with respect to his allotment, the labourer has not unfrequently to complain of the difficulties which are thrown in his way. The rent which they pay for these allotments is in too many cases greatly above the value of the neighbouring property. Many of them pay as much as 20s. and even 25s. for the quarter of an acre, while land of the same character is let in the neighbourhood at even less than £2 per acre. In the Hartismere union, in Suffolk, there are six acres of land belonging to the parish; the land is not worth more than £2 per acre, including rates and tithes. The guardians, however, have divided it into twenty-four allotments, which they let at the rate of £3 per acre to the poor people. The Rev. Mr. Knevitt, chaplain to the union, states that during the last four years that the land has been allotted there has not been a single instance of default in the payment of the rent. In several places horticultural societies are established in connection with the allotment system, the object of which is to distribute rewards to the cottagers for the best articles of different kinds which they can produce upon their allotments. One of the most extensive societies of this kind is the "Eye Horticultural Society," in the northern part of Suffolk, of which Sir Edward Kerrison, Bart., is the patron, and a considerable amount was this year distributed in prizes to the cottagers.

Admitting, for a moment, to the fullest extent, the advantages which are generally claimed for the large-farm system, and that even the occupiers had gained the point for which they had so long been striving, viz., that of producing the greatest quantity at the least possible cost, still it certainly does appear to be a matter of regret, that the labourer should be so completely debarred from all the means of cultivating the land upon his own account, and of raising himself to a position of comparative independence. As an invariable rule, the agricultural labourer commences his career as a weekly labourer; and, whatever may be his talents and industry, he must inevitably end his days as a labourer, or, when unfitted through old age to continue his work, die as a pauper.

In a future letter I shall have occasion to refer to several instances of this kind which have come under my knowledge. Without wishing to speculate upon the advantages which would ensue from opening up to the labourer some prospect of his being able to rise in the world, or to be admitted into the ranks of the toiling and industrious, but rapidly diminishing, class of small farmers, there is no doubt but that the condition of the labourer would not be worse under such a system than it is at present; and it is not a very extravagant opinion to form—seeing the results which have already attended the partial adoption of the allotment system—that a more industrious, sober, and intelligent class of labourers would be produced, and that a state of greater contentment, prosperity, and happiness would exist in the agricultural districts than are at present to be found in them, if such a system were more generally adopted. To adopt the words of a gentleman residing in Suffolk, who has paid considerable attention to the subject, "Let the labourers feel that they have a stake in society, and the great discontent, want, misery, crime, and incendiarism which pervade the county, will recede like a mist before the morning sun— many an Eden will spring up in the desert, and many a human being will become a better and a happier man."

For ability and practical skill in the various occupations of husbandry the peasantry of Norfolk, Suffolk, and some parts of Essex have few competitors who could excel them. The ploughing of Norfolk is, perhaps, superior to that of any other county in England. The proficiency of the labourer in this department is, perhaps, in a great measure owing to the very frequent use of the plough upon the land. Notwithstanding the neglect and ungenerous treatment which they have experienced too often at the hands of their employers, and the small advance which has been made towards affording them a good education, they are, generally speaking, a manly and industrious class of persons, and are possessed of a considerable amount of practical intelligence and skill. Towards each other they possess a considerable amount of good feeling, and are always anxious to afford assistance to the utmost extent of their means. Many instances of self-denying charity upon their part have come under my notice. I might refer, upon this point, to the case of a poor woman residing at Woolpits, in Suffolk, who, with tears in her eyes, was telling me of the want and wretchedness of many of her neighbours. Her husband was in constant work, and the cottage she lived in was left to her by her father. Her sole employment appeared to be that of looking up cases of distress, and endeavouring to afford every assistance in her power. "I know the condition," said she, "of a'most all the people about here, and many of 'em go through a world of trouble, but there are some a great deal worse off than they are about here. In Rattlesdeen there's a *hape* of people who are very *wanting;* oh dear! that's a great poverty place indeed. My poor dear mother knowed the circumstances of all the poor people about, and when the poor creature died—and she was above seventy when she died—a'most the last word she said was, 'Betsy, don't forget to take the poor folk next door a bit of tay tomorrow, and a 'crem of sugar, if they want it;' and ever since she's dead—and I pray God her good soul is in heaven—I have always done all as ever laid in my power to help the poor people, though I can't afford to do much. The poor dear clargyman who was here afore this one used to leave it all to my mother. Poor dear man! he is gone too, and if a good soul ever goes to heaven I'm sure he's there—that I am. When the new clargyman came, he asked me to do the same for the poor people as my mother used to do, and I said I would; and many and many's the score shilling that I've got out of the 'sacrament money' for the poor people. Afore I go to church on Sundays I always consider in myself who's the people that's the most desarving of it and as wants it most; and then I pray to God to put it in my heart what to spake when I go to ask the clargyman for the money. Last Sunday of all, I got 9s. from him. There was two shillings for a poor man that had lost his wife and got nine children. There was a shilling for a poor man that was nearly blinded with some dust he'd got in his eyes when *throshing*. There was two shillings and some wine for a poor woman as was just confined, and hadn't a bit of clothes for the babby till I got some from the clargyman's wife. I borrowed the loan of a few little things from my daughter that's married. There was three shillings for two poor *widur* women, and then there was a shilling for a woman with a large family as had her husband lave her; and I gave the poor woman as was confined a shilling out of my own pocket, and made her a little stew with some bones like—I sharn't lose any thing, I know, for it—I'm so plased to do a little good if I can. Lor' bless you, the poor dear people all round here look up to me as if I was their mother. I'd go through fire and water to sarve 'em, poor things—that I would. I hope and pray God that something will be done for the poor people."

In the Mulford and Lochryland hundred this charitable feeling on the part of the poor people towards each other is turned to useful account by the guardians of the poor. The poor-law is there administered simply with the view of affording partial assistance to the applicants for relief, by giving them something to help them, as it were, over their difficulties; and is not, as in other places, calculated to remove all their immediate wants. Thus, when an applicant comes before the board and makes out a strong and pressing case for relief, all that is given is something to help him, and not anything sufficient to support him entirely till the next board day. In support of this mode of administering relief, the guardians contend that it tends to keep alive the charitable feelings of the poor people, and that when they know that any of their neighbours have not sufficient to support them, they are more likely to render them assistance than when they know they can obtain a sufficiency from the parish. I was informed, by one of the overseers, that the system had been found to work admirably well for many years, and they had no wish whatever to alter it for the more general mode of administering relief. "The condition of the poor people," said he, "is far better in our hundred than in any parish in Suffolk." As to the policy of such a system, whether sound or unsound, I have nothing to say; it is sufficient for me that it is founded upon the display of what I have very generally observed throughout the three counties of Norfolk, Suffolk, and Essex, viz., the kind and charitable feelings of the poor people themselves.

Having touched upon the question of pauperism and relief, I shall before I conclude briefly refer to the state of pauperism in the three counties. Since the new poor-law came into operation—notwithstanding some few objections with respect to the workhouse test—an improved state of feeling has been brought about between the employer and the employed. The greatest possible abuses formerly existed with respect to what was termed the "scale allowance." "I have known" says the Rev. Mr. Knevitt, chaplain of the Oxne Union, "men come before the board in the rudest possible manner, with their hats on and pipes in their mouths, and insolently demand their scale allowance." The scale allowance was the amount in flour or in money which the applicant would be entitled to, and was calculated according to the number of his family, one stone of flour being the proportion for the man, the same for the wife, and half a stone for each of the children; and as soon as a man was out of work he became entitled to this allowance. "In one case that I knew," said Mr. Knevitt, "a man applied to the board for his scale allowance, amounting to 7s. 6d. The overseer offered the man 5s.; and a most undignified scene took place between the board, who wanted to cut him down, and the man, who was determined to have his full amount. After contesting the point for some time, the parties agreed to split the difference, and the man received 6s. 3d. When the money was given to the man, he told the overseer that if he had not paid him his allowance he would have gone home with him to his own house, and compelled him to find a bed for himself and family till he could go to the magistrates in the morning, who would be sure to give an order for the payment of the money." This system has been completely done away with, and the poor people now know that if they want any relief, they will be unable to get it unless they go into the house. The consequence of this alteration has been, that many of the most idle and dissolute characters have been compelled to settle down to work of some kind or other, as it would not at all square with their wishes to come into the workhouse. The numbers of persons of both sexes and of all ages receiving in-door relief on the 29th of September, 1849, were—in Norfolk, 2,935; Suffolk, 2,524; Essex, 2,610; at the same period of 1848, the numbers were—Norfolk, 2,932; Suffolk, 2,498; Essex, 2,060; being an increase over the corresponding quarter of last year—in Norfolk, of 3; Suffolk, 26; and in Essex, 550. The amount expended for out-door relief for the same period was—1849, Norfolk, £2,219; Suffolk, £1,541; Essex, £1,503; in 1848—Norfolk, £2,315; Suffolk, £1,573; Essex, £1,393; being a decrease in Norfolk, for 1849, as compared with 1848, of £96; and in Suffolk of £32; and an increase in Essex of £110. From the mode in which the pauper returns are made up it is impossible to ascertain the number of persons receiving these several amounts of out-door relief, as the same person may probably apply more than once in the year, and in each case of his application he is set down as a fresh applicant. A man who applies for his wife and three children will, upon this principle, if he applies four times in the year, be entered as twenty paupers. The numbers of able-bodied poor who were receiving in-door relief on the 29th of September, 1849, were—Norfolk, 142; Suffolk, 166; Essex, 99. At the same period of 1848 the numbers were—Norfolk, 116; Suffolk, 101; Essex, 85; being an increase in 1849, as compared with 1848, of 26 in Norfolk, 65 in Suffolk, and 14 in Essex. The average number of able-bodied in-door poor for the quarter ending the same period in 1849 was—Norfolk, 155; Suffolk, 174; Essex, 100. In 1848 the numbers were—Norfolk, 127; Suffolk, 119; Essex, 69; showing an increase, on the average of the quarter, of 28 for Norfolk, 55 for Suffolk, and 31 for Essex.

The workhouses which I visited in each of the three counties are, for the most part, excellently conducted. The best managed of any which I have seen is the one at Chelmsford, in Essex. It is built to accommodate 450 persons. There are five acres of ground in connection with the house, which are cultivated by the inmates, and produce a supply of vegetables for the whole establishment. A most perfect system of classification is carried out. There are two classes of able-bodied men—the well-behaved and the troublesome; a third for the aged men; a fourth for the idiots; a fifth for single women with illegitimate children; a sixth, able-bodied women; a seventh, aged women; the boys and girls form two separate classes; and there are three divisions for the sick; one for girls and women of bad character; one for men, and another for women. The bed-rooms are all remarkably clean and well-ventilated. The bedsteads are of iron; and during the day-time the bedding and bed-clothes of the boy's and men's beds are neatly rolled up, and placed at the foot of the bedsteads, in order to allow of a thorough ventilation. The chapel is a commodious apartment; a partition running down the centre separates the sexes, and is so constructed as to afford the chaplain a view of the whole of the persons present. The whole of the cooking is performed by an extensive system of steam apparatus. The perfect cleanliness, order, and decorum of the establishment and its inmates were such as to reflect the highest credit upon the able and intelligent master of the workhouse, Mr. Beckham. His constant attention to the inmates, and the interest which he takes in promoting their comfort, are such as to entitle him to their warmest thanks, and many of the paupers spoke to me in the highest terms of his kindness and assiduous attention to their wants. The whole of the inmates were remarkably healthy—indeed there was no case of illness in the house, except that of two persons who had been brought in ill a few days previously. The children, especially, looked particularly ruddy and well, and the mode in which they dealt with their dinners showed that in their catalogue of wants want of appetite had no place. The subjoined dietary table will show how greatly superior is the food of the paupers to that of great numbers of the labourers. The number of inmates in this workhouse on the 6th of December was 285; upon the same day in 1848 the numbers were 338; and in 1847, 330; showing a diminution, as compared with 1848, of 53, and with 1847, of 45.

ABLE-BODIED MEN AND WOMEN.

	Breakfast.		Dinner.						Supper.	
	Bread.	Porridge.	Cooked Meat.	Vegetables.	Bread.	Cheese.	Suet or Rice Pudding.	Soup.	Bread.	Cheese.
	Oz.	Pints.	Oz.	Oz.	Oz.	Oz.	Oz.	Pts.	Oz.	Oz.
Sunday:										
Men	8	1½	..	..	8	1½	..	..	8	1
Women ..	6	1	..	..	7	1½	..	..	6	1
Monday:										
Men	8	1½	5	12 } or { 4	..	..	..	8	1
Women ..	6	1	5	12 } { 4	..	..	..	6	1
Tuesday:										
Men	8	1½	..	..	4	..	..	1½	8	1
Women ..	6	1	..	..	4	..	..	1½	6	1
Wednesday:										
Men	8	1½	..	..	..	..	14	..	8	1
Women ..	6	1	..	..	..	..	14	..	6	1
Thursday:										
Men	8	1½	5	12 } or { 4	..	..	..	8	1
Women ..	6	1	5	12 } { 4	..	..	..	6	1
Friday:										
Men	8	1½	..	..	4	..	..	1½	8	1
Women ..	6	1	..	..	4	..	..	1½	6	1
Saturday:										
Men	8	1½	..	..	..	..	14	..	8	1
Women ..	6	1	..	..	..	..	14	..	6	1

INFIRM MEN AND WOMEN.

	Breakfast.		Dinner.						Supper.	
	Bread.	Tea or Coffee.*	Cooked Meat.	Vegetables.	Bread.	Cheese.	Suet or Rice Pudding.	Soup.	Bread.	Tea or Coffee.*
	Oz.	Pint.	Oz.	Oz.	Oz.	Oz.	Oz.	Pts.	Oz.	Pint.
Sunday:										
Men	7	1	..	..	7	1½	..	..	7	1
Women ..	6	1	..	..	7	1½	..	..	6	1
Monday:										
Men	7	1	5	12 } or { 4		..	..	..	7	1
Women ..	6	1	5	12 } or { 4		..	..	..	6	1
Tuesday:										
Men	7	1	..	..	4	..	..	1½	7	1
Women ..	6	1	..	..	4	..	..	1½	6	1
Wednesday:										
Men	7	1	..	..	..	..	14	..	7	1
Women ..	6	1	..	..	..	..	14	..	6	1
Thursday:										
Men	7	1	5	12 } or { 4		..	..	..	7	1
Women ..	6	1	5	12 } or { 4		..	..	..	6	1
Friday:										
Men	7	1	..	..	4	..	..	1½	7	1
Women ..	6	1	..	..	4	..	..	1½	6	1
Saturday:										
Men	7	1	..	..	..	..	14	..	7	1
Women ..	6	1	..	..	..	..	14	..	6	1

* The tea or coffee to be sweetened with an allowance of sugar, after a rate not exceeding half an ounce of sugar to each pint of tea or coffee.

"And we do hereby empower the guardians to allow to each infirm person, in addition, an allowance of butter not exceeding six ounces per week.

"And we do hereby further order and direct, that children under the age of nine years, resident in the said workhouse, shall be fed, dieted, and maintained with such food and in such manner as the said guardians shall direct; and that boys of the age of nine years, and under the age of fourteen years, and girls above the age of nine years, shall be allowed the same quantities as are prescribed in the above table for able-bodied women."

The Morning Chronicle, Saturday, December 29, 1849.

LABOUR AND THE POOR.

THE RURAL DISTRICTS.

[FROM OUR SPECIAL CORRESPONDENT.]

NORFOLK, SUFFOLK, AND ESSEX.

Letter XXI.

Of the three counties above enumerated Essex is the most southern. The Thames forms its southern boundary, the German Ocean washes its eastern coast, Suffolk and a portion of Cambridge bound it on the north, while the county of Hertford and the eastern portion of Middlesex form together its western boundary. It is in shape an irregular four-sided figure; the distance between its extreme north-west and north-east portions is about 53 miles—from the north-east to the south-west, about the same—and from north-east to south-west, measuring along its water frontier, the length would be 63 miles. Its area is 1,533 square miles, or about 981,120 acres. Its proximity to the metropolis affords advantages to this county which are not possessed by any other in the eastern districts, and its inland and coast navigation gives the greatest facilities for the conveyance of its agricultural produce, and for the supply of those requisites which are indispensably necessary to the cultivation of the soil.

The principal rivers of Essex are the Stour, the Colne, the Blackwater, the Crouch, the Chelmer, and the Lea. The Eastern Counties and the North-Eastern railways traverse the county—the former along the western side, the latter through the more central portions, while various branches from the main line connect the principal towns. The people pride themselves—and not without some reason—on the excellence of their highway and turnpike roads. The soil varies very considerably: its principal substratum is chalk, which passes beneath nearly the whole extent of the county, showing itself at Saffron Walden in the north, and at Grays Thurrock on the Thames, at which place there are some very extensive lime-works. A strong tenacious soil, chiefly composed of London clay, is superimposed upon the chalk formation, varying in thickness from 100 to 300 feet. Loam, gravel, sand, clay, and various other strata, are found in almost every variety of admixture. Along the course of the principal rivers there is a considerable quantity of fine alluvial soil.

An extensive chalky-clay district is found to prevail round Dunmow, to the boundaries of Cambridgeshire and Hertfordshire, to Epping, and nearly to Chelmsford. The mixed-soil district extends throughout nearly the whole of that portion of the county between Colchester and Harwich, while the heavy clay is principally in the neighbourhood of the Dengey hundred. Along the shore of the Thames the country is flat, marshy, and uninteresting; in the central and northern parts it is considerably undulated and well wooded. Some of the hills rise to a considerable height; among which may be mentioned those about Billericay, Highbeach, Danbury, and Langdon-hills. Mr. Young, in his "Survey," speaking of the latter of these places, says—"Such a prodigious valley, everywhere bounded with the finest verdure, and intersected with numberless hedges and woods, appears beneath you that it is past description. The Thames, winding through it full of ships, and bounded by the hills of Kent—nothing can exceed it, except that which Hannibal exhibited to his disconsolate troops when he bade them behold the glories of the Italian plains."

Essex is famous for its wheat, which is always quoted in the markets, with that of Kent, higher than that of any other district. Large quantities of barley are also grown in the county, which for its malting properties is not excelled by any elsewhere. This barley is principally sold to maltsters at Stortford, Sawbridgeworth, and other places, and is usually sold in the London markets as "Ware malt."

A considerable diminution took place in the rate of increase in the population of Essex during the ten years between 1831 and 1841, as compared with the previous decades. In 1801 the population was 226,437; in 1811 it amounted to 252,478, being an increase of 11 per cent.; in 1821 there was an increase of 15 per cent., the numbers then being 289,424; in 1831 the numbers were 317,507, being an increase of 10 per cent.—while in the subsequent ten years, up to 1841, the increase was only at the rate of 8.6 per cent., the population of the county then being 344,979, or about 4.4 per cent. below the average of the whole country. Of the population, as returned in 1841, there were under 20 years of age, males 81,284, females 81,076; above 20 years of age, males 91,064, females 91,555. The number of persons born in the county was 297,671; born elsewhere 47,308. The number of inhabited houses was 67,618, which would give a proportion of about 5.1 persons to each house. There were within the county 5,121 farmers and graziers, who employed among them 43,672 agricultural labourers of both sexes and of all ages—being about 8.5 labourers to each occupier. The rate of wages per annum paid to each was on an average about £20 7s.—the aggregate sum paid for wages being, as near as could be ascertained, about £904,000. Although Essex is principally an agricultural county, still employment is afforded within it to a large number of persons who do not come under the designation of agricultural labourers—such as straw-plait workers, weavers, fishermen, shipwrights, and others.

In the district around Castle Hedingham, and including Halstead, Sudbury, Clare, and Haverhill, on the borders of Suffolk, an enormous amount of straw-plaiting is carried on. In fact there is scarcely a cottage in this district in which this branch of industry is not exercised. Till within the last two or three months the trade has been somewhat slack; there is, however, at present a very great demand for it. Many merchants from Luton, in Bedfordshire, I was informed, were in the habit of coming to Castle Hedingham to purchase the straw-plait. For the best kinds of work the makers get 3s. 6d. a score, and one of the best hands can make a score and a half in the week. For the inferior kind of work the rate of pay varies from 8d. to 10d. and 1s. per score. The earnings of children and girls may be taken to be from 3d. to 4d. per day. These, as well as boys, are principally employed upon the coarser kinds. The straw is usually purchased of the farmers in the neighbourhood at 6d. a bundle, being, in quantity, about as much as a person can conveniently carry. The rate of wages paid to the agricultural labourer in this district is wretchedly low, not more than 6s. or 7s. per week, and were it not for the straw plait, the people would generally be in a far worse condition than they are at present. When the plaiting is depressed, a considerable quantity of work is done by the women for the cheap tailors of London, Colchester, and other places, who send the different articles to Castle Hedingham and other places in the neighbourhood to have them made up. I inquired of several of the workpeople the rate of wages paid for this kind of work, and received among others the following statement:—
"I am generally pretty well employed for one house at Colchester. The things are all given out ready to make. I get for making a pair of the best cloth trowsers from 10d. to 1s. We are obliged to put the best of work in them, or we should have them thrown back on our hands.

When we first did the work, two or three years ago, we didn't use to put such good work in them, but they get more particular now. We are obliged to sew them all with double thread. You must work very hard indeed to make a pair in a day. I don't believe that there's many as can make a pair in a day. For fustian or cord trowsers we get 9d. We used to get 10d., but they've taken us a little off lately. A pair of this sort of trowsers takes us almost as long to make as a pair of cloth ones—the stuff is generally so hard. Sometimes I am employed in making small coats for boys, and I generally get from 1s. to 1s. 3d. for them, but I can't make one of them in a day, do all I will. For a pair of cord breeches the usual price is from 10d. to 1s.—the same as for the cloth trowsers. There is always constant work to be got at it, except just at this time of the year, when they're taking stock. They are nearly all women who work at the tailoring about here. I don't know of any man who is employed at it in this place. Mr. —— came down from London, or somebody from him, with a lot of things, and said he would send regularly, but he didn't. I think our prices was too high for him, and besides, we was working for Mr. ——, of Colchester, and we didn't like to give up a certainty for an uncertainty."

Essex, some years since, was famous for its silk and worsted manufactures; Colchester was known for its "bays" and "says," and Lindsey for its "Lindsey woolsey." These manufactures have now almost entirely passed away. There are, however, several mills at Braintree, Bocking, Halstead, Coggeshall, and Colchester, for the manufacture of silk. The principal manufacturers are the Messrs. Courtauld, who have a mill at Braintree for "throwing" the silk, at which 180 hands are employed; one at Halstead, at which 800 or 900 persons are employed; and a third at Bocking, employing not less than 500 persons. Upon making application to the different manufacturers of Braintree as to the rates of wages, I was refused any information whatever, and in one instance my inquiry was met by the counter question, whether I was prepared to make up any deficiency to the workpeople, as that would be the only condition upon which any information would be vouchsafed. As I was unable to procure what I desired from the employers, I at once proceeded in search of some of the weavers themselves. The first person of this class that I discovered was one who was then engaged upon some work at his own house for the parties who had requested me to make up deficiencies in the people's wages. His statement was as follows:—"I am at present at work on the fancy silk, with a Jacquard loom. Trade has been wonderfully bad with us for the last two years, but I'm in hopes it's about to take a turn for the better now. The piece that I've got to weave will be about 54 yards long when wove, and I shall get £2 5s. for it. I expect to finish it in a month. Out of that I shall have to pay one shilling a week for winding, three-pence a week for the hire of the loom, and if I didn't work at home I should have to pay 1s. a week for loom hire. Then the oil to burn at night will be 6d. a week at least, for I know I must work fifteen hours a day to get it done in the month. The piece that I'm at work on is what some people call a 'shotted' silk, it is a green cane and pink shoot; they pay extra for that in London, but they don't give us nothing extra here for it. Well, out of my £2 5s., I shall have to take off 4s. for winding, 1s. for loom hire, and 2s. at least for oil—that makes 7s.; 7s. from 45s. leaves 38s.—that's 9s. 6d. a week. I'm certain that what I've told you is quite correct, and if you ask any other weaver, I am sure he will tell you the same as I have done. I should think there are about 350 hand-loom weavers in Braintree, and perhaps 150 in Halstead. When a man is at work on the richer kinds of satins, figured ones and that, he can earn more than at the plain ones. I dare say he could earn 12s. a week if he was to work hard and stick close to it. I pay 3s. a week rent, and have only five children." This account of the man's earnings was fully corroborated by the statement of another person who was employed upon precisely the same kind of fabric.

The next person I called upon was a weaver of silk handkerchiefs. He stated that it would take him, working very hard, four days to make a dozen of them, the price for which would be 10s. or 11s., and the winding would cost him 9d. a dozen, and the oil perhaps 6d. a week. The rent of his cottage, containing four rooms, was 3s. a week, and the poor-rate 6s. a quarter. He had been but recently married, and had one child. He was at present in pretty constant work, but had had to "play" a good deal previously. Last spring he "played seven weeks right off," and there was always great delay in getting the cane. After some trouble I succeeded in finding a velvet weaver. The statement of the young woman employed upon the velvet was to the effect that the trade was very slack. That she was "the only velvet going in the place." That the piece upon which she was at work would, when finished, be about 30 yards in length, and that the price for it would be 2s. 10d. per yard, and that by working very late at it she could make four yards in the week. The father of the young woman employed on the velvet was weaving black silk scarfs (for gentlemen), of two yards in length, for which he would get 9s. per dozen. He was able to make a dozen in the week, but frequently had to "play" a great deal. At Sudbury, in Suffolk, the price for making velvet does not exceed 1s. 6d. per yard, and some of it is as low as 1s.

With respect to the persons employed at the mills on power-looms and otherwise, I succeeded in obtaining the following information from several persons in the mills:—"I was at work," said a young woman, "as winder at the mill ever since I was 16 years old. I get 3s. and 3s. 3d. a week. I don't think there are any get higher than I do, and a good many I know get less; some 1s. 6d., some 1s. 9d. a week. They won't let any one work at the mill under twelve years old, if they know it." A young woman employed in the mill at "picking" informed me that she got 5s. a week; the "throwsters" can earn from 4s. to 5s. per week, the "drawers" from 3s. to 4s. No persons are allowed to work as drawers under fourteen years of age. The "plug winders," whose duty it is to wind the silk on the "plugs," are the best paid, and get from 6s. to 7s. a week; some of the best hands get even as much as 8s., but there are not many of them. One of the weavers employed at the Halstead mill said that she "could earn in weaving crape from 4s. to 6s. per week—5s. was about the average." At Coggeshall and at Colchester the rate of wages was similar to those above mentioned. I should regret to give publicity to erroneous statements on the subject of the wages of the weavers; but as all assistance was denied me by the employers, the only course open to me was to obtain the statements of the persons employed. I have reason to believe, from the manner in which they gave the information, and the evident desire on their part to avoid anything like misrepresentation, that their accounts were substantially correct.

Some portions of the population of Essex derive employment from oyster-dredging—the principal places where this occupation is carried on being, Donald, Rowbridge, Brightlingsea, Wivenhoe, and Colchester. About 160 boats are engaged in the oyster trade, and about 500 men. The persons so employed are mostly freemen of the river Colne, and they are allowed to dredge in the river for a certain quantity every morning—a portion of the proceeds being handed over to the widows of the freemen of Colchester and the other places where the trade is carried on. Another portion of the produce is set apart for the boat, and the remainder is divided among the men. In the oyster season, which lasts from August to April, their earnings will average about 12s. per week. At the close of the season the men usually start off with their boats to Guernsey, Jersey, and the Channel

Islands to dredge for "spat" (which is the young oysters). When a sufficient quantity is obtained it is brought home and deposited in beds in the river, where it remains for three or four years before the oysters are allowed to be dredged up, as it takes that period to allow the oyster to arrive at a proper size for the market. The small oyster known as the "native" is the sort indigenous to the river—being, as their name implies, "natives" of the river Colne. Upwards of 500 persons are almost constantly employed in connection with the port of Harwich in dredging for stone, which is very extensively used in the manufacture of cement. When the weather is favourable the men usually earn from 4s. to 4s. 6d. per day; and the wages of the persons employed in the manufacture of the cement vary from 14s. to 16s. per week. There is probably no town in the whole of the three Eastern counties where the population are, generally speaking, so well off as at Harwich. When any of the people are out of work, they have only to go out on the sands and collect oysters, whelks, "pin-patchers" (periwinkles), and other things, for which they can always find a ready sale in the town, whence they are sent to the Ipswich and the London markets. Large quantities of wild-fowl are also shot by the poor people, which can be disposed of without difficulty in the market. There are also a considerable number of salvors, or "salt wager men," as they are called, whose employment it is to afford assistance to shipwrecked vessels; and since great numbers of wrecks are constantly taking place on the Gunfleet Sands, the amount of salvage which they obtain is frequently very considerable.

Among the other occupations of the county there are, according to the census, domestic servants 19,733; labourers of various sorts, 6,655. The number of persons returned as "independent," for Essex, was 23.4 below the average of England and Wales—while the number of paupers returned in 1844 was 50 per cent. above the average. The amount of deposits in the savings banks is 13.5 below the average, and the amount of real property in 1842 was 4.2 above the average.

Agricultural labour, however, forms by far the most important portion of the labour of Essex, the number of persons so employed being not less than 43,672. Of this number there are above twenty years of age, males, 35,744; females, 6,516; under twenty years of age, males, 1,072; females, 310. The wages vary very considerably in different parts of the county. In the neighbourhood of the metropolis and among the principal farmers who grow for the London markets, the rate is about 10s. per week. In the parish of Writtle, which is nearly the largest agricultural parish in the county, wages vary from 8s. to 9s. per week. At Roxwell, and in the immediate neighbourhood of the property of Mr. Bramston, M.P., they are about 8s. per week. In the Tendring hundred they average about 8s. per week for married men, 6s. for unmarried. About Great Baddow the highest wages are at present about 9s.—formerly some were paid as high as 12s. per week. The harvest work is usually done either by the month, or at a certain price per acre—the amount varying from 9s. to 11s. per acre. From ten to twelve acres is commonly the quantity allotted to one man, for which he would receive about £5 at the end of the harvest. During the harvest the men are usually allowed eight pints of ale, or six pints of strong beer, and four of table-beer, per day. The allowance given by Mr. Robert Baker, of Writtle, to his men, last harvest, was six pints of ale, made at the rate of four bushels of malt to the hogshead and a half, and as much table-beer as they liked to have. Many of the men, he informed me, would drink sixteen pints of beer in the day; most of them from ten to twelve. The quantity of beer consumed upon Mr. Baker's farm last harvest was 1,200 gallons. In cases where beer is not allowed, it is usual to give three or four bushels of malt and four pounds of hops to each man, with the use of brewing utensils and casks, to allow him to brew his own beer. The custom of giving what is called the "horkey," or harvest-home supper, also very generally prevails throughout the county. Where the supper is not given, 5s. is allowed to each man instead. It is, however, in the northern and western portions of the county that the lowest rate of wages is found to prevail. Throughout the whole of this district the wages are invariably 2s. or 3s. per week lower than in the other portions of the county. It is in this district, bordering upon parts of Suffolk, Cambridge, and Hertfordshire, and including Saffron Walden, Clavering, and other places where the wages are equally low, that the greatest amount of distress and discontent is to be found, and that incendiary fires are of the most frequent occurrence. With respect to the quality of the farming in this district, Mr. Robert Baker, in his prize essay on the agriculture of Essex, says—"Throughout this district, the farm premises are ill-arranged—large barns, sheds, and waggon-lodges being placed inconveniently, and detached from each other, the accumulation of water from their thatched roofs falling into yards having large hollows and excavations made by constant scooping out the clay from time to time as the manure is carted out, so that a person unacquainted with their inequalities is liable to be engulfed in them, as the surface, being covered with the accumulated barley-straw, exhibits all smooth to the eye; and it is only by the rising of the water and sinking of the straw that he is awakened to the situation he is placed in. This, however, has been remedied by the more spirited occupiers, but still prevails to an extent deserving their attention, as, upon a moderate estimate, one-fourth of the most valuable properties of the manure is thus annually lost."

The Harvest

Perhaps it is unnecessary to inquire further into the cause of the extremely low wages which prevail in this district; the wretched condition of the farms may be considered as affording a pretty fair index to the condition of the labourer.

When speaking to several of the farmers on this subject, I have always been told the condition of the labourer is not so bad as would at first sight appear. The rent of his cottage is, they say, 1s. a week lower here than elsewhere. I have not, however, found upon inquiry that the rents are lower than in many of the districts where higher wages are paid. At Clavering the rents vary from £2 10s. to £3 10s.; and some of the larger cottages, containing four rooms, are £4 per annum. In addition to the advantages which the labourer in this district is assumed to possess in the shape of low rents, I was also informed that he eats a coarser description of flour—that his fuel is not so expensive to him as in other parts of the county—and that, therefore, the difference of wages is not so great as would appear to a superficial observer. A large farmer in Clavering informed me that "a man with a family of five children will be *nearly* able with 6s. a week to buy bread enough, if he buys the coarsest flour; his rent he generally pays out of his harvest money; his clothes he gets by some means or other—people sometimes give them to him—and then, when he is unemployed, why we keep him in the workhouse. So you see, sir, he is amply provided for, even with wages at 6s. per week." How far the word "amply" applies to such a state of existence is a matter upon which, probably, there may be more than one opinion. The statement given above is one that I have heard from the farmers, not once, but many times, and it affords a key to the whole system of paying the agricultural labourer. Calculations are made with the greatest possible nicety, not so much to ascertain how much he can live upon, as how much he can live without. A scale just immediately above starvation point is fixed upon for his subsistence, and when he is unable to work, they are content to provide him an asylum at the expense of the ratepayers. The labourer is, of course, unable to lay by a shilling for old age or other casualties, and he invariably ends his days a pauper.

A more striking instance of the ill effects of such a system is, perhaps, nowhere to be found than in the different workhouses of the county. One of the most affecting sights in an agricultural county is the "old men's" ward of the different unions. In the case of the Chelmsford union, situated in a district where the wages are somewhat higher than in the neighbourhood of Saffron Walden, there were, in the "old men's" ward, 19 paupers whose united ages were 1,577 years, the average age being rather more than 83. I put a number of questions to each of them, with a view of ascertaining their previous employment, and the rates of wages which they had received. Several, from their extreme imbecility and old age, were unable to give any-thing like a coherent answer to any question put to them. From some, however, I was able to obtain answers; and as it will show, perhaps, more forcibly than anything else, the condition of the agricultural labourers, I will give the information which I was enabled to elicit. The first three whom I questioned were confined to their beds, being too infirm to sit up. They were eating their dinners, consisting of beef and potatoes, mixed up together, the potatoes being peeled for them, and the meat minced; and as they were unable to use either knife or fork, spoons where provided for them. The first to whom I addressed myself was an old man aged 89; he was sitting up in his bed, sup-ported by his pillow, and was vainly endeavouring to raise the food to his mouth with the spoon. A more pitiable spectacle of helpless imbecility could perhaps nowhere be found than he presented. Of the food which he endeavoured to raise to his lips, at least one-half lay scattered over his person and on the bed clothes—it being either tilted out of the spoon before it arrived at his mouth, or upset by com-ing in contact with some other part of his face. So far as his health was concerned it was not bad: he was not labouring under any attack of sickness. He complained of a cough, but his imbecility arose from sheer weakness and exhaustion. His statements, rambling and inco-herent as they were, were to the following effect:—"I reckon I'm 89, or thereabouts. My father lived near Braintree; he was taken for a sol-dier for the American war. I was a parish boy. I think I can remember his going, but I don't recollect much about it. I was born before he went, I think. I had a brother once, but he was *drownded* when he went in the water to get a poor fellow out as had tumbled in. Poor fellow! I began to work when I was seven years old. I run away from the parish then to help my mother. I used to live with her. I used to get sometimes eighteenpence a day—sometimes fourteen pence. For a particular job at mowing or reaping, I used to get more—sometimes two shillings. I always worked on the farm. I was married once, and had five children. Some of 'em didn't turn out well; some of 'em did. I think there's only two of 'em living now, but I don't know where they are; in London I think. I kept on working till about two years ago, when I come in here, because I couldn't work any longer. I never had any relief from the parish after I left the workhouse, when I was a parish-boy." According to this old man's statement, he had worked as a farm-labourer for 80 years. Another old man who was in the adjoining bed, was, if possible, more feeble than the one already mentioned. With a great deal of difficulty I succeeded in obtaining some intelligible answers to my questions:—"I think I'm 88; I don't know exact—may be more than that. I began work when I was 14, and was pretty lucky, for I always got work. Sometimes I used to get eighteen-pence a day, sometimes less; two shillings once. I've brought up ever so many children. I got a prize once for it," said the old man, with a laugh, the exertion of which appeared to produce considerable pain in his chest. "I think there was nine of 'em. The last work I got was at a gentleman's house, but I couldn't do much, so they turned me off, and I came here. I've been here—I don't know how long." The master informed me that he had been in the house about four months. The number of years that he had worked as a farm-labourer was about 62. For two years he had been at the gentleman's house that he spoke of. The third man that I spoke to said, "I was a farm-labourer all my life. My father had a farm of his own. He was a wonderful man to spend money on the poor. That's a long while ago. I don't know how long since he gave up the farm. I used to get when I worked, sometimes 2s. a day, sometimes less. I had to work for myself when I was ten years old, and I've been at work ever since, till a little while ago, and never had no parish relief. I reckon I'm about 85. I had eight children; some of 'em are in London, and some are dead. One of my daughters is a cook at a gentleman's at Ingatestone."

Another labourer, who was also confined to his bed, said, with considerable excitement, "I'm 85 years old. I've been a farm-labourer all my life, ever since I was a boy, and this is what it's all come to. The last job I did was for Master ——. I went hoeing a few turnips, and they told me I was to get four shillings a week. When I was there one week they took off a shilling. I told 'em that they said they'd give me four, and they said if I didn't like to have that, I might have none at all, for I hadn't worked enough to arne more. I grumbled, but it was no use, and I went to work the next week, and then they sarved me worse again, for they only gave me half-a-crown, took off eighteenpence; and I said, d——d if I stand it any longer, and if they took it off any more I'd go to the workhouse. Well, then I come in here, and I've been here since. I know I'm very old and weak, and can't do much, and p'raps didn't arne more than half-a-crown, but then they said they'd give me four shillings, and I wouldn't put up with it, to have it took off when they come to pay me." The old man continued for some time to denounce the acts of his employer in a state of the greatest excitement, which he displayed by gnashing his gums—for there were no teeth in his head—clenching his fist, and shaking his head as he muttered indistinctly his imprecations on the person whom he considered had wronged him.

A hearty and healthy-looking old man, "just turned of 91," said, "I was at work at one farm above fifty years, and I used to get sometimes 10s. a week, sometimes less; in harvest I used to get more. I have had twelve children; there's only five alive now, and two of the daughters are at the Hall, where I worked for fifty years. After I left the Hall, I worked at different places. I begun when I was under twelve years old, and I've been hard at it all my life till I come here, and that's not long—two years I think; so I have had in my time nearly eighty years of it, and seen a many different things. It's a bad job to come here, after all, and die in the workhouse; but I might have been worse off out of the house than in it, in my time of life, with nobody to look after me. I'm as comfortable as anybody can be in such a place like, but I wouldn't have come in yet if I could do anything out o' doors." Another old man, of 88 years of age, said, "I began work when I was a young boy, and I kept on until just before I come in here, because I couldn't do much. I used to get a little help from the parish just before I came into the house, because I couldn't get enough to keep me by my own work. At one time we used to get 10s. or 12s. a week, sometimes more than that. I've had eight children. I think they're most of 'em alive and married. I recollect, when I was a boy, flour used to be 10d. a peck and cheese 2½d. a pound. I've heard my mother say that she knowed when it was only 9d. a peck." "That was in 1772 or 1773, when I was at school," said the old man of ninety-one. "I recollect taking the money to buy the flour with when I used to go home from school." One old man, who informed me he was 82, said, "At the time flour was dear I used to pay the men, for I was in a little way of business myself then, about 18s. a week; that was when flour was 7s. a bushel all but a penny; I don't know how long that was ago, it's a long time I know, for I've been at work on another farm more than fifty years since that. I have brought up twelve children; my wife had six before I had her, but we brought them up and all, and I never had any relief from the parish till just when I come in here." "I am in my 80th come April," said another; "I worked for fifty-eight years on Mr. ——'s farm, and afore I went to him I worked nine years on another farm. I wasn't able to work any longer, or else I wouldn't have come in here. I am afeard I shall never be able to do much more work, I hurt my toe on the farm, and can't hardly walk. I have had, I s'pose, half a dozen children; my oldest boy was in his sixtieth when he died, and the parish buried him just afore I come in here. It is sixty years last May Fair since I was married. I was bred and born at High Easton, not far from Masborough, and when I was first married the wages used to be only 7s. a week." "I," said another of the paupers, "was 82 the 13th of last month, and I've been at work ever since I was a boy. I've not left off long either, and wouldn't be here now if I could get any work to do as I could get on with. I never received any relief in my life till now, for I'd scorn to be under their control. The wages I got was just as it happened—sometimes 1s. a day, sometimes 1s. 6d. Once or twice I got 2s."

Perhaps the most miserable-looking specimen of any in the affecting group of paupers who were clustered round the fire-place in their day-room was an old shepherd. Owing to the constant shaking of every part of his frame, it was almost impossible to understand a single word that he uttered. What I was enabled to gather from him was to the following effect:—"I was a shepherd, and so was my father and grandfather before me. I'm 82. All my life I've been a shepherd, and nothing else. I'm a Suffolk man. I used to be by the year, and was boarded and farmed in the house. Sometimes I used to get £7 a year, sometimes £8; and the highest I ever got was £9. The lowest, I think, was £6—except when I got 6s. a week, and had to board myself. That was about a dozen years ago. I've left off some time, but I used to go out with my father when I was very young, and look after the sheep. I s'pose I have had sixty years of looking after the sheep on my own account." Another labourer, of 84 years of age, said "I've been at work on the farm ever since I was a youngster, and I got into mischief at Mr. ——'s farm, at Writtle, or else I wouldn't have been here now. I was driving some horses, and they got frightened at a thrashing machine as was at work, and ran away, and drove me on to a bank and broke my leg. I had two or three falls, too, after my leg was set to rights, that made me a good deal worse. If it hadn't been for that I don't think I should have come in here for a long while to come. I was getting into years before I came in, and I didn't get so much as I used to get. 7s. a week was what I got, and they then got down to 6s. 6d. When I was a *yunker* I used to earn a good bit more money—sometimes 2s. a day; but they went on and went on getting of 'em down till now." "I am four score and four or five," said one who was sitting next, "I won't be sure which. I worked mostly on the marshes; they give you more there than they do in the uplands. It is very damp work, and gives you a strange lot of colds and such things like. The last wages I got was 9s. a week; I used once to get 10s. I've been at farm-work—lor' bless me, how long?—aye, ever since about 1770. When I was six or seven years old I recollect I used to puddle about adoing of something or other. I never had no relief from the parish till I came in here." "I shall be 70 if I live till next Tuesday week—that is my birth-day, I think," said a lame old man, who was hobbling about on crutches. "I have been at work on a farm, too, all my life. In very dear times I used to get 2s. and 2s. 6d. a-day—that must be 40 years ago, or near upon 50, when bread was so dear. I've not been able to do any work for a long time, since I've hurt my back and my hip. If I could only get right again I should be able to do a little more work I think—not much perhaps, but still enough to keep me out of here." The other persons to whom I spoke were all above 70 years of age—one 73, one 76, one 77, two 78, and one 79, the whole of whom had been farm labourers, and had been so nearly the whole of their lives. One of the old men of 77 said that the reason he came into the house was because he could not get anything to do, but he thought he was able still "to go and do a good day's work, but his grey hairs was against him, and they wouldn't employ him when they saw 'em." There were one or two old men in the idiots' ward, but we could get no information from them. There was, however, one individual among them who presented a most extraordinary contrast to those whom I had just left. He had the greatest horror of all kinds of work, and never could be brought to do any. He would never sleep in any house, preferring to sleep under the hedges. On one occasion, during some very severe weather, the frost caught both his legs, and he was compelled to have them cut off. "They can't make me work now," said the poor creature to me, with an idiotic smile upon his face, "for I've got none but these wooden legs; it was a good job when they cut 'em off."

From the consideration of the wages of the agricultural labourer of Essex, I pass on to a description of his dwelling; and in this respect much requires to be done. Mr. Robert Baker, of Writtle, has done a good deal towards setting an example in this respect. He has built several cottages of four and five rooms each, with about ten roods of garden ground attached, with ovens, and a good supply of water from wells, which he has caused to be sunk for the use of the cottages—the expense of building a pair of these having been about £150. They are let for £5 per annum. More recently he has built some commodious and comfortable dwellings of dried clay, the outer walls of which are covered with gas tar, which has the effect of making them impervious to rain. The floors of the cottages are formed of a species of asphalte, which is laid upon a bed of concrete, which effectually prevents any damp from rising from the ground. About Chelmsford a great many new dwellings have recently been built, in consequence of some portions of the estate of Lady Mildmay having been sold, in small lots, for building purposes; but the destruction of a number of cottages at a short distance from Chelmsford has tended to drive a considerable number of persons from the outskirts into the town, who are glad to obtain any kind of shelter. In some portions of the town, but more especially in a portion of Moulsham, which is considered as a part of Chelmsford, the condition of the cottages is most disgraceful, some of them, if not exceeding, at all events fully equalling many of the wretched places in Norwich and Bury, to which I have previously referred. To enumerate these miserable hovels would be to mention nearly the whole of the little courts and alleys which lead off to the right and left from Moulsham. In Weatherhall-passage there are four small houses containing two rooms each, with no back premises whatever, the space in front of the houses being not more than a few feet, which is closely packed with a pig-sty, a dust-bin, and a privy, all of which are connected together. There is no water to any of the houses, and the rent is 4s. 6d. per week. At another place close by, which the inmates told me "they didn't call anything, for it never had no name," though it would not be difficult to find an appropriate one for it—the cottages, which were merely run up one brick thick, were fast falling into decay; the water and filth from the yard ran into the lower rooms, and the rain streamed down the walls almost as fast as if it had not met with the partial obstruction of a roof. In another place, called Talmer's Cottages, where the inspector of nuisances had ordered some privies to be emptied, I was happy to hear him state that he was determined to do his duty. The whole of the night-soil out of these receptacles lay in one corner of the yard intermixed with the vegetable and other refuse from the surrounding cottages, which were inhabited, I was told, by about fifty persons. In another wretched dark little passage, near the "Masons' Arms," where there was scarcely room for two persons to pass each other, were six cottages, one of which was inhabited by an old woman, who informed me that she was "eighty-five, and as gay as a lark." She requested me to come in and see her two little rooms. They were more clean and tidy than any person could have expected to see, but the water was trickling down the walls continually. "I'm not ashamed for nobody to see my rooms," said the old woman; "I keeps them as clean as I can. I have been here twenty years, come Easter, and have paid 1s. a week rent, and don't owe a farthing." She informed me that she was with her husband in Ireland during the Rebellion; that upon his discharge he went up to London, and brought down some boys, and commenced the "chimbley" trade, and did all the principal sweeping business of the town. After his death, she took to the manufacture of "bull's-eyes," for children, and at one time made 60 or 70 lbs. in a week. Her business had lately fallen off so much, that she did not make more than two lbs. in the week, the profit upon which was 2½d. A shilling a week was allowed her by some charitable person in the town, and two shillings from the parish. While she was giving me her history her daughter came in to borrow the bellows. "I don't mind lending 'em you," said the old woman, "but pray don't put the nose of 'em in the fire. I always keeps 'em bright, sir, for my husband's sake; he bought 'em for me a long many years ago."

Perhaps the most wretched places of any in or about the town were to be found in Old Barrack-lane or road. Many were falling down from sheer neglect; one or two of them, which were uninhabited, were used by the neighbouring houses as a place of common convenience, besides being a receptacle for the ashes and the refuse of the other houses in cases where the people choose to take the trouble of carrying it beyond the front of their own dwellings. In one of these cottages lived a man and his wife and five children. An old stool was the only article of what might be called furniture in the house; a few bricks, collected from some of the ruins about it, piled above one another in four or five different heaps, showed where the inmates were in the habit of seating themselves. There was not a single piece of bedding or bed-clothes in the upper room, nor an article of furniture of any kind, while the floor of the room and the walls were dripping with the wet and rain that came through the roof. The mother of the family, a wretched-looking woman, with an old ragged gown, said, "My eldest boy is 19 and my Eliza 16; them and the four other young'uns and us sleep up stairs. We've got no clothes, so we sleeps as close together as we can, and that keeps us warm. My husband sometimes gets a job in the market; sometimes he doesn't. We get nothing from nobody, and if we likes to go without and *pinch* ourselves that's no matter to nobody either." The statement that she "got nothing from nobody," in the sense in which she intended it to be understood, was a perfect falsehood; bedding and furniture had several times been furnished by the parish and some charitable persons, but they were always made away with immediately after. "I was very ill," continued the woman, "a few days since, and my husband went to the doctor's to get some medicine, but he threw it at him, because he wouldn't give him some money. I will allow that he oughtn't to have done that, though I know he don't think much of the doctors, nor I neither. My husband owes seven weeks' rent at 1s. a week, and he is employed by the landlord to work it out. He gets 1s. 6d. a day, and I am quite agreeable that he should do it, and when he comes home he brings the 6d. that he's yearned after paying the rent, and then him and me and five of us goes to supper off it, and then we goes without till he comes home again the next night—that's the way we does it." A greater amount of callousness and indifference to misery and wretchedness I never saw than was exhibited by this woman. I was informed, that a day or two previous to my visit, a gentleman had given the man a truss of straw to take home, for his family to lie upon, but that he sold it almost immediately after for 6d., which he spent in drink. Characters of this sort are, it is to be hoped, for the sake of human nature, comparatively rare, but even in Chelmsford, I was told by the relieving officer that there are great numbers of persons, who, through habits of improvidence, idleness, or drunkenness, are seldom off the relief-lists of the parish.

In the rural districts many of the cottages are exceedingly bad, but in the northern and western part of the county this is peculiarly the case. Along the whole line of country from Castle Hedingham to Clavering, there is an almost continuous succession of bad cottages. Among the worst of these might be mentioned those in the neighbourhood of Sible Hedingham, Weathersfield, Bardfield, Wicken and Clavering. Great numbers of these cottages are situated in low and damp situations, and their heavy and grass-covered thatches appear as if they had almost crushed the buildings down into the earth. Little or no light can ever find its way into the wretched little windows, many of which are more than half stopped up with rags and pieces of paper. In point of fact, there are many of them which, but for the possession of a chimney, would be nothing superior to many of the most wretched cabins which I have witnessed in Tipperary and many other parts of Ireland. At Manningtree there are also a considerable number of wretched one-room cottages, and those which are larger are generally tenanted by as many families as there are rooms. In some cases the number of families exceeds that of the rooms. It is customary in Manningtree to rate every one of the lodgers in such a house. In one case, of a house with three rooms, the persons living in the lower room, consisting of a husband and wife, and three grown-up children, were rated at £1 5s. The second compartment, occupied by a man and his wife, and one son, was rated at £1. The occupiers of the third room, who consisted of a man and his wife, and five children, were rated at 15s., the poor-rates being 6s. in the pound for the year. There are also some wretched holes situated upon Back-hill, where the amount of rates enforced averages about 3d. to each house. The cottages in the Tendring hundred are, generally speaking, pretty good, and overcrowding does not exist to so great an extent as in other parts of the county. At Beaumont there are a considerable number of cottages which belong to Guy's Hospital, which are kept in very good condition. For some years past it has been the custom of the managers of the property to purchase, wherever they could, cottage property, and improve it as soon as it came into their hands, when the property was susceptible of improvement—and, in cases where it had been suffered to proceed too far towards decay, to pull down the cottages and erect new and more commodious ones in their stead. The rents of the dwellings in this parish vary from about £3 10s. to £4, and some are let as high as £5. At Castle Hedingham the cottages are, generally speaking, good, and the rents moderate. Great numbers of them, however, have but two rooms.

Among those who have endeavoured to improve the physical and moral condition of the people are the following:—Lord Petre, Lord Braybrooke, Mr. Bramston, M.P., Sir J. Tyrell, M.P., Mr. Magendie, of Castle Hedingham, Mr. Robert Baker, of Writtle, Rev. J. Wilkins, of Wickes, &c. Among the most enterprising and successful of the farmers, are Mr. Tabrum, of High Roothing; Mr. Glasscock, Mr. Adams, of Westham; Mr. Seabrook, of Dagenham; Mr. Blewitt, of Rayham; and Mr. Crossley, of Baddow. Mr. Adams grows an enormous quantity of produce for the London markets. Last year he had 500 acres of potatoes and 100 acres of onions. Mr. Seabrook and Mr. Blewitt also grow large quantities of potatoes, peas, and beans for the London markets. Mr. Crossley, of Baddow, is noted for his great success in obtaining the prizes at the agricultural shows for enormous vegetables.

I will now endeavour to describe the state of education in Essex, as well as in the adjoining counties of Norfolk and Suffolk. In a former letter, when speaking of the education of Suffolk, I had occasion to allude to the want of anything like statistical information upon so important a subject. It is not necessary to repeat the observations then made; but I will endeavour, according to the best means at my disposal, to state the extent of education in these three counties. The education, or rather the ignorance, of the inhabitants of Norfolk, Suffolk, and Essex, as indicated by the number of persons who signed the marriage register by marks instead of with their name, was, according to recent returns, very considerable. In thirty-seven counties the proportion per cent. of persons so signing the marriage register was less than in Norfolk. There were thirty-nine less than Suffolk, and forty less than Essex; there are but three counties, Bedford, Monmouth, and Hertford, in which the proportion was greater. The proportion per cent. above the average for England and Wales was for Norfolk, 38.1; Suffolk, 42; Essex, 42.4. The number of persons who signed the marriage register with marks in 1845 were—

	Males.	Females.	Total.
Norfolk	1,495	1,625	3,120
Suffolk	1,167	1,269	2,436
Essex	1,069	1,176	2,245
Total of three counties			7,801

In 1839 the numbers were—

	Males.	Females.	Total.
Norfolk	1,172	1,313	2,485
Suffolk	1,007	1,166	2,173
Essex	906	1,058	1,964
Total of three counties			6,622

Showing an increase for 1845, as compared with 1839, of not less than 1,179, which considerably exceeds the rate of increase in the population during those two periods. Turning from the state of ignorance among the adults, let us inquire to what extent exertions are being made to educate the rising generation. In Norfolk there are 39,417 scholars in connection with the National Society's school; in Suffolk, 32,667; and in Essex, 35,870. To the kindness of the Rev. Mr. Vosey, the secretary of the Wesleyan Education Committee, I am indebted for the following account of the state of education in the three counties, in connection with the Wesleyan body:—

	Total number of Scholars.	Average attendance.	Numbers attending Day School.
Norfolk	9,071	6,762	3,534
Suffolk	2,454	1,944	926
Essex	2,773	2,226	1,132

The number of teachers in connection with the schools being—for Norfolk, 1,548; Suffolk, 388; Essex, 369. In the week-day and infant schools, there are—in Norfolk, 118 scholars; Suffolk, 110; and in Essex, 99. Among the Catholics the number of scholars is very small indeed. In Norwich there are about 200 children in connection with the school, at Cossey about 100. At Lynn there is no Catholic school. At Ipswich there is no school at present; the number of children belonging to the Catholic working classes of the congregation of that town are about fifty, of these but few receive any education. At Bungay there is no Catholic school, the children receiving what education they get in their respective neighbourhoods. At Bury there is a Catholic school in connection with the chapel, at which about fifty children receive education. The school is supported by the Catholic minister of the town, the children paying 1d. a week. It is not confined to Catholics, but is open to the children of any denomination. At Brentwood there are about twenty children in connection with the Catholic chapel of that place. With respect to Ingatestone I was informed that there were three small schools under Catholic mistresses, that the scholars were not all Catholics, but that there was no interference with the religion of non-Catholic children. The numbers in the three schools might be over forty, and under fifty. In connection with the Sunday-school Union the number of scholars is 1,676. The Primitive Methodists about 1,680. Of various classes of dissenters the number of scholars is, for the three counties, as far as I have been enabled to collect the information, about 9,500. The total number of children receiving education, including Sunday and day schools, in connection with the various religious and educational societies in the three counties would, therefore, be:—

National Society 107,954
Wesleyans (average attendance)   10,932
Week-day and infant schools . .   327
Other Dissenters   9,500
Sunday-school Union   1,676
Primitive Methodists   1,680
Catholics   450
                                         ――――
          Total 132,519

The population of the three counties was, in 1841, 1,072,716; of whom there were, under fifteen years of age, males 198,431, females 198,072. Assuming that the population has increased in the same ratio since 1841 as before that period, and that the number under fifteen years of age bears the same proportion to the entire population, the present population would amount to 1,130,716, and the number of persons under fifteen years of age to 416,844. Of this number, 132,519 are receiving education in connection with the various societies above-named, being somewhat less than one-third of the entire number. Great numbers of these, however, receive only a Sunday-school education; comparatively few attend any week-day schools, and even where they do attend they are unable to do so regularly, their instruction being consequently afforded to them in the most irregular manner. There are two classes of children, however, which these returns do not include—those of the more wealthy, and those of the paupers. With respect to the former, it is impossible for me to obtain any accurate information. Of the schools of the latter, which are under Government inspection, the statistics are more easily ascertainable: being—Norfolk, 1,117; Suffolk, 1,043; Essex, 1,220. Total in the three counties, 3,480. The education afforded in these schools is in many respects superior to that which is given in many of the other schools; and it is not at all an uncommon complaint to hear among the farmers that the pauper children are receiving too much education. A few days since I met with one who said that he was opposed to all the new-fangled education that they were giving to the paupers. "I am," said he, "one of the guardians of our union; and I just happened to go into the school-room, and there if the master wasn't telling the boys to point out with a stick, on some big maps that were hanging up, where South Amerikey was, and France, and a lot of other places; and they did it, too. Well, when I went home, I told my son of it, and asked him if he could tell me where them places was; and he couldn't. Now, is it right that these here pauper children should know more than the person who will have to employ them?" "Certainly not," would be the natural reply of almost every thinking person to a question of this kind; but if the farmer's son chooses to remain in ignorance, that can surely be no reason why even the pauper should. If the farmer's son is distanced in learning by the pauper, and if it be a grievance to him, the remedy is in his own hands. The objection entertained by many to the introduction of geography, for instance, into the education of paupers, appears to be founded entirely on the supposition that the latter are naturally of a distinct and inferior caste, that they must always continue so, and that the education, if any, imparted to them, must be made to descend to their supposed level. That pauperism forms to a great extent a distinct and most degraded class, is unfortunately but too true, and the adult pauper is generally too far degraded to be raised by education. With the children, however, the case is far different. In the great majority of cases the debasing effects of pauperism have not been as yet felt by them. From all that I have seen in the various schools which I have visited, I believe them to be fully equal in natural capacity to any of the children of the unpauperized labourer. The Boys' Home at Norwich shows also most incontestably, that when they are reared in morality and religion, trained to industry, and removed from the contaminating influences of the other inmates of the workhouse, they render themselves remarkable in after life for intelligence, industry, and good conduct.

Complaints have not unfrequently been made to me—not by the labourers, but by those above them—that the pauper children are receiving a better education than those of the labourer. It is one of the anomalies of the poor-law, that the pauper is better fed, better clothed, and better lodged than the labourer; and the same person who would find fault with the pauper receiving a better education than the child of the labourer, must also in justice complain that he is better fed, clothed, and lodged, and that he is so there can be no doubt. Let those who are able adjust the inequality. In the case of the labourer, as of the farmer, the real cause of complaint is, not that the child of the pauper is educated well, but that his own is not. The community which provides education for the pauper only fulfils but a portion of its obligations; and to it is applicable, in its strongest sense, the rebuke "This ought ye to have done; but not to have left the other undone."

The partial introduction of the system of industrial training in connection with the pauper schools, has hitherto been attended with the most complete success in those unions where it has been adopted.

In order to facilitate the carrying out of the plan of industrial training, the 7th and 8th Vic., c. 101, and the 11th and 12th Vic., c. 82,
were passed, which gave power to the Poor-law Board, under certain
restrictions, to unite together a number of parishes and districts for
the more effectual education and training of pauper children. The act,
however, at present remains a dead letter, none of the guardians feeling disposed to give effect to it in any of their unions. At many of the
unions, however, a system of industrial training is carried on, and the
boys are either employed in cultivating a piece of land in connection
with the workhouse, or in making boots and shoes, tailoring, making
mats, straw hats, and a variety of things, while the girls are employed
in various household duties. At Wortham the pauper school is entirely
disconnected with the workhouse, and the establishment affords on
a small scale the advantages which would be derived from the establishment of district schools.

In counties where ignorance is so prevalent it is natural to expect
a considerable amount of crime and immorality. The number of persons committed for trial or bailed in the three counties in 1847, were—
Norfolk, males 608, females 143; Suffolk, males 423, females 82; Essex, males 538, females 65: total of three counties, 1,859. The proportion per cent. of commitments for the six years 1842-47, for Norfolk,
was 17.6 above the average of England and Wales; malicious offences
against property 193 per cent. above the average. For Suffolk the total
commitments were 7.4 per cent., and malicious offences against property 278.9 per cent. above the average. In Essex the total commitments
were 17.2 per cent., and malicious offences against property 198.5 per
cent. above the average.

One species of immorality which is peculiarly prevalent in Norfolk and Suffolk is that of bastardy. With the exception of Hereford
and Cumberland there are no counties in which the per centage of bastardy is so high as it is in Norfolk—being there 53.1 per cent. above
the average of England and Wales; in Suffolk it is 27 per cent. above,
and in Essex 19.1 per cent. below the average. In the two first-named
counties, and even in the latter one, though not to the same extent,
there appears to be a perfect want of decency among the people. "The
immorality of the young women," said the rector of one parish to me,
"is literally horrible, and I regret to say it is on the increase in a most
extraordinary degree. When I first came to the town, the mother of
a bastard child used to be ashamed to show herself. The case is now
quite altered; no person seems to think anything at all of it. When I

first came to the town there was no such thing as a common prostitute in it; now there is an enormous number of them. When I am called upon to see a woman confined with an illegitimate child, I endeavour to impress upon her the enormity of the offence; and there are no cases in which I receive more insult from those I visit than from such persons. They generally say they'll get on as well, after all that's said about it, and if they never do anything worse than that, they shall get to Heaven as well as other people." Another clergyman stated to me that he never recollected an instance of his having married a woman who was not either pregnant at the time of her marriage, or had had one or more children before her marriage. Again, a third clergyman told me that he went to baptize the illegitimate child of one woman, who was 35 years of age, and it was absolutely impossible for him to convince her that what she had done was wrong. "There appears," said he, "to be among the lower orders a perfect deadness to all moral feeling upon this subject." Many of the cases of this kind which have come under my knowledge evince such horrible depravity that I dare not attempt to lay them before the reader. Speaking to the wife of a respectable labourer on the subject, who had seven children, one of whom was then confined with an illegitimate child, she excused her daughter's conduct by saying, "What was the poor girls to do; the chaps say that they won't marry 'em first, and then the girls give way. I did the same myself with my husband." There was one case in Cossey, in Norfolk, in which the woman told me, without a blush crimsoning her cheek, that her daughter and herself had each had a child by a sweep who lodged with them, and who promised to marry the daughter. The cottage in which these persons slept consisted of but one room, and there were two other lodgers who occupied beds in the same room; in one of which "a young woman occasionally slept with the young man she was keeping company with." The other lodger was an old woman of seventy-four years of age. To such an extent is prostitution carried on in Norwich, that out of the 656 licensed public-houses and beer-shops in the city, there are not less than 220 which are known to the police as common brothels. And although the authorities have the power of withholding the licenses, nothing is done to put a stop to the frightful vice. "At Bury," said one of the guardians of the poor to me, "there is, I believe, a larger amount of prostitution, in proportion to the size of the place, than is to be found in any town or city in England." Harwich appears to be remarkably free from this vice. "There are not," I was informed by the police, "more than six prostitutes in the town, and there is not a single brothel."

The progress of religion, as indicated by the number of new churches, is remarkably small. It appears, from the Twenty-sixth Annual Report of the Commissioners for Building New Churches, presented to the House of Commons on the 26th of August, 1846, that 27 new churches had been erected by the aid of grants placed at their disposal; that there were 32 erected towards which they had subscribed; that there were 18 churches of which the plans had been approved; and they had made conditional grants, which are still pending, to 89 other places, but of the whole number there is not a single place in the three counties of Essex, Suffolk, and Norfolk which has come in for any portion of the funds, with the exception of the port of Lynn.

With regard to the progress of education among the adults, there is scarcely a town or good sized village in the county which has not its mechanics' institute—one of the most zealous in promoting institutions of this kind, as well as schools in his own parish, being the Rev. Mr. Wilkes, of Wickes, in Essex. Once in every week he travels six or seven miles from his own house to Manningtree, to deliver lectures to the members of the institution, and he is known throughout the county for his strenuous advocacy of an improved and scientific education of the farmers.

LABOUR AND THE POOR.

THE RURAL DISTRICTS.

[FROM OUR SPECIAL CORRESPONDENT.]

NORFOLK, SUFFOLK, AND ESSEX.

Letter XXII.

I propose in the present letter to consider the state of the labourer with regard to his habits of providence—if such a term be not misapplied when used in connection with a body of men whose earnings appear to be barely sufficient to procure them the means of present existence, much less to enable them to provide for the future. Out of the scanty pittance of his wages, the labourer, however, by a process mysterious to the most sagacious economist, does contrive to devote a portion to the means of providing himself with assistance in the time of sickness and death. In order to accomplish this laudable end, he has recourse to the machinery of benefit societies—which in too many instances are, to him, only such in name—and clubs. Of these associations, thus called into being by the wants, and supported by the hard-earned pence of the labourer, it is my intention in the present letter to treat. By far the most important of the class, though happily not the most numerous, are the "Burial" or "Death" Clubs. The disclosures which have recently been made with respect to the mischievous effects of these clubs have given to the county of Essex an unenviable notoriety in the criminal annals of the country. Before proceeding to describe the numbers and the effects of clubs of this kind, it will be as well if I allude to their objects, to the mode in which they are generally conducted, and to the chief causes of their establishment.

Although the Burial Clubs have been brought prominently before the notice of the public in connection with the county of Essex, they are by no means peculiar to that county. Great numbers of them exist in various other parts of the country, in the manufacturing districts, and in the metropolis. The clubs for the labouring classes in Essex are almost invariably got up by an undertaker and by the publican at whose house their meetings are generally held; and in passing along

the streets the passenger may frequently see placards in the windows
of the public-houses, bearing such headings as, "All flesh is grass," "In
the midst of life we are in death," and other texts or mottos. Beneath
these may also be occasionally seen a ghastly-looking death's head
and bones. In cases where the clubs are the joint speculation of the
publican and the undertaker, mutual agreements appear to be entered
into for the promotion of their respective interests. Provision is made
in the rules of the society that the "box" shall not be removed from the
publican's house—the publican being almost invariably appointed the
treasurer; and the undertaker is guaranteed the exclusive right to the
performance of his professional duties for such members of the club as
may require it. Indeed, in the case of one club, a portion of the rules of
which I have before me, I perceive that the office of undertaker is not
only vested permanently and immovably in the originator of the club,
but it is even made hereditary in his family. One of the fundamental
rules of the society is—"That ——, being the founder of this society,
shall be the undertaker, and no future articles shall remove him, as
long as he gives general satisfaction to the society; and in case of his
death, his eldest son shall claim the same for the benefit of the widow,
and at her decease the same shall devolve on the eldest son living."

The ostensible object of these societies may perhaps be gathered
from the following somewhat obscure preamble, prefixed to the rules
of one of the clubs:—

> "In contemplating the many vicissitudes and changes incident
> to all persons of every station in life, and the many anxieties that
> crowd about our advancing years, more particularly the labouring
> class, through the uncertainty of employment, by long illness, or for
> want of friends, reduced to extreme distress, and after a long and
> miserable life, and in expectation of that awful change which we
> must one time or other undergo, without ever providing for a decent
> interment, it will be some alleviation to our sufferings to remember
> that we bring no pecuniary burthen on our commiserating friends
> and relations, that at least we have divested our suffering families of
> that anxiety respecting our mortal remains which would add another
> pang to their already lacerated hearts: it too frequently occurs, to the
> sorrow of many a feeling heart, who mourns over the deplorable loss
> of a beloved husband, wife, or friend: to obtain this desirable object,
> this society offers to the public, on easy terms, advantages worthy the
> consideration of persons in all stations of life."

The contributions to these societies, and the amount derived from
them in cases of death, vary considerably in different clubs. In some

cases the subscriptions are 1d. per week, and 2d. or 4d. per quarter for expenses; in others the payments are 4d. per quarter for expenses, and 6d. at the time of a death, from each member; in a few of them the amount of subscription is regulated according to the age of the party, and the amount paid upon death is dependent upon the class to which the member may belong; while in others, persons of all ages admitted into the club pay a like sum, and the survivors or nominees receive an equal amount upon the death of the member.

The reason which I have most frequently heard assigned for the existence of these clubs is, the great desire felt by the poor of procuring decent interment. There appears to be nothing more repugnant to the feelings of great numbers of the labouring population than the idea of being buried as a pauper by the parish. Several old persons in the different workhouses have, after telling me that so far as their present existence was concerned they were tolerably comfortable, added, with evident emotion, "But I suppose I shall be buried by the parish." "There," said another to me, pointing to a small enclosed spot, which the small green mounds marked as the paupers' burial ground—"There will be my home at last, and it's not a pleasant thought neither—is it?—to be buried like a pauper." Another person, who was employed as an agricultural labourer, said to me, when speaking of the hard struggle which he had to maintain for an existence, "So as I can but rub through, master, and pay up the club, and be buried decently after all, I don't mind working hard." The enormously high price which the labourer has to pay for the gratification of this, the almost only object of his ambition, forces him to become a member of one or more of the numerous clubs which hold out to him the prospect of a realization of his wishes; and he will endure almost any amount of privation, and subject himself to any inconvenience, in order to pay up his "death money," or the subscription to his benefit club. So strongly does this desire for decent interment prevail among the working classes, that many of them who are in a condition to do so will leave deposits in the savings bank, or in provident institutions, for the purpose of ensuring the object of their wishes; and in not a few cases it has happened that upon the death of the party he has been found to have died an inmate of a poor-house, and destitute of every kind of property save the little fund which he had set apart for his funeral. There is nothing perhaps which has tended more to the establishment and growth of these badly constituted clubs, than the enormous expense to which the poor are invariably put at the time of a funeral. The expenses upon these occasions are seldom less than £4, and they not unfrequently exceed £6. I have found upon inquiry, that, for a person in the condition of an agricultural labourer, in cases where the survivor does not receive gratuitous assistance in one form or other, the expense of the funeral is upon an average about £4 10s. At the time of death, the widow, generally speaking, knows not to whom to apply for assistance and counsel under the distressing circumstances in which she is placed; she is consequently led to apply to the nearest person whom she thinks can afford her any advice, and she not unfrequently becomes the prey of some unprincipled individual, whose sole desire is to make as much as he can out of the transaction. I was informed, that at Harwich and some other large towns, funerals were frequently performed what is called "three deep"—that is, the person really conducting the funeral does it for another person, who in his turn is employed by the party to whom the order was originally given. The men who act as bearers or attendants frequently find themselves thus raised to the dignity of undertakers, although in all probability it may be the first affair of the kind they ever attempted. Each of the parties through whose hands the work goes receives his share of the profit, and the price is consequently greatly enhanced to the family of the deceased, who too frequently are reduced to the greatest possible straits in order to pay the expense. In great numbers of cases there is no doubt that, if it were not for the undertaker giving them a little time for payment, by allowing them to defray the funeral charges by weekly or monthly instalments, they would not be able to bury the corpse at all.

In the course of my inquiries in Essex, I was enabled to collect information with respect to eight of these burial clubs, which are confined to the Tendring hundred. I was not able to ascertain the existence of any burial clubs in Norfolk. At Ipswich there are two or three, I believe, but I could obtain no information respecting them. The information which I succeeded in procuring with respect to the clubs in the Tendring hundred I will now proceed to lay before the reader. These clubs are distributed in the following places:—At Thorpe, there is one held at the Rose and Crown; in Great Oakley there are two—one of them being held at the May Bush Inn, and the other at the Cups Inn. The Hand-in-Hand Burial Society is held at St. Coyth, and adopts as its motto, "Bear ye one another's burdens." At Brightlingsea there are two clubs, each of which is called the Mourner's Friend Society. At Harwich there is one bearing a similar title, which is held at the Globe Inn; and another, of which the notorious Mary May was a member, is called "The New Society for rendering mutual Assistance in Cases of Mortality," and meets at the Privateer Inn, in Harwich. In one of these clubs no person is admitted as a member whose age exceeds 50 years, or is less than 14; in two others, the respective ages are 60 and 14; in four, the age at which persons are admitted is from 14 to 65; while in the eighth the minimum age is set down at 16, the maximum being left blank—"60" being the age, as I understood, which has been actually adopted. In the majority of the clubs the number of members is limited to 420. In seven of the clubs the entrance money is 1s. "for the use of the society," and 3d. for the rules and regulations, the person admitted being requested to appoint a nominee. In the eighth the entrance money is 9d. The mode in which seven of the clubs are conducted is contained in the following rule:—"It is also agreed that this society be under the direction of a collector or collectors, who shall be chosen by the committee; and the said collector or collectors shall collect 6d. from every member at the death of either a member or nominee; 4d. per quarter to be sent to the collector from every member; 1s. of the same to be allowed the collector a quarter, and 4s. at the death of every member or nominee for his trouble and loss of time in collecting the said money for deaths, &c., the remainder to pay the secretary's salary and other expenses, and the surplus (if any) to form a fund till there be a sufficiency to pay at a death or deaths." A secretary is chosen annually, and is allowed the sum of one pound per annum. A following rule provides—"That should it be discovered and proved by the committee that he (the secretary) has acted dishonestly, he shall be dismissed from the society and forfeit all claims thereon." Another rule provides—"That if one or more of the committee, secretary, or collectors, shall lose any of the moneys or property belonging to the society, they shall replace the same at their own expense, or be excluded from all benefits of this society." Other regulations set forth the duties of the president and of the secretary, the latter of whom, upon receiving notice of the death of a member or nominee, is to give a written order to the collector to collect the sixpences from the members, "all defaulters to be excluded." All causes of complaint against members or nominees are to be reported "to the committee, and five or more of them have power to act as they shall think proper." The committee are also "empowered to alter or amend any of the foregoing rules, as may appear to them for the benefit of the society." "The Provident Mourner's Friend Society," held at the Rose and Crown, in Thorpe, is conducted upon the plan of paying thirteenpence per quarter, instead of sixpence, upon the death of a member or nominee. The numbers of members in the different clubs vary considerably. The average for the whole, as calculated upon the numbers given to me for each club, and with the details of which it will be unnecessary to trouble the reader, is 2,395; but as each member is required to appoint a nominee, the clubs have "to stand the mortality" of 4,790, or double the number of members. Upon the death of a nominee, the member who may have appointed him of course receives the money, and in the event of the death of the member, the nominee whom he may have appointed receives the money. The average number of deaths per annum is 96.6; this is exclusive of ten deaths in the two Harwich clubs, the dues on which were in course of collection; these I have not included in the average mortality, as I was informed there had been ten cases of cholera in connection with those clubs, and my object was to ascertain the proportion of deaths among members of the clubs, uninfluenced by any visitation such as that of the cholera. The lowest amount paid in any of the societies is in the one at Thorpe, where the amount paid was only £2 14s.; in the St. Asyth Club the amount was £5 15s.; and in the larger ones, in most cases, between £9 and £10 has been the amount paid upon the death of a member or nominee.

Having thus stated the principle upon which the burial clubs in Essex are conducted, the number of members who belong to them, and the amount of benefit received by them, I now proceed to consider whether any sufficient grounds exist for the general opinion that there is a higher rate of mortality among persons connected with these societies than among those who are not so connected. The question is a difficult one to decide, and, involving as it does matters of so grave and serious a character, I feel some reluctance in expressing an opinion upon it; but if the information which I have received be correct—and I have every reason to believe that it is so, since it was furnished to me by the presidents, secretaries, or collectors of the different clubs—the results which it discloses are such as to call for at least some more extensive inquiry, and for the adoption of some very stringent measures for the regulation of these clubs.

I have stated that the average annual number of deaths of persons connected with the clubs of Essex is 96.6, being a per centage of 2.1 upon the number of their members and nominees. Now, in order to ascertain whether the per centage of deaths is higher in the clubs than out of them, it is necessary in the first place to discover what is the rate of mortality for the district in which they are situated. The whole of these clubs are situated in the Tendring hundred, a district in which the rate of mortality is considerably lower than in any other part of Essex. The annual mortality for the whole of Essex upon an average of seven years—1838-44—was at the rate of one death to 49.5 persons living; while for the Tendring hundred for the same period, it was only at the rate of one death to 53 persons living—being in the former case 2.019 per cent. and in the latter 1.884. This rate of mortality, however, applies to all ages, and does not, of course, bear upon the mortality of the clubs; and I only use it in order to show that there is nothing in the Tendring hundred to lead us to suppose that the natural mortality is higher there than elsewhere. In point of fact, there are 39 counties in which the rate of mortality is higher than that of the hundred of Tendring—only 24 in which it is higher than that of Essex—and but eighteen in which it is higher than in the burial clubs of Tendring. In order fairly to compare the mortality of the burial clubs with that of the surrounding district, it will of course be necessary to take the same conditions as to age in both cases. No person is admitted into these clubs under the age of fourteen, and in the case of some of them they are admitted up to the age of sixty-five; but it is only within the last year or two that restrictions as to the maximum age have been imposed at all, and it may be fairly assumed that among the members of the burial clubs are included persons of all ages above fourteen years; and we have already seen that this number, including nominees, is 4,790, the average rate of mortality since the formation of the clubs being 96.6. The population of Essex, which we will take as a point of comparison, was, in 1841, 320,811 of all ages. Of this number there were under fourteen years of age, males, 61,212; females, 61,365; making a total of 122,577. This number, deducted from the total population, will give us the population of Essex above fourteen years of age equal to 198,234. The amount of mortality for the whole of Essex for the seven years 1838-44, was 45,364, including all ages. The returns of this amount of mortality are given in quinquennial periods; and in order to obtain the proportion out of this number which would represent the deaths under fourteen years of age, I have taken one-fifth from the number of deaths as between the ages of ten and fifteen, adding the remainder to the total number under ten years of age: the result of this is, that there were in the seven years above-mentioned 22,584 deaths under fourteen years of age, which, taken from the number of all ages, would leave the mortality above fourteen years of age 22,780. As the seven years 1838-44 include the three years before and the three years after 1841—the year in which the census was taken—it may be supposed to be a fair average of the mortality. The population above fourteen years of age was 198,234, and the deaths above fourteen years of age for the seven years were 22,780, being equal to 11.45 per cent., or 1.63 per cent. per annum. The mortality of the Tendring hundred is lower, as we have already seen, than that of Essex generally; and, to avoid a wearisome multiplication of figures, it will be necessary to give the mortality of that district—a larger area, like Essex, affording also a better criterion by which to judge of the mortality of the burial clubs. In the whole of Essex, then, the mortality above fourteen years of age is 1.637 per cent., while for the clubs it is 2.1 per cent.—showing an increase as against the clubs of 0.463. The value of this decimal, as applied to the whole population of Essex, would increase its mortality by not less than 700 persons annually. Supposing the same rate of mortality to apply to the burial clubs as prevails in Essex, the proportion of deaths to the 4,790 members and nominees of the clubs ought to be only 75.2 instead of 96.6—or 22.4 less than the returns which I have obtained show to be the existing rate of mortality among them. Making every allowance for any incorrect statements which may have been made—deduct even one-half from the excess—and still a fearful and grave suspicion must rest upon these clubs, which it would be well if a more extensive and searching investigation were able to remove.

In addition, however, to the great disparity in the rates of mortality in and out of the clubs, as shown by a comparison with the mortality of the seven years from 1838 to 1844, suspicion is also aroused by the evidence contained in the register of burials in some of the districts where these societies are situated. None of the clubs in Essex have been established more than four or five years; and I was curious to ascertain whether the parish registers of burials would throw any light upon the working of these associations. I found, upon looking over the register of the parish of Wickes, that in the four years previous to the establishment of the clubs the number of deaths had been 36—whereas in the four years of the existence of the clubs the number had increased to 47. In both of the periods the deaths only are included of persons above the age of fourteen. The population of Wickes is about 800; there has been no cholera nor any other epidemic disease to explain the increased mortality; neither can it be accounted for by any increase in the population, as the numbers are at present somewhat lower than they were in 1841. In Great Oakley parish I was only able to obtain the number of deaths of persons of all ages; it cannot therefore be considered as of much value for the purposes of comparison. In the one period, however, the number of deaths was 90, as compared with 76 in the period preceding the formation of the clubs. The suspicion that a great deal of "foul play" exists with respects to these clubs is supported not only by a comparison of the different rates of mortality, but it is considerably strengthened by the facts proved upon the trial of Mary May. The Rev. Mr. Wilkins, the vicar of Wickes, who was mainly instrumental in bringing the case before a court of justice, stated to me, that from the time of Mary May coming to live in his parish, he was determined to keep a very strict watch upon her movements, as he had heard that fourteen of her children had previously died suddenly. A few weeks after her arrival in his parish, she called upon him to request him to bury one of her children. Upon his asking her which of the children it was, she told him that it was "Eliza"—a fine, healthy-looking child of ten years old. Upon his expressing some surprise that she should have died so suddenly, she said, "Oh, sir, she went off like a snuff; all my other children did so, too." A short time elapsed, and she again waited upon the vicar, to request him to bury her brother as soon as he could. His suspicions were aroused, and he endeavoured to postpone the funeral for a few days, in order to enable him to make some inquiries. Not succeeding in obtaining any information which would warrant further delay in burying the corpse, he most reluctantly proceeded in the discharge of his duty. About a week after the funeral Mary May again waited upon him, to request him to sign a certificate to the effect that her brother was in perfect health a fortnight before he died—that being the time at which, as it subsequently appeared, she had entered him as nominee in the Harwich Burial Club. Upon inquiring as to the reason of her desiring this certificate, she told him that unless she got it she could not get the money for him from the club. This at once supplied the vicar with what appeared to be a motive for "foul play" on the part of the woman. He accordingly obtained permission to have the body of her brother exhumed; doses of arsenic were detected, and the woman was arrested. With the evidence given upon the trial the reader is no doubt perfectly conversant, and it will be unnecessary for me to detail it. She was convicted. Previously to her execution, she refused to make any confession, but said, "If I were to tell all I know it would give the hangman work for the next twelvemonths." Undue weight ought not to be attached to the declaration of such a woman as Mary May—but, coupled with the disclosures that took place upon the trial with respect to some of her neighbours and accomplices, and with the extraordinary rate of mortality among the clubs, it certainly does appear that the general opinion with respect to the mischievous effects of these societies is not altogether without foundation.

Although there are not in Essex, at present, any burial clubs in which children are admitted under 14 years of age, as members or nominees, still, as illustrating the evils arising from these clubs, I may state that many persons who are fully conversant with the working of such institutions have stated that they have frequently been shocked by hearing women of the lower classes, when speaking of a neighbour's child, make use of such expressions as—"Oh, depend upon it, the child'll not live; it's in the burial club." When speaking to the parents of a child who may be unwell, it is not unfrequently that they say, "You should do so and so," or "you should not do so and so;" "you should not treat it in that way; is it in the burial club?" Instances of the most culpable neglect, if not of graver offences, are continually occurring in districts where clubs exist in which children are admitted. A collector of one of the most extensive burial societies gave it as his opinion, founded upon his experience, that it had become a constant practice to neglect the children for the sake of the allowance from the clubs, and he supported his opinion by several cases which had come under his own observation.

But setting aside for a moment all considerations with respect to "foul play" among adults, and neglect of children arising from the existence of these clubs, there are other points of view in which they are productive of the greatest evils; and foremost among many others may be mentioned their demoralizing influence upon the members of the clubs. Great numbers of persons enter these societies as a speculation; they have the power of appointing as nominee a person of any age, or in any state of health, for although some of the rules of the society state that none but healthy members can be admitted, still no care is taken to prevent the admission of unhealthy lives. One of the persons to whom I was speaking on the subject of burial clubs—a small tradesman of a village—said:—"Well, I never joined any of 'em but once, and that was one close by here. I put in an old aunt of mine who was 82—and she was in the workhouse—and I thought she'd be a good 'un to name, but I paid three years for her and she wouldn't die, so I gave it up, I wouldn't pay no longer. Well, do you know, two or three months after I'd left off paying on her, she went off, and hang me if I didn't lose ten pound by her, for the club just then was paying full." I was told of another instance, in which a person had paid in for some time upon another old woman, of upwards of eighty, but he also left the club in consequence of his not seeing any immediate prospect of gain from the decease of the poor woman. Another instance, which illustrates the feeling with which the death of a member of one of these clubs is generally regarded, was afforded me by the secretary of one of them. While I was with him, he received a letter from one of the members, which he read to me for the purpose of showing the benefit which these societies were to the poor people, and the mode in which the money was usually obtained from the club. The letter was dated London, and was as follows:—"I am sorry to inform you of the death of poor dear Mr. ——, which took place last Monday night, as he was a member of the Mourner's Friend Society, of which you are secretary. Mrs. ——, who was Mr. ——'s nominee, will sign the order, if you forward it to her at Mr. ——'s, farmer, as I have written to inform her of it." The secretary having read the letter, repeated the words at its commencement—"*I am sorry* to inform you of the death of poor dear Mr. ——" "That's what I laugh at always in these kind of letters—'*I am sorry;*' if they were to say what they mean, they'd all say 'I am glad.' This woman has been wishing for a long time that poor dear —— would go off; when he was alive she was living with another man, and now he's gone they'll have a jollification with the money." I asked him if there was no regulation in the club compelling the party receiving the money to see that the deceased was decently interred, and I was told, "that there was none whatever; that it was no part of their business to look after that; it was no odds to them who buried 'em, or how they were buried, whether it was by the parish or anybody else; all they wanted was proof of the death of the party."

To this almost entire obliteration of the feelings with which the occasion of a death ought to be regarded, is to be added the evil, inseparable from most of the clubs, of compelling the survivors to find large quantities of drink for their friends and the undertaker's men. A working man, who is the secretary to one of these societies, stated that he had known drink to be given to such excess, that the undertaker's men were frequently unfit to perform their duty, and sometimes even reeled while carrying the coffin. "The men," he says, "who stand as mutes at the door, as they stand out in the cold, are supposed to re-quire most drink, and receive it most liberally. I have seen these men reel about the road, and after the burial we have been obliged to put these mutes and their staves into the interior of the hearse, and drive them home, as they were incapable of walking. After the return from the funeral, the mourners commonly have drink again at the houses." In the case of a death, the publican at whose house the club is held claims that a certain portion of the "funeral allowances" should be spent with him. It has been calculated that in 90 of these societies, if one year's expenditure on drink, feast, and decoration money were placed out in the savings banks at interest, together with the amount of losses from mismanagement, the amount due to the contributors would, at the end of ten years, amount to not less than £5,328.

The excessive amount of the subscriptions paid by the members is also an evil deserving of the most serious attention. In the case, for instance, of one of the clubs in Essex, the number of members and nominees might be taken to be about 800. The average age of the members was, I was informed, about 45; of this number about 75 die in five years. Their places, we may assume, are supplied by persons of the same age as the original members; the club will then consist of 725 persons at the average age of 50, they being five years older than when it first started, and 75 of the age of 45. At the end of the next five years, assuming the rate of mortality to be the same, the club will consist of 650 persons of 55 years of age, 75 at 50, and 75 at 45, the average age of the whole club being 52. But, notwithstanding the increased risk in consequence of the greater age of the members, the rate of subscription remains the same. The 50th member of the club who may die will have paid, supposing that the nominees die at the same rate as the members—for the deaths of 99 members and nominees, together with his quarterly subscriptions, £2 17s. 9d.; the 100th member, £5 16s. 1d.; the 200th member, £11 12s. 9d.; the 300th, £17 9s. 5d.; and the 400th, supposing the club to exist so long, £23 6s. 1d.; while the amount that may be paid upon his death will not exceed £10, and in every probability it would be considerably less than that sum. Taking the expense of the funeral at £5, there would not be more than 80 members who would have paid into the club a less sum than would be sufficient to provide for the expense of their funeral, while the remaining 320 would pay in more than that sum; and in the case of some of them they would pay four or five times the amount of their funeral expenses—to say nothing of the loss of the interest of their money, which they might have obtained had they invested it in other funds, and the extra expenses which they had incurred for drink in connection with the various meetings of the club at the public-house.

A comparison of the rates charged in the different burial clubs for the benefits insured, with similar rates charged by assurance societies, shows that for a risk for which, if the Northampton tables were taken as the basis of the assurance, a premium of 3s. 9d. only would be demanded by an assurance office, 7s. 10d. is taken from the contributors to the club; in another, for a risk for which 3s. 9d. would suffice in the Northampton tables, 11s. 5d. is received; instead of an average premium of 5s. 2d., a third society takes 11s. 1d. If we add 25 per cent. to the premium that would be charged according to the Northampton rate (which is supposed to represent a higher mortality than the average), for expenses of management, including books, stationery, &c.—and to cover the loss of interest occasioned by weekly or monthly contributions, instead of annual premiums payable at the beginning of each year—in nearly all these clubs the poor man pays an excess for burial of at least one-third, independently of the extra expenses of drink in connection with these clubs, and his quarterly subscriptions.

The following graduated table of weekly contributions has been drawn up by Mr. Finlaison, the actuary to the Commissioners for the Reduction of the National Debt, and it is matter for regret that it is not more generally acted upon by the managers of these clubs:—

Age of Members.	Free to Receive Benefits at end of	CONTRIBUTIONS PAYABLE.		BENEFITS.	
		On Entrance.	Weekly for the whole of Life.	Sum payable at Death of Member.	Sum payable at Death of Member's Wife.
6 and under 12	....	6d.	¼d.	£4.	Nil.
12 „ „ 18	....	1s.	½d.	£7.	Nil.
18 „ „ 23	....	1s. 6d.	¾d.	£10.	£3.
23 „ „ 28	Twelve	2s.	1d.	£10.	£4.
28 „ „ 33	....	2s. 6d.	1¼d.	£10.	£5.
33 „ „ 38	....	3s.	1½d.	£10.	£5.
38 „ „ 43	Months	3s. 6d.	1¾d.	£10.	£5.
43 „ „ 48	....	4s.	2d.	£10.	£5.
48 „ „ 53	....	4s. 6d.	2½d.	£10.	£5.
53 „ „ 60	....	5s.	3d.	£10.	£5.

The majority of burial clubs have no funds from which they are enabled to pay the amount on the death of a member; the plan adopted is, as may be seen by one of their rules, that of collecting so much money from each member upon the occasion of a death. Clubs of this kind cannot therefore be said to become insolvent, in the true sense of the word. The members of the club find it impossible to keep up the payments of from 10s. to 12s. per year, in clubs consisting of about 400 members; they are excluded for default—the number of defaulters gradually increases, till the amount payable on death is reduced to a mere trifle—and the club then becomes extinct. In Manningtree there were three of these societies which were dissolved in this manner; and there is every probability that the whole of them, in Essex at least, will follow in the same track. None of the clubs have at present their full complement of members, and in two of those at Harwich they have ten deaths in the course of collection, the subscriptions for which they are unable to obtain. Of course when the clubs break up, the members lose all that they have subscribed, for there is no property to divide: they are left helpless and unprovided for—their previous subscriptions have been, at least so far as their own benefit is concerned, completely thrown away—they have perhaps passed the age at which they can be admitted into a friendly society—and nothing remains for them but the dreaded prospect of a parish shell and a pauper's grave. I was informed by a clergyman of a case of hardship of this kind. A poor man had paid for several years to his club, which however had broken up. Upon his death the widow came to him, begging for some assistance. He had helped the family to a considerable extent during the husband's life-time. The woman begged hard that he would do something for her, and not allow her husband to be buried by the parish. He very readily waived his burial fees, and by the assistance of her neighbours a coffin was obtained, which cost 14s.; the charge to the sexton was 2s.; passing the bell, 1s. Four of the poor man's neighbours gave up half of their day's wages to carry the corpse to the ground—the clerk was paid 6d.—and 6d. was also paid for the use of the pall, which was kept by the clerk. By this means the funeral was performed at an expense of only 18s. to the widow, who had the satisfaction of knowing that her husband was not buried as a pauper.

Unreasonable as may be the charges which are usually made for the burial of the labourer, still they are considerably more than covered by the amount received from the clubs—and it is this excessive amount paid to the members which constitutes one of the worst features of these associations. The usual charge for the funeral of an adult of this class is between £3 and £4. This charge is made up of the following items:—Coffin, 30s.; shroud and pillow, 5s. 6d.; church fees, including grave-digger, 10s.; bearers, 6s.; use of pall, 5s.; scarfs and bands for mourners, 15s.—leaving a margin of upwards of £6 of the club money, the greater portion of which is mostly spent in drink, and in treating the mourners and undertaker's men.

There is one other point in connection with these clubs which ought not to be overlooked—and that is, that no precautions whatever are taken either with respect to the admission of members, or in ascertaining the cause of the death of the party. With respect to the admission of members, Mr. Jenkins, the secretary to one of the societies, stated before a committee of the House of Commons, in answer to a question as to how they ascertained whether the applicants for admission were in good health—"We take their word for it; we do not submit them to any medical examination; and as to their age, the same with regard to that, we take their word for it. If we think they appear to be anything like the age, we take it for granted. We take what they represent to be the fact as to their health and age. We ask the question, 'Are you in good health?' They say 'Yes.' Then we take them." In answer to the question put to the same witness, "Supposing a parent proposed to you to admit a child that any one of you who might have the direction of affairs knew to be unhealthy, do you object to it?"—the answer was, "If a whole family be entered, we do not object to it." Indeed, it is, in almost all cases, to the interest of the managers of the club to admit unhealthy lives, as, in the words of one of the managers, who was an undertaker, "it brings grist to the mill." Every one connected with the clubs, except the unfortunate members upon whom this species of "black mail" is levied, has a direct interest in the number of deaths that may take place. To the treasurer, who is mostly the publican, the news of a death is equivalent to an order for so much liquor; to the secretary it gives an additional fee; and to the collectors their per centage upon the amount collected by them. There is, therefore, no person whatever to look after the interests of the poor people who may belong to the club. All that they have to do is to pay their contribution when called upon, or be excluded from the society; or, if they attempt to inquire for themselves into its affairs, or to make any charge against any of its managers, they are forthwith stopped by the terrors of one of the rules—"That if any member charge the committee or any member thereof, or trustees or secretary, with any improper practice in the management of the society, and cannot make it appear just"—and that to the satisfaction of a self-constituted committee—"he or she shall be fined 5s. or be excluded."

Among numerous cases of fraud in connection with the clubs might be mentioned a case which has been kindly furnished to me by a gentleman who has devoted considerable time and attention to the subject—and which, but for the visit of one of the officers of the clubs, whose duty it was to see the corpse, would no doubt have been perfectly successful. A man and his wife agreed that one of them— namely, the husband—should pretend to be dead, in order that the wife might receive his funeral money. Accordingly the wife proceeded in due form to give notice of his death. The visiting officer on behalf of the society, whose duty it was to see the corpse, repaired to the house, entered the chamber, and inquired for the deceased; the would-be disconsolate widow pointed him to the body of her late husband, whose chin was tied up with a handkerchief in the attitude of death. He surveyed the corpse, the eyelids seemed to move; he felt the pulse, the certain signs of life were there; the officer pronounced him not dead; she in return said—"*He is dead*, for there has not been a breath in him since twelve o'clock last night." The neighbours were called in; a discussion ensued between the wife and the officer; some declared they saw the husband at the door that morning, giving a light. The officer required her to bring a doctor; she went, and said she could not get one to come; the officer went and brought one, who ordered the man to be raised up in the bed—and, having obtained some water, the doctor, while the man was sitting up, dashed it in his face. It need scarcely be added that the effect of the cold water was perfectly invigorating upon the pretended corpse.

The well-known insecurity of these clubs among the labourers has had the effect of inducing them to join several, in the hope that one at least of the number may be able to stand. Several of the persons with whom I entered into conversation on the subject informed me that they were members of two, three, and four of these clubs. In case of death their survivors would, of course, receive the money from each of the societies, but at the same time they were compelled, to use their own words, "to stand the mortality of the members and nominees of four clubs," the expense of which could not be less than £2 per annum. The amount received from the whole of the clubs being enormously disproportioned to the amount required for burial, naturally increases the inducement to have recourse to "foul play," in order to obtain so large a sum of money.

Of the whole of the burial clubs in Essex, there is not one that is enrolled—which is an additional injury to the poor people, inasmuch as they have no remedy against the dishonesty of the managers. The rule requiring that if any of the collectors or others should lose any of the moneys or property of the club, it should be made good at their own expense, is a perfect dead letter—the only means which they have of compelling the party to make good the loss being the expulsion of the defaulting member. In the case of one of the clubs at Great Oakley, application was made to Mr. Tidd Pratt on the subject of enrolment, and a copy of the rule was transmitted to him. Before allowing the club to be enrolled, he required, however, the insertion of rules to the effect, that three trustees should be elected on a quarterly night to continue in office during the pleasure of the society, vacancies to be filled in the same manner; that the funds should be invested with the consent of the members on each quarterly night; that the stewards should prepare annually a statement of the funds and effects belonging to the society, to a copy of which every member should be entitled upon payment of twopence; and that, in cases of dispute between the society and any of its members, reference should be made to justices of the peace. He also required that books should be kept, in which all moneys received or paid on account of any particular fund or benefit should be entered in separate accounts. The sixth requirement was, that the returns of the rates of mortality in the clubs, together with an account of the assets and liabilities, should be sent to the registrar of friendly societies once in every year. The seventh article imposed penalties, recoverable by the sale of the chattels and goods, upon the persons neglecting to make the required returns. To one and all of these reasonable requirements the managers of the clubs demurred, and they refused to have the club enrolled "upon any such conditions." Regulations of this kind could not be too strict with respect to these clubs, especially with regard to their accounts, for anything more slovenly or disgraceful than the state of what by courtesy were called their books, I never saw, than was shown me by the collectors and secretaries of some of them. In scarcely one of the clubs was there any account kept of the number of deaths that had taken place—the only way of arriving at the result being by extracting from a series of dirty-looking papers, the number of "crosses" and "sixes" jotted

down with lead pencil against the names of the members in the collector's books. The appointment of trustees and the investment of the
funds would have the effect of taking from the secretaries the privilege of holding the little money belonging to them in their own hands,
which is the case at present. Reference to the magistrate in cases of
dispute was strongly protested against by the secretary of one of the
societies, on the ground "that they didn't want to have nothing to do
with law or lawyers, and that they were quite able to manage their
own affairs without either of 'em." And as to levying a penalty upon
the officers for neglect of duty, "by the sale of goods and chattels,"—
it was "a thing they wasn't used to." And so, until these societies are
by some means or other brought under efficient control, the labourer
must continue to be defrauded of a portion of his scanty earnings; he
will be called upon to pay excessively for an object which, after all,
is but poorly obtained; the demoralization of the people will spread
wider and wider, and a total disregard of human life will usurp the
place of the better feelings of our nature.

I have gone somewhat more fully into the question of the burial
clubs than I had intended; the mischievous effects which are produced by them, and the urgent necessity which exists for the adoption of some measures for their regulation, have led me beyond the
bounds which I had assigned to myself for the consideration of the
subject. The next associations in connection with the provident habits
of the labouring classes, are the Benefit and Friendly societies. Many
of the observations with respect to the government and management
of the burial clubs apply with equal propriety to large numbers of the
friendly societies. The payments of the members are regulated without reference to the amount of risk; the meetings are mostly held at
public-houses; and a large portion of the contributions is required to
be expended in drink by the members. The objects which they embrace are more extensive in their character than those of the burial
clubs—the one having reference only to death—the other to a state
of both sickness and death, and even to the prevention of want, as
may be gathered from the following preamble to the Union Benefit
Society held at the Bell Inn, Thorpe, Essex:—

> "LET US LOVE ONE ANOTHER.—Man is formed a social being. The
> Sovereign Ruler of the world has been pleased to place us in this life as
> dependent upon each other, and in continual need of mutual assistance
> and support, and has interwoven in our constitutions those humane
> and sympathetic affections which we always feel at the distresses of

our fellow-creatures; how greatly is the beneficent and generous spirit rewarded in contributing to relieve that distress. Of all the delights human nature is capable of enjoying, the most lively and transport-ing are those which flow from sympathy and social passion, as they are not only the most pleasing in their immediate exercise, but also in contemplation and reflection; every benevolent mind, therefore, that sincerely delights in the good of others, will not fail to improve every opportunity to promote their happiness and comfort, particularly of those who are afflicted with sickness, lameness, blindness, or any such calamity by which they are deprived of the means and power of sup-porting, not only themselves, but perhaps a numerous family. That this is the true and laudable intent of this society, the following articles will sufficiently explain; where every disorder with which any of its mem-bers may be afflicted is, as far as is consistent with the general good of the whole society, so relieved as at least to prevent want from com-ing within his doors."—Signed "Gabriel Bones," and other members of the committee."

In order to give effect to the very laudable purpose expressed in the above preamble, the rules of the society go on to declare, that ev-ery member must pay to the society 1s. 9d. per month, and 4d. to be spent at each meeting; the benefits promised in return being, an an-nual feast at Whitsuntide (for the arrangement of which the officers are to receive each 1s.)—the sum of £5 upon the death of any member, to be paid to his widow, heirs, or executors—and if at any time it shall please God to afflict any free member with hurt, sickness, lameness, or other infirmity, the said member shall receive 10s. per week for three calendar months; and if not recovered from his affliction within that period, he shall receive 8s. per week for three months longer; if he continues unwell at the expiration of that period, he receives 6s. per week for a further period of three months—and if he still remains unwell, the sum of 4s. per week for three further months, and a sum of 2s. for each and every week afterwards, so long as he may continue so afflicted as not to be able to earn his livelihood. There are numerous minor rules for the regulation of the proceedings at the meetings of the club, and of the mode in which the drink is to be ordered and paid for by the members. Among other things, it is declared, that, in order to preserve decency, good order, &c., "any member who may call for or order liquor to be brought into the club-room during club hours, without first asking leave of the president, shall pay for it himself," and further on, "if any member feels disposed to drink his share, or spend his fourpence aforesaid by himself, he may; and if any member drink the same without his or their consent, he shall pay for it." The regulations with respect to the drinking department of the clubs appear to have occupied by far the greater share of the attention of the framers of the regulations, some of which are so obscurely worded that it is difficult at first sight to understand their import. In one of the clubs, called the Rock Club, held at Kirby, it is provided, among other things, "that there shall be a sixpenny club for beer, at which every member shall attend or forfeit 3d., besides his eighteenpence, or be excluded. Also, that all the members shall meet every year, by 12 o'clock, at the house where the club is kept, or send their money, or in failure thereof to forfeit 6d. each; and there shall be a feast provided for them by order of the stewards and assistants." In one of the clubs it is agreed "that if any member sits down to drink with the stewards he shall be fined sixpence." In another, "if any person sits down to drink with the committee, he is to pay sixpence." There are other regulations, which provide "that if any member shall call for liquor out of the club-room, without being ordered by the steward, and the club be charged with the same, he shall forfeit one shilling for every sixpence so charged." The fair sex are strictly prohibited from entering the club-room; for, "if the wife of any member shall come into the club-room without the consent of the society, her husband shall forfeit sixpence: no woman to be present at any public or other meeting, the mistress or servant of the house excepted." With respect to the custody and disposal of the funds, it is ordered in the Rock Club "that there shall be a chest with five locks and keys provided, the stewards' assistants and clerks shall each of them have one"—whether lock or key is not stated—in which the money is to be deposited. Anxious to provide for every possible contingency, the same club have agreed, "that every member belonging to this society shall have liberty to dispose of his privilege therein *before* his departure out of this life, viz., the stewards shall pay £3 to *the widow of the deceased if married*—if single, to any friend whom the deceased shall have named." It is also provided, "that if the wife of any member, *who shall have been a member* for the space of two years shall die, the stewards shall pay the said member the sum of 40s. for the wife only, and on the next quarterly meeting night every member shall bring or send one *extraordinary shilling* towards *raising the same again;*" from the fact of an "*extraordinary shilling*" being required, one would almost suppose, upon reading the above, that it was the "one wife only" who was to be "raised again."

Of benefit and friendly societies there are enrolled in Essex 138, in Suffolk 112, and in Norfolk 109. These numbers, however, by no means represent the whole of the societies of this kind in existence in those counties. The number of unenrolled clubs is probably equal to, if not more numerous than, those which are enrolled. The greatest distress is frequently felt by the members of the clubs in consequence of the "box" being closed at the time when they stand in need of the assistance which they had a right to expect in return for their contributions. As illustrating the instability and injurious effects of these clubs, it was stated by Mr. Tidd Pratt, in the course of one of the late sanitary inquiries, that, at a recent election of a poor man to a vacancy in the Metropolitan Benefit Societies' Asylum—a condition of which was that the candidate must be above sixty years of age, and have been a member of a benefit society more than ten years—there were 32 candidates, from whose documents it appeared that the societies of no less than 14 out of the 32 had been dissolved, and that some of them had belonged to two societies, and that both had failed them. Such societies are, nevertheless, constantly renewed on the old and unsafe foundations; and so intense is the prevalent feeling on the subject of decent interments, and the desire to obtain some assistance in case of sickness, that numbers of poor people, as in the case of the burial clubs, join several, in the hope that one may at the last avail them. I have met with several cases in which poor people have told me that they had been compelled to apply to the parish for relief solely in consequence of the clubs having failed to supply them with the assistance upon which they had calculated. "I paid fourteen years," said one man to me, "to my club, and never had a farthing out of it in my life, and I've paid towards twelve deaths; but now, when I come to be ill myself, I can't get a ha'penny from 'em; the box is shut, they say." Another woman told me that her husband had also paid for a long time, and never had but one week's money from the club. "If I had," said she, "but all the money he has paid to the bothering club, my children wouldn't be in the ragged state they're now in, nor be so hungry as they are sometimes."

When treating of the wages of the labourer, it was shown that it was impossible for him to do more than merely obtain a bare sufficiency of food for himself and family with the amount which he usually received. The means by which he obtains his clothing is admitted by almost every one to be a mystery. So impressed have many of the more wealthy persons residing in the neighbourhood of small towns been with the utter impossibility of the labourer obtaining clothing for himself and his family, that they have formed in many places what are called "clothing clubs." These clubs are conducted on the principle of allowing the labourer to contribute one penny or more per week, according as he can afford it, and at the end of the year the person so contributing receives an order upon some tailor or draper in the town, to the amount of 10s. or 15s. for every 5s. which he may have subscribed himself; the increased sum being made up from the contributions of charitable individuals in the town, some of whom are contributors to the extent of £1, £2, and £5 each. In the town of Halesworth, upwards of £200 is thus annually distributed for clothing for the labourers in the immediate neighbourhood. In many other parts of the country, clubs of a similar character abound. The supply of coals, too, is not unfrequently obtained through the same agency by the labourers.

Without these associations for enabling the labourer to obtain fuel, clothing, relief in sickness, and burial at his death, his condition would be, if possible, far worse than it is at present. Even from the friendly and burial clubs, badly constructed as they are, an enormous amount of assistance is afforded to the poor man, but under an improved system of management the benefits would be increased tenfold. Unfortunately the present state of the labourer, in the absence of any material improvement in his condition, imperatively demands the assistance of associations of this kind. His whole life appears to be constantly wavering between toil and charity. The parish doctor attends at (in all probability) his illegitimate birth; he is swathed in linen provided for him by the hands of some charitable individual, or benevolent association. A charity school doles out to him his scanty education in the irregular intervals of his youthful labour; as he advances in years the subscriptions of the more affluent are necessary to provide him with clothing; when unemployed, or unable through old age or infirmity to do a fair day's work, the workhouse is his refuge; in sickness the parish doctor attends him, and his club supports him; in death, if his club be in existence, the funds for his burial are provided by a portion of the hard earnings of his club-mates—for many of whom, who may have passed away before him, he had been called upon to perform the like act of self-denying charity. If his club be closed, as is frequently the case, the parish will find him a shell; four of his neighbours, perhaps poorer than himself, sacrifice their half-day's wages to bear him gratuitously to the spot which the guardians of the poor have appointed as the pauper's final resting-place, and in which his ancestors and some of his offspring were perhaps laid before him. The clergyman waives his burial fees, or the union chaplain consigns him to the ground which for half a century, in seed time and in harvest, he had moistened with his sweat and enriched by his toil.

Such is by no means an exaggerated description of the mode of existence and end of vast masses of the agricultural labourers in the three counties which are named at the head of this letter. I have endeavoured calmly, temperately, and I trust impartially, to describe what I have myself seen and heard among them—and I now leave them in the hands of those whose duty it may be, to consider and devise the best means for the improvement of their social, moral, and physical condition.

Index

Titles Available in the Series

LABOUR AND THE POOR

Volumes I to IV: The Metropolitan Districts
Henry Mayhew

ISBN 978-1-913515-11-9, 978-1-913515-12-6, 978-1-913515-13-3, 978-1-913515-14-0

Volume V: The Manufacturing Districts
Angus B. Reach

ISBN 978-1-913515-15-7

Volumes VI & VII: The Rural Districts
Alexander Mackay & Shirley Brooks

ISBN 978-1-913515-16-4, 978-1-913515-17-1

Volume VIII: Wales
Special Correspondent

ISBN 978-1-913515-18-8

Volume IX: Birmingham
Charles Mackay

ISBN 978-1-913515-19-5

Volume X: Liverpool
Charles Mackay

ISBN 978-1-913515-20-1

For information on these and other titles available please visit:

DittoBooks.co.uk

www.ingramcontent.com/pod-product-compliance
Lightning Source LLC
Chambersburg PA
CBHW060303030426
42336CB00011B/919